The Practical Guide to

EVIDENCE
IN
CRIMINAL CASES

Eighth Edition

The Honourable
Roger E. Salhany, Q.C.

DISCARDED

CARSWELL®

A cataloguing record for this publication is available from Library and Archives Canada.

ISBN 978-0-7798-5500-1

Printed in Canada by Thomson Reuters.

⊗ The acid-free paper used in this publication meets the minimum requirements of American National Standard for Information Sciences — Permanence of Paper for Printed Library Materials, ANSI Z39.48-1984.

TELL US HOW WE'RE DOING
Scan the QR code to the right with your smartphone to send your comments regarding our products and services. Free QR Code Readers are available from your mobile device app store. You can also email us at carswell.feedback@thomsonreuters.com

CARSWELL, A DIVISION OF THOMSON REUTERS CANADA LIMITED

One Corporate Plaza
2075 Kennedy Road
Toronto, Ontario
M1T 3V4

Customer Relations
Toronto 1-416-609-3800
Elsewhere in Canada/U.S. 1-800-387-5164
Fax 1-416-298-5082
www.carswell.com
Contact www.carswell.com/contact

PREFACE TO THE EIGHTH EDITION

It has been over 55 years since I attended my first lecture in evidence at Osgoode Hall. I recall that the course in evidence involved learning a series of complex rules, and exceptions to those rules. Confusion reigned, at least for me, if not for some of my fellow students. Over the years, I have discovered that the law of evidence is not so complex at all. It is, as Professor James Bradley Thayer observed over a hundred years ago in the introduction to his scholarly Preliminary Treatise on Evidence, ". . .this institution of the jury which accounts for the common-law system of evidence". To understand the law of evidence, one has to understand its historical development *vis-à-vis* the jury system.

Today, more trials are conducted before judges sitting alone than with juries, but the same foundation for the law of evidence continues to pervade and influence its development. In its search for the truth, the common-law system of justice — the adversary system — has only a few underlying fundamental principles. The first is that truth can never emerge unless first hand evidence (subject to certain exceptions in chapter 3) is presented to the trier so that its honesty and reliability can be tested by cross-examination. The second is that only evidence that is relevant to a fact in issue is admissible to ensure that an accused receives a fair trial. Thirdly, that the trier reaches a decision based on the evidence presented and common experience; expert evidence on a fact in issue is only admissible if it is necessary, assists the trier and does not usurp the independence of the trier in reaching his or her judgment. In recent years, a fourth principle has emerged — the right and obligation of a trier to exclude relevant evidence where its prejudicial effect outweighs its probative value.

The first edition was written in 1990 when I was a trial judge during my sabbatical at the University of Western Ontario. It was titled, A Basic Guide to Evidence in Criminal Cases. My purpose was to encourage counsel appearing before me who objected to the introduction of certain evidence to explain the rationale for their objection rather than to simply cite a case or two in support of their objection. It was an attempt to demystify the law of evidence — to make it more logical and in the end more understandable. Subsequent editions had this goal in mind. Unfortunately, over the last 24 years and eight editions, it has unexpectedly grown larger at the request of students, lawyers and colleagues.

In this edition, the law of evidence, as developed by cases decided since the seventh edition, is brought up to date. In particular: *I.(D.)* (the mentally incompetent witness), *Prokofiew* (commenting on the silence of a co-accused), *Nedeclu* (cross-examination on civil discovery evidence), *Barros* (the identity of an informer), *Ahmad* (section 38 of the *Canada Evidence Act*, *Côté* (discoverability in section 24 *Charter* analysis) in the Supreme Court, *Li* (introducing transcript evi-

Preface to the Eighth Edition

dence), *Figliola* (adverse vs. the hostile witness), *Bucik* (the W.D. formula for exculpatory statements), *Berhe* (non-expert identification), *Green* (admissibility of recanting evidence), *Baldree* (hearsay) and *Burgar* (cross-examination on a criminal record) in provincial appellate courts. A number of other areas have been added dealing with Parliamentary changes to the treatment of child and mentally incompetent witnesses, preliminary inquiry evidence at trial and prohibited cross-examination of the accused. At the suggestion of some of my former judicial colleagues, there is expanded discussion in areas such as the rule against collateral facts, the evidence of children and persons who may be mentally incompetent, the derivative confessions rule and the right to remain silent and specific presumptions.

I want to thank my editor Val McIntyre for putting this edition together, and my partner Tannis who patiently corrected my grammatical errors and encouraged me when my energy waned.

R.E.S.

Kitchener, Ontario

June 2013

TABLE OF CONTENTS

TABLE OF CONTENTS

TABLE OF CONTENTS

TABLE OF CONTENTS

TABLE OF CASES

Table of Cases

Table of Cases

Table of Cases

Table of Cases

Table of Cases

Table of Cases

Table of Cases

Table of Cases

Table of Cases

Table of Cases

Table of Cases

Table of Cases

Table of Cases

Table of Cases

Table of Cases

Table of Cases

Table of Cases

Table of Cases

Table of Cases

Table of Cases

Table of Cases

Table of Cases

Table of Cases

Table of Cases

Table of Cases

Table of Cases

Table of Cases

Table of Cases

Table of Cases

Table of Cases

Table of Cases

Table of Cases

Table of Cases

Table of Cases

Table of Cases

Table of Cases

Table of Cases

Table of Cases

Table of Cases

Table of Cases

Table of Cases

Table of Cases

Table of Cases

Table of Cases

Table of Cases

Table of Cases

Table of Cases

Table of Cases

Table of Cases

Table of Cases

Table of Cases

Table of Cases

PART A

Admissibility

1
GENERAL PRINCIPLES

1. THE NATURE OF THE TRIAL PROCESS

The Canadian trial process under the common law is known as the adversary system, and has a thousand year history of development and refinement in the common law of England. The theory of the adversary system is that if one pits two equal champions in a process of examination and cross-examination of witnesses who have information about a fact in issue, truth will probably emerge. What is important to the discovery of truth is what takes place only in the courtroom — the actual trial itself.

Under the adversary system, the investigation of a crime is entirely in the hands of the police. It is the police who decide what charges should be laid against an accused; and it is the lawyers for the Crown that present the evidence against the accused in a courtroom. Judges play no role in the investigation. They are expected under the adversary system to be impartial as well as independent. They are not supposed to know anything about the case against an accused until they hear the evidence for the first time in the courtroom. Every step is taken to ensure that there is no hint of influence in favour of the Crown or the accused.

The adversary system must be contrasted with the inquisitorial justice system, the method of trial in most countries of continental Europe, and introduced to those countries that came under their colonial rule. Under the inquisitorial system, judges play a pivotal role from the very beginning of the investigative process, long before the trial begins. Although the investigation of a crime is usually conducted by the police, in a serious case, a judge, called an examining magistrate, or the French "juge d'instruction", will often be instructed by the state to take over the investigation of a crime. The examining magistrate will question witness and prepare a brief or dossier for the trial court. Under the inquisitorial system, the trial judges are expected to read the brief prepared by the examining magistrate and know everything about the evidence against the accused before the trial begins.

In Canada, Crown prosecutors in a criminal trial are required to make full and complete disclosure to the defence of all of the evidence that has been gathered by the police, for and against the accused.[1] The defence has no reciprocal obligation to reveal its defence, subject to a few exceptions, such as alibi evidence.[2] The defence need not reveal anything until all of the Crown's evidence has been presented to the judge and/or jury, and tested by the defence. Moreover, the obligation of the defence to reveal its position will not arise unless the state has presented sufficient evidence on every essential element of proof to the extent that a judge or jury, fully instructed and acting rationally, could convict the accused. Indeed the accused has no obligation to say anything at any time, and neither the judge nor jury is entitled to draw an adverse inference from the accused's silence. The accused has the right to remain silent until the very end of the trial and say to the state — "You prove your case against me". It is only when the Crown has passed the threshold of presenting sufficient evidence on all elements of a charge and the trial judge is satisfied that a jury properly instructed and acting rationally could convict the accused that the defence is required to reveal its position.[3]

To prove its case, the Crown must establish three things. The first is that the crime charged against the accused was committed — what is called the *"actus reus"*. The second is that it was the accused who committed the crime — the identity of the perpetrator. The third and final thing that must be established is that the accused intended to commit the crime, in the sense

[1] *Stinchcombe*, 1991 CarswellAlta 559, 1991 CarswellAlta 192, 68 C.C.C. (3d) 1, 8 C.R. (4th) 277 (S.C.C.)

[2] *Cleghorn*, 1995 CarswellOnt 126, 1995 CarswellOnt 802, [1995] 3 S.C.R. 175, 100 C.C.C. (3d) 393, 41 C.R. (4th) 282

[3] *Chaulk*, 1990 CarswellMan 385, 1990 CarswellMan 239, [1990] 3 S.C.R. 1303, 62 C.C.C. (3d) 193, 2 C.R. (4th) 1 ". . . the Crown must tender, as part of its case, evidence that will establish the existence of *all* elements of the offence with which the accused is charged".

that it was his deliberate act, or in some cases, a result of his recklessness or gross negligence. This is what is called the "*mens rea*". However, intention should not be confused with motive. Why a person commits a crime is not really something that concerns the court, although it may be relevant, as a matter of circumstantial evidence, to prove one of the three issues. There are also certain crimes where intention is not a relevant issue; sometimes the accused may not even be aware that he was committing the crime. These are called strict liability offences and are not necessary to this discussion.

Proof of a fact in issue may be made either by way of direct evidence or circumstantial evidence. Direct evidence is simply evidence that directly proves a fact in issue. For example, if the issue is whether A walked across the street, evidence given by B that he saw A walk across the street is direct evidence. Circumstantial evidence, on the other hand, is evidence of surrounding circumstances from which an inference may be drawn by the judge or jury that a fact in issue occurred. For example, B may not have seen A walk across the street but may have observed him on one side of the street one minute and then on the other side a minute later. In such instance, testimony by B of that observation is circumstantial evidence from which an inference may be drawn by the judge or jury that A must have walked across the street. Circumstantial evidence allows the trier of fact to draw the inference that a fact occurred, provided that the inference is a reasonable one and not inconsistent with any other rational conclusion.

2. TEST OF RELEVANCY

In a criminal trial, neither the Crown nor defence is entitled to introduce, as of right, every piece of evidence in their possession that may or may not be relevant to the case. Evidence is only admissible if it is relevant to prove one of the three issues in the case: the act, the identity or the intent. If the trial judge concludes that the evidence is relevant and should not be excluded because it runs afoul of a specific exclusionary rule, or if a balancing of its probative value against its prejudicial effect does not warrant its exclusion, then the judge will admit it. It then becomes the responsibility of the trier of fact (whether the judge or the jury) to decide what importance or weight should be attached to the evidence.

What is relevant will be decided by logic and human experience. As Pratte J. said in *Cloutier*,[4] referring to Cross, On Evidence, 4th ed. (1974) p. 16.

> For one fact to be relevant to another, there must be a connection or nexus between the two which makes it possible to infer the existence of one from the existence of the other. One fact is not relevant to another if it does not have real probative value with respect to the latter.

Moreover, the relevance of any piece of evidence must be determined only in relation to the issues that the prosecution must establish.

If the evidence is logically probative of one of the three issues that the Crown must prove, then it is said to be relevant and admissible so long as it is not contrary to one of the exclusionary rules of evidence that will be discussed in the next two sections. No minimum probative value is required for evidence to be deemed relevant.[5] In *Corbett*, Mr. Justice LaForest described the rule this way:

> All relevant evidence is admissible, subject to a discretion to exclude matters that may unduly prejudice, mislead or confuse the trier of fact, take up too much time, or that should otherwise be excluded on clear grounds of law or policy. Questions of relevancy and exclusion are, of course, matters for the trial judge, but over the years many specific exclusionary rules have been developed for the guidance of the trial judge, so much so that the law of evidence may superficially appear to consist simply of a series of exceptions to the rules of admissibility, with exceptions to the exceptions, and their subexceptions.[6]

Although evidence, to be relevant and admissible, must be logically probative of one of the three issues, there is no requirement that it must go directly to the proof of one of the those issues. As Doherty J. pointed out in *P. (R.)*:

> Evidence may, however, be relevant even though it does not go directly to the proof of a material fact, or even alone provide the basis for an inference that the material fact exists. Evidence may be relevant by its combination with other evidence adduced in the case. Such is the essence of circumstantial evidence.[7]

---

[4] 1979 CarswellQue 15, 1979 CarswellQue 164, [1979] 2 S.C.R. 709, 48 C.C.C. (2d) 1, 12 C.R. (3d) 10 at p. 731 [S.C.R.]

[5] *Corbett*, 1988 CarswellBC 756, 1988 CarswellBC 252, [1988] 1 S.C.R. 670, 28 B.C.L.R. (2d) 145, 41 C.C.C. (3d) 385, 64 C.R. (3d) 1, [1988] 4 W.W.R. 481, 34 C.R.R. 54, 85 N.R. 81.

[6] *Ibid.*, at pp. 33-34 [C.R.].

[7] 1990 CarswellOnt 2696, 58 C.C.C. (3d) 334 (H.C.) at pp. 339-40 [C.C.C.].

This means that where evidence offered by one side is circumstantial in nature, the trial judge, in deciding whether the evidence is relevant and admissible, is required to examine that evidence in light of all of the factual issues that are raised and the respective position taken by the Crown and the defence in the case.[8] Although, generally, relevance will depend on the ultimate issue in the case (whether it be the act, identity or intent, or a combination of any or all of the three), the evidence, although not directly relevant to one of those issues, may be relevant to another fact that is relevant to one of those issues.

Thus, the relevance of any piece of evidence requires a determination by the trial judge whether, as a matter of human experience and logic, the existence of fact A makes the existence of fact B more or less probable than it would be without the existence of fact A. If it does, then fact A is relevant to fact B. As long as fact B is itself a material fact in issue or is relevant to a material fact in issue in the case, then fact A is relevant and *prima facie* admissible.[9]

Unfortunately, when it comes to circumstantial evidence, even the courts often have difficulty in deciding what is relevant to a fact in issue. Whether evidence is considered relevant will usually depend upon the facts and the individual view of the judge hearing the case. For example in *Cloutier*,[10] the accused was charged with importing marijuana. Marijuana had been found concealed in a dresser imported into Canada and stored at the home of the accused's mother on the accused's instructions. At trial, the judge had refused to admit certain items found by the police during a search of the accused's home. These included a glass jar containing a green substance analyzed as marijuana, certificates of analysis of a cigarette butt made of marijuana and traces of marijuana found on scales and pipes in the premises. The Supreme Court of Canada, in a majority decision, held that the trial judge was correct in his ruling. The majority said that the fact the accused used marijuana did not create a logical inference that he knew or ought to have known that the dresser contained a narcotic at the time it was

---

[8] *Sims*, 1994 CarswellBC 574, 87 C.C.C. (3d) 402, 28 C.R. (4th) 231 (C.A.) at pp. 420–27 [C.C.C.].

[9] *Morris* (1983), 1983 CarswellBC 695, 1983 CarswellBC 730, [1983] 2 S.C.R. 190, 7 C.C.C. (3d) 97, 36 C.R. (3d) 1, 1 D.L.R. (4th) 385, [1984] 2 W.W.R. 1, 48 N.R. 341; *Watson*, 1996 CarswellOnt 2884, 30 O.R. (3d) 161, 108 C.C.C. (3d) 310, 50 C.R. (4th) 245, 92 O.A.C. 131 (C.A.). Expert evidence, however, also has a cost-benefit analysis to determine whether its value is worth what it costs in terms of its impact on the trial process. See *Mohan*, 1994 CarswellOnt 1155, 1994 CarswellOnt 66, 89 C.C.C. (3d) 402, 29 C.R. (4th) 243 (S.C.C.).

[10] *Supra*, note 4.

imported. All it showed was that a user of a narcotic was more likely to import the substance illegally than a non-user. Nor could the evidence be used to prove motive since it did not "disclose a sufficiently close logical connection between the facts that are to be proven as a motive and the crime committed".[11]

The minority came to the exact opposite conclusion. They concluded that since guilty intent cannot be established by direct evidence in such cases, it is "necessary to admit in evidence every bit of circumstantial evidence".[12] As far as they were concerned, there was a clear connection between the fact that the accused was a user of a prohibited narcotic and the presence of that narcotic concealed in the dresser. So long as there was some connection, even though not conclusive, the evidence had to be admitted for what it was worth. It was up to the trier to decide what weight should be attached to the evidence. If the accused was a marijuana user, then his motive in importing it was obvious.

A little over four years later, the Supreme Court, in a majority decision, came to the opposite conclusion on similar facts. In *Morris*,[13] the accused and several others were charged with conspiracy to import and traffic in heroin from Hong Kong. The Crown's case was based on surveillance and wiretap evidence. When the accused was arrested, a newspaper article headed "The Heroin Trade Moves to Pakistan", which had been written two years prior to the offence, was found in the accused's apartment. This time the majority held that an inference could be drawn from the presence of the newspaper article in the accused's apartment that he had informed himself of the sources of supply of heroin, a subject of vital interest to an importer of heroin. It raised the inference that the accused had taken preparatory steps to import heroin or had contemplated it, even though the article referred to the heroin trade in Pakistan and not Hong Kong. The minority, relying on *Cloutier*, held that the sole relevancy of the evidence was to show that it was more likely that persons who are traffickers keep such information than people who are not. Since the newspaper article only went to the disposition of the accused to commit the offence, it should not have been admitted by the trial judge.

---

[11] *Ibid.*, *per* Pratte J. at SCR, p. 735, (C.R.) p. 81.

[12] *Ibid.*, *per* Pigeon J. at SCR p. 746.

[13] (1983), 1983 CarswellBC 695, 1983 CarswellBC 730, [1983] 2 S.C.R. 190, 7 C.C.C. (3d) 97, 36 C.R. (3d) 1, 1 D.L.R. (4th) 385, [1984] 2 W.W.R. 1, 48 N.R. 341.

A subsequent decision of the Supreme Court in *Lepage*[14] plainly demonstrates that relevancy will usually depend upon the facts and the individual view of the judge hearing the case. *Lepage* was charged with possession of LSD for the purposes of trafficking. A plastic bag containing the drug was seized from the common area of the home that he shared with two others. One of the co-residents was allowed to testify that the drugs were not his and that *Lepage* was a drug trafficker, although he could not identify a relationship between *Lepage* and the specific drugs in issue. Sopinka J., for the majority of the Court, held that the evidence was admissible because it was relevant to show possession "which is a key issue". He wrote:

> In the circumstances of this case, there were three people living in the house and it was clear that the drugs belonged to one of the three. Surely, it is relevant to the issue of possession to have one of the three testify that the drugs were not his and, furthermore, indicate that the respondent is in the business and, therefore, it was more likely that he was the owner of the drugs.[15]

Major J., however, dissented, holding that the evidence was only evidence of propensity and nothing more. It did not provide any evidence that actually connected the accused to the drugs.

Let us assume that an accused is seen crouching down in an empty field, 30 to 40 feet off the highway. The accused then gets up and gets into his automobile parked on the side of the road and drives away. The area where the accused was observed is searched and a bag containing nine pounds of marijuana is found. The accused is later arrested by the police, who search his car and find a small amount of cocaine and a large amount of cash. The accused is charged with possession for the purposes of trafficking of the nine pounds of marijuana found in the field. Is the evidence of the finding of cocaine in the accused's car admissible on the charge of possession of marijuana for the purposes of trafficking? The accused's defence is that it was mere coincidence that the marijuana was in the place where he had been observed.

That very issue faced the Manitoba Court of Appeal in *Caslake*.[16] Here again the Court was divided. Lyons J.A. held that such evidence was admissible. As far as he was concerned, the evidence went beyond mere propen-

---

[14] 1995 CarswellOnt 3, 1995 CarswellOnt 517, [1995] 1 S.C.R. 654, 95 C.C.C. (3d) 385, 36 C.R. (4th) 145, 178 N.R. 81, 79 O.A.C. 191.

[15] *Ibid.*, at p. 399 [C.C.C.].

[16] 1995 CarswellMan 470, 101 C.C.C. (3d) 240, 45 C.R. (4th) 98, 107 Man. R. (2d) 24, 109 W.A.C. 24, [1995] M.J. No. 383 (C.A.); affirmed (1998), 1998 CarswellMan 1, 1998 CarswellMan 2, [1998] 1 S.C.R. 51, 121 C.C.C. (3d) 97, 13

sity because it largely discredited the defence's position that the accused's presence at the location of the cache of marijuana was only a coincidence and that he was a mere victim of circumstances. The other two members of the Court, however, disagreed. Helper J.A, who delivered the majority judgment, felt that the evidence was not admissible. The evidence of the possession of cocaine was not probative of any element on the charge of possession of the marijuana for the purposes of trafficking. As far as she was concerned, it had no relevance beyond mere propensity.

3. HABIT OR DISPOSITION

The common law prohibits the prosecution from leading evidence in chief that the accused is a person of bad character and one who is in the habit of committing criminal acts to prove that he committed the particular offence charged.[17] The prohibition is not based on irrelevance. The disposition of the accused to engage in certain kinds of conduct may be very relevant to the facts in issue. However, evidence of an accused's disposition is excluded because of its potential prejudicial effect. The common law has consistently reaffirmed its belief that the overall fairness of the criminal trial process requires an accused to stand trial for what is specifically alleged in the indictment, not for what he may have done in the past. Propensity reasoning alone has been excluded because of the concern that it may impair the proper functioning of the criminal justice system.

Martin J.A. expressed the rule this way in *Scopelliti*:

> The law prohibits the prosecution from introducing evidence for the purpose of showing that the accused is a person who by reason of his criminal character (disposition) is likely to have committed the crime charged, on policy grounds, not because of lack of relevance.[18]

Although evidence of an accused's disposition is generally excluded, not because of lack of relevance, but because of its prejudicial effect, evidence of habit or disposition of a third party may sometimes be relevant and there-

---

C.R. (5th) 1, 155 D.L.R. (4th) 19, [1999] 4 W.W.R. 303, 48 C.R.R. (2d) 189, 123 Man. R. (2d) 208, 221 N.R. 281, 159 W.A.C. 208.

[17] *Makin v. Attorney General for New South Wales* (1893), [1894] A.C. 57, [1891–94] All E.R. Rep. 24, 17 Cox C.C. 704, 58 J.P. 148, 63 L.J.P.C. 41, 69 L.T. 778, 6 R. 373, 10 T.L.R. 155 (New South Wales P.C.) at p. 65 [A.C.]; *Koufis*, 1941 CarswellNS 24, [1941] S.C.R. 481, 76 C.C.C. 161, [1941] 3 D.L.R. 657 at p. 170 [C.C.C.].

[18] 1981 CarswellOnt 814, 34 O.R. (2d) 524, 63 C.C.C. (2d) 481 (C.A.) at p. 493 [C.C.C.].

fore admissible because it is a reliable predictor of conduct. For example, in *Watson*,[19] the accused (who was charged with murder) and two associates, H and C, visited the deceased at his place of business, which consisted of a small office and a large warehouse area behind. The deceased was shot dead by H in a confrontation at the back of the warehouse, while Watson remained in the front office. C was also shot in the chest. At least two of the bullets that hit the deceased came from a different gun than the one used to shoot C. In support of its theory that the deceased was killed during a spontaneous gun battle between H and the deceased, and that the deceased's death was not planned by H, C and Watson, the defence sought to call a witness who had given a statement to the police that the deceased was in the habit of carrying a gun. The purpose was to show that since the deceased always carried a gun, it was less likely that Watson was a party to a plan to kill or harm him. The trial judge, however, refused to allow the defence to call that evidence because there was no evidence that the deceased had a gun on the day in question, or that he fired a gun if he had one.

The Ontario Court of Appeal disagreed and held that the trial judge had erred. Doherty J.A., delivering the judgment of the Court, reasoned as follows:

> The fact that a person is in the habit of doing a certain thing in a given situation suggests that on a specific occasion in which those circumstances arose the person acted in accordance with established practice. It makes the conclusion that the person acted in a particular way more likely than it would be without the evidence of habit. Evidence of habit is therefore properly viewed as circumstantial evidence that a person acted in a certain way on the occasion in question.
>
> Evidence of habit is closely akin to, but not identical to, evidence of disposition. Evidence of habit involves an inference of conduct on a given occasion based on an established pattern of past conduct. It is an inference of conduct from conduct. Evidence of disposition involves an inference of the existence of a state of mind (disposition) from a person's conduct on one or more previous occasions and a further inference of conduct on the specific occasion based on the existence of that state of mind. Evidence of habit proceeds on the basis that repeated conduct in a given situation is a reliable predictor of conduct in that situation. Evidence of disposition is premised on the belief that a person's disposition is a reliable predictor of conduct in a given situation.[20]

---

[19] 1996 CarswellOnt 2884, 30 O.R. (3d) 161, 108 C.C.C. (3d) 310, 50 C.R. (4th) 245, 92 O.A.C. 131 (C.A.).

[20] *Ibid.*, at p. 325 [C.C.C.].

Doherty J.A. felt that the evidence that the deceased always carried a gun was therefore relevant to the question whether he had a gun when he was shot. The availability of the inference from the deceased's possession of the gun, to the use of it, required a consideration of the rest of the evidence which revealed that there were only two possibilities. Either C was shot by the deceased, or H fired two different guns hitting the deceased with one and C with the other. The jury, having concluded that the deceased was armed, could have inferred that C was shot, not by his friend H, but by the deceased who was the target of H's assault. Had the jury inferred that the deceased was armed and fired a weapon, those inferences could logically have influenced their conclusion as to the origins of the shooting. If the deceased was unarmed, the circumstances strongly suggested a preconceived plan to shoot the deceased. If the deceased was armed and used his weapon, then the possibility that the shooting was as a result of a spontaneous competition between H and the deceased, both of whom were armed, became a viable one. Evidence supporting the inferences that the deceased was armed and used a weapon during the confrontation made the defence position as to Watson's non-involvement in any plan to kill or do harm to the deceased more viable than it would have been if those inferences were not available.

Although the Crown is not entitled to call evidence of the accused's disposition to prove its case, evidence of the accused's disposition may also be relevant where the defence advanced blames a third party or a co-accused for the offence. For example, in *McMillan*,[21] the accused, who was charged with the murder of his infant son, denied hurting the child. The trial judge had permitted the defence to call psychiatric evidence to the effect that the accused's wife had a psychopathic personality disturbance with brain damage, that she was immature, impulsive, and that she had poor appreciation of the difference between right and wrong, in order to show that it was more likely that she had committed the offence. It was held that evidence of the disposition of the accused's wife in these circumstances was relevant because it went to the probability of the accused doing or not doing the act charged. At the same time, the door was now opened to permit the Crown to call evidence *in reply* of the accused's disposition for violence.

Evidence of the victim's disposition has also been permitted where the defence raised is self-defence. For example, in *Scopelliti*,[22] the defence

[21] 1975 CarswellOnt 7, 7 O.R. (2d) 750, 23 C.C.C. (2d) 160, 29 C.R.N.S. 191 (C.A.); affirmed 1977 CarswellOnt 474, 1977 CarswellOnt 474F, [1977] 2 S.C.R. 824, 33 C.C.C. (2d) 360, 73 D.L.R. (3d) 759, 15 N.R. 20.
[22] 1981 CarswellOnt 814, 34 O.R. (2d) 524, 63 C.C.C. (2d) 481 (C.A.).

raised was that the accused killed the two deceased in self-defence when they attempted to rob him. The trial judge permitted the defence to lead evidence of previous acts of violence by the deceased, even though at the time of the killing the accused was not aware of those acts. Martin J.A. held that, although evidence of a person's disposition is not generally admissible, it was relevant and admissible in the circumstances to support the accused's version of the events. Again, evidence by the defence of the victim's disposition for violence opened up the door for the Crown to call, *in reply*, evidence of the accused's disposition for violence.

In all of these cases, evidence of the disposition of a third party was permitted where it was relevant to the defence raised. The Crown was not entitled to lead evidence of the accused's disposition as part of its case in chief, even though such evidence may have been relevant to the facts in issue. Policy considerations prevented the Crown from leading in chief evidence of the accused's disposition for violence until the issue of disposition was raised as part of the accused's defence. However, where the defence raised the disposition for violence of a third party, this opened the door for the Crown to lead disposition evidence of the accused.

Although an accused's propensity towards certain conduct is generally not admissible, there may be occasions where propensity reasoning will be admitted because it is critical to the proper functioning of the criminal trial process. For example, in *Batte*,[23] Doherty J.A. argued:

> The criminal law's resistance to propensity reasoning is not, however, absolute. There will be situations in which the probative force of propensity reasoning is so strong that it overcomes the potential prejudice and cannot be ignored if the truth of the allegation is to be determined. The probative force of propensity reasoning reaches that level where the evidence, if accepted, suggests a very strong disposition to do the very act alleged in the indictment. For example, if an accused is charged with assaulting his wife, evidence that the accused beat his wife on a regular basis throughout their long marriage would be admissible. Evidence of prior beatings does much more than suggest that the accused is a bad person or that the accused has a general disposition to act violently and commit assaults. The evidence suggests a strong disposition to do the very act in issue — assault his wife. In such cases, the jury is permitted to reason, assuming it accepts the evidence of prior assaults, that the accused was disposed to act violently towards his wife and that he had that disposition on the occasion in issue. The existence

---

[23] 2000 CarswellOnt 2113, 49 O.R. (3d) 321, 145 C.C.C. (3d) 449, 34 C.R. (5th) 197, 134 O.A.C. 1, [2000] O.J. No. 2184 (C.A.).

of the disposition is a piece of circumstantial evidence that may be considered in deciding whether the accused committed the alleged assault.[24]

Marital violence, as in the *Batte* case, usually involves issues of credibility. The defence to an allegation by a wife that she was assaulted by her husband will often be a simple denial that it happened. If the Crown seeks to lead evidence of previous assaults as evidence supporting the wife's credibility on the particular occasion in question, the issue then becomes — who is telling the truth? Evidence of previous acts of violence by the accused on his wife, if admitted, will undoubtedly be very persuasive as to whether he did, in fact, assault his wife on the occasion in question. However, the Supreme Court in *Handy*[25] warned trial judges that they must take care not to open the door too wide to admit propensity evidence since credibility is an issue that pervades most trials, and at its broadest may amount to a decision on guilt or innocence. Similar fact evidence should not be used simply to bolster the credibility of the complainant.

Before admitting disposition evidence, judges must be careful to identify the issue that the evidence is being led to prove. Unfortunately, this was not done in *C.(D.A.R.)*.[26] There the accused was charged with sexually assaulting his common law spouse by ripping off her panties and digitally penetrating her. The accused admitted that he had assaulted her but stated that the complainant's panties had ripped accidently, and that he did not digitally penetrate her. The trial judge admitted, as similar fact evidence, previous instances of assault or threatened assault by the accused upon the complainant because he suspected her of having relationships with other men. On appeal, it was held that the trial judge had not erred since feelings of jealously and other emotions were relevant in proving not only the intent but also the actual doing of the act — *sexually* assaulting her. This reasoning is difficult to reconcile with the decision of the Supreme Court in *Handy* which the Court of Appeal relied upon to support its conclusion that the evidence was relevant to the issue in question. Since the accused had admitted assaulting the complainant on previous occasions and the issue in question was only whether he had *sexually* assaulted her by ripping her panties and digitally penetrating her, it is difficult to understand to what issue the evidence of previous conduct was relevant.

---

[24] *Ibid.*, at p. 481 [C.C.C.].

[25] 2002 CarswellOnt 1968, 2002 CarswellOnt 1969, 164 C.C.C. (3d) 481, 1 C.R. (6th) 203 (S.C.C.). See also *K. (C.P.)*, 2002 CarswellOnt 4408, 171 C.C.C. (3d) 173, 7 C.R. (6th) 16 (C.A.).

[26] 2002 CarswellPEI 89, 170 C.C.C. (3d) 64 (C.A.).

4. JUDICIAL DISCRETION TO EXCLUDE EVIDENCE

The general rule at common law was that, apart from the question of confessions, the court was not concerned with how evidence was obtained. So long as the evidence was relevant to a fact in issue, the court allowed the evidence to be admitted. It was not until the *Wray*[27] case in 1989 that the Supreme Court of Canada was finally prepared grudgingly to recognize a limited judicial discretion to exclude evidence that was otherwise admissible. However, the Court stressed that judicial discretion existed only where that evidence had little probative value and was so gravely or highly prejudicial to the accused that it would prevent a fair trial.

Following the *Wray* case, Canadian courts struggled over the extent of a judge's discretion to exclude evidence. Even the Supreme Court was divided on the issue. That division was summed up by Mr. Justice LaForest in *Potvin*,[28] in these words:

> As my colleague notes, some have interpreted Martland J.'s dictum (in *Wray*) as limiting the discretion solely to situations where the evidence is highly prejudicial to the accused and is of only modest value. I do not accept this restrictive approach to the discretion . . . under English law a judge in a criminal trial always has a discretion to exclude evidence if, in the judge's opinion, its prejudicial effect substantially outweighs its probative value . . . The discretion is grounded in the judge's duty to ensure a fair trial.[29]

Today, the Supreme Court regards the *Wray* formula as superseded by the more expansive formula expressed by La Forest J. in *Potvin*. In *Seaboyer*,[30] the Court said that "admissibility will depend upon the probative effect of the evidence balanced against the prejudice caused to the accused by its admission".[31] Moreover, when it comes to evidence offered by the defence, the courts have said that the discretion of a trial judge to exclude relevant

---

[27] (1970), 1970 CarswellOnt 207F, 1970 CarswellOnt 22, [1971] S.C.R. 272, [1970] 4 C.C.C. 1.

[28] 1989 CarswellQue 16, 1989 CarswellQue 104, [1989] 1 S.C.R. 525, 47 C.C.C. (3d) 289, 68 C.R. (3d) 193, 42 C.R.R. 44, 93 N.R. 42, 21 Q.A.C. 258.

[29] *Ibid.*, at p. 243 [C.R.].

[30] 1991 CarswellOnt 109, 1991 CarswellOnt 1022, [1991] 2 S.C.R. 577, 66 C.C.C. (3d) 321, 7 C.R. (4th) 117, 83 D.L.R. (4th) 193, 6 C.R.R. (2d) 35, 128 N.R. 81, 48 O.A.C. 81.

[31] *Ibid.*, at p. 139 [C.R.], quoting *Sweitzer*, 1982 CarswellAlta 552, 1982 Carswell-Alta 132, [1982] 1 S.C.R. 949, 37 A.R. 294, 21 Alta. L.R. (2d) 97, 68 C.C.C. (2d) 193, 29 C.R. (3d) 97, 137 D.L.R. (3d) 702, [1982] 5 W.W.R. 555, 42 N.R. 550.

evidence should only be exercised where the prejudice *substantially* outweighs its probative value.[32]

There are some instances where the right to exclude evidence which is highly prejudicial has been specifically recognized by the Supreme Court. One is where the Crown is seeking to introduce evidence under section 715(1) of the *Criminal Code*.[33] Section 715 provides that the Crown *may* read in at trial evidence given by a witness at the previous trial of the accused on the same charge, or in the investigation of the charge against the accused, or on the preliminary inquiry into the charge, where the witness refuses to be sworn or to give evidence, or is dead, insane, too ill to travel or testify, or is absent from Canada. The rationale underlying section 715 is necessity — the fact that the witness is unavailable to testify. At one time, the rule was that the judge had no discretion to refuse to admit the evidence where the conditions set out in section 715(1) had been met, even though the section said that the evidence *may* be admitted. However, in *Potvin*,[34] the Supreme Court decided that the word "may" does confer on the trial judge the discretion not to allow the previous testimony to be admitted in circumstances that would operate unfairly to the accused. An example of the exercise of that discretion would occur where the accused satisfies the judge that he did not have full opportunity to cross-examine the witness. In *Potvin*, Wilson J. explained how that discretion should be exercised by trial judges:

> In my view there are two main types of mischief at which the discretion (to refuse to admit evidence under section 715) might be aimed. First, the discretion could be aimed at situations in which there has been unfairness in the manner in which the evidence was obtained . . . An example of unfairness in obtaining the testimony might be a case in which, although the witness was temporarily absent from Canada, the Crown could have obtained the witness's attendance at trial with a minimal degree of effort. Another example might be a case in which the Crown was aware at the time when the evidence was initially taken that the witness would not be available to testify at the trial but did not inform the accused of the fact so that he could make best use of the opportunity to cross-examine the witness at the earlier proceeding . . . A different concern at which the discretion might have been aimed is the effect of the admission of the previously-taken evidence on the

---

[32] *Seaboyer, supra* note 30 at pp. 611-12, [1991] 2 S.C.R; *Watson*, 1996 Carswell-Ont 2884, 30 O.R. (3d) 161, 108 C.C.C. (3d) 310, 50 C.R. (4th) 245, 92 O.A.C. 131 (C.A.); *Clarke*, 1998 CarswellOnt 3447, 129 C.C.C. (3d) 1, 18 C.R. (5th) 219 (C.A.) at para. 33.

[33] R.S.C. 1985, c. C-6.

[34] *Supra*, note 28.

fairness of the trial itself. This concern flows from the principle of the law of evidence that evidence may be excluded if it is highly prejudicial to the accused and of only modest probative value . . .[35]

In Ontario, the Court of Appeal has gone further and said that it is not sufficient for the Crown to simply show that a witness is not compellable because he or she is out of the jurisdiction to satisfy the necessity requirement. Section 715 evidence is hearsay and requires the judge to undertake a necessity/reliability analysis before it should be admitted. This means that efforts should be made to pursue other options for presenting the evidence, such as teleconferencing or taking commission evidence, before one reaches the conclusion that admitting evidence by way of a hearsay statement is necessary.[36] The Court noted that the additions to the *Criminal Code* in 1999 of sections 714.2 and 714.4 require the trial judge to consider the possibility of taking the evidence in a live manner via audio or video technology.[37] As Feldman J.A for the Court put it, "It seems to me that when s. 715(1)(d) is read together with ss. 714.2 and 714.4, it is incumbent on a trial judge to include, as a consideration before making the order, the possibility of taking the evidence in a live manner via audio or video technology.[38]

Another instance where the Supreme Court has held that there is a discretion to exclude evidence which may be probative, but also gravely prejudicial, is where the Crown seeks to cross-examine the accused under section 12 of the *Canada Evidence Act*[39] on his criminal record. Section 12 of the Act permits the accused or a witness to be asked whether he has been convicted of any offence and, if he denies or refuses to answer the question, allows the criminal record of the accused or witness to be proved. In *Corbett*,[40] the Supreme Court held that the trial judge has a limited discretion to

---

[35] *Ibid.*, at pp. 237-38 [C.R.].

[36] *Li*, 2012 ONCA 291, 2012 CarswellOnt 5530, 284 C.C.C. (3d) 207, *Finta*, 1992 CarswellOnt 96, 73 C.C.C. (3d) 65, 14 C.R. (4th) 1 (C.A.); affirmed on other grounds (1993), 1994 CarswellOnt 61, 1994 CarswellOnt 1154, [1994] 1 S.C.R. 701, 88 C.C.C. (3d) 417, 28 C.R. (4th) 265; reconsideration / rehearing refused (June 23, 1994), Doc. 23023, 23097 (S.C.C.), *Orpin*, 2002 CarswellOnt 1327, 165 C.C.C. (3d) 56 (C.A.), and *O'Connor*, 2002 CarswellOnt 3955, 62 O.R. (3d) 263, 170 C.C.C. (3d) 365, 7 C.R. (6th) 205 (C.A.).

[37] *Li, supra* at para. 56.

[38] *Supra* at para. 56

[39] R.S.C. 1985, c. C-5.

[40] 1988 CarswellBC 756, 1988 CarswellBC 252, [1988] 1 S.C.R. 670, 28 B.C.L.R. (2d) 145, 41 C.C.C. (3d) 385, 64 C.R. (3d) 1, [1988] 4 W.W.R. 481, 34 C.R.R. 54, 85 N.R. 81.

prevent cross-examination of an accused on his previous criminal record where it might unduly prejudice, mislead or confuse the trier of fact.

Thus, there is an obligation upon a trial judge to determine whether to exclude evidence that is otherwise admissible. This obligation requires an assessment of the value of the evidence, the strength of the inferences, its reliability, and whether admitting the evidence would be fair to the witnesses for the Crown and the defence. Crown evidence that impairs the ability of an accused to make full answer and defence will be more readily excluded whereas defence evidence may be excluded as a matter of discretion "only where the prejudice *substantially* outweighs the probative value".[41]

5. CONSTITUTIONAL REQUIREMENT TO EXCLUDE EVIDENCE

The *Charter of Rights and Freedoms*,[42] enacted in 1982, has substantially broadened the court's powers to exclude evidence where a right or freedom guaranteed by the *Charter* has been denied or infringed. Section 24 provides:

> 24. (1) Anyone whose rights or freedoms, as guaranteed by this Charter, have been infringed or denied may apply to a court of competent jurisdiction to obtain such remedy as the court considers appropriate and just in the circumstances.

> (2) Where, in proceedings under subsection (1), a court concludes that evidence was obtained in a manner that infringed or denied any rights or freedoms guaranteed by this Charter, the evidence *shall* be excluded if it is established that, *having regard to all the circumstances*, the admission of it in the proceedings would bring the administration of justice into disrepute. [Emphasis added].

It is important to note at the outset that section 24(2) is concerned not only with the fairness of an accused's trial, but also with the method by which the evidence was obtained by the prosecution. For example, in *Manninen*,[43] the accused told a police officer that he did not want to say any-

---

[41] *Seaboyer*, 1991 CarswellOnt 109, 1991 CarswellOnt 1022, [1991] 2 S.C.R. 577, 66 C.C.C. (3d) 321, 7 C.R. (4th) 117 at pp. 611-12 [S.C.R.].

[42] *Canadian Charter of Rights and Freedoms*, Part 1 of the *Constitution Act, 1982*, being Schedule B to the Canada Act 1982 (U.K.), 1982, c. 11.

[43] 1987 CarswellOnt 967, 1987 CarswellOnt 99, [1987] 1 S.C.R. 1233, 61 O.R. (2d) 736 (note), 34 C.C.C. (3d) 385, 58 C.R. (3d) 97, 41 D.L.R. (4th) 301, 38 C.R.R. 37, 76 N.R. 198, 21 O.A.C. 192.

thing until he had seen his lawyer. However, the officer continued to question the accused and obtained an incriminating answer that the trial judge relied upon in convicting him. It was held that the officer's conduct was a deliberate and flagrant disregard of the accused's right to counsel as guaranteed by section 10(b) of the *Charter of Rights and Freedoms*.

Section 24(2), however, does not say that every breach of the *Charter* will result in the exclusion of evidence obtained by that breach. It is only where it is established by the accused that, "having regard to all the circumstances, the admission of it in the proceedings would ["could", *i.e.*, "susceptible" under the French version] bring the administration of justice into disrepute". In 1987, the *Collins*[44] case, the first in a series of decisions by the Supreme Court interpreting section 24, decided that a trial judge should consider three factors in determining whether the administration of justice would [could] be brought into disrepute. The first was whether the admission of the evidence would affect the fairness of the trial. Here the Court drew a distinction between evidence that was already pre-existing, such as a murder weapon, and evidence that was obtained purely as a result of a *Charter* violation, such as a confession. It said that a *Charter* violation relating to pre-existing evidence was not as serious as one where the evidence was obtained after a violation of the *Charter*. The Court reasoned that the use of evidence obtained after a violation of the *Charter*, such as a person's confession, strikes at one of the fundamental tenets of a fair trial — the right against self-incrimination. It stressed that where the evidence existed prior to the *Charter* violation, then the more serious the offence, the less likely the evidence would be excluded, as that, in itself, would bring the administration of justice into disrepute. On the other hand, where the evidence was obtained as a result of a *Charter* violation, the more serious the offence, the more damaging to the system's repute would be an unfair trial, in which case the evidence should be excluded.

Lamer J. wrote:

> The trial is a key part of the administration of justice, and the fairness of Canadian trials is a major source of the repute of the system ... If the admission of the evidence in some way affects the fairness of the trial, then the admission of the evidence would tend to bring the administration of justice into disrepute and, subject to a consideration of other factors, the evidence generally should be excluded.[45]

---

[44] 1987 CarswellBC 94, 1987 CarswellBC 699, [1987] 1 S.C.R. 265, 13 B.C.L.R. (2d) 1, 33 C.C.C. (3d) 1, 56 C.R. (3d) 193, *(sub nom. Collins v. R.)* 38 D.L.R. (4th) 508, [1987] 3 W.W.R. 699, 28 C.R.R. 122, 74 N.R. 276.

[45] *Ibid.*, at (C.R.) p. 211.

The second factor that a trial judge was required to consider was the seriousness of the violation. Relevant to this issue was whether the violation was committed in good faith, whether it was inadvertent or of a merely technical nature, whether it was motivated by urgency or to prevent the loss of evidence, and whether the evidence could have been obtained without a *Charter* violation.

The last factor that the judge had to consider was the effect excluding the evidence would have on the administration of justice. Here the focus again was on the fairness of the trial. Evidence was not automatically admissible even where the breach was trivial, the charge serious and the evidence essential to substantiate the charge, if it would result in an unfair trial.

Lamer J. explained:

> Real evidence that was obtained in a manner that violated the Charter will rarely operate unfairly for that reason alone. The real evidence existed irrespective of the violation of the Charter and its use does not render the trial unfair. However, the situation is very different with respect to cases where, after a violation of the Charter, the accused is conscripted against himself through a confession or other evidence emanating from him. *The use of such evidence would render the trial unfair, for it did not exist prior to the violation and strikes at one of the fundamental tenets of a fair trial, the right against self-incrimination.* [Emphasis added].[46]

Although the *Collins* case required judges to consider all three factors, the Supreme Court in 1992 began to focus its attention on the first factor, trial fairness. In *Elshaw*[47] and *Broyles*,[48] the Court said that where the tainted evidence affects the fairness of the trial, the second set of factors, that is, good faith on the part of the police, cannot reduce the seriousness of the violation. Mr. Justice Iacobucci, delivering the judgment of the Court in *Elshaw*, re-affirmed that the test for the admissibility of self-incriminating evidence under section 24(2) was more stringent than the test for real evidence. This was because the breach of the right against self-incrimination was directly related to a *Charter* violation and its admission would dramati-

---

[46] *Ibid.*

[47] 1991 CarswellBC 215, 1991 CarswellBC 922, [1991] 3 S.C.R. 24, 59 B.C.L.R. (2d) 143, 67 C.C.C. (3d) 97, 7 C.R. (4th) 333, 3 B.C.A.C. 81, 6 C.R.R. (2d) 1, 128 N.R. 241, 7 W.A.C. 81.

[48] (1991), 1991 CarswellAlta 212, 1991 CarswellAlta 560, [1991] 3 S.C.R. 595, 120 A.R. 189, 84 Alta. L.R. (2d) 1, 68 C.C.C. (3d) 308, 9 C.R. (4th) 1, [1992] 1 W.W.R. 289, 8 C.R.R. (2d) 274, 131 N.R. 118, 8 W.A.C. 189.

cally affect the presumption of innocence of an accused, as well as his or her right not to testify. He wrote:

> A proper approach would have been premised on the principle that, as a general rule, such evidence (self-incriminating remarks as a result of the breach of right to counsel) is not admissible because it would adversely affect the fairness of the trial and bring the administration of justice into disrepute.[49]

In 1995, the Supreme Court again dealt with the issue of the admissibility of self-incriminating evidence obtained through a violation of the accused's section 10(b) right to counsel. In *Burlingham*,[50] the accused, who was charged with first-degree murder, had been repeatedly questioned by the police intensively and in a manipulative way, even though he indicated that he wished to consult with his lawyer. The police had also denigrated the integrity of his counsel. Burlingham ultimately accepted a deal to plead guilty to second-degree murder in exchange for a full confession and assisting the police in locating the murder site and the murder weapon. The accused complied with his end of the agreement. However, the deal fell through because Burlingham misunderstood that he had to plead guilty to second-degree murder. The Crown then tried him for first-degree murder and he was convicted.

At trial, the judge had refused to admit the evidence of Burlingham's confession, the disclosure of the location of the weapon and his directions and gestures to the police. He did, however, admit the fact of the finding of the gun and the testimony of the accused's girlfriend regarding statements that he had made to her. Burlingham appealed his conviction to the Supreme Court, arguing that the judge had erred in admitting the evidence of the finding of the gun. The Court set aside his conviction.

Adopting the "but for" approach to derivative evidence, the Court held that such evidence should not have been admitted by the trial judge because it brought the administration of justice into disrepute. The Court observed that "but for" the unconstitutional behaviour of the police, the derivative evidence, that is, the gun would not have been found.

In vigorous dissent, Madam Justice L'Heureux-Dubé expressed concern that the Supreme Court's broad interpretation of the term "trial fairness" in the first branch of the *Collins* test resulted in virtually automatic exclusion of evidence whenever there is a finding of "trial unfairness". She felt that

---

[49] *Supra*, note 44, at p. 351 [C.R.].

[50] 1995 CarswellBC 71, 1995 CarswellBC 639, [1995] 2 S.C.R. 206, 97 C.C.C. (3d) 385, 38 C.R. (4th) 265, 124 D.L.R. (4th) 7, 58 B.C.A.C. 161, 28 C.R.R. (2d) 244, 181 N.R. 1, 96 W.A.C. 161.

this approach was inconsistent with a court's obligation under s. 24(2) to determine whether the evidence should be excluded "having regard to all of the circumstances". To do so would allow "trial fairness . . . to wag the section 24(2) dog". As far as she was concerned, the only evidence that could result in an unfair trial would be evidence that was not reliable by reason of some connection with state action amounting to a *Charter* breach.

Mr. Justice Sopinka felt it necessary to address her concerns. He wrote:

> A fair trial is the sine qua non of our justice system and it is hard to conceive of a situation in which it could be said that an unfair trial resulting in a conviction did not depreciate the repute of our system of justice.[51]

In 1997, the Supreme Court in *Stillman*,[52] finally clarified the direction it had been taking since its seminal interpretation of section 24(2) in *Collins*. In *Stillman*, the Court said that the distinction between real or testimonial evidence was no longer relevant in a section 24(2) remedy analysis. Evidence must now be classified as "conscriptive" or "non-conscriptive" depending upon how the evidence was obtained. Evidence was "conscriptive" when an accused, in violation of his *Charter* rights, was compelled to incriminate himself at the behest of the state by means of a statement, the use of the body, or the production of bodily samples. "Non-conscriptive" evidence was that which the accused was not compelled to participate in its creation or discovery because it existed independently of the *Charter* breach in a form useable by the state. If the evidence was non-conscriptive, its admission would not render the trial unfair and courts would proceed to consider the two other tests in *Collins*, namely, the seriousness of the breach and the effect that exclusion would have on the repute of the justice system. If the evidence was conscriptive, then the Crown had to establish on a balance of probabilities that the evidence would have been discovered by alternative non-conscriptive means. If the Crown failed to do so, then its admission would render the trial unfair. In such instance, it would not be necessary to consider the remaining tests, since an unfair trial would automatically bring the administration of justice into disrepute (the third test). However, if the Crown demonstrated on balance that the conscriptive evidence would have been discovered by alternative means, then its admission would generally not render the trial unfair. In such instance, the trial judge would have to consider the second and third tests, namely the seriousness of

---

[51] *Ibid.*, at p. 455 [C.C.C.].
[52] 1997 CarswellNB 107, 1997 CarswellNB 108, [1997] 1 S.C.R. 607, 185 N.B.R. (2d) 1, 113 C.C.C. (3d) 321, 5 C.R. (5th) 1, 144 D.L.R. (4th) 193, 472 A.P.R. 1, 42 C.R.R. (2d) 189, 209 N.R. 81, [1997] S.C.J. No. 34.

the breach and the effect that exclusion would have on the repute of the justice system.

In *Stillman*, the issue was whether hair samples, buccal swabs and dental impressions taken from the accused, using threats and contrary to his express wishes and the explicit written directions of his lawyers, should have been excluded. A majority panel of the Court (6-3) held that they should have been excluded because they were taken in violation of Stillman's right to security of the person as protected by section 7 of the *Charter* and could not have been obtained otherwise. However, a tissue discarded by the accused that contained nasal mucous suitable for DNA analysis was admissible. Although the tissue was conscriptive, it could have been obtained by a warrant to seize the tissue. Moreover, the violation was not serious and there was no interference with the accused's bodily integrity.

Complaints by provincial appellate courts that the Supreme Court had developed a rule of automatic or near automatic exclusion began to surface and the Court was called upon to revisit the issue.[53] Finally, the Supreme Court in *Grant*,[54] acknowledged that existing jurisprudence on the issue of exclusion of evidence was difficult to apply and could lead to unsatisfactory results. McLachlin C.J.C. observed:[55]

> ... the concepts of trial fairness and conscription under the first branch of *Collins* introduced new problems of their own. Moreover, questions arose about what work (if any) remained to be done under the second and third categories, once conscription leading to trial unfairness had been found. Finally, issues arose as to how to measure the seriousness of the breach under the second branch and what weight, if any, should be put on the seriousness of the offence charged in deciding whether to admit evidence.

In *Grant*, the Court decided that the approach to admissibility of bodily evidence under section 24(2) that asked simply whether the evidence was conscripted should be replaced by a flexible test based "on all of the circumstances", as the wording of section 24(2) requires. As for other types of evidence, it was decided that admissibility should be determined by inquiring into the effect admission may have on the repute of the justice system, having regard to the seriousness of the police conduct, the impact of the

---

[53] See Laskin J.A. in *Grant*, 2006 CarswellOnt 3352, 81 O.R. (3d) 1, 209 C.C.C. (3d) 250, 38 C.R. (6th) 58, 143 C.R.R. (2d) 223, 213 O.A.C. 127, [2006] O.J. No. 2179, 70 W.C.B. (2d) 390 (C.A.); reversed in part 2009 SCC 32, 2009 CarswellOnt 4104, 2009 CarswellOnt 4105, 245 C.C.C. (3d) 1, 66 C.R. (6th) 1, 84 W.C.B. (2d) 241.

[54] 2009 SCC 32, 2009 CarswellOnt 4104, 2009 CarswellOnt 4105, 245 C.C.C. (3d) 1, 66 C.R. (6th) 1, 84 W.C.B. (2d) 241

[55] *Supra* at para. 62.

Charter breach on the protected interests of the accused, and the value of a trial on the merits.

The Court accepted that criteria relevant to determining when, in "all the circumstances", admission of evidence obtained by a *Charter* breach "would bring the administration of justice into disrepute" had to be clarified. It noted that the purpose of section 24(2) was to maintain the good repute of the administration of justice. It noted as well that viewed broadly, the term "administration of justice" embraces maintaining the rule of law and upholding *Charter* rights in the justice system as a whole; the phrase "bring the administration of justice into disrepute" must be understood in the long-term sense of maintaining the integrity of, and public confidence in, the justice system. The Court said that while exclusion of evidence resulting in an acquittal may provoke immediate criticism, section 24(2) does not focus on the immediate reaction to the individual case. Rather, it looks to whether the overall repute of the justice system, viewed in the long term, will be adversely affected by admission of the evidence. The inquiry is objective, the Court said, and asks whether a reasonable person, informed of all relevant circumstances and the values underlying the *Charter*, would conclude that the admission of the evidence would bring the administration of justice into disrepute. Moreover, the focus of section 24(2) should be not only long-term, but also prospective. The fact of the *Charter* breach means damage has already been done to the administration of justice and section 24(2) starts from that proposition and seeks to ensure that evidence obtained through that breach does not do further damage to the repute of the justice system. Its focus is also societal; not aimed at punishing the police or providing compensation to the accused, but rather at systemic concerns.

The Court said that when faced with an application for exclusion under section 24(2), a court is now required to assess and balance the effect of admitting the evidence on society's confidence in the justice system having regard to: (1) the seriousness of the *Charter*-infringing state conduct, (2) the impact of the breach on the *Charter*-protected interests of the accused, and (3) society's interest in the adjudication of the case on its merits. At the first stage, the nature of the police conduct that infringed the *Charter* and led to the discovery of the evidence must be considered. The more severe or deliberate the state conduct that led to the *Charter* violation, the greater the need for the courts to dissociate themselves from that conduct by excluding evidence linked to that conduct in order to preserve public confidence in and ensure state adherence to the rule of law. The second stage of the inquiry calls for an evaluation of the extent to which the breach actually undermined the interests protected by the infringed right. The more serious the incursion on these interests, the greater the risk that admission of the evidence would bring the administration of justice into disrepute. At the third stage, a court should ask whether the truth-seeking function of the criminal trial process would be better served by admission of the evidence or by its exclusion. Factors such as the reliability of the evidence and its importance to the Crown's case should be considered at this stage. The weighing process and the balancing of these concerns is a matter for the trial judge in each case.[56] Where the trial judge has considered the proper factors, appellate courts should accord considerable deference to his or her ultimate determination.

The Court also reaffirmed that *discoverability* remains relevant to the section 24(2) analysis.[57]

> Discoverability retains a useful role, however, in assessing the actual impact of the breach on the protected interests of the accused. It allows the court to assess the strength of the causal connection between the *Charter*-infringing self-incrimination and the resultant evidence. The more likely it is that the evidence would have been obtained even without the statement, the lesser the impact of the breach on the accused's underlying interest against self-incrimination. The converse, of course, is also true. On the other hand, in cases where it cannot be determined with any confidence whether evidence would have been discovered in absence of the statement, discoverability will have no impact on the s. 24(2) inquiry. [para. 122]

6. ADMISSIBILITY VERSUS WEIGHT

It is important to draw a distinction between the admissibility of evidence and its weight. When one side seeks to introduce evidence and the other side objects, the trial judge must rule as to its admissibility. This a threshold question that the trial judge must decide before allowing the evidence to be introduced. The decision generally involves a question of law that only the trial judge can decide, and in some instances may involve an assessment of the strength of the evidence or both. An example is where the trial judge must decide whether a confession by the accused is voluntary. Another is

---

[56] In *Harrison*, 2009 SCC 34, 2009 CarswellOnt 4108, 2009 CarswellOnt 4109, [2009] 2 S.C.R. 494, 245 C.C.C. (3d) 86, 66 C.R. (6th) 105, the Supreme Court stressed that *Charter* protections must be construed so as to apply to everyone, even those alleged to have committed the most serious criminal offences para. [40]; see also *Blake*, 2010 ONCA 1, 2010 CarswellOnt 23, 251 C.C.C. (3d) 4, 71 C.R. (6th) 317.

[57] *Côté*, 2010 QCCA 303, 2010 CarswellQue 1175, 2010 CarswellQue 15137, (sub nom. *R. v. Côté*) 276 C.C.C. (3d) 30, 74 C.R. (6th) 130; reversed 2011 CarswellQue 10407, 2011 CarswellQue 10408, 276 C.C.C. (3d) 42, 87 C.R. (6th) 1 (S.C.C.).

whether hearsay evidence which one side seeks to introduce has satisfied the tests of necessity and reliability. If the judge rules that the evidence has passed the threshold test and is admissible, then the question of what importance or weight should be attached to the evidence is a matter solely for the trier of fact, either a jury or the judge sitting without a jury.

This distinction is of particular importance when we come to Chapter 3 dealing with hearsay evidence and recent developments in the law of hearsay authorizing a trial judge to admit hearsay evidence that meets the twin tests of necessity and reliability. Whenever such evidence is admitted, the trial judge must remind the jury (or himself, where he sits alone) of the potential unreliability of such evidence and instruct the jury that the question of the weight to be attached to such evidence is for them alone.

7. THE RULE AGAINST COLLATERAL FACTS

(a) The Rule

The fundamental rule governing the adversary system is that evidence must be relevant to a fact in issue, otherwise it will be considered collateral and inadmissible. The purpose of the rule against introducing collateral facts is to ensure that the focus of a trial is only on the events that form the basis of a prosecution. The rule is designed to ensure that answers given by a witness during cross-examination on matters that are not directly related to the facts in issue are treated as final, and cannot be contradicted by extrinsic evidence.

A number of reasons have been advanced for the rule. Although questions considered collateral may show that the witness is not a credible person, such questions are considered too remote, may mislead the jury and may detract the trier from the main issue in the case. There is also the concern that it would only encourage a series of mini-trials on the credibility of each witness and unduly prolong the length of the trial. As one author has said,

> On cross-examination, every permissible type of impeachment that may be employed during cross-examination has as one of its purposes the testing of the credibility of the witness. The use of extrinsic evidence to contradict is more restricted due to considerations of confusion of the issues, misleading the jury, undue consumption of time, and unfair prejudice raised by the introduction of so-called collateral matters. If a matter is considered collateral, the testimony of the witness on direct or cross-examination stands — the cross-examiner must take the witness' answer; extrinsic evidence, i.e., evidence offered other than through the witness himself, in contradiction is not permitted. If the matter is not collateral, extrinsic evidence may be in-

troduced disputing the witness' testimony on direct examination or denial of truth of the facts asserted in a question propounded on cross-examination.[58]

While there are critics of the rule,[59] the more difficult question is — what is a collateral fact? One of the earliest attempts at a definition is that of Baron Pollock in *Attorney General v. Hitchcock*,[60]

> The test whether a matter is collateral or not is this: if the answer of a witness is a matter which you would allow on your part to prove evidence — if it have such connection with the issues, that you would be allowed to give it in evidence — then it is a matter on which you may contradict him.

In other words, the rule restricts a party from calling extrinsic evidence which contradicts an opposing witness' testimony *on a collateral matter*. While the rule is clear, what is a collateral matter is not always clear. This was pointed out by the English Court of Criminal Appeal in *Funderburk (Roy)*.[61]

> The difficulty we have in applying that celebrated test is that it seems to us to be circular. If a fact is not collateral then clearly you can call evidence to contradict it, but the so-called test is silent on how you decided whether that fact is collateral. The utility of the test may lie in the fact that the answer is an instinctive one based on the prosecutor's and the court's sense of fair play rather than any philosophic or analytic process.

Craig J.A. offered an explanation as to the meaning of collateral in *Krause*,[62]

> One sometimes reads, or hears, a statement that credibility is a collateral issue. This is misleading. Credibility may be a secondary issue in a particular case, the primary issue being whether the Crown is able to establish the guilt of the accused beyond a reasonable doubt, but it is always an underlying issue. Evidence of the former words and conduct of a witness which is unrelated to the circumstances in issue is inadmissible either because it is immaterial or because it is irrelevant. It is collateral in both senses of the word. To the extent, however, that the former words and conduct of a witness may bear on his credibility in the case before the court, he may be questioned about them, but his answers may not be contradicted because to permit such a contradiction would cause confusion of issues, surprise and

---

[58] *McCormick on Evidence* (4th ed. 1992), vol. 1, at pp. 182-83.

[59] J. A. Andrews, "Issues as to the Credibility of Witnesses", [1965] Crim.L.R. 461.

[60] (1847), 154 E.R. 38, 1 Exch. 91.

[61] (1989), [1990] 2 All E.R. 482 (C.A.) at p. 491.

[62] 1984 CarswellBC 845, 12 C.C.C. (3d) 392 (C.A.) at p. 405 [C.C.C.], ; reversed 1986 CarswellBC 330, 1986 CarswellBC 761, 29 C.C.C. (3d) 385, 54 C.R. (3d) 294 (S.C.C.).

unfair prejudice. On the other hand, a person's words and conduct in relation to the case before the court are not collateral. They are very relevant.

The first question that must be asked in determining whether a question is collateral is what is the question designed to prove. If is designed to prove a fact in issue, of course, it is not collateral. However, if it is designed to prove some potentially relevant fact that may not be in issue at the time, but may be later, then whether or not it is collateral will depend upon the evidence that is later presented. If the sole relevance of the question is to test the credibility of the witness on a matter unrelated to the issues in the case, then it will be considered collateral and no evidence may be called to contradict the witness on that matter.[63] However, where the evidence of the witness is critical to the issues in the case, it is arguable that in some instances contradictory evidence should be admissible to show that that the witness is not credible even if the contradictory evidence is considered collateral.

Questions testing the veracity of a witness are particularly problematic in a sexual assault case where an accused wishes to establish that the accusation is false and that the complainant should not be believed because she has made a similar accusation against another person that was dismissed by the court. Since there are usually no witnesses to the assault, such cases are known as "she said, he said" cases — the credibility of a complainant will be critical to a successful defence. If the complainant accuses another person of sexual assault and the charge was dismissed, is the fact that she was not believed on another occasion relevant to the issue whether she should be believed on this occasion? In *Riley*[64] it was held that it was not and that such evidence was collateral and not admissible. The Court said,

> To have Rowsell (the acquitted accused) testify that the complaint was false, would only introduce a collateral issue of credibility which would be as difficult to resolve as those contained in the complaints of which the trial judge was seized. Even if we had a proper record of Rowsell's trial, a not guilty verdict, standing by itself, could not establish that the prosecution was based on fabricated testimony by the complainant.

Should the same reasoning apply where the defence seeks to cross-examine a police officer whose evidence was rejected by a trial judge in another case, specifically where the judge found that the police officer had lied? In other words, is the expression "once a liar always a liar", evidence

---

[63] *Crane*, 1991 CarswellSask 133, 69 C.C.C. (3d) 300 (C.A.) per Wakeling J.A. at p. 309.

[64] 1992 CarswellOnt 707, 11 O.R. (3d) 151 (C.A.); leave to appeal refused [1993] 2 S.C.R. x.

of a witness's lack of credibility. That issue arose in *Ghorvei*.[65] The issue there was whether the defence was entitled to cross-examine a police officer with respect to a finding made by a judge in a prior proceeding that the officer was a "compulsive liar. I do not believe his evidence at all". The accused had been convicted of trafficking in heroin and breach of recognizance and attempted, on appeal, to lead fresh evidence of the finding against the officer in the form of the transcript of the previous trial. In dismissing the appeal, it was held that the previous trial judge's finding was nothing more than a rejection of the officer's testimony. The Court said that if the fact that the officer had lied under oath formed the basis of a conviction for perjury or giving contradictory evidence by the officer, he could have been subjected to cross-examination on that conviction and on its underlying facts.

(b) Exceptions to the Rule

There are certain exceptions to the no-collateral-evidence rule. The most commonly recognized exception is the use of a prior criminal record of the witness. Although it is not permitted to lead evidence to show that a witness has not been believed in a previous proceeding,[66] a cross-examiner has the right to prove that a witness has previously been convicted of a criminal offence. Section 12 of the *Canada Evidence Act* provides for this well-known exception.

> 12. (1) A witness may be questioned as to whether the witness has been convicted of any offence, excluding any offence designated as a contravention under the *Contraventions Act*, but including such an offence where the conviction was entered after trial on an indictment.
>
> (1.1) If the witness either denies the fact or refuses to answer, the opposite party may prove the conviction.

If the witness either denies the fact or refuses to answer, the opposite party may prove the conviction by producing a certificate of the conviction and proof of identity. Although the plain language of section 12 seems to restrict the question to the particulars of the conviction and not the underlying facts, case law confirms that the cross-examiner is not restricted to questioning the witness only on the particulars of the conviction. The witness may be cross-examined on the underlying facts of a conviction, subject

---

[65] 1999 CarswellOnt 2763, 138 C.C.C. (3d) 340, 29 C.R. (5th) 102 (C.A.).
[66] *Ghorvei, supra.*

to the trial judge's general discretion to limit the cross-examination within the bounds of relevance and propriety.[67]

The purpose of section 12 is to permit the judge or jury to conclude that because the witness has been convicted of an offence, he or she is less worthy of belief.[68] Of course, not every conviction is an indication that the witness is not worthy of belief. A conviction for fraud is evidence that a person is not worthy of belief but a conviction for assault indicates that the witness may be a violent person but not necessarily a liar. Yet the authorities draw no such distinction in the case of the ordinary witness. For example, in *Miller*,[69] Charron J.A. (as she then was) pointed out that such cross-examinations may be relevant to discreditable conduct and associations, unrelated to the subject-matter of the testimony, as a ground for disbelieving the witness's testimony. In other words, a judge or jury is entitled to disbelieve what the witness is saying because he or she has been a bad person in the past. The character of the witness is a factor in deciding whether he is worthy of belief.

On the other hand, where the witness is the accused, the rule is different. The Supreme Court has said that while it is permissible under section 12 to ask an accused whether he or she has been convicted of a criminal offence, the trial judge has the discretion to exclude evidence in situations where its probative value is substantially outweighed by its prejudicial effect.[70] In *Corbett*,[71] the Court said that the right to cross-examine an accused on a prior criminal record should not be automatic. It questioned the fairness of cross-examining an accused on a prior criminal record unless the record was in some way indicative of the accused's credibility with respect to the charge he or she was now facing. For example, if the accused was charged

---

[67] *Davison*, 1974 CarswellOnt 559, 20 C.C.C. (2d) 424 (C.A.); leave to appeal refused (1974), 20 C.C.C. (2d) 424n (S.C.C.); *Gassyt*, 1998 CarswellOnt 3241, 127 C.C.C. (3d) 546 (C.A.); leave to appeal refused (1999), 136 C.C.C. (3d) vi (S.C.C.); *Miller*, 1998 CarswellOnt 4983, 131 C.C.C. (3d) 141, 21 C.R. (5th) 178 (C.A.)

[68] *Corbett*, 1988 CarswellBC 756, 1988 CarswellBC 252, [1988] 1 S.C.R. 670, 41 C.C.C. (3d) 385, 64 C.R. (3d) 1; *Watson*, 1996 CarswellOnt 2884, 30 O.R. (3d) 161, 108 C.C.C. (3d) 310, 50 C.R. (4th) 245, 92 O.A.C. 131 (C.A.) at para. 76.

[69] *Supra* note 67. Relying upon *Davison*, 1974 CarswellOnt 559, 20 C.C.C. (2d) 424 (C.A.); leave to appeal refused (1974), 20 C.C.C. (2d) 424n (S.C.C.) and *Gassyt*, 1998 CarswellOnt 3241, 127 C.C.C. (3d) 546 (C.A.); leave to appeal refused (1999), 136 C.C.C. (3d) vi (S.C.C.).

[70] *Corbett*, 1988 CarswellBC 756, 1988 CarswellBC 252, [1988] 1 S.C.R. 670, 41 C.C.C. (3d) 385, 64 C.R. (3d) 1.

[71] *Ibid.*

with arson, it was permissible to cross-examine on a prior criminal record involving fraudulent conduct because a person who commits arson to collect insurance money is dishonest.[72] But what if there was no insurance on the building that the accused was alleged to have burnt. Would a conviction for arson automatically be an indication of prior dishonesty?

Once the cross-examiner is allowed to go into the details of the conviction, the risk of prejudice may be greater depending on the nature of the details. If details of very serious conduct are allowed to emerge that are not readily apparent from the plain words of a conviction, supporters of permitting detail will argue that this will permit the trier to have clearer information about the nature of the accused and to better assess the kind of person giving evidence, and therefore his or her credibility. To ensure that the details do not prejudice the fair trial of the accused, the general rule is that cross-examination of an accused on a prior criminal record should be restricted to the nature of the offence, the date and place of conviction and the penalty imposed.[73] On the other hand, it is open for counsel for the accused to bring out in chief details of the convictions where they are not as serious as one would expect from the wording of the convictions.

Another exception to the general rule will arise where the accused places his or her character in issue. If an accused says that he is a person of good character, then it is only fair that the Crown be allowed to cross-examine the accused on prior acts of discreditable conduct, including details of prior convictions, subject to the right to exclude such evidence where its prejudicial effect outweighs its probative value.[74] Similarly, if the accused attacks the character of a Crown witness, then it is only fair that his or her own character should be open to attack. Unless the Crown is given the right to attack the accused, the judge and jury may be left with the impression that the accused has lead an exemplary life while the Crown's witness has not.[75]

---

[72] *Watkins*, 1992 CarswellOnt 1062, 70 C.C.C. (3d) 341 (C.A.) where the accused had 19 prior convictions under the *Unemployment Insurance Act*.

[73] *Laurier*, 1983 CarswellOnt 825, 1 O.A.C. 128 (C.A.) at p. 131 [O.A.C.]; *W. (L.K.)*, 1999 CarswellOnt 3014, 138 C.C.C. (3d) 449 (C.A.); leave to appeal refused 2000 CarswellOnt 4252, 2000 CarswellOnt 4253 (S.C.C.).

[74] *McNamara (No. 1)*, 1981 CarswellOnt 1243, 56 C.C.C. (2d) 193 (C.A.); leave to appeal refused [1981] 1 S.C.R. xi; affirmed 1985 CarswellOnt 939, 1985 CarswellOnt 96, (sub nom. *Canadian Dredge & Dock Co. v. R.)* 19 C.C.C. (3d) 1, 45 C.R. (3d) 289 (S.C.C.); *Farrant*, 1983 CarswellSask 132, 1983 CarswellSask 235, 4 C.C.C. (3d) 354, 32 C.R. (3d) 289 (S.C.C.).

[75] *Tremblay*, 2006 CarswellQue 14116, 2006 CarswellQue 299, 209 C.C.C. (3d) 212 (C.A.).

Evidence which demonstrates bias or partiality by a witness is another exception to the no-collateral evidence rule. Facts to establish bias or partiality on the part of a witness may be elicited on cross-examination and, if denied, may be independently proved. As Doherty J.A, explained in *Watson*,[76]

> A witness's credibility may be impeached by cross-examination intended to show that the witness has a bias for or against a party to the litigation or a personal interest to be served by testifying in a particular manner. Because impeachment by the demonstration of bias or partiality is potentially so helpful to the trier of fact in assessing a witness's credibility, the opposing party is allowed to call evidence to contradict a witness's denial of partiality or bias.

An example is *Green*.[77] At issue in that case was whether evidence that the complainant had on two prior occasions alleged that she had been sexually assaulted by other persons only to later recant those allegations was relevant to the credibility of her allegation against the accused. The trial judge had refused to admit the evidence holding it was collateral to the issue of whether the accused had sexually assaulted the complainant. It was held that the trial judge had erred. The questions were proper questions to put to the complainant on cross-examination. Moreover, evidence of her recantations to the very witness to whom she had complained of sexual assault by the accused was relevant in assessing the complainant's general credibility and the reliability of her statement to the witness that she had just been sexually assaulted by the accused.

Evidence of a witness's reputation for untruthfulness has also been accepted as an exception to the no-collateral evidence rule. It allows a party to call a witness and to ask that witness whether he or she knows the reputation of an impugned witness for veracity. If the witness says that he or she does, then the witness may be asked whether they would believe the impugned witness on oath.[78] This exception, an old one, has been the subject of much criticism. The concern is that there is a risk that in some cases the

---

[76] 1996 CarswellOnt 2884, 30 O.R. (3d) 161, 108 C.C.C. (3d) 310, 50 C.R. (4th) 245, 92 O.A.C. 131 (C.A.) at para. 77 referring to *Martin*, 1980 CarswellOnt 1262, 53 C.C.C. (2d) 425 (C.A.) at pp. 434–36 [C.C.C.]; *Attorney General v. Hitchcock* (1847), 1 Exch. 91 (Eng.) at pp. 101–103; E. Ratushny, "Basic Problems in Examination and Cross-examination" (1974), 52 Can. Bar Rev. 209 at 240-41; *U.S. v. Abel*, 105 S.Ct. 465 (1984) at pp. 468-69; McCormick on Evidence, *supra* at pp. 130–36.

[77] 2013 ONCA 74.

[78] *Gonzague*, 1983 CarswellOnt 81, 4 C.C.C. (3d) 505, 34 C.R. (3d) 169 (C.A.); *T. (S.)*, 1986 CarswellOnt 144, 31 C.C.C. (3d) 1, 55 C.R. (3d) 321 (C.A.).

jury will simply over value that opinion and defer to the opinion of the character witness because that witness obviously knows the impugned witness and is in a much better position to assess the witness's credibility.[79]

Medical evidence that is capable of establishing that a witness suffers from a mental disease or abnormality of the mind that may affect the reliability of his or her evidence is another exception to the rule.[80] Here evidence is not confined to a general opinion of the unreliability of the witness. Evidence may be given to show, not only the foundation and reason for the diagnosis, but also the extent to which the credibility of the witness is affected

Is it open for an accused to question the methods used by an expert in the behavioral, social and emotional characteristics of sexual abused children on the interview techniques used by the expert during interviews of children who allege that they have been sexually assaulted? If the defence denies the abuse and the credibility of the children is in question, it would follow that the defence should be allowed to cross-examine the therapist on the interview techniques used to prove that they had been coached or manipulated even though the credibility of the children is a collateral matter.

In *R. (D.)*,[81] it was held that the trial judge had erred in ruling that the transcripts of the methods used in interviewing children's complaints of sexual abuse should not be used to show that there had been coaching or manipulation because it was collateral. Major J., who delivered the majority decision, wrote,[82]

> The credibility of the children was at the heart of the case against the appellants. The appellants would have been entitled to lead evidence on the effect of the interview techniques on the memories of the children, and, accordingly, met the test in *Hitchcock*. Any evidence that might have cast doubt on the children's credibility, or that might show that the children had been subject to coaching and manipulation, was evidence that would have been crucial to the appellants' case.

---

[79] *Clarke*, 1998 CarswellOnt 3447, 129 C.C.C. (3d) 1, 18 C.R. (5th) 219 (C.A.).

[80] *Hawke*, 1975 CarswellOnt 4, 22 C.C.C. (2d) 19, 29 C.R.N.S. 1 (C.A.); *French*, 1977 CarswellOnt 1011, 37 C.C.C. (2d) 201 (C.A.); affirmed 1979 CarswellOnt 709F, 1979 CarswellOnt 709, 47 C.C.C. (2d) 411 (S.C.C.).

[81] 1996 CarswellSask 448, 1996 CarswellSask 449, 107 C.C.C. (3d) 289, 48 C.R. (4th) 368 (S.C.C.).

[82] *Supra* at p. 305.

2
KINDS OF EVIDENCE

1. INTRODUCTION

The law recognizes two methods of proof: direct evidence and circumstantial evidence. There is no particular magic in these terms. Direct evidence is simply evidence that directly proves a fact in issue. For example, if the fact in issue is whether Smith stabbed Jones, a witness who testifies that he saw Smith stab Jones is giving what is known as direct evidence.

Circumstantial evidence, on the other hand, is evidence of surrounding circumstances from which an inference may be drawn that a certain event occurred. If, in our previous example, the witness did not see Smith stab Jones, but saw Smith walking down the street all covered in blood with a knife in his hand and Jones, a short distance away, lying in a pool of blood, it would be reasonable to infer from all of the surrounding circumstances that Smith did in fact stab Jones. This is circumstantial evidence of a fact in issue, as opposed to direct evidence of the fact.

Although both kinds of evidence are admissible, the court scrutinizes circumstantial evidence more carefully. The burden of proof will be discussed later. It is only necessary to say at this stage that the burden is always upon the Crown to prove the guilt of an accused, and such proof must be established beyond a reasonable doubt. Where proof is based upon circumstantial evidence, either in whole or in part, a judge will usually caution a jury (or him or herself when trying the case without a jury) that before they can rely on circumstantial evidence, they must be satisfied that the guilt of the accused is the only logical inference to be drawn from such evidence.

There are three kinds of evidence that are generally recognized as admissible to establish a fact in issue. They are: oral testimony or *viva voce* evidence; real evidence, which includes documents or things such as weapons, etc.; and demonstrative evidence, which includes photographs, maps, etc.

2. ORAL TESTIMONY

(a) Generally

The most common way that evidence is given is by a witness entering the witness box and testifying in open court. In Canada, as well as throughout other common law jurisdictions, the order of questioning a witness is strictly controlled. The witness is first examined by the side that calls the witness; the witness may then be cross-examined by the other side; and finally the witness may be re-examined by the side that called him or her. Unlike the inquisitorial system, which allows a witness to repeat his evidence with little interruption, the evidence of a witness is tightly controlled by the questions asked. This does not mean that the witness must answer either yes or no. However, the witness is expected to be responsive to the questions put to him. A witness is not entitled to make a speech unconnected with the question asked.

There is a distinction, however, between the type of questions that may be asked in chief (that is, by the side who calls the witness) and the questions that may be asked in cross-examination (that is, by the opposing side). When a witness is examined in chief, the examiner must not lead the witness or suggest the answer, except on matters that are not disputed or in issue. For example, a witness may be led on all preliminary background matters such as age, marital status, number of children, occupation, *etc.*, unless those issues are disputed or in issue. Often a judge will permit the examiner to lead a witness of tender years or one who is intellectually challenged and is having difficulty expressing him or herself. Such evidence, however, may not be given the same weight as evidence that is not led by the examiner.

On the other hand, there are few restrictions on the cross-examiner. The cross-examiner may lead the witness or suggest answers. One purpose of cross-examination is to test the accuracy of what the witness has said in chief. Another is to test the honesty of the witness. And another is to bring out new evidence that the witness did not give in chief that is favourable to the cross-examiner's case. Once cross-examination is completed, the side that called the witness is entitled to re-examine him. Here, however, re-examination is restricted solely to matters that were raised in cross-examination, and then only to clarify those answers that were given.

(b) Competence of the Witness

(i) Generally

Not everyone is allowed to enter the witness box and give oral evidence. A person called as a witness must be competent to give testimony. Competence refers to the legal qualification of a person to give evidence. Competence must also be distinguished from compellability. Compellability refers to the right of either side of a dispute to call a witness to give evidence and the legal obligation of that witness to testify.

It was not until the end of the eighteenth century that a great many individuals were considered incompetent to give evidence. For example, a person who had an interest in the case was not allowed to testify because his evidence was not considered reliable. In fact, it was not until 1640 that a person charged with a felony (*i.e.*, a serious crime), was allowed to call witnesses for his defence. And, until the end of that century, witnesses for the defence were not allowed to give their evidence under oath. The rationale was that such witnesses, if they contradicted the witnesses for the Crown, were probably lying.

Today, generally all witnesses (subject to the exceptions below) are presumed competent to testify if they understand the nature and obligation of an oath. Until recently, that meant that the proposed witness had to understand the spiritual consequences of an oath. In other words, he or she had to believe in God or a Supreme Being. That requirement is no longer necessary. When a witness takes an oath to tell the truth, it means that the witness understands the moral obligation to tell the truth.[1] It also means that the witness understands the legal consequences of lying, namely, the possible prosecution for perjury or giving contradictory evidence. As McLachlin J. (as she then was) wrote in *Khan*:

> Before a person can give evidence under oath, it must be established that the oath in some way gets a hold on his conscience, that there is an appreciation of the significance of testifying in court under oath.[2]

For a long time, a person who would not or could not take an oath because of his or her religious beliefs, or lack of it, was not allowed to testify at all. In Canada today, a person may give sworn testimony without the necessity of taking an oath. Section 14 of the *Canada Evidence Act*[3] allows a person to solemnly affirm if the traditional oath is objected to on the grounds of conscientious scruples or because the person would not be bound by it. In such instance, the person is required to solemnly affirm that the evidence to be given by him or her "shall be the truth, the whole truth and nothing but the truth". This means that if the witness tells a lie, he or

---

[1] *Fletcher*, 1982 CarswellOnt 1229, 1 C.C.C. (3d) 370 (C.A.); leave to appeal refused (1983), 48 N.R. 319 (S.C.C.).

[2] 1990 CarswellOnt 108, 1990 CarswellOnt 1001, [1990] 2 S.C.R. 531, 59 C.C.C. (3d) 92, 79 C.R. (3d) 1, 113 N.R. 53, 41 O.A.C. 353, [1990] S.C.J. No. 81 at p. 7 [C.R.].

[3] R.S.C. 1985, c. C-5.

she is liable to prosecution for perjury or giving contradictory evidence, just as if the traditional oath had been taken. The evidence of a witness who solemnly affirms has the same effect as if given under oath.

Although all witnesses are now presumed competent to testify, a witness may be declared incompetent if the witness suffers from a mental or psychiatric condition that renders it unsafe for the trier of fact to rely on his or her testimony. However, the mere finding that the witness suffers from a particular mental or psychiatric condition does not necessarily disqualify the witness from giving evidence. In order to disqualify a witness, the court must be satisfied that the particular condition is such as to substantially negative the trustworthiness of the witness's evidence on the specific subject.

The general rule, as we shall see later, is that an expert is not permitted to give opinion evidence as to the credibility of a witness. However, where the opposing side seeks to challenge the competency of a witness because of a particular mental or psychiatric condition, experts are permitted to go further and say that the witness suffers from some "hidden defect" which affects the reliability of the testimony. Moreover, the expert's evidence is not confined to a general opinion about the unreliability of the witness. The expert will be permitted to testify about all of the matters necessary to show not only the foundation of and the reasons for the diagnosis, but also the extent to which the credibility of the witness is affected.[4]

(ii) The Accused

Historically, the most serious restriction on the right to testify was on the accused. An accused was not allowed to testify because it was believed that since the accused had an interest in the outcome of the trial, he or she would probably lie. It was not until 1898 that an accused in England was allowed to give evidence under oath on his or her own behalf. In Canada, that right was granted a few years earlier. Today, section 3 of the *Canada Evidence Act* specifically provides that "a person is not incompetent to give evidence by reason of interest or crime".

Section 4(1) of the Act goes on to provide:

> Every person charged with an offence ... *is a competent witness for the defence* whether the person so charged is charged solely or jointly with any other person. [Emphasis added].

This means that although an accused is competent to testify *for the defence*, he or she is still not competent (and therefore not compellable) at the

---

[4] *Hawke*, 1975 CarswellOnt 4, 7 O.R. (2d) 145, 22 C.C.C. (2d) 19, 29 C.R.N.S. 1 (C.A.); *Toohey v. Metropolitan Police Commissioner*, [1965] A.C. 595, [1965] 1 All E.R. 506, 49 Cr. App. R. 148 (U.K. H.L.).

instance of the prosecution to testify against him or herself. It also means that an accused who is jointly tried with others is not competent at the instance of the prosecution to testify against a co-accused; moreover, he or she is not compellable to testify at the instance of a co-accused. The fact that an accused is competent to testify in her own defence means that she becomes an ordinary witness like any other witness once she takes the witness stand. The accused is required to answer any question asked by the prosecution or counsel for a co-accused regarding his involvement in the offence or the involvement of a co-accused.

An accused who fails to testify is protected by section 4(6) of the Act from any adverse comment by the judge or counsel for the prosecution. The purpose is to ensure that the accused's right to silence is not diminished. The protection also extends to an accused where the accused's spouse fails to testify. An accused who had raised an alibi defence but does not give evidence is also protected from adverse comment by the judge or prosecutor. Although it is open for the jury to draw an adverse inference from accused's failure to testify in cases where an alibi defence is offered, the trial judge and prosecutor are prohibited from making an adverse comment on the silence of accused even where the comment is related strictly to the alibi defence.[5]

The Supreme Court has drawn a distinction between a prohibitive comment by a trial judge on the failure of the accused to testify and an instruction by a trial judge to the jury that they are not to draw an adverse inference from the accused's failure to testify. The Court has said that section 4(6) does not prohibit a trial judge from instructing the jury that, as a matter of law, no adverse inference may be drawn from the failure of the accused to testify. Such instruction, it has been suggested, is not a comment on the accused's failure to testify; rather, its regarded as a protection of the accused's right not to testify, and is considered not to be prejudicial.[6] Ritchie J. explained the distinction in *McConnell*.[7]

> Here the language used by the trial judge to which objection is taken was not so much a "comment" on the failure of the persons charged to testify as a statement of their right to refrain from doing so, and it does not appear to

---

5 *Miller*, 1998 CarswellOnt 4983, 131 C.C.C. (3d) 141, 21 C.R. (5th) 178 (C.A.).

6 *McConnell*, 1968 CarswellOnt 17, [1968] S.C.R. 802, [1968] 4 C.C.C. 257; *Avon*, 1971 CarswellQue 39, 1971 CarswellQue 39F, [1971] S.C.R. 650, 4 C.C.C. (2d) 357; and *Potvin*, 1989 CarswellQue 16, 1989 CarswellQue 104, [1989] 1 S.C.R. 525, 47 C.C.C. (3d) 289, 68 C.R. (3d) 193; *Prokofiew*, 2012 SCC 49, 2012 CarswellOnt 12411, 2012 CarswellOnt 12412, 290 C.C.C. (3d) 280, 96 C.R. (6th) 57.

7 *McConnell, ibid.* at p. 809 [S.C.R.].

me that it should be taken to have been the intention of Parliament in enacting s. 4(5) (now 4(6)) of the *Canada Evidence Act* to preclude judges from explaining to juries the law with respect to the rights of accused persons in this regard. . . .

> I think it is to be assumed that the section in question was enacted *for the protection of accused persons against the danger of having their right not to testify presented to the jury in such fashion as to suggest that their silence is being used as a cloak for their guilt.* [Emphasis added]

Similarly, in *Avon*,[8] the Supreme Court said,

> I would say that the language used by [the trial judge] is a "statement" of an accused's right not to testify, rather than a "comment" on his failure to do so. In my opinion, the instructions complained of cannot be construed as prejudicial to the accused or such as to suggest to the jurors that his silence was used to cloak his guilt.

The distinction between a comment on the failure to testify and an instruction that no adverse inference may be drawn from a failure to testify may be difficult for the judge to express and for the jury to understand. For example, in *Prokofiew*,[9] the Crown alleged that P and his co-accused, S, participated in a fraudulent scheme involving the fictitious sale of heavy equipment to generate harmonized sales tax that was then not remitted to the federal government as required. The fraudulent nature of the scheme was never challenged by the defence nor was the involvement of P and S in the scheme. The question for the jury was whether either or both accused were aware of the fraudulent nature of the scheme. P did not testify, but was incriminated by S's testimony. In his closing address, S's counsel invited the jury to infer P's guilt from P's failure to testify. Although accepting that counsel's comment might prejudice P, the trial judge nevertheless refrained from giving a remedial instruction to the jury about P's right to silence because he was concerned that any comment would breach section 4(6). P was convicted. Although a majority panel of the Supreme Court applied the curative proviso of section 686(1)(b)(iii) of the *Criminal Code* and dismissed P's appeal, it was held that the trial judge had erred in failing to affirm the accused's right to silence. Section 4(6) does not prohibit trial judges from instructing the jury that, as a matter of law, no adverse inference may be drawn from the failure of the accused to testify. Such instruction is not a comment on the accused's failure to testify but rather a protection of the accused's right not to testify, and is not prejudicial.

---

[8] *Supra*, at p. 655.

[9] 2012 SCC 49, 2012 CarswellOnt 12411, 2012 CarswellOnt 12412, 290 C.C.C. (3d) 280, 96 C.R. (6th) 57.

(iii) *The Spouse of the Accused*

Historically, another person who was not allowed to give evidence was the spouse of an accused, unless the offence charged affected the spouse's person, health or liberty. This was initially based on the theory that husband and wife were one. Thus, if the accused was incompetent to testify, so was his or her spouse. Eventually, this reason was abandoned and justification for the rule was based on the natural repugnance of using the law to compel a wife to betray her husband or *vice versa*, if marital harmony was to be preserved. The rule was even applied if the parties were not husband and wife at the time of the offence, so long as they were married at the time of the trial.[10] Ironically, the same rule was not applied to prevent a child from betraying a parent, or a sister or brother from betraying a sibling.

The rule rendering a spouse incompetent to testify was eventually abolished in Canada at the end of the 19th century by section 4 of the *Canada Evidence Act*. Section 4(1) of the Act now makes a spouse "a competent witness for the defence", but not for the prosecution, subject to certain exceptions outlined in subsections (2) and (4). Those exceptions relate generally to certain sexual offences or assaults against children under the age of 14. Here a spouse is a competent witness for the prosecution, without the consent of the accused. Another exception is contained in section 4(5). It gives statutory recognition to the common law rule that allowed the prosecution to call a spouse to give evidence where the offence charged affected the spouse's person, health or liberty.

Over the last couple of decades, the courts have indicated that they intend to restrict the spousal non-competency rule to the policy considerations underlying it. For example, in *Salituro*,[11] the Supreme Court said that if the parties, although legally married, are separated with no reasonable prospect for reconciliation, then the public policy of promoting marital harmony would have no rational foundation and spousal incompetence will no longer apply. It has also been held that the time for determining whether spouses have irreconcilably separated is at the time of the trial.[12] Moreover, the so-

---

[10] *Hoskyn v. Commissioner of Police for the Metropolis* (1978), [1979] A.C. 474, [1978] 2 All E.R. 136, 67 Cr. App. R. 88 (U.K. H.L.).

[11] 1990 CarswellOnt 101, 56 C.C.C. (3d) 350, 78 C.R. (3d) 68, 38 O.A.C. 241 (C.A.); affirmed 1991 CarswellOnt 1031, 1991 CarswellOnt 124, [1991] 3 S.C.R. 654, 68 C.C.C. (3d) 289, 9 C.R. (4th) 324, 8 C.R.R. (2d) 173, 131 N.R. 161, 50 O.A.C. 125.

[12] *Jeffrey*, 1993 CarswellAlta 84, 141 A.R. 299, 12 Alta. L.R. (3d) 153, 84 C.C.C. (3d) 31, 25 C.R. (4th) 104, 106 D.L.R. (4th) 442, 17 C.R.R. (2d) 95, 46 W.A.C. 299 (C.A.).

called "common law marriage" or "common law relationship" has not been recognized by the courts so as to render one of the parties to that relationship incompetent to testify for the Crown against the other.[13]

Although the Supreme Court has indicated a willingness to adapt and develop common law rules to reflect changing circumstances in society at large, it has also stressed that such changes should only be made incrementally to the common law.[14] A good example of where the Court refused to make any changes was *Hawkins*.[15] There the Crown had suggested that a spouse should be rendered competent if the marriage was solemnized after the issuance of an information or indictment and where an accused married a witness for the purpose of insulating that witness from being called by the prosecution. The Court rejected this suggestion for a number of reasons. First of all, it would strike at the heart of the traditional rule of spousal incompetency. Secondly, such a marriage may be perfectly valid and genuine, a marital bond worthy of protection. Thirdly, even if the marriage were motivated by a desire to take advantage of the incompetency rule, it may nonetheless be a true marriage deserving of the law's protection. Finally, the Supreme Court said that it would be unworkable because it would require the courts to examine the motivation for the marriage, and there would be no justification for such an inquiry unless there was concrete evidence that the marriage was legally invalid. The Court, however, did not absolutely rule out such an inquiry where the evidence clearly established that the only purpose of the marriage was to avoid criminal responsibility by rendering a key witness non-compellable and the partners had no intention of fulfilling their mutual obligations of care and support.

In refusing the Crown's suggestion, the Court stressed that complex changes to the law with uncertain ramifications that could result should be left for resolution by Parliament. Although the Crown had relied upon *Salituro*[16] to support the Court's authority to change the law, the Court noted that the change which it made in that case did not strike at the original

---

[13] *Duvivier*, 1990 CarswellOnt 958, 75 O.R. (2d) 203, 60 C.C.C. (3d) 353 (Gen. Div.); affirmed 1991 CarswellOnt 87, 64 C.C.C. (3d) 20, 4 C.R. (4th) 378 (C.A.); *Martin*, 2009 CarswellSask 159, 244 C.C.C. (3d) 206, 64 C.R. (6th) 377 (C.A.). But see *Masterson*, 2009 CarswellOnt 4069, 245 C.C.C. (3d) 400, 69 C.R. (6th) 266 (S.C.J.).

[14] *Couture*, 2007 CarswellBC 1365, 2007 CarswellBC 1366, [2007] 2 S.C.R. 517, (sub nom. *R. c. C. (D.R.)*) 220 C.C.C. (3d) 289, 47 C.R. (6th) 1.

[15] 1996 CarswellOnt 4063, 1996 CarswellOnt 4062, [1996] 3 S.C.R. 1043, 30 O.R. (3d) 641 (headnote only), 111 C.C.C. (3d) 129, 2 C.R. (5th) 245, 141 D.L.R. (4th) 193, 204 N.R. 241, 96 O.A.C. 81, [1996] S.C.J. No. 117.

[16] *Supra*, note 11.

justifications of marital harmony and repugnance which animated the substance of the common law rule.

As will be discussed later in this chapter (Compellability of the Witness), the *compellability* of a witness must be distinguished from the question of a witness's *competence* to give evidence. Although a spouse of an accused may be competent to testify by common law or statute, he or she is not necessarily compellable to give testimony against the accused

(iv) Children

Until recently, section 16(1) of the *Canada Evidence Act* contemplated that there were two persons who *might* not be competent to give evidence: the first was a person under the age of fourteen years; the second was a person whose mental capacity was challenged. Before a person under the age of fourteen was allowed to give evidence, the court was required to conduct an inquiry to determine whether that person understood the nature of an oath or a solemn affirmation, and whether he or she was able to communicate the evidence. The rule was based upon the belief that children were generally incompetent to testify because they were incapable of distinguishing fact from fiction, and did not appreciate the importance of an oath and the obligation to tell the truth. Before permitting a child to testify, judges were required to question the child to determine whether the child understood the nature of an oath and was able to articulate their evidence.

The belief that children were generally incompetent was rejected by Parliament's enactment of section 16.1 of *the Canada Evidence Act* that came into force on January 2, 2006. Section 16.1 removes the presumption that a person under the age of fourteen does not have the capacity to testify. It was passed following Parliament's receipt of the findings of the *Child Witness Project* at Queen's University. The *Child Witness Project* was composed of an interdisciplinary research team headed by Professor Nicholas Bala. Its purpose was to investigate the impact of pre-testimonial competency inquiries on child witnesses. The project concluded that,

> Child witnesses can be equally as reliable as adult witnesses, and often provide essential evidence for the criminal justice process;
>
> There is no relationship between a child's ability to answer questions about such abstract concepts, as "truth" and "lie", and whether they will actually tell the truth or lie;
>
> If a child promises to tell the truth, the child is more likely to tell the truth, even if the child cannot give a definition of a "promise";
>
> The CCTV, screen and videotape provisions of the *Code* have facilitated the giving of evidence by children in the criminal justice system without compromising the rights of accused persons, but they are insufficiently used; and

Applications for orders for the use of testimonial aids were inefficiently made and inconsistently granted.

Section 16.1 provides that "A person under fourteen years of age is presumed to have the capacity to testify". Subsection 3 further provides that "the evidence of a proposed witness under fourteen years of age shall be received if they are able to understand and respond to questions". Moreover, subsection 2 no longer requires that a witness under fourteen years of age take an oath or make a solemn affirmation "despite a provision of any Act that requires an oath or a solemn affirmation". Subsection 6 only requires a witness under fourteen years of age to promise to tell the truth; and subsection 8 provides that such evidence shall have the effect "as if it were taken under oath".

Although the competence of a witness under fourteen years of age to testify may still be challenged, the burden is now on the side that challenges the witness's competence. Section 16.1(4) provides:

> (4) A party who challenges the capacity of a proposed witness under fourteen years of age to testify has the burden of satisfying the court that there is an issue as to the capacity of the proposed witness to understand and respond to questions.

If the challenger satisfies the judge that there is an issue as to the witness' capacity to understand and respond to question, subsection 5 requires the judge to conduct an inquiry into that capacity. This means that the challenger must present some evidence to show incapacity. It is not enough simply to allege incapacity. However, any challenge to incapacity may not be based upon the witness's understanding of the promise to tell the truth.

> (7) No proposed witness under fourteen years of age shall be asked any questions regarding their understanding of the nature of the promise to tell the truth for the purpose of determining whether their evidence shall be received by the court.

Attacks on section 16.1 as infringing sections 7 and 11(d) of the *Charter* have been unsuccessful. In *S. (J.)*,[17] the Supreme Court said that section 16.1 of the *Canada Evidence Act* does not infringe ss. 7 and 11(d) of the *Charter*. The Court affirmed the decision of the British Columbia Court of Appeal that had held that in enacting section 16.1 of the *Canada Evidence Act*, Parliament has decided that a promise to tell the truth is sufficient to engage the child's moral obligation to tell the truth. Section 16.1 placed a child witnesses on a more equal footing with an adult witness by presuming testimonial competence. Under section 16.1, potential concerns about a

---

[17] 2008 CarswellBC 2132, 238 C.C.C. (3d) 522, 61 C.R. (6th) 282 (C.A.); affirmed 2010 CarswellBC 91, 2010 CarswellBC 92, 251 C.C.C. (3d) 1, 72 C.R. (6th) 42 (S.C.C.).

child's credibility, reliability and understanding of the nature of the promise to tell the truth go to the weight of the evidence, not its admissibility. The provision changes the focus in the context of the children's evidence from one of admissibility to one of reliability. It discards the former rigid pre-testimonial requirements which often prevented a child from testifying because of their inability to articulate an understanding of abstract concepts that even many adults have difficulty explaining.

(v) Persons Who May be Mentally Incompetent

Section 16 of the *Canada Evidence Act* permits the other side to challenge a witness fourteen years of age or older who may be mentally incompetent to testify. Where that challenge is made, the court must conduct an inquiry to determine whether the person understands the nature of an oath or a solemn declaration and whether the person is able to communicate the evidence. Section 16 of the Act provides:

> 16. (1) If a proposed witness is a person of fourteen years of age or older whose mental capacity is challenged, the court shall, before permitting the person to give evidence, conduct an inquiry to determine
>
> > (a) whether the person understands the nature of an oath or a solemn declaration; and
> >
> > (b) whether the person is able to communicate the evidence.
>
> (2) A person referred to in subsection (1) who understands the nature of an oath or a solemn affirmation and is able to communicate the evidence shall testify under oath or solemn affirmation.
>
> (3) A person referred to in subsection (1) who does not understand the nature of an oath or a solemn affirmation but is able to communicate the evidence may, notwithstanding any provision of any Act requiring an oath or a solemn affirmation, testify on promising to tell the truth.
>
> (4) A person referred to in subsection (1) who neither understands the nature of an oath or a solemn affirmation nor is able to communicate the evidence shall not testify.
>
> (5) A party who challenges the mental capacity of a proposed witness of fourteen years of age or more has the burden of satisfying the court that there is an issue as to the capacity of the proposed witness to testify under an oath or a solemn affirmation.

In *I. (D.)*,[18] the Supreme Court was asked to decide whether section 16(3) required an adult witness with mental disabilities to demonstrate an understanding of the nature of the obligation to tell the truth in order to be

---

[18] 2012 CarswellOnt 1089, 2012 CarswellOnt 1090, (sub nom. *R. v. D.A.I.*) [2012] 1 S.C.R. 149, 280 C.C.C. (3d) 127, 89 C.R. (6th) 221.

deemed competent to testify and whether a finding of testimonial competence without a demonstration of an understanding of the obligation to tell the truth breached an accused's right to fair trial. In a majority decision, it was held that section 16(3) imposes only two requirements for the testimonial competence of an adult with mental disabilities: (1) the ability to communicate the evidence; and (2) a promise to tell the truth. It is unnecessary, and indeed undesirable, to conduct abstract inquiries into whether the witness understands the difference between truth and falsity, the obligation to give true evidence in court, and what makes a promise binding. The Court noted that the plain words of section 16(3) focus on the concrete acts of communicating the evidence and promising to tell the truth. Judges should not add other elements to the dual requirements imposed by section 16(3). The Court rejected the argument that this approach transforms the promise into an empty gesture. It reasoned that adults with mental disabilities may have a practical understanding of the difference between the truth and a lie, and know they should tell the truth without being able to explain what telling the truth means in abstract terms. When such a witness promises to tell the truth, the seriousness of the occasion and the need to say what really happened is reinforced.

The Court rejected those authorities that had suggested that section 16(3) requires an abstract understanding of the obligation to tell the truth. That requirement, it was pointed out, was based on a version of section 16 that explicitly required the witness to "understand the duty of speaking the truth". Although Parliament had deleted that requirement in 1987, courts continued to require proof that children understand the duty of telling the truth. Parliament responded by enacting section 16.1(7), which expressly forbids such inquiries of a child. The Court said that the section 16.1(7) ban for children does not require an inference that mentally disabled adults are to be questioned on the obligation to tell the truth for a number of reasons. First, because section 16(3) only requires a promise to tell the truth, Parliament had no need to ban such questioning of adults with mental disabilities. Second, section 16(3) requires only a promise to tell the truth, so there was no need for Parliament to enact a similar provision with respect to section 16(3). Third, the enactment of section 16.1(7) did not imply that the earlier judicial interpretation of section 16(3), as it applied to children, had been endorsed for adult with mental disabilities. Fourth, the fact that section 16 does not have a provision equivalent to section 16.1(7) does not mean that adults with mental disabilities must demonstrate an understanding of the nature of the duty to speak the truth. Finally, there is no need to prove that, unless it can be shown that adults with mental disabilities are the same as, or like, child witnesses, they must be subjected to an inquiry into their understanding of the nature of the obligation to tell the truth before they can be held competent to testify.

The Court said that the underlying policy concerns — bringing the abusers to justice, ensuring fair trials and preventing wrongful convictions — also support allowing adults with mental disabilities to testify. Rejecting the evidence of alleged victims on the ground that they cannot explain the nature of the obligation to tell the truth in philosophical terms would exclude reliable and relevant evidence, immunize an entire category of offenders from criminal responsibility for their acts, and further marginalize the already vulnerable victims of sexual predators. Allowing an adult with mental disabilities to testify when the witness can communicate the evidence and promises to tell the truth does not render a trial unfair. Generally, the reliability threshold is met by establishing that the witness has the capacity to understand and answer the questions put to her and by bringing home the need to tell the truth by securing an oath, affirmation or promise.

Eight considerations were listed by the Supreme Court for applying section 16(3). First, the *voir dire* on the competence of a proposed witness is an independent inquiry: it may not be combined with a *voir dire* on other issues. Second, the *voir dire* should be brief, but not hasty. It is preferable to hear all available relevant evidence that can be reasonably considered before preventing a witness to testify. Third, the primary source of evidence for a witness's competence is the witness herself. Questioning an adult with mental disabilities requires consideration and accommodation for her particular needs; questions should be phrased patiently in a clear, simple manner. Fourth, persons familiar with the proposed witness in her everyday situation may be called as fact witnesses to provide evidence on her development. Fifth, expert evidence may be adduced if it meets the criteria for admissibility, but preference should always be given to expert witnesses who have had personal and regular contact with the proposed witness. Sixth, the trial judge must make two inquiries during the *voir dire* on competence: (a) does the proposed witness understand the nature of an oath or affirmation, and (b) can she communicate the evidence? Seventh, the second inquiry into the witness's ability to communicate the evidence requires the trial judge to explore in a general way whether she can relate concrete events by understanding and responding to questions. It may be useful to ask if she can differentiate between true and false everyday factual statements. Finally, the witness testifies under oath or affirmation if she passes both parts of the test, and on promising to tell the truth if she passes the second part only.

The majority decision had three strong dissenters. Binnie J, with whom LeBel and Fish J.J concurred felt that to permit a witness with a mental disability to testify on a promise to tell the truth, without any inquiry into whether the promise has any significance for the witness, turns the promise to tell the truth into an empty formality and dilutes the protection Parliament intended to provide to accused persons. When Parliament amended the *Canada Evidence Act* to prohibit asking child witnesses "any questions regarding their understanding of the nature of the promise to tell the truth", the empirical evidence before Parliament related exclusively to children. No such empirical studies were carried out with respect to adults with mental disabilities. In their case, no "don't ask" provision was proposed, let alone adopted. Thus, it was argued, the majority judgment has the effect of turning Parliament's direction permitting a person "whose mental capacity is challenged" to testify only "on promising to tell the truth" into an empty formality — a mere mouthing of the words "I promise" without any inquiry as to whether the promise has any significance to the potential witness.

Since it is the judge who must determine whether a witness is incompetent, the usual practice is for the trial judge to question the challenged witness, although the judge may permit counsel to ask questions. Although Crown and defence counsel are permitted to put questions to the challenged witness, the trial judge must ensure that the inquiry is fairly conducted and under his or her control.[19]

Although section 16(1) does not require the inquiry to be conducted in the jury's presence, some Canadian courts have said that it is generally preferable to do so.[20] Support for this practice is found in the decision of Lord Goddard C.J. in *Reynolds*, (dealing with the evidence of a child) where he noted:

> . . . although the duty of deciding whether the child may be sworn or not lies on the judge and is not a matter for the jury, it is most important that the jury should hear the child's answers and see its demeanour when questioned, because those matters will enable the jury to come to a conclusion as to the weight they should attach to its evidence.[21]

That view was echoed by the British Columbia Court of Appeal in *Ferguson*.[22] There the Court noted that the evidence given by a prospective child witness on the inquiry under the former provision might well assist the jury in weighing the child's evidence on the substance of the complaint, if the child is subsequently found competent to testify. The Court felt that the sub-

---

[19] *Peterson*, 1996 CarswellOnt 628, 106 C.C.C. (3d) 64, 47 C.R. (4th) 161 (C.A.); leave to appeal refused (1996), 109 C.C.C. (3d) vi (S.C.C.); *Ferguson*, 1996 CarswellBC 2888, 112 C.C.C. (3d) 342 (C.A.).

[20] *Ibid.*

[21] (1950), 34 Cr. App. R. 60 (C.A.) at p. 64.

[22] *Supra*, note 19.

ject of the child's competence, which is to be determined by the judge, and the child's credibility, which is to be determined by the jury, are tightly entwined. Evidence relevant to one issue will be relevant to the other. The Court acknowledged that there might be the possibility of prejudice to an accused if the child was found by the trial judge not to be competent to testify. However, it also felt that this could be avoided if counsel sat down with the judge before the inquiry began and reviewed ways of avoiding it.

The view that the jury should be present during the inquiry is not universally held by all common law jurisdictions. For example, in Australia, it has been said that where "a question of competency is likely to be prejudicial to the accused, it should be received in the absence of the jury".[23] Similarly, the English Court of Appeal in *Hampshire*[24] said that the above passage by Lord Goddard was not necessary for the decision in *Reynolds* and the practice should not be followed. The Court reasoned that since a proposed witness, whose competence is attacked, is not a witness until the judge has investigated and ruled on the witness's competency, the jury should not be present during the competency hearing. The logic in this argument seems more compelling.

On the other hand, where the competency of a witness is questioned and third party experts (such as psychologists or psychiatrists) are called to give evidence on the issue of a witness's competency, the practice is clear that their evidence should be heard on a *voir dire* in the absence of the jury. In this way, the risk that the jury may draw the conclusion that the experts believe that the witness is telling the truth is avoided. Moreover, it would prevent a breach of the rule against oath helping and the likelihood of prejudice to the accused.[25]

The first branch of the test in section 16(1) requires the judge to question the witness to determine if he or she "understands the nature of an oath or solemn affirmation". Here, the judge's (or counsel's) questions must be directed towards determining whether the witness understands the legal consequences of lying under oath and the special obligation to tell the truth in court. As noted earlier, the test is whether "the oath in some way gets a hold on his (the witness) conscience, that there is an appreciation of the significance of testifying in court under oath".[26] Unfortunately the cases offer lit-

---

[23] *Demirok*, [1977] 137 Crim. L.R. 21.

[24] [1995] 2 Cr. App. R. 319 (C.A.).

[25] *Deakin (Richard Albin)*, [1995] 1 Cr. App. R. 471 (C.A.).

[26] *Khan*, 1990 CarswellOnt 108, 1990 CarswellOnt 1001, [1990] 2 S.C.R. 531, 59 C.C.C. (3d) 92, 79 C.R. (3d) 1, 113 N.R. 53, 41 O.A.C. 353, [1990] S.C.J. No. 81 at p. 7 [C.R.].

tle assistance to the trial judge on how far he or she must go to satisfy the test. This was probably because the nature and extent of the inquiry generally depended upon the age of the witness. In other words, the courts considered that an intensive inquiry was not necessary when the witness was close to 14,[27] while it was for a younger child.[28] Since an inquiry into the capacity of a child under the age of 14 to understand the nature of the promise to tell the truth is no longer permitted,[29] the nature and the extent of the inquiry for persons 14 or older will undoubtedly depend upon their answers to the questions of counsel or the judge.

The second branch of the test obligates the trial judge to determine whether the person whose mental competency is challenged "is able to communicate the evidence". Reference to "the evidence" indicates the ability to testify about the matters before the court. Here the inquiry by the judge is into the capacity of the proposed witness to observe, recollect and communicate generally, not into whether the witness actually observes, recollects and can communicate about the events in question.[30] In other words, any deficiencies in the particular witness's perception, recollection or narration of the events in question will go to the weight of the witness's evidence; it will not go to the witness's competence to testify.[31] However, it has been said that the ability to "communicate the evidence" must mean more than mere verbal ability.[32] It means that the judge who conducts the inquiry must ensure that the proposed witness has the capacity to give his or her evidence with some independence, and not simply in response to suggestive questions.[33] It requires the witness to demonstrate some ability, not only to distinguish between fact and fiction, but also a capacity and a willingness, to relate to the court the essence of what happened to him or her.[34]

If the court is satisfied that a witness whose competency is challenged "understands the nature of an oath or a solemn affirmation and is able to

---

[27] *Fletcher*, 1982 CarswellOnt 1229, 1 C.C.C. (3d) 370 (C.A.); leave to appeal refused (1983), 48 N.R. 319 (S.C.C.).

[28] *L. (J.)*, 1990 CarswellOnt 895, 54 C.C.C. (3d) 225, 37 O.A.C. 269 (C.A.).

[29] Section 16.1(7) C.E.A.

[30] *Marquard*, 1993 CarswellOnt 995, 1993 CarswellOnt 127, [1993] 4 S.C.R. 223, 85 C.C.C. (3d) 193, 25 C.R. (4th) 1, 108 D.L.R. (4th) 47, 159 N.R. 81, 66 O.A.C. 161, [1993] S.C.J. No. 119.

[31] *Marquard, ibid.*

[32] *Marquard, ibid.*

[33] *Caron*, 1994 CarswellOnt 866, 19 O.R. (3d) 323, 94 C.C.C. (3d) 466, 72 O.A.C. 287, [1994] O.J. No. 1591 (C.A.).

[34] *Ibid.*

communicate the evidence", the witness will be entitled to testify under oath or solemn affirmation.[35] However, the fact that a mentally incompetent person does not understand the nature of an oath or of a solemn affirmation will not necessarily result in an exclusion of the witness's testimony. Section 16(3) of the *Canada Evidence Act* provides that if a witness is "able to communicate the evidence" and promises "to tell the truth", the witness will be allowed to give unsworn or unaffirmed testimony.[36]

Ironically, section 16 does not attach any evidentiary distinction in terms of weight to the evidence of someone who is only required to promise "to tell the truth" as opposed to someone who gives evidence under oath or affirmation. Both are entitled to the same weight. Logically, if no lesser weight is to be attached to evidence given after a simple "promise to tell the truth", then it would seem that the requirement of an oath or a solemn affirmation is redundant and of no significance. Although, the language of section 16 viewed in its totality would appear to indicate that evidence given upon a promise "to tell the truth" is at the bottom of the scale in descending order of weight, the courts have said that the weight to be given to a young person's evidence "is not affected by the form of the witness's commitment to tell the truth".[37] In *D. (R.R.)*, Bayda C.J.S. wrote:

> The purpose of an oath, a solemn affirmation and a promise are the same: to put an additional impact on the person's conscience and to give further motivation for the person to tell the truth . . . There is no reason in logic to treat one class of witness as belonging to a higher level than another class. Nor is there any reason in logic to treat differently, from the standpoint of need and importance, the three prerequisites: an oath, a solemn affirmation and a promise.[38]

(c) Compellability

(i) The Accused and Co-Accused

When it is said that a witness is "compellable", it means that the law authorizes either side to call the witness to give evidence. However, the fact that a person may be competent to testify does not necessarily mean that he or she is automatically compellable to testify. Although the general rule is that all competent witnesses are also compellable, there are a number of exceptions.

---

[35] *Canada Evidence Act*, s. 16(2).

[36] *D. (R.R.)*, 1989 CarswellSask 66, 47 C.C.C. (3d) 97, 69 C.R. (3d) 267, 20 R.F.L. (3d) 1, 72 Sask. R. 142 (C.A.).

[37] *McGovern, supra*, note 36 *per* Twaddle J.A. at p. 365 [C.R.].

[38] *Supra*, note 36, at pp. 274-75 [C.R.].

The most notable is the accused. Although an accused is competent to testify for the defence, the accused is not compellable. An accused who elects to testify cannot refuse to answer any question that may incriminate him. The accused must submit to cross-examination on any issue relating to the case, subject to a limited discretion in the trial judge to prevent cross-examination on a previous criminal record where it might unduly prejudice, mislead or confuse the trier of fact.[39]

A person who is jointly charged and tried with another accused is not compellable either by the prosecution or by a co-accused to give evidence at his own trial. But if the accused's trial is severed from the trial of a co-accused by a judge's order for a separate trial, or if the accused is charged in a separate information or indictment by the Crown with the same offence as a co-accused, he or she becomes an ordinary witness at the trial of the co-accused. Although an accused is not compellable to testify at his own trial, he is compellable to testify either for the prosecution or for the defence at the separate trial of his co-accused.

(ii) Spouse of the Accused

When section 4(1) of the *Canada Evidence Act* made an accused's spouse a *competent* witness for the defence, the accused's spouse also became a *compellable* witness for the defence. However, since a spouse is not *competent* to testify for the prosecution, a spouse is not *compellable* to testify for the prosecution, subject to two exceptions.

The first is the common law exception, preserved by section 4(5) of the *Canada Evidence Act*, which allows the prosecution to call the accused's spouse as a witness without the accused's consent where the common law permitted it. The common law made an exception where the evidence disclosed that the spouse's person, liberty or health had been threatened by the accused. The second exception is set out in subsections 4(2) and (4) of the *Act*. Those subsections make husbands and wives compellable against one another with respect to certain specified offences (generally sexual offences and assaults against children under the age of 14). The purpose is to ensure that spouses will testify against one another where an offence has been committed against children, particularly their own. Before the enactment of these sections, children who had been physically or sexually assaulted by one parent could not count upon the other parent to testify against the accused parent.

---

[39] *Corbett*, 1988 CarswellBC 756, 1988 CarswellBC 252, [1988] 1 S.C.R. 670, 28 B.C.L.R. (2d) 145, 41 C.C.C. (3d) 385, 64 C.R. (3d) 1, [1988] 4 W.W.R. 481, 34 C.R.R. 54, 85 N.R. 81.

It is important at this stage to draw a distinction between a "communication" made by husbands and wives to one another and an "observation" by one spouse of the conduct of the other. The two exceptions already discussed, which allow the prosecution to compel a husband or wife to testify against the other, are clearly applicable to "observations" made by that spouse. However, section 4(3) of the *Canada Evidence Act* has preserved the common law rule that prohibits a husband or wife from being compelled by the prosecution to disclose a marital "communication". Section 4(3) provides that:

> 4 (3) No husband is compellable to disclose any communication made to him by his wife during their marriage, and no wife is compellable to disclose any communication made to her by her husband during their marriage.

Not all authorities have been convinced that section 4(3) was intended to preserve the common law exception relating to marital communications. For example, in *St-Jean*,[40] Kaufman J.A. observed:

> It seems to me that it would not make sense to make a spouse competent and compellable, only to put severe restrictions on the scope of his or her testimony.

However, the appellate courts of Alberta and Ontario have not agreed with that observation.[41] They have held that the language of section 4(3) is unambiguous and must be given its plain meaning. Although a spouse may be otherwise competent and compellable to give evidence, a spouse is not compellable to disclose any *communication* (but not observation) made by his or her spouse "during their marriage". Thus a wife who is giving evidence is entitled to invoke the protection of section 4(3) at any time during her testimony and to refuse to disclose a martial communication made to her by her husband, who is an accused.[42] It must be remembered, however, that the privilege extends only to a marital communication received by her

---

[40] 1976 CarswellQue 12, 32 C.C.C. (2d) 438, 34 C.R.N.S. 378 (C.A.) at p. 441 [C.C.C.].

[41] *Jean*, 1979 CarswellAlta 169, 15 A.R. 147, 46 C.C.C. (2d) 176, 7 C.R. 338, 7 C.R. (3d) 338 (C.A.); affirmed 1980 CarswellAlta 312, 1980 CarswellAlta 157, [1980] 1 S.C.R. 400, 20 A.R. 360, 51 C.C.C. (2d) 192, 16 C.R. (3d) 193, 31 N.R. 410; *Mailloux*, 1980 CarswellOnt 77, 55 C.C.C. (2d) 193 at 196, 30 C.R. (3d) 121 (C.A.) at p. 196 [C.C.C.]; *Zylstra*, 1995 CarswellOnt 124, 99 C.C.C. (3d) 477, 41 C.R. (4th) 130, 82 O.A.C. 394 (C.A.).

[42] *Zylstra, ibid.*

from her husband. Section 4(3) does not protect her from revealing any marital communication which she has made to her husband.[43]

It must also be remembered that the protection given by section 4(3) may only be invoked for a verbal communication. If a wife has received a written communication from her husband, the privilege ceases to apply and the written communication is admissible in evidence.[44] Similarly, if a third person overhears a verbal marital communication made by an accused to his wife, the privilege ceases to apply and the person who has heard it may repeat it in court.[45]

(d) Refreshing the Witness's Memory

At the foundation of the common law adversarial system are two notions. The first assumes that a witness will have a memory of the events that he or she is relating to the court. The second assumes that the other side will be allowed to test the accuracy of that memory and the truth of that testimony by cross-examination.

Frequently a witness who is called upon to testify weeks, months or even years after an event, may find that once he or she steps into the witness box, their memory has failed on some critical issue. Historically, the rule was that a witness was entitled to refresh his memory while in the witness box from any record of the event which he had with him made or verified by himself concerning, and contemporaneously with, the facts to which he testified; or by others, providing in the latter case that it was read by him when the facts were fresh in his memory, and he knew the statement to be correct. It was expected that the record was written either at the time of the transaction or so shortly afterwards that the facts were still fresh in his memory. A delay of a fortnight was not considered fatal, but an interval of several weeks, or six months, was held to preclude use of the record to refresh the witness's memory[46]

---

[43] *Lloyd*, 1980 CarswellBC 441, 53 C.C.C. (2d) 121, 16 C.R. (3d) 221 (C.A.); reversed 1981 CarswellBC 633, 1981 CarswellBC 404, [1981] 2 S.C.R. 645, 35 B.C.L.R. 145, 64 C.C.C. (2d) 169, 31 C.R. (3d) 157, 131 D.L.R. (3d) 112, 39 N.R. 474.

[44] *Kotapski*, 1981 CarswellQue 255, 66 C.C.C. (2d) 78 (S.C.); affirmed 1984 CarswellQue 222, 13 C.C.C. (3d) 185 (C.A.); leave to appeal refused (1984), 57 N.R. 318 (S.C.C.); leave to appeal refused 1984 CarswellQue 222, 13 C.C.C. (3d) 185 (C.A.).

[45] *Jean*, *supra* note 41; *Kotapski, ibid.*

[46] *Gwozdowski* (1972), 1972 CarswellOnt 944, [1973] 2 O.R. 50, 10 C.C.C. (2d) 434 (C.A.), quoting *Phipson on Evidence*, 11th ed. (1970), pp. 632-3, art. 1528-29.

In recent years, the strictness of this rule has been relaxed. The courts no longer require that the note be made by the witness or, if made by another, verified by the witness *shortly after the event*. What now appears to be required is that the note be made either by the witness or by another and verified by the witness, *when the event was fresh in the witness's mind*.[47] Common sense tells us that, unless the note was made at least when the event was fresh in the witness's mind, there is a serious risk that the note will contain errors that the witness will probably rely upon when giving testimony. Although delay in making the note will not necessarily prevent the witness from using the note to refresh his or her memory, delay will go to the weight of the witness's testimony.

English courts have also relaxed the strictness of the rule.[48] There the question is one for the discretion of the trial judge applying the requirements of fairness and justice. Such a rule is obviously more sensible. It seems rather arbitrary to say that a witness is only entitled to refresh his or her memory if the note is made shortly after the event. A police officer doing undercover work or on surveillance duty may be unable to make notes until hours after the event in question. Nevertheless, the risk of possible error from the delay cannot be ignored and should be the subject of a caution by the judge to the jury when assessing the weight of the witness's testimony.[49] It is a common and accepted practice for the Crown to give witnesses the transcript of the preliminary inquiry and to ask them to read their testimony at the inquiry in order to refresh their memory of the events in issue before they testify at trial.[50] Although evidence given at the preliminary inquiry is obviously closer to those events in issue, today's preliminary inquiries are often held months or sometimes a year after the event. Presumably, justification for allowing witnesses to refresh their memory from the transcript of the inquiry is based on the fact that before they testified at the inquiry, they refreshed their memory from notes made or a statement given to the police shortly after the event, or at least when the events were fresh in their minds.

---

[47] *Coffin*, 1956 CarswellQue 1, [1956] S.C.R. 191, 114 C.C.C. 1, 23 C.R. 1; *Shergill*, 1997 CarswellOnt 5225, 13 C.R. (5th) 160, 23 O.T.C. 218 (Gen. Div.); *B. (K.G.)*, 1998 CarswellOnt 1914, 125 C.C.C. (3d) 61, 109 O.A.C. 138, [1998] O.J. No. 1859 (C.A.).

[48] *South Ribble Stipendiary Magistrate Ex p. Cochrane*, [1996] 2 Cr. App. R. 544; *Da Silva (Michael Reginald)* (1989), (1990) 90 Cr. App. R. 233 (C.A.).

[49] *B. (K.G.)*, *supra* note 47.

[50] *Coffin*, *supra* note 47.

At one time, the rule was that a witness was only required to produce his notes to the cross-examiner if the witness relied upon the notes while testifying in court; if the witness used the notes to refresh his or her memory before entering the witness box, the witness did not have to produce them to the cross-examiner.[51]

The logic of this distinction is difficult to understand. All it did was encourage witnesses to memorize their notes before they came to court. This meant that neither the judge nor the cross-examiner was aware whether notes existed, and if they did, when they were made in order to test the reliability of the witness's evidence. Today, it is generally accepted that any witness who refreshes his or her memory from any notes or statement made prior to trial, or uses those notes to assist during his or her testimony, must produce them to the cross-examiner.[52] This makes more sense. If a witness refreshes his or her memory before trial or relies upon notes or any documents at trial, then what the witness says when he or she gives testimony may be essentially the information contained in those notes. The cross-examiner should be allowed to examine the notes to consider whether they are consistent with the witness's oral testimony. The cross-examiner may also wish to attack the accuracy of the notes by questioning the timeliness of the record or raising the possibility of invention.

It is, of course, important for a witness relying on notes to be able to advise the court that he or she has an independent memory of the matters upon which they are giving evidence and that the notes are being used only to refresh that memory.[53] The trial judge has a duty to receive this assurance before the witness is allowed to use the notes while giving evidence. Moreover, the witness should not be permitted simply to read the notes since it does not demonstrate that the witness has an independent memory of the events which are being related to the court. Unfortunately, witnesses, particularly police officers, are too often permitted to read their notes into evidence without examining counsel first asking whether the witness has an independent memory of the events and whether he or she requires notes only to refresh that memory.

The discussion so far has proceeded on the assumption that the witness has some memory of the events in issue, but wishes to use the notes to jog

---

[51] *Kerenko* (1964), 1964 CarswellMan 65, [1965] 3 C.C.C. 52, 45 C.R. 291, 49 D.L.R. (2d) 760, 51 W.W.R. 53 (C.A.).

[52] *Catling*, 1984 CarswellAlta 391, 73 A.R. 61, 29 C.C.C. (3d) 168 (Q.B.); *Morgan*, 1993 CarswellOnt 795, 80 C.C.C. (3d) 16 (C.A.); leave to appeal refused (1994), 87 C.C.C. (3d) vi (note), 172 N.R. 246 (note), 72 O.A.C. 82 (note) (S.C.C.).

[53] *Wilks*, 2005 CarswellMan 326, 201 C.C.C. (3d) 11, 35 C.R. (6th) 172 (C.A.).

or refresh that memory. This is what is known as "present memory revived". What happens, however, if the notes do not refresh the witness's memory and that memory is lost forever? Is testimony of that witness lost forever, even though the witness may have made notes of the event? Can the written word ever replace the lost memory?

Professor Wigmore recognized that total memory loss did not necessarily result in lost testimony where certain conditions were met.[54] He called it "past recollection recorded". Those conditions were,

1. The past recollection must have been recorded in some reliable way.

2. At the time, it must have been sufficiently fresh and vivid to be probably accurate.

3. The witness must be able *now* to assert that the record accurately represented his knowledge and recollection at the time. The usual phrase requires the witness to affirm that "he knew it to be true at the time."

4. The original record itself must be used, if procurable.

In other words, the notes or record made at the time replace the memory of the witness and become "past memory recorded".

Canadian courts have been slow to recognize past recollection recorded as an exception to the hearsay rule.[55] The reason may be because of the difficulty in effectively cross-examining a witness who has made a record of the event, but has no memory of it. All that the witness can say is that he or she made a note at the time and, when the note was made, believed it to be true. The witness cannot be cross-examined as to the accuracy of the contents of the note because the witness cannot recall the events contained in the note. Although the necessity for admitting the note is the lack of recollection by the witness, the only basis for the note's reliability is the assurance of the witness that he or she believed the note to be true at the time it was made.

Few Canadian authorities have paid much attention to the distinction between "present memory revived" and "past recollection recorded".[56] This

---

[54] *Wigmore on Evidence* (Chadbourn rev. 1970), Vol. 3, c. 28, para.744 *et seq.*

[55] See *Rouse* (1978), 1978 CarswellBC 508, 1978 CarswellBC 561, (sub nom. *McInroy v. R.)* [1979] 1 S.C.R. 588, 42 C.C.C. (2d) 481, 5 C.R. (3d) 125, 89 D.L.R. (3d) 609, [1978] 6 W.W.R. 585, 23 N.R. 589; *Green*, 1994 CarswellOnt 96, 32 C.R. (4th) 248 (Gen. Div.).

[56] See *Meddoui* (1990), 1990 CarswellAlta 187, 111 A.R. 295, 77 Alta. L.R. (2d) 97, 61 C.C.C. (3d) 345, 2 C.R. (4th) 316, [1991] 2 W.W.R. 289, 5 C.R.R. (2d) 294 (C.A.); leave to appeal refused (1991), [1991] 3 S.C.R. ix, 114 A.R. 80

may be due to the fact that a witness who is asked to refresh their memory from a statement or note before testifying will usually be reluctant to admit that they have absolutely no memory of an event. The problem is that once the witness has reviewed the statement or the note, it is almost impossible for the cross-examiner to determine whether the witness is relying on the note, or his or her memory of the event, or both.

(e) The Adverse or Hostile Witness

(i) The General Rule

The rule, already noted, is that the side who calls a witness is not allowed to ask that witness leading questions, that is, questions that directly or indirectly suggest the answer to the witness. Nevertheless, there may be occasions when a witness will have a lapse of memory and not be responsive to the questions asked by the examiner. In the case of a written statement, this situation may be remedied by simply showing the witness his previous statement and asking him to read it over.[57] It may jog the witness's memory. When this happens, the witness is, in effect, being allowed to refresh his memory. If the previous statement was an oral one, then counsel is entitled to draw the witness's attention to the circumstances surrounding the making of the statement and ask him if he made it.

If the witness cannot remember making the previous inconsistent statement, or denies making it, or admits making it but says that it is false, counsel who called the witness is entitled to call other witnesses to contradict the witness's testimony. This remedy is rarely satisfactory since the witness's in-court testimony, although contradicted by the testimony of other witnesses, may still be considered by the trier with all of the other testimony. Counsel who called the witness is now faced with a problem. Unless that counsel is able to impeach his own witness's testimony with the prior inconsistent statement, the trier will be entitled to consider the witness's in-court testimony for what it is worth.

(note), 82 Alta. L.R. (2d) lxv (note), 69 C.C.C. (3d) vi, [1992] 1 W.W.R. lxv (note), 6 C.R.R. (2d) 192 (note), 137 N.R. 389 (note); *B. (A.J.)*, 1994 CarswellNfld 206, 120 Nfld. & P.E.I.R. 147, 90 C.C.C. (3d) 210, 373 A.P.R. 147 (C.A.); reversed 1995 CarswellNfld 43F, 1995 CarswellNfld 43, [1995] 2 S.C.R. 413, 133 Nfld. & P.E.I.R. 231, 98 C.C.C. (3d) 95, 413 A.P.R. 231, 182 N.R. 384 and *F. (C.)*, 1997 CarswellOnt 4448, 1997 CarswellOnt 4449, (sub nom. *R. v. F. (C.C.)*) [1997] 3 S.C.R. 1183, 120 C.C.C. (3d) 225, 11 C.R. (5th) 209, 154 D.L.R. (4th) 13, 220 N.R. 362, 104 O.A.C. 321, [1997] S.C.J. No. 89.

[57] *Coffin, supra* note 47.

Section 9(1) of the *Canada Evidence Act* offers the examiner a solution. It provides:

> 9. (1) A party producing a witness shall not be allowed to impeach his credit by general evidence of bad character, but if the witness, in the opinion of the court, proves adverse, the party may contradict him by other evidence, or, by leave of the court, may prove that the witness made at other times a statement inconsistent with his present testimony, but before the last mentioned proof can be given the circumstances of the supposed statement, sufficient to designate the particular occasion, shall be mentioned to the witness, and he shall be asked whether or not he did make the statement.

It should be noted at the outset that section 9(1) starts off by stating the general rule that a person calling a witness may not "impeach his credit by general evidence of bad character". The section then goes on to say illogically, "but if the witness, in the opinion of the court, proves adverse," he may be contradicted by other evidence or a prior inconsistent statement. Unfortunately, the draftsman of this legislation misstated the common law and put the cart before the horse. At common law, an examiner was not required to prove that the witness was *adverse* before the witness could be contradicted by other inconsistent evidence. An examiner was entitled to use the prior inconsistent evidence to prove the witness adverse. Fortunately, the courts have ignored this apparent condition precedent and have allowed the calling of other evidence to contradict a witness.

Section 9(1) goes on to allow the examiner to use the cross-examination on the previous inconsistent evidence to have the witness declared "adverse" by the trial judge. The Ontario Court of Appeal has said that a ruling that a witness is "adverse" pursuant to s. 9(1) of the *Canada Evidence Act* is not the equivalent of a common law declaration of "hostility" entitling the examiner to cross-examine the witness at large.[58] An "adverse" witness is one who is opposed in interest or unfavourable in the sense of opposite in position to the party calling that witness. On the other hand, a hostile witness is one who, "from the manner in which he gives his evidence, shows that he is not desirous of telling the truth to the court" or "does not give his or her evidence fairly and with a desire to tell the truth because of a hostile *animus* towards the prosecution".[59] In other words, the witness must

---

[58] *Hanes v. Wawanesa Mutual Insurance Co.* (1961), 1961 CarswellOnt 116, [1961] O.R. 495, [1963] 1 C.C.C. 176 (C.A.); reversed 1963 CarswellOnt 61, [1963] 1 C.C.C. 321 (S.C.C.); *Cassibo*, 1982 CarswellOnt 850, 39 O.R. (2d) 288, 70 C.C.C. (2d) 498 (C.A.); *Figliola*, 2011 ONCA 457, 2011 CarswellOnt 4983, 105 O.R. (3d) 641, 272 C.C.C. (3d) 518.

[59] *Coffin*, 1956 CarswellQue 1, [1956] S.C.R. 191, 114 C.C.C. 1 at p. 213 [S.C.R.], p. 24 [C.C.C.], where Kellock J. equates hostile with adverse under s. 9; See also

demonstrate "an antagonistic attitude or hostile mind toward the party calling him or her".[60] The judge must determine this hostility by observing the witness's general attitude or demeanour in the witness stand and the substance of witness's evidence. Once a witness is declared hostile, the witness may be cross-examined, not only with respect to his previous inconsistent evidence or statement, but on the whole of his evidence, or what is commonly called "at large".

The appellate courts of New Brunswick,[61] and Nova Scotia,[62] have not drawn a distinction between an adverse witness and a hostile one. They have held that the word "adverse" meant "hostile", and not simply "unfavourable".[63] Before a witness called by a party may be cross-examined, the court "must come to the conclusion that the witness bears a hostile *animus* towards that party (in this case the prosecution); in other words, there must be a ruling, either express or implied, that the witness is hostile".[64]

Section 24 of the Ontario *Evidence Act*[65] also codifies the common law with respect to civil proceedings. Although cast in similar language, it does not require the court to first make a finding of adversity before the witness can be impeached by other evidence. Moreover, in *Hanes v. Wawanesa Mutual Insurance Co.*,[66] the Ontario Court of Appeal said that the word "adverse" should be given its ordinary meaning of "opposed in interest" and not the restricted meaning of "hostile". This means that in determining whether the witness is "adverse", the judge is not limited to a consideration only of the witness's demeanour or attitude in the witness box. The trial judge is also entitled to consider the witness's prior inconsistent statement in determining whether he was adverse.

In 1969, section 9(2) was added in an attempt to give some clarification.

> 9 (2) Where the party producing a witness alleges that the witness made at other times a statement in writing, reduced to writing, or recorded on audio tape or video tape or otherwise, inconsistent with his present testimony, the

---

Figliola, 2011 ONCA 457, 2011 CarswellOnt 4983, 105 O.R. (3d) 641, 272 C.C.C. (3d) 518 at para. 50.

[60] *Figliola, supra.*

[61] *Wyman*, 1958 CarswellNB 6, 122 C.C.C. 65, 28 C.R. 371 (C.A.).

[62] *McIntyre*, 1963 CarswellNS 7, [1963] 2 C.C.C. 380, 43 C.R. 262 (C.A.).

[63] Relying upon *Greenough v. Eccles* (1859), 28 L.J.C.P. 160 (Eng. C.P.).

[64] *McIntyre, supra* per Ilsley C.J. at para. 11.

[65] R.S.O. 1990, c. E.23.

[66] (1961), 1961 CarswellOnt 116, [1961] O.R. 495, [1963] 1 C.C.C. 176, 28 D.L.R. (2d) 386 (C.A.); reversed 1963 CarswellOnt 61, [1963] S.C.R. 154, [1963] 1 C.C.C. 321, 36 D.L.R. (2d) 718.

court may, without proof that the witness is adverse, grant leave to that party to cross-examine the witness as to the statement and the court may consider the cross-examination in determining whether in the opinion of the court the witness is adverse.

This section appears to be legislative recognition that the trial judge is not first required to make a finding of adversity before cross-examination may be permitted on a prior inconsistent statement. However, it should be noted that section 9(2) only applies to "a statement in writing, reduced to writing, or recorded on audio tape or video tape or otherwise". It does not apply to an oral statement made by the witness.

The trial judge must hold a *voir dire* to determine whether evidence of the witness is inconsistent with the witness's prior statement. In *Milgaard*,[67] the Saskatchewan Court of Appeal suggested the following procedure be used where this situation arises:

1. Counsel should advise the court that he desires to make an application under section 9(2) of the *Canada Evidence Act*.

2. When the court is so advised, the court should direct the jury to retire.

3. Upon retirement of the jury, counsel should advise the trial judge of the particulars of the application and produce for him the alleged statement in writing or the writing to which the statement has been reduced.

4. The trial judge should read the statement, or writing, and determine whether, in fact, there is an inconsistency between the statement or writing and the evidence the witness has given in court. If he decides that there is no inconsistency, then that is the end of the matter. If he finds that there is an inconsistency, he should then call upon counsel to prove the statement or writing.

5. Counsel should then prove the statement or writing. This may be done by producing the statement or writing to the witness. If the witness admits the statement, or the statement reduced to writing, such proof is sufficient. If the witness does not admit it, counsel should then provide the necessary proof by other evidence.

6. If the witness admits making the statement, counsel for the opposing party should have the right to cross-examine as to the circumstances under which the statement was made. A similar right to cross-examine

---

[67] 1971 CarswellSask 26, 2 C.C.C. (2d) 206, [1971] 2 W.W.R. 266, 14 C.R.N.S. 34 (C.A.); leave to appeal refused 1971 CarswellSask 124, 4 C.C.C. (2d) 566 (note) (S.C.C.). See also *Cassibo*, 1982 CarswellOnt 850, 39 O.R. (2d) 288, 70 C.C.C. (2d) 498 (C.A.).

should be granted if the statement is proved by other witnesses. It may be that counsel will be able to establish that there were circumstances which would render it improper for the trial judge to permit the cross-examination, notwithstanding the apparent inconsistencies. The opposing counsel, too, should have the right to call evidence as to factors relevant to obtaining the statement, for the purpose of attempting to show that cross-examination should not be permitted.

7. The trial judge should then decide whether or not he will permit the cross-examination. If so, the jury should be recalled.

If the judge is not satisfied that there is an inconsistency between the witness's evidence and the statement, then the witness will not be declared adverse. If the judge finds an inconsistency and declares the witness adverse, the examiner may cross-examine the witness. Here, cross-examination is limited to the statement that the court finds is a previous inconsistent statement.[68] That cross-examination may be the basis for persuading the judge that the witness is also hostile, in which case the witness may be cross-examined at large. In deciding whether a witness is hostile, the court is not restricted to relying only on the inconsistency in his testimony with a previous statement or the answers that he gives in his testimony. The court may also determine that a witness is hostile by observing his general attitude or demeanour in the witness stand, the substance of his evidence and any other contradictory evidence.

What steps may counsel take if the previous statement is an oral one? Until the decision of the Ontario Court of Appeal in 1982 in *Cassibo*,[69] the general view was that a judge could not consider a previous inconsistent oral statement in determining whether a witness was adverse because section 9(2) was restricted to previous written statements or ones reduced to writing. However, the *Cassibo* case rejected the notion that section 9(2) was such a compromise and held that a previous oral statement could still be considered under section 9(1) of the *Canada Evidence Act* in deciding whether the witness is adverse.

(ii) Use That Can be Made of a Prior Inconsistent Statement

(A) The Orthodox Rule

What use can be made of a prior inconsistent statement? Until recently, the common law rule was that if the witness denied making the statement or

---

[68] *Figliola*, 2011 ONCA 457, 2011 CarswellOnt 4983, 105 O.R. (3d) 641, 272 C.C.C. (3d) 518.

[69] 1982 CarswellOnt 850, 39 O.R. (2d) 288, 70 C.C.C. (2d) 498 (C.A.).

said that it was false, no use could be made of it on the issue of its truth. The jury was not entitled to accept the prior inconsistent statement for its truth, even if they did not believe the witness's testimony. The jury was only entitled to accept the prior inconsistent statement for its truth if the witness adopted the statement as the truth while giving testimony in the witness stand.[70] Unless adopted as the truth, the prior inconsistent statement could only be used to cancel out or neutralize the witness's damaging in-court testimony. In other words, it could only be used in assessing the credibility of the harmful testimony given by the witness.

In applying the common law rule, courts were careful to ensure that the prosecution did not try to use a prior inconsistent statement to unfairly cancel out or cast doubt on the credibility of the defence witnesses. For example, in *Soobrian*,[71] two accused, who were friends, were charged with sexual assault. A third friend, who was present during the alleged assault, told the police that he did not observe any sexual activity. Later, however, at the preliminary inquiry, he told the police that he had observed consensual sexual activity between the accused and the complainant. At trial, the Crown called the witness in expectation that he would testify in a manner consistent with his preliminary inquiry testimony. The Crown's purpose in calling the witness was to demonstrate the inconsistency between the witness's first statement to the police and his later testimony at the preliminary inquiry in an effort to obtain leave to cross-examine him under section 9(2) of the *Canada Evidence Act* and possibly have him declared adverse under section 9(1) of the Act. In other words, it was to prove that since the witness was lying, so were his friends, the accused. It was held that since a finding that the witness was adverse would serve no purpose other than to neutralize his evidence and would have no bearing on whether the accused were credible, the Crown should not have been permitted to proceed in this fashion. It was unfair because it was an attempt by the Crown to prove that the entire defence was a fabrication without any evidence of either accused's involvement in fabricating it.

---

[70] *Deacon*, 1947 CarswellMan 1, [1947] S.C.R. 531, 89 C.C.C. 1, 3 C.R. 265, [1947] 3 D.L.R. 772; *Mannion*, 1986 CarswellAlta 190, 1986 CarswellAlta 715, [1986] 2 S.C.R. 272, 75 A.R. 16, 47 Alta. L.R. (2d) 177, 28 C.C.C. (3d) 544, 53 C.R. (3d) 193, 31 D.L.R. (4th) 712, [1986] 6 W.W.R. 525, 25 C.R.R. 182, 69 N.R. 189; *Kuldip*, 1990 CarswellOnt 62, 1990 CarswellOnt 1010, [1990] 3 S.C.R. 618, 61 C.C.C. (3d) 385, 1 C.R. (4th) 285, 1 C.R.R. (2d) 110, 114 N.R. 284, 43 O.A.C. 340.

[71] *Soobrian*, 1994 CarswellOnt 202, 21 O.R. (3d) 603, 96 C.C.C. (3d) 208, 76 O.A.C. 7 (C.A.).

One reason why a prior inconsistent statement was not admissible for its truth is because what the witness said on a prior occasion is hearsay (which will be discussed in Part B). The courts have been concerned that what the witness said on a prior occasion was not said under oath or solemn affirmation and the judge or jury had no opportunity to observe the witness's demeanour when the statement was made in order to assess the credibility of the witness. Probably the strongest reason why a prior inconsistent statement was not admissible for its truth was that the other side did not have the opportunity to cross-examine the witness when he made the statement.

(B) The Modern Rule

Not everyone agreed with the logic of the orthodox rule that restricted the use of a prior consistent statement to an assessment of the credibility of its maker. Mr. Justice Estey, in a dissenting judgment in *Rouse*[72] could not understand why a witness's prior inconsistent statement should not be considered for its truth as well as for the credibility of the witness. Even though the prior inconsistent statement was hearsay, he could not see why the rule should be enforced where the witness was in the witness box and available for cross-examination. Others argued that the lack of opportunity by the judge and jury to observe the demeanour of the witness at the time that the statement was made, and thus to assess credibility based on that demeanour, was overstated. They pointed out that the opportunity to observe the witness at trial denying or professing not to remember making the statement gave the judge and jury insight into the truthfulness of the prior statement. They argued that the power of an oath as a means of ensuring reliability of evidence should be discounted. Moreover, they noted that the witness was under oath when he testified at trial.

All of these various attacks on the orthodox rule were finally considered by the Supreme Court of Canada in *B. (K.G.)*.[73] There the Court decided that the time had come for the orthodox rule to be replaced by a new one that recognized the changed means and methods of proof in modern society. It was felt that changing the rule was not a matter best left to Parliament, since it was a judge-made rule. The rule lent itself to judicial reform, and was a natural and incremental progression in the development of the law of hearsay in Canada.

Chief Justice Lamer, delivering the majority judgment of the Court, stressed that the focal issue for consideration by the trial judge is the com-

---

[72] *Supra* note 55.

[73] 1993 CarswellOnt 76, 1993 CarswellOnt 975, [1993] 1 S.C.R. 740, 79 C.C.C. (3d) 257, 19 C.R. (4th) 1, 148 N.R. 241, 61 O.A.C. 1, [1993] S.C.J. No. 22.

parative reliability of the prior statement and the testimony offered at trial. That criterion of reliability is satisfied when the circumstances in which the prior statement was made provide sufficient guarantees of its trustworthiness with respect to the dangers of the absence of oath and the inability of the trier of fact to assess the declarant's demeanour. It was his view that there would be sufficient guarantees of reliability to allow the jury to make substantive use of a prior statement if,

1. It was made under oath, solemn affirmation or solemn declaration following an explicit warning to the witness as to the existence of severe criminal sanctions for the making of a false statement;

2. It was videotaped in its entirety; and

3. The opposing party, whether the Crown or the defence, had a full opportunity to cross-examine the witness at trial respecting the statement.

In his reasons, the Chief Justice explained that he was not restricting the admissibility of a prior inconsistent statement for its truth to the fulfillment of the three conditions. He left it open to the trial judge to consider other guarantees of reliability, so long as the judge was satisfied that the circumstances provided adequate assurances of reliability in place of those which the hearsay rule traditionally required. He summed up the role of the trial judge this way:

... in the part of the *voir dire* addressing the new rule, the trial judge must first satisfy him or herself that the indicia of reliability necessary to admit hearsay evidence of prior statements — a warning, oath, solemn affirmation, or solemn declaration, and videotape record, or sufficient substitutes — are present and genuine. If they are, he or she must then examine the circumstances under which the statement was obtained, to satisfy him or herself that the statement supported by the indicia of reliability was made voluntarily if to a person in authority, and that there are no other factors which would tend to bring the administration of justice into disrepute if the statement was admitted as substantive evidence. In most cases, as in this case, the party seeking to admit the prior inconsistent statements as substantive evidence will have to establish that these requirements have been satisfied on the balance of probabilities. The trial judge is not to decide whether the prior inconsistent statement is true, or more reliable than the present testimony, as that is a matter for the trier of fact. Once this process is complete, and all of its constituent elements satisfied, the trial judge need not issue the standard limiting instruction to the jury, but may instead tell the jury that they may take the statement as substantive evidence of its contents, or, if he or she is sitting alone, make substantive use of the statement, giving the evidence the appropriate weight after taking into account all of the circumstances. In either case, the judge must direct the trier of fact to consider carefully these circumstances in assessing the credibility of the prior inconsistent statement relative to the witness' testimony at trial. For example, where appropriate the trial judge might make specific reference to the significance of the demeanour of the witness at all relevant times (which could include when making the statement, when recanting at trial, and/or when presenting conflicting testimony at trial), the reasons offered by the witness for his or her recantation, any motivation and/or opportunity the witness had to fabricate his or her evidence when making the previous statement or when testifying at trial, the events leading up to the making of the first statement and the nature of the interview at which the statement was made (including the use of leading question, and the existence of pre-statement interview or coaching), corroboration of the facts in the statement by other evidence, and the extent to which the nature of the witness' recantation limits the effectiveness of cross-examination on the previous statement. There may be other factors the trier of fact should consider, and the trial judge should impress upon the trier of fact the importance of carefully assessing all such matters in determining the weight to be afforded prior inconsistent statements as substantive evidence.

Where the prior statement does not have the necessary circumstantial guarantees of reliability, and so cannot pass the threshold test on the *voir dire*, but the party tendering the prior statement otherwise satisfied the requirements of ss. 9(1) or (2) of the *Canada Evidence Act*, the statement may still be tendered into evidence, but the trial judge must instruct the jury in the terms of the orthodox rule.[74]

The Chief Justice's statement that he was not restricting the admissibility of a prior inconsistent statement for its truth to the fulfillment of the three conditions has, as expected, caused some judicial disagreements as to what must be established before the statement will be admitted. For example, in *Trieu*[75] the accused was convicted of home invasion offences. The case against him was that he had masterminded the crime although he had not participated in the home invasion. To support its case, the Crown relied upon the video statements of the two perpetrators who committed the crime implicating the accused. However, the statements were *not under oath and the declarants were not given the B.(K.G.) warning.* At the accused's trial, both of the declarants testified disavowing the role of the accused. The accused's appeal was dismissed but the members of the court were divided. Moldaver J.A., who wrote the majority decision, held that although the statements were not under oath and the declarants not given the warning, they were still available for cross-examination. As far as he was concerned, lack of *contemporaneous* cross-examination was the most important of the hearsay dangers. Rosenberg J.A., disagreed, holding that the circumstances

---

[74] *Ibid.*, at pp. 45-46 [C.R.].

[75] 2005 CarswellOnt 1073, 195 C.C.C. (3d) 373, 29 C.R. (6th) 174 (C.A.).

in which the declarant *N's* statement was taken (absence of an oath and the warning) did not produce ideal substitutes for the hearsay danger.[76]

In *U. (F.J.)*,[77] the Supreme Court noted that the gravest danger associated with hearsay evidence, namely, the absence of contemporaneous cross-examination, simply does not exist in the case of prior inconsistent statements because the witness is available for cross-examination. It also noted that the other two dangers, namely, the absence of an oath and absence of demeanour evidence, can be met through appropriate police procedures and occasionally appropriate substitutes can be found. The Court stressed that a prior statement is necessary evidence when a witness recants.

In *U.(F.J.)* both the accused and the complainant had made separate statements containing similarities to the police. However, both had recanted at trial. The Court held that a threshold of reliability can be established in cases where the witness is available for cross-examination by a striking similarity between two statements. In order to eliminate, or at least substantially reduce, the likelihood of a similarity between two statements arising through coincidence, the similar factual assertion must be so striking that it is unlikely two people would have independently fabricated it. In some cases, the necessary degree of similarity will result from the unique nature of particular factual assertions in both statements. In other situations, it may be that the cumulative combination of similar points renders the overall similarity between the two statements sufficiently distinctive to reject coincidence as a likely explanation.

The Court set out the procedure that should be followed where the party invokes section 9 of the *Canada Evidence Act* and fulfils its requirements on the *voir dire* under that section:

1. The party must state its objectives in tendering the statement. If the statement is only to be used to impeach the witness, the inquiry ends at this point. If, however, the party calling the witness wishes to make substantive use of the statement, the *voir dire* must continue so that the trial judge can assess whether a threshold of reliability has been met. However, the necessity criterion need not be assessed as it is met whenever a witness recants.

---

[76] A similar result was reached by the Manitoba Court of Appeal in *Abazi*, 2006 CarswellMan 243, 211 C.C.C. (3d) 190 (C.A.) relying upon the reasoning of Moldaver J.A. in *Trieu*.

[77] 1995 CarswellOnt 555, 1995 CarswellOnt 1175, [1995] 3 S.C.R. 764, 101 C.C.C. (3d) 97, 42 C.R. (4th) 133, 128 D.L.R. (4th) 121, 186 N.R. 365, 85 O.A.C. 321.

2. If the reliability criterion is to be met, in rare cases, by the striking similarity between the statement being assessed and another statement which is already clearly substantively admissible, the trial judge must be satisfied on a balance of probabilities that there are striking similarities between the two statements, and there was neither reason nor opportunity for the declarants to collude, nor improper influence by interrogators or other third parties. The trial judge must also ascertain that the prior statement relates to evidence which would be admissible as the witness's sole testimony.

3. If the trial judge determines that the statement meets the threshold reliability criterion and is thus substantively admissible, he or she must direct the jury to follow a two-step process in evaluating the evidence.

(a) The jury must first be certain that the statement which is being used as a reliability referent was made, without taking into account the prior inconsistent statement under consideration.

(b) Once the jury is satisfied that the other statement was made, they may compare the similarities between the two statements. If they are sufficiently striking that it is unlikely that the two people independently fabricated them, then they may draw conclusions from that comparison about the truth of the statements.

One of the difficulties with Step 3, which requires that the jury "*must first be certain* that the statement which is being used as a reliability referent, was made", is how the trial judge should instruct the jury as to how the statement may be used by them. The requirement that the jury *must first be certain*" presumably means proof beyond a reasonable doubt. However, the same Court in *MacKenzie*,[78] approved the judgment of the Ontario Court of Appeal in *Minhas*,[79] where Martin J.A. held that "the instruction that the jury must be satisfied beyond a reasonable doubt that the statements alleged to have been made by the appellant were, in fact, made by her . . . was . . . more favourable to the appellant than the instructions to which she was by law entitled". Moreover, in *Evans*,[80] the Supreme Court held that the judge must tell the jury that they must determine whether the Crown has estab-

---

[78] 1993 CarswellNS 12, 1993 CarswellNS 270, [1993] 1 S.C.R. 212, 118 N.S.R. (2d) 290, 78 C.C.C. (3d) 193, 18 C.R. (4th) 133, 327 A.P.R. 290, 146 N.R. 321.

[79] 1986 CarswellOnt 125, 29 C.C.C. (3d) 193, 53 C.R. (3d) 128, 16 O.A.C. 42 (C.A.); leave to appeal refused (1987), 36 C.C.C. (3d) vi (note), 86 N.R. 320 (note) (S.C.C.).

[80] 1993 CarswellAlta 111, 1993 CarswellAlta 567, [1993] 3 S.C.R. 653, 145 A.R. 81, 13 Alta. L.R. (3d) 1, 85 C.C.C. (3d) 97, 25 C.R. (4th) 46, 108 D.L.R. (4th) 32, 158 N.R. 278, 55 W.A.C. 81.

lished on a balance of probabilities that the statements were those of the accused, and if that threshold is met, then the jury may consider the statements with all of the other evidence in the case to determine whether or not guilt has been proven beyond a reasonable doubt.[81] The decision of the Supreme Court in *U.(F.J.)* will undoubtedly create difficulties for the trial judge and confusion for the jury where they must be instructed that *they must be certain* the accused's statement was made when the statement is used as a reliability referent on a *B. (K.G.)* (now *U.(F.J.)*) application, but they must only be satisfied on balance where the statement is tendered by the Crown to prove that the statement, in fact, was made by the accused.

Since the goal of the Crown in attempting to introduce a prior inconsistent statement is to contradict the truth of the declarant's sworn testimony, it would seem to follow that the test for reliability should be more stringent than for other forms of hearsay.[82] On the other hand, authorities have suggested that the trial judge should not apply the same strict standards for reliability of the prior out-of-court statements to the defence as it does to the Crown.[83] As Martin J.A. noted in *Williams*:[84]

> It seems to me that a court has a residual discretion to relax in favour of the accused a strict rule of evidence which is necessary to prevent a miscarriage of justice and where the danger against which an exclusionary rule aims to safeguard does not exist.[85]

Although the trial judge may be satisfied as to the reliability of the prior inconsistent statement of a witness, it is an error for the judge to tell the jury that he has found it sufficiently reliable to warrant its reception as original evidence.[86] It is up to the jury to assess the reliability of the statement and

---

[81] See also *Dickson*, 1993 CarswellOnt 3811, 13 O.R. (3d) 489, 63 O.A.C. 254 (C.A.).

[82] *Diu*, 2000 CarswellOnt 1727, 49 O.R. (3d) 40, 144 C.C.C. (3d) 481, 33 C.R. (5th) 203, 133 O.A.C. 201, [2000] O.J. No. 1770 (C.A.).

[83] *Eisenhauer*, 1998 CarswellNS 65, 165 N.S.R. (2d) 81, 123 C.C.C. (3d) 37, 14 C.R. (5th) 35, 495 A.P.R. 81 (C.A.); leave to appeal refused (1998), 171 N.S.R. (2d) 200 (note), 126 C.C.C. (3d) vi (note), 519 A.P.R. 200 (note), 230 N.R. 400 (note) (S.C.C.) at p. 64 [C.C.C.]; *F. (G.)*, 1999 CarswellOnt 129, 43 O.R. (3d) 290, 132 C.C.C. (3d) 14, 116 O.A.C. 345 (C.A.).

[84] *Williams*, 1985 CarswellOnt 86, 50 O.R. (2d) 321, 18 C.C.C. (3d) 356, 44 C.R. (3d) 351, 14 C.R.R. 251, 7 O.A.C. 201 (C.A.); leave to appeal refused [1985] 1 S.C.R. xiv, 50 O.R. (2d) 321n, 18 C.C.C. (3d) 356n, 44 C.R. (3d) 351n, 59 N.R. 160, 10 O.A.C. 319 (note).

[85] *Ibid.*, at p. 378 [C.C.C.].

[86] *Gilling*, 1997 CarswellOnt 2353, 34 O.R. (3d) 392, 117 C.C.C. (3d) 444, 101 O.A.C. 297 (C.A.).

the weight to be given to it relative to the witness's evidence at trial and the judge is required to instruct them to this effect.

(f) Protection or Privilege from Answering Questions

(i) Generally

When a witness enters the witness box, he is required to answer all questions that are relevant to the facts in issue. The common law, however, has recognized that, for reasons of public policy, certain persons should be protected from answering questions touching on certain matters. This does not mean that the questions asked by examining counsel or the answers counsel seeks are irrelevant to the issues in the case. They may be very relevant. It simply means that the courts have concluded that society, as a whole, would be better served if some witnesses were protected from revealing certain information, even though that information was important and crucial to the determination of the issues in the case.

What kind of information is protected?

(ii) The Privilege Against Self-Incrimination

In the early common law, anyone accused of heresy or some other crime could be brought before a judge or some other public official and ordered to take an oath to answer truthfully all the questions that might be put to him. He was not told of the specific crime that he was suspected to have committed nor the names of the witnesses against him. If he refused to take the oath or answer the questions put to him, he was thrown into prison and kept there until he agreed to answer the questions.

By the beginning of the seventeenth century, many persons summoned for questioning refused to take the oath and claimed that "no man should be required to incriminate himself". The prosecution of John Lilburne[87] brought the matter to the attention of the courts and Parliament and, by the end of the seventeenth century, the claim of privilege became firmly established in all courts. It was enshrined in the American *Bill of Rights* as the Fifth Amendment on September 25th, 1789. In Canada, it was given constitutional recognition by section 11(c) of the *Charter of Rights and Freedoms* in 1982. Section 11(c) provides that,

> Any person charged with an offence has the right
>
> (c) not to be compelled to be a witness in proceedings against that person in respect of the offence.

---

[87] *John Lilburne* (1649), 4 St. Tr. 1270.

Section 11(c) thus protects an accused from being forced to enter the witness box to give evidence in any proceedings against him or her. However, an accused who chooses voluntarily to testify loses the privilege of silence and is treated like any other witness. Once an accused chooses to testify, section 5(1) of the *Canada Evidence Act* requires the accused to answer all questions that are put by counsel or the judge. Any testimony that the accused gives may be considered by the trier in determining the accused's guilt or innocence of the charge.

However, section 5(2) of the *Canada Evidence Act* guarantees the accused (or any witness who testifies) that in exchange for being compelled to answer a question, his or her testimony at trial is protected from being used against him or her *in any other criminal proceeding*, except a later prosecution for perjury in the giving of that evidence or for giving contradictory evidence. Similar protection is guaranteed an accused under provincial evidence statutes. The same protection is also given constitutional recognition by section 13 of the *Charter*.

Section 13 provides:

> A witness who testifies in any proceedings has the right not to have *any incriminating evidence so given used to incriminate the witness in any other proceedings*, except in a prosecution for perjury or for the giving of contradictory evidence.

It is important to note that although section 5(2) of the *Canada Evidence Act* and section 13 of the *Charter* appear to overlap in their protection of an accused's right to silence, there is a distinct difference between the two sections. Section 5(2) requires the witness at the first proceeding to object to answering the question in order to trigger the protection given by that section. Section 13 of the *Charter* automatically gives the witness protection.

Both sections, on their face, seem to indicate that a witness or an accused is immune from being confronted with testimony given in a previous proceeding that is inconsistent with what he or she is saying in a subsequent proceeding. This raises the question whether an accused, who has been convicted of an offence and is granted a new trial, should be allowed to go into the witness box at his or her retrial and give evidence different from that given at the earlier trial, and not be confronted with that earlier testimony. Understandably, there is a concern that an accused should not be allowed to use section 13 in a retrial to give different testimony with impunity. To get around this problem, the Supreme Court, in an early case, drew a distinction between cross-examination on the prior evidence for the purpose of impeaching credibility and cross-examination to incriminate the accused, that is, to establish guilt.[88] This left it open for the Crown to ask the accused questions about the apparent inconsistencies between testimony given at the previous proceedings and the testimony that he or she was now giving, provided that questions were not designed to incriminate the accused. This imposed upon the trial judge the responsibility of warning the jury that the purpose of the cross-examination was to test the credibility, not to establish the truth of the prior evidence.

The subtle difference between cross-examination on prior evidence *for the purpose of impeachment* and cross-examination *to incriminate* was obviously difficult for juries to understand. It caused one judge, Martin J.A., to observe that "where the prior evidence is used ostensibly to impeach the accused's credibility only, it nevertheless does assist the Crown in its case and, in a broad sense, may help to prove guilt".[89]

In 2005, the Supreme Court was asked to reconsider its earlier decisions because of problems arising out of the application of section 13. The distinction between cross-examination for the purpose of impeachment and cross-examination to incriminate had become unnecessarily complex and technical. Both the defence and the prosecution viewed with skepticism the belief that triers of fact could isolate the purpose of impeaching credibility from the purpose of incrimination. In *Henry*,[90] the accused, in their re-trial on a charge of first-degree murder, told a different story under oath than they did five years earlier at their first trial on the same charge. The trial judge allowed the Crown to cross-examine the accused on their prior inconsistent testimony for the purpose of impeaching their credibility and they were convicted. Their appeal to the British Columbia Court of Appeal was dismissed, as was their appeal to the Supreme Court of Canada.

The Supreme Court decided that section 13 was not available to an accused who chooses to testify at his or her retrial on the same indictment. The Court said that the purpose of section 13 is to protect individuals from being indirectly compelled to incriminate themselves. Section 5 of the *Canada Evidence Act* and section 13 of the *Charter* embody a *quid pro quo*. When a witness who is compelled to give evidence in a proceeding is exposed to the risk of self-incrimination, the state offers, in exchange for that witness's testimony, protection from subsequent use of that evidence

---

[88] *Kuldip*, 1990 CarswellOnt 62, 1990 CarswellOnt 1010, [1990] 3 S.C.R. 618, 61 C.C.C. (3d) 385, 1 C.R. (4th) 285.

[89] *Kuldip*, 1988 CarswellOnt 50, 40 C.C.C. (3d) 11, 62 C.R. (3d) 336 (C.A.) at p. 23 [C.C.C.] ; reversed 1990 CarswellOnt 62, 1990 CarswellOnt 1010, 61 C.C.C. (3d) 385, 1 C.R. (4th) 285 (S.C.C.).

[90] 2005 CarswellBC 2972, 2005 CarswellBC 2973, (sub nom. *R. c. Henry)* [2005] 3 S.C.R. 609, 202 C.C.C. (3d) 449, 33 C.R. (6th) 215.

against them. Binnie J. for the Court defined incriminating evidence as something "from which a trier of fact may infer that an accused is guilty of the crime charged".[91]

In *Henry*, the Court found that the compulsion, which is the source of the *quid pro quo*, was missing. The accused had freely testified at their first trial and freely testified at their second trial. The Court also said that the Crown was precluded from filing the testimony given by the accused at their prior trial as part of the Crown's case in-chief. To do so would indirectly compel the accused to testify at their retrial in circumstances where section 11(c) of the *Charter* would not permit such compelled self-incrimination. The Crown had to prove its case without recruiting the accused to incriminate themselves.

Recently, however, the Supreme Court in *Nedelcu*,[92] has decided to redefine the meaning of "incriminating evidence" in section 13. There the accused who was charged with dangerous driving causing bodily harm had taken the victim for a ride on his motorcycle and crashed into a curb, causing the victim permanent brain damage. During his examination for discovery in a civil lawsuit brought by the victim, the accused testified that he had no memory of the events from the day of the accident until he woke up in the hospital the following day. At his criminal trial, however, he gave a detailed account of the events leading up to and during the accident. The trial judge gave Crown counsel leave to cross-examine the accused on his discovery evidence. He was asked him about his memory of the events and stated, "I have a recollection about 90, 95 percent". His trial testimony was found to be unreliable and he was found guilty.

In Ontario, rule 31.04(2) of the Ontario *Rules of Civil Procedure* compels a defendant in a civil action to be examined for discovery as a litigant in a civil action. In *Nedelcu*, the issue was whether section 13 applies to all compelled testimony at a prior proceeding or to only incriminating evidence. On appeal, the Ontario Court of Appeal had decided that section 13 applied to all prior compelled testimony, not just prior compelled *incriminating* testimony, and had ordered a new trial. The Supreme Court, however, in a split (6-3) decision, disagreed and restored the conviction. It was held that although the accused was statutorily compellable and therefore compelled to testify at his examination for discovery in the civil action, the use of his non-incriminating discovery evidence for impeachment purposes could not and did not trigger the application of section 13. Relying upon the

---

[91] *Supra* at para. 25.
[92] 2012 SCC 59, 2012 CarswellOnt 13663, 2012 CarswellOnt 13664, 290 C.C.C. (3d) 153, 96 C.R. (6th) 391.

decision of Arbour J. in *Noël*,[93] it was held that if the original evidence was not incriminating, the *quid pro quo* was never engaged. There she had stated,[94] for the majority:

> ... the witness cannot ask of the state that he be prevented from being cross-examined as to his credibility should he assert matters differently in a subsequent proceeding, even if the ultimate effect of that subsequent cross-examination may be adverse to his interest. This is consistent with the language of s. 13 which grants to every witness the right not to have any "incriminating evidence so given used to incriminate that witness in any other proceedings".

In *Nedelcu*, the Court said that, on its own, the accused's discovery testimony was not incriminating because it could not have been used by the Crown to prove or assist in proving one or more of the essential elements of the criminal charges he was facing. While his inconsistent discovery evidence might lead the triers of fact to reject his trial testimony, rejection of an accused's testimony does not create evidence for the Crown.

Lebel J., delivering the dissenting judgment, argued that the focus should not be on the nature of the statements. While section 13 refers to using "incriminating evidence" to "incriminate", parsing an accused person's testimony to distinguish what is "incriminating" from what is "innocuous" in order to determine on what parts of his or her testimony the accused may be cross-examined could result in a protracted and unpredictable classification exercise. As far as he was concerned that distinction was just as unworkable as the previously abolished distinction between using prior compelled testimony to impeach credibility and using it to incriminate the accused. Any evidence that might assist the Crown in proving its case would have an incriminating effect and was subject to section 13 protection. Despite the rather blatant inconsistencies in the accused's testimony, he felt that section 13 dictated that the truth-seeking function of the trial should give way to the right of the accused against self-incrimination.

(iii) Spousal Privilege

As noted earlier, an accused's spouse is not competent nor compellable as a witness for the prosecution unless the offence charged is one of those listed in subsections (2) and (4) of section 4 of the *Canada Evidence Act* or is subject to the common law exception preserved by section 4(5) of the Act. The common law exception arises in those cases where the charge af-

---

[93] 2002 CarswellQue 2167, 2002 CarswellQue 2168, [2002] 3 S.C.R. 433, 168 C.C.C. (3d) 193, 5 C.R. (6th) 1.

[94] *Supra* at para. 47.

fects the person, health or liberty of the accused's spouse. For a long time, the law was uncertain whether the charge had to specifically allege a threat against the spouse or if it was enough that the evidence itself disclosed such a threat. In England, the Court of Criminal Appeal had decided that the nature of the charge had to affect a spouse's health or liberty.[95] Canadian authorities, however, eventually began to adopt a liberal approach allowing a spouse to testify where the evidence revealed that his or her health or liberty was affected.[96]

Although the common law exception extends to cases involving the health or liberty of a spouse, it does not, ironically, apply where the health or liberty of a child of the accused is involved. In other words, at common law a wife was able to testify against her husband where he assaulted her, but not where he assaulted their child. An attempt to rectify this situation was made in 1903 by an amendment to the *Canada Evidence Act*. That amendment listed a number of offences, primarily sexual offences, where a spouse was both competent and compellable for the prosecution, but it omitted simple assaults. In 1983, that omission was corrected by a further amendment to section 4(4).

Spousal privilege against compellability by the prosecution will extend only as long as the parties are married at the time of trial and are living together. If the parties are married at the time of the offence, but are divorced at the time of trial, then the privilege does not apply.[97] Since the modern justification for the rule is that it promotes marital harmony, it is against common sense that spousal privilege should continue after divorce.

That view has given support to the argument that spousal privilege should not continue if the parties are separated and there is no reasonable possibility of reconciliation;[98] nor should spousal incompetence or non-compellability be extended to so-called "common law marriages" or similar rela-

---

[95] *Director of Public Prosecutions v. Blady*, [1912] 2 K.B. 89 (Eng.).

[96] *Sillars* (1978), 1978 CarswellBC 541, 45 C.C.C. (2d) 283, 12 C.R. (3d) 202, [1979] 1 W.W.R. 743 (C.A.); *Czipps*, 1979 CarswellOnt 56, 25 O.R. (2d) 527, 48 C.C.C. (2d) 166, 12 C.R. (3d) 193, 101 D.L.R. (3d) 323 (C.A.).

[97] *Marchand*, 1980 CarswellNS 95, 39 N.S.R. (2d) 700, 55 C.C.C. (2d) 77, 115 D.L.R. (3d) 403, 71 A.P.R. 700 (C.A.); *Bailey*, 1983 CarswellOnt 62, 4 C.C.C. (3d) 21, 32 C.R. (3d) 337 (C.A.).

[98] *Salituro*, 1990 CarswellOnt 101, 56 C.C.C. (3d) 350, 78 C.R. (3d) 68, 38 O.A.C. 241 (C.A.); affirmed 1991 CarswellOnt 1031, 1991 CarswellOnt 124, [1991] 3 S.C.R. 654, 68 C.C.C. (3d) 289, 9 C.R. (4th) 324, 8 C.R.R. (2d) 173, 131 N.R. 161, 50 O.A.C. 125.

tionships since they are not recognized by law.[99] In *Salituro*, Mr. Justice Iacobucci argued:

> Absent parliamentary intervention, I would conclude that changing the common law rule to make spouses who are irreconcilably separated competent witnesses for the prosecution would be appropriate. Although the principles upon which this change is based would appear to favour abolishing the rule entirely and making all spouses competent witnesses under all circumstances, policy considerations and uncertainty as to the consequences of such change suggest that a more cautious approach is appropriate. The parties before us did not argue for such a change, and in my opinion a far reaching change of this kind is best left to the legislature. However, expanding the exceptions to the common law rule to include irreconcilably separated spouses is precisely the kind of incremental change which the courts can and should make. The courts are custodians of the common law, and it is their duty to see that the common law reflects the emerging need and value of our society.[100]

As noted previously, a distinction must be drawn between a "communication" made by husbands and wives to one another and an "observation" by one spouse of the conduct of the other. Section 4(3) of the *Canada Evidence Act* provides that no spouse is compellable "to disclose any communication made [to him or her by the other spouse] during their marriage". The prevailing view seems to be that all marital communications continue to be protected by section 4(3) of the Act.[101] What is clear, however, is that any protected marital communication must be testimonial in nature. Spousal privilege will not prevent the admission into evidence of a document written by the accused and sent to his wife which is found during a search of the accused's house.[102] Moreover, the privilege is limited to the spouses them-

---

[99] *Duvivier*, 1990 CarswellOnt 958, 75 O.R. (2d) 203, 60 C.C.C. (3d) 353 (Gen. Div.); affirmed 1991 CarswellOnt 87, 64 C.C.C. (3d) 20, 4 C.R. (4th) 378, 6 C.R.R. (2d) 180 (C.A.).

[100] *Supra* note 98, at p. 344 [C.R.].

[101] *Jean*, 1979 CarswellAlta 169, 15 A.R. 147, 46 C.C.C. (2d) 176, 7 C.R. 338, 7 C.R. (3d) 338 (C.A.); affirmed 1980 CarswellAlta 312, 1980 CarswellAlta 157, [1980] 1 S.C.R. 400, 20 A.R. 360, 51 C.C.C. (2d) 192, 16 C.R. (3d) 193, 31 N.R. 410; *Mailloux*, 1980 CarswellOnt 77, 55 C.C.C. (2d) 193 at 196, 30 C.R. (3d) 121 (C.A.); *Zylstra*, 1995 CarswellOnt 124, 99 C.C.C. (3d) 477, 41 C.R. (4th) 130, 82 O.A.C. 394 (C.A.).

[102] *Kotapski*, 1981 CarswellQue 255, 66 C.C.C. (2d) 78 (S.C.); affirmed 1984 CarswellQue 222, 13 C.C.C. (3d) 185 (C.A.); leave to appeal refused (1984), 57 N.R. 318 (S.C.C.); leave to appeal refused 1984 CarswellQue 222, 13 C.C.C. (3d) 185 (C.A.).

selves. Although a spouse may not be compelled to disclose what his or her spouse has said, third persons who overhear, either intentionally or accidentally, a marital communication are compellable by the prosecution to testify about what they overheard.[103]

It should be noted that section 4(3) speaks of "any communication made ... during their marriage". This would seem to exclude communications made before marriage. However, since the purpose of the section is to promote marital harmony, then it would seem to follow that all communications made prior to or during marriage should be included provided that the marriage is *bona fide* and subsisting at the time of the trial of the accused spouse.[104]

(iv) Solicitor/client Privilege

What a person says to his or her lawyer in the latter's professional capacity and intended to be confidential is privileged. Neither the lawyer nor the client can be compelled to disclose the contents of that information.[105] Such communications are protected not because they are irrelevant, but because there are overriding policy reasons for upholding the confidentiality. The rule is based on the fact that the relationship and the communications between solicitor and client are essential to the effective operation of the legal system.[106] It is in the best interests of society as a whole that a person be allowed to consult with his or her legal adviser openly and freely, knowing that what the person tells their legal adviser cannot be revealed.

Despite its importance, solicitor-client privilege is not absolute. It is subject to certain clearly defined exceptions where other societal values are more compelling.[107] For example, danger to the public will, in appropriate

---

[103] *Rumping v. Director of Public Prosecutions* (1962), [1964] A.C. 814, [1962] 2 All E.R. 233 (C.A.); affirmed (1962), [1964] A.C. 814 at 822, [1962] 3 All E.R. 256, 46 Cr. App. R. 389 (U.K. H.L.); *Siniscalchi*, 2010 CarswellBC 1932, 257 C.C.C. (3d) 329 (C.A.).

[104] *Hawkins, supra* note 15.

[105] *Bencardino*, 1973 CarswellOnt 51, 2 O.R. (2d) 351, 15 C.C.C. (2d) 342, 24 C.R.N.S. 173 (C.A.).

[106] *Fosty*, 1991 CarswellMan 206, 1991 CarswellMan 285, (sub nom. *R. v. Gruenke*) [1991] 3 S.C.R. 263, 67 C.C.C. (3d) 289, 8 C.R. (4th) 368, [1991] 6 W.W.R. 673, 7 C.R.R. (2d) 108, 75 Man. R. (2d) 112, 130 N.R. 161, 6 W.A.C. 112, [1991] S.C.J. No. 80.

[107] *Smith v. Jones*, 1999 CarswellBC 590, 1999 CarswellBC 3425, [1999] 1 S.C.R. 455, 62 B.C.L.R. (3d) 209, 132 C.C.C. (3d) 225, 22 C.R. (5th) 203, 169 D.L.R. (4th) 385, [1999] 8 W.W.R. 364, (sub nom. *Jones v. Smith*) 120 B.C.A.C. 161, 60 C.R.R. (2d) 46, 236 N.R. 201, 196 W.A.C. 161, [1999] S.C.J. No. 15.

circumstances, provide the requisite justification for setting aside the privilege. Here three factors must be considered: the first is whether there is a clear risk to an identifiable person or group of persons; the second is whether there is a risk of serious bodily harm or death; the last is whether there is imminent danger.

Nevertheless, the Supreme Court has said that solicitor-client privilege must be as close to absolute as possible to ensure public confidence and retain relevance.[108] It does not involve a balancing of interests on a case-by-case basis. In order for the communication to be privileged, it must arise from a communication between a lawyer and his client where the client seeks *lawful* advice.[109] For example, privilege does not attach to a communication by a client to his lawyer seeking advice on how to commit a crime.[110] Such a communication is outside the scope of the rule and is not protected from being revealed by the lawyer.

The communication does not have to be given directly to the lawyer. It may be given to the lawyer's assistant or anyone acting under the lawyer's supervision. For example, privilege has been held to extend to statements made by a client to a law clerk to obtain legal aid.[111] Privilege has also been extended to communications between an accused and an expert where counsel requires the services of the expert in order to help counsel prepare the accused's defence.[112] Even if a person changes lawyers, the information that the person gave to his previous lawyer is still protected from disclosure.[113] The protection also extends to information given by two or more persons to their lawyer in connection with the same matter, unless there is a dispute and one of the persons demands disclosure in order to establish his or her innocence.[114]

It is important to stress that the privilege extends only to a communication made by the client to his or her solicitor. It does not extend to any real evidence that a client may have given to his or her solicitor for safekeeping.

---

[108] *McClure*, 2001 SCC 14, 2001 CarswellOnt 496, 2001 CarswellOnt 497, [2001] 1 S.C.R. 445, 151 C.C.C. (3d) 321, 40 C.R. (5th) 1, 195 D.L.R. (4th) 513, 266 N.R. 275, 142 O.A.C. 201, [2001] S.C.J. No. 13.

[109] *McClure, ibid.*

[110] *Cox*, 15 Cox C.C. 611, 14 Q.B.D. 153, 33 W.R. 396 (Eng. C.C.R.).

[111] *Littlechild*, 1979 CarswellAlta 265, 19 A.R. 395, 51 C.C.C. (2d) 406, 11 C.R. (3d) 390, 108 D.L.R. (3d) 340, [1980] 1 W.W.R. 742 (C.A.).

[112] *Perron*, 1990 CarswellQue 13, 1990 CarswellQue 1900, 54 C.C.C. (3d) 108, 75 C.R. (3d) 382 (C.A.).

[113] *Bell v. Smith*, 1968 CarswellOnt 79, [1968] S.C.R. 664, 68 D.L.R. (2d) 751.

[114] *Dunbar*, 1982 CarswellOnt 74, 68 C.C.C. (2d) 13, 28 C.R. (3d) 324 (C.A.).

For example, clients cannot claim privilege with respect to any item given to their solicitor that is evidence of a crime, such as a weapon or bloody shirt. Indeed, the solicitor may be compelled to testify for the prosecution that he or she received these items from the client, although the solicitor need not reveal what the client said about the items.

The client, but not the lawyer, may waive a solicitor-client privilege either intentionally or even inadvertently. For example, waiver may occur where the accused asks his solicitor to send the communication to a third person, such as his wife, even though he does not intend to waive the privilege.[115] Moreover, the accused is not entitled to pick and choose which part of the communication he will waive. Once the accused waives part of the communication, he cannot claim protection for the balance of the communication. If he waives any part of the privilege, he loses protection for the entire communication.[116]

Does the court have the right to set aside solicitor-client privilege where, for example, an accused relies upon the communication of another person to his or her solicitor that might establish the accused's innocence, such as a confession of guilt? The Supreme Court has said that the court does have that right but only where the accused's innocence is at stake.[117] The test is so stringent that the privilege should only be infringed where core issues going to the guilt of the accused are involved and there is a genuine risk of a wrongful conviction. Unless the solicitor-client communication goes directly to one of the elements of the offence, it will not be sufficient to meet the stringent requirements. Before doing so, the accused must establish that the information sought to be disclosed is not available from any other source and it is not possible to raise a reasonable doubt as to his guilt in any other way.[118] To ensure that the privilege is not breached, except where the accused does not have access to any other information that will be admissible at trial which will raise a reasonable doubt as to the accused's guilt, the application for disclosure should be delayed until the very end of the Crown's case. If the Crown fails to prove its case, there will be no need to violate solicitor-client privilege. If disclosure is ordered, it should be limited to that information necessary to provide the accused with a fair trial. Moreover, the privilege is entitled to the protection of section 7 of the

---

[115] *Kotapski, supra* note 102.

[116] *Ibid.*

[117] *McClure, supra* note 108.

[118] *Brown*, 2002 CarswellOnt 916, 2002 CarswellOnt 917, 162 C.C.C. (3d) 257, 50 C.R. (5th) 1 (S.C.C.).

Charter. Since disclosure is only for the purpose of preventing a wrongful conviction, it should not be used to incriminate the privilege holder.

An area of the law that causes some concern for solicitors is whether the police are entitled to search their office for evidence of a crime that may have been committed by their client and, if so, what documents can be seized. Parliament, in an attempt to resolve the problem, passed section 488.1 of the *Criminal Code* which set out rules that the Crown must follow before searching a solicitor's office. However, in *Lavallee, Rackel & Heintz*,[119] the Supreme Court held that section 488.1 was unconstitutional violating section 8 of the *Charter* for a number of reasons: the privilege could be lost through the solicitor's absence or inaction; a lawyer asserting privilege was required to reveal the client's name to the police; there were no provisions for notice to the client; the time limits for objecting to the seizure and asserting privilege were strict; the judge was not given remedial discretion to relieve the privilege holder from his or her default; and there was the possibility that the Crown could have access to the material prior to the judicial determination on the privilege issue.

The Supreme Court then set out ten constitutional imperatives that govern searches of law offices that, as a matter of common law, must be respected if Parliament chooses to re-enact section 488.1. They are:

1) No search warrant can be issued for documents known to be protected by solicitor-client privilege;

2) Before searching a law office, the investigative authorities must satisfy the issuing justice that there exists no reasonable alternative to the search.

3) The issuing justice must be rigorously demanding to afford maximum protection of solicitor-client confidentiality;

4) Unless otherwise authorized by warrant, all documents in the lawyer's possession must be sealed before being examined or seized;

5) Every effort must be made to contact the lawyer and client when the search warrant is executed. Where the lawyer or client cannot be contacted, a representative of the bar should oversee the sealing and seizure of documents;

6) The investigating officer executing the warrant should report to the justice of the peace the efforts made to contact all potential privilege holders, who should then be given a reasonable opportunity to assert a

---

[119] 2002 CarswellAlta 1818, 2002 CarswellAlta 1819, (sub nom. *Lavallee, Rackel & Heintz v. Canada (Attorney General)*) 167 C.C.C. (3d) 1, 3 C.R. (6th) 209 (S.C.C.).

claim of privilege and, if that claim is contested, to have the issue judicially decided;

7) If notification of potential privilege holders is not possible, the lawyer who had custody of the documents seized, or another lawyer appointed by the Law Society or the court, should examine the documents to determine whether a claim of privilege should be asserted, and should be given a reasonable opportunity to do so;

8) The Attorney General may make submissions on the issue of privilege, but should not be permitted to inspect the documents beforehand. The prosecuting authority can only inspect if and when determined by a judge that the documents are not privileged;

9) Where sealed documents are found not to be privileged, they may be used in the normal course of the investigation; and

10) Where documents are found to be privileged, they are to be returned immediately to the holder of the privilege, or to a person designated by the court.

To date, Parliament has not chosen to re-enact section 488.1.

(v) Work Product (Litigation) Privilege

The work product of the Crown, such as Crown counsel's notes and memorandum on a file, correspondence, research, theories, analysis, opinions and trial strategy in preparation for trial, may or may not have work product privilege. Unlike solicitor-client privilege, there is no presumption of privilege. Whether the privilege exists must be decided on a case-by-case basis. The onus is upon the Crown to establish privilege. If the Crown does, then the onus shifts to the defence to establish waiver by the Crown or that the information sought might affect the outcome of the trial. If the defence establishes that the accused's rights are paramount, then disclosure will be ordered.[120] Work product privilege and solicitor-client privilege are driven by different policy considerations and generate different legal consequences. Work product privilege is not directed at, still less restricted to, communications between solicitor and client. It contemplates, as well, communications between a solicitor and third parties, or, in the case of the unrepresented litigant, between litigant and third parties. The purpose of the work product privilege is to create a zone of privacy in relation to pending or apprehended litigation. Unlike solicitor-client privilege, it is neither ab-

---

[120] *Trang*, 2002 CarswellAlta 153, 168 C.C.C. (3d) 145, 50 C.R. (5th) 242 (Q.B.); *Chan*, 2002 CarswellAlta 396, 164 C.C.C. (3d) 24, 50 C.R. (5th) 280 (Q.B.); *Armstrong*, 2005 CarswellOnt 8293, 77 O.R. (3d) 437 (S.C.J.).

solute in scope nor permanent in durations. It comes to an end, absent related proceedings, upon termination of the litigation that gave rise to the privilege.[121]

(vi) Identity of Informers

Law enforcement officers often depend upon professional informers to furnish them with information about criminal activities. The law therefore recognizes that it is in the best interests of society as a whole that people with important information about the commission of a crime be encouraged to come forward and give that information to the police without fear of disclosure. The law thus protects a witness for the Crown from answering questions that would have the effect of disclosing the identity of the informer.[122] This protection in turn encourages cooperation with the police for future potential informers. The general protection is considered so important that it renders informer privilege a matter beyond the discretion of a trial judge.

Once a trial judge is satisfied that the privilege exists, a complete and total bar on any disclosure of the informer's identity applies.[123] Neither the police nor the courts possess the discretion to abridge it. The privilege belongs to the Crown and cannot be waived without the informer's consent.[124] The privilege prevents not only disclosure of the informer's name, but also any information that might implicitly reveal the informer's identity.[125] No case-by-case weighing of the justification for the privilege is permitted. All information that might tend to identify the informer is protected by the privilege. Neither the Crown nor the court has any discretion to disclose this information in any proceeding, at any time.[126]

---

[121] *Blank v. Canada (Department of Justice)*, 2006 SCC 39, 2006 CarswellNat 2704, 2006 CarswellNat 2705, 40 C.R. (6th) 1.

[122] *Hunter*, 1987 CarswellOnt 89, 59 O.R. (2d) 364, 34 C.C.C. (3d) 14, 57 C.R. (3d) 1, 19 O.A.C. 131 (C.A.); *Escoffery*, 1996 CarswellOnt 935, (sub nom. *R. v. Grey)* 28 O.R. (3d) 417, 47 C.R. (4th) 40, 89 O.A.C. 394 (C.A.); *Leipert*, 1997 CarswellBC 101, 1997 CarswellBC 102, [1997] 1 S.C.R. 281, 112 C.C.C. (3d) 385, 4 C.R. (5th) 259, 143 D.L.R. (4th) 38, [1997] 3 W.W.R. 457, 85 B.C.A.C. 162, 41 C.R.R. (2d) 266, 207 N.R. 145, 138 W.A.C. 162.

[123] *Application to proceed in camera, Re*, 2007 SCC 43, 2007 CarswellBC 2418, 2007 CarswellBC 2419, 224 C.C.C. (3d) 1, 51 C.R. (6th) 262.

[124] *Gordon*, 1999 CarswellOnt 1146, 136 C.C.C. (3d) 64 (Gen. Div.).

[125] *Leipert*, *supra* note 122.

[126] *Omar*, 2007 CarswellOnt 946, 84 O.R. (3d) 493, 218 C.C.C. (3d) 242, 46 C.R. (6th) 174 (C.A.).

This protection, however, is not absolute. If the court is persuaded that the identity of the informant would be material to demonstrate the innocence of the accused, then the court may order the Crown to disclose the informant's identity.[127] Section 7 of the *Charter of Rights and Freedoms* ensures that everyone has the right "to life, liberty and security of the person and the right not to be deprived thereof except in accordance with the principles of fundamental justice". The principles of fundamental justice entitle everyone accused of a crime to make "full answer and defence".

Thus, it is only where innocence is at stake that the privilege yields and information tending to reveal the identity of the informant can be disclosed.[128] In order to raise this exception, there must be a basis on the evidence for concluding that the disclosure of the informer's identity is necessary to demonstrate the innocence of the accused. For example, in *Leipert*,[129] the police had investigated the accused following a "Crime Stoppers" tip that drugs were being grown in his house. The tip was mentioned in the information to obtain a warrant to search the accused's house. The Crown had refused to produce the tip sheet on the ground of informer privilege. The trial judge viewed the document and attempted to edit out all references to the identity of the informer and then ordered disclosure. When the Crown ceased to call evidence, the trial judge acquitted the accused. The British Columbia Court of Appeal ordered a new trial and that order was upheld by the Supreme Court of Canada. The Supreme Court held that the rule of informer privilege is of such importance to the workings of a criminal justice system that it cannot be balanced against other interests relating to the administration of justice. There was concern that it would undermine the efficacy of programs such as Crime Stoppers, which depends on guarantees of anonymity to those who volunteer information on crimes. The Court said that where it is impossible, in the case of the anonymous informer, to determine which details of the information provided by the informer will or will not result in that person's identity being revealed, none of those details should be disclosed unless there is a basis to conclude that the innocence at stake exception applies.

The police, the Crown, and the courts have a duty to protect and enforce informer privilege. However, the defence, including a private investigator

---

[127] *Bisaillon c. Keable*, 1983 CarswellQue 384, 1983 CarswellQue 28, [1983] 2 S.C.R. 60, 4 Admin. L.R. 205, 7 C.C.C. (3d) 385, 37 C.R. (3d) 289, 2 D.L.R. (4th) 193, 51 N.R. 81.

[128] *Basi*, 2009 SCC 52, 2009 CarswellBC 3869, 2009 CarswellBC 3870, 248 C.C.C. (3d) 257, 70 C.R. (6th) 18.

[129] *Supra* note 122.

working for the defence, is not bound by any such duty in undertaking its own investigation independently of the courts and the prosecution.[130] The defence is entitled to do what it can to identify the informant and otherwise make full answer and defence, provided that the methods used are lawful. The right to make full answer and defence is fundamental to criminal justice and is protected by section 7 of the *Charter*. However, not all attempts to identify an informant will be linked to that right. Some defence enquiries may amount to an obstruction of justice, or extortion, depending on the manner in which the enquiries are carried out and their intended purpose, and the other circumstances of the case. A veiled reference may constitute a threat if it is sufficient, in light of all the circumstances, to convey to the victim the consequences which he or she fears or would prefer to avoid.

A police informer must be distinguished from a police agent.[131] Unlike an informer who merely furnishes information to the police, an agent will usually act on the direction of the police and go "into the field" to gather information about a criminal activity, or may even participate in an illegal transaction which will be the subject of the charge against an accused. Although the police informer is protected by a *strong privilege that is not disclosable subject to the innocence at stake exception*, the identity of the agent is disclosable to the defence.

An example of where disclosure of the name of the informant was ordered is *Hunter*.[132] There the defence was seeking to attack a search warrant that had been used to search the accused's residence where narcotics were discovered. It was held that, in the circumstances of that case, disclosure of the identity of the informer was crucial to the defence. The Crown was given the option either of disclosing the informant's identity, proceeding on a warrantless search or withdrawing the prosecution.

Another exception that allows the court to order disclosure is where the informer has acted as an *agent provocateur*. Disclosure may also be ordered where the accused seeks to establish that a search and seizure of his premises was not undertaken on reasonable grounds and therefore contravened section 8 of the *Charter*.[133]

---

[130] *Barros*, 2011 CarswellAlta 1724, 2011 CarswellAlta 1725, 273 C.C.C. (3d) 129, 88 C.R. (6th) 33 (S.C.C.).

[131] *B. (G.)*, 2000 CarswellOnt 2750, 146 C.C.C. (3d) 465 (C.A.); leave to appeal refused 2001 CarswellOnt 874, 2001 CarswellOnt 875, 151 C.C.C. (3d) vi (S.C.C.).

[132] *Supra* note 122.

[133] *Scott*, 1990 CarswellOnt 65, 1990 CarswellOnt 1012, [1990] 3 S.C.R. 979, 61 C.C.C. (3d) 300, 2 C.R. (4th) 153, 1 C.R.R. (2d) 82, 116 N.R. 361, 43 O.A.C. 277.

(vii) Surveillance Location Privilege

Another claim of privilege that has become the subject of judicial consideration in recent years is "surveillance location privilege". Persons who assist the police by providing them with a safe location from which to conduct surveillance of suspected criminal activity have been held to be entitled to the same protection as persons assisting the police by providing information.[134] Such people are vulnerable to retribution from criminals who may resent the fact that they have cooperated with the police and may attempt to make an example of them in order to discourage others from doing the same. Unless their identities are kept confidential, they may be reluctant to help the police. Moreover, disclosure could destroy the value of the location and possibly threaten the safety of officers using that location.

Against these considerations must be balanced the right of an accused to full answer and defence. Whether the officer was able to make the observations claimed in his evidence may depend on the location of the observation post. Unless the defence is provided with the location of the post, it would be virtually impossible for the defence to test the credibility of the officer when he gives evidence of his observation. Thus, it would appear that the admissibility of the location and the reliability of the officer's observations have to be decided on a case-by-case basis.[135]

Section 37(1) of the *Canada Evidence Act* provides,

> Subject to sections 38 to 38.16, a Minister of the Crown in right of Canada or other official may object to the disclosure of information before a court, person or body with jurisdiction to compel the production of information by certifying orally or in writing to the court, person or body that the information should not be disclosed on the grounds of a specified public interest.

It has been held that the Crown is entitled to claim surveillance location privilege either by common law or under section 37(1) of the CEA of the location of an observation post used by the police in investigating crime.[136]

(viii) Public Interest Privilege

The law recognizes that it is not in the public interest to disclose certain information regarding governmental activities. At the same time, it also recognizes that litigants should have access to all evidence that may be of assistance to the fair disposition of issues arising in litigation in order for the

---

[134] *Thomas*, 1998 CarswellOnt 1331, 124 C.C.C. (3d) 178, [1998] O.J. No. 1400 (Gen. Div.); *Lam*, 2000 BCCA 545, 2000 CarswellBC 1928, 148 C.C.C. (3d) 379, 38 C.R. (5th) 189, 143 B.C.A.C. 193, 235 W.A.C. 193.

[135] *Lam, ibid.*

[136] *Lam, supra.*

administration of justice to operate properly and fairly. What the court must try to do is balance these two competing interests. It will depend, as one judge has said, on "changing social conditions and the role of government in society at various times".[137]

Sections 37(1) to 37.3 of the *Canada Evidence Act* set up a procedure to permit a Minister of the Crown in the right of Canada or other official to apply to the courts to assert a claim of privilege denying disclosure of any information on the basis of a special public interest. If the objection is made before a superior court or any other court of the province, the object must be determined by the superior court. However, the superior court does not have exclusive jurisdiction. The Federal Court also has jurisdiction.[138] Section 37(4.1) provides that disclosure may be ordered unless it would encroach upon the specified public interest. Even where the court concludes that disclosure would encroach upon a specified public interest, but the court is of the view that the public interest in disclosure outweighs in importance the specified interest, disclosure may be ordered. Section 37(5) requires the court to balance competing interests, including the public interest in disclosure, and the form and conditions of disclosure that are most likely to limit any encroachment of the specified public interest.

(ix) Jurors

No juror may be required to divulge what another juror said during deliberations except for the purposes of an investigation of a juror for obstructing justice. Not only is a juror protected from being compelled to disclose that information, a juror is guilty of contempt of court if he or she does. Moreover, section 649 of the *Criminal Code* makes it an offence for a juror to disclose such information.

There are several reasons for the rule. One reason is that verdicts are intended to be final and jurors should not be required to explain why they reached a particular verdict. If a juror was required to disclose what took place during deliberations, it would encourage dissatisfied litigants from using every means to find out what went on in the jury room in an effort to show that the result was not according to law, and this would be contrary to

---

[137] *Carey v. Ontario*, 1986 CarswellOnt 1011, 1986 CarswellOnt 472, [1986] 2 S.C.R. 637, 58 O.R. (2d) 352n, 22 Admin. L.R. 236, 30 C.C.C. (3d) 498, (sub nom. *Carey v. R.*) 14 C.P.C. (2d) 10, 35 D.L.R. (4th) 161, 72 N.R. 81, 20 O.A.C. 81, *per* La Forest J. at p. 506 [C.C.C.].

[138] Section 37(3)(a).

public policy.[139] Another reason is to encourage jurors while deliberating their verdict to engage in full and frank discussion without fear that what they say may be publicly disclosed by another juror. Finally, the recent attention by the media to high-profile cases gives added importance to the rule. It ensures that jurors are protected from harassment by investigative reporters and prevents jurors from financially exploiting their duties by selling accounts of their deliberations to the media.

(x) Diplomats

Diplomats are also protected from disclosure of information. The basis of this common law rule is that the courts should respect representatives of the government of another country, even though they have jurisdiction over foreign subjects who are present in Canada. Such immunity, however, is not absolute where the safety of the country is imperilled.[140]

(xi) No Automatic Privilege

There is a misconception by the public generally that persons such as doctors, psychiatrists, priests and journalists are entitled to claim privilege and to refuse to divulge information given to them by patients, penitents and informants. No such common law privilege exists. The reason is that the courts have considered that the public interest in the search for truth far outweighs the protection of confidentiality in such cases.[141]

Similarly, the privilege contained in section 10(5) of the *Divorce Act* which precludes the admissibility of "anything said or of any admission or communication made in the course of assisting spouses to achieve a reconciliation" only applies where the statements for which the claim is made are "in a divorce proceeding" and to a "person nominated by a court under this section to assist spouses to achieve a reconciliation".[142] Although the com-

---

[139] *Perras (No. 2)*, 1974 CarswellSask 69, 18 C.C.C. (2d) 47, 48 D.L.R. (3d) 145, [1974] 5 W.W.R. 187 (C.A.); *Pan*, 2001 CarswellOnt 2261, 2001 CarswellOnt 2262, 155 C.C.C. (3d) 97, 43 C.R. (5th) 203 (S.C.C.).

[140] *Rose* (1946), 1946 CarswellQue 16, 88 C.C.C. 114, 3 C.R. 277, [1947] 3 D.L.R. 618 (K.B.).

[141] *S. (R.J.)*, 1985 CarswellOnt 93, 19 C.C.C. (3d) 115, 45 C.R. (3d) 161, 8 O.A.C. 241 (C.A.); leave to appeal refused (1985), 61 N.R. 266n, 11 O.A.C. 317n (S.C.C.).

[142] *Pabani*, 1994 CarswellOnt 69, 17 O.R. (3d) 659, 89 C.C.C. (3d) 437, 29 C.R. (4th) 364, 70 O.A.C. 118 (C.A.); leave to appeal refused (1994), 19 O.R. (3d) xvi, 91 C.C.C. (3d) vi, 33 C.R. (4th) 405n, 179 N.R. 79 (note), 77 O.A.C. 400 (note).

mon law recognizes a privilege in matrimonial disputes for the purpose of promoting spouses to reconcile, there is no such common law privilege recognized by the criminal law outside of the plea bargaining structure.

Nevertheless, some judges, particularly in civil cases, have been loath to compel witnesses to disclose information given in confidence to them;[143] other judges have ordered the information to be disclosed but have refused to impose any penalty, or have imposed a nominal one, for the refusal to do so. By doing so, the judges have not recognized a legal privilege. They have simply refused to impose sanctions on the witness for refusing to divulge the confidential information.

In recent years, however, the Supreme Court of Canada has recognized that there may be case-by-case instances where a judge may allow a person to withhold disclosure of a confidential communication. In *Fosty*,[144] the Court recognized that there are two types of privilege: the first is "blanket privilege" (or what is also known as *prima facie*, common-law or class privilege); the other is "case-by-case privilege". Blanket privilege has been discussed previously. On the other hand, an accused may be able to show that the relationship between himself and his confessor satisfies certain pre-conditions. In such instance, the courts will generally rule that the communication was privileged.

In *Fosty*, the Supreme Court recognized that the courts may declare a confidential communication protected from disclosure where the witness satisfies the following pre-conditions set out by the late Professor Wigmore in his text, *Evidence in Trials at Common Law*:

1. The communication must originate in a confidence that it will not be disclosed;

2. The element of confidentiality must be essential to the full and satisfactory maintenance of the relationship between the parties;

3. The relationship must be one which in the opinion of the community ought to be sedulously fostered;

4. The injury that would inure to the relationship by the disclosure of the communication would be greater than the benefit gained for the correct disposal of the litigation.

In *National Post*,[145] the Supreme Court considered a claim of privilege by a journalist. The Court said that although the common law does not rec-

---

[143] *Dembie v. Dembie*, 1963 CarswellOnt 50, 21 R.F.L. 46 (S.C.).

[144] *Supra* note 106.

[145] 2010 CarswellOnt 2776, 2010 CarswellOnt 2777, (sub nom. *National Post v. Canada*) 254 C.C.C. (3d) 469, 74 C.R. (6th) 1 (S.C.C.).

ognize a class privilege protecting journalists from compelled disclosure of secret sources, a journalist's claim for protection of secret sources can be assessed properly using the case-by-case model of privilege. The Wigmore criteria provide a workable structure within which to assess, in light of society's evolving values, the sometimes-competing interests of free expression and the administration of justice and other values that promote the public interest. It provides the necessary flexibility and an opportunity for growth that is essential to the proper function of the common law.

The Court said that scope of the privilege may be total or partial. It is capable, in a proper case, of being asserted against the issuance or execution of a search warrant. A promise of confidentiality will be respected if: the communication originates in a confidence that the identity of the informant will not be disclosed; the confidence is essential to the relationship in which the communication arises; the relationship is one which should be sedulously fostered in the public good; and the public interest in protecting the identity of the informant from disclosure outweighs the public interest in getting at the truth. This approach, the Court said, properly reflects *Charter* values and balances the competing public interests in a context-specific manner. The media party asking the court to uphold a promise of confidentiality must prove all four criteria and no burden of proof shifts to the Crown. This includes, under the fourth criterion, proving that the public interest in protecting a secret source outweighs the public interest in a criminal investigation. The weighing up under this criterion will also include the nature and seriousness of the offence under investigation, and the probative value of the evidence sought to be obtained measured against the public interest in respecting the journalist's promise of confidentiality. The underlying purpose of the investigation is relevant as well. Until the media have met all four criteria, no privilege arises and the evidence is presumptively compellable and admissible. Therefore, no journalist can give a secret source an absolute assurance of confidentiality.

3. DOCUMENTARY EVIDENCE

(a) Generally

Direct or circumstantial evidence of a fact in issue may also be proved by a document. In order to prove the authenticity of a document, it is usually necessary to call as a witness the person who made the document so that he can identify it. However, proof as to authorship can also be established by circumstantial evidence, such as the finding of the document in the possession of the accused, by an admission of the accused of ownership or authorship, or proof by a handwriting expert.[146] In such instance, it is still necessary for a witness to be asked to identify the document and to give evidence that will tend to connect it with a fact in issue.

Assume, for example, that the accused is charged with forging a cheque. If someone is able to testify that he saw the accused writing out the cheque and can identify the particular document, that is direct evidence from which a judge or jury can conclude that the accused committed the crime. However, if no one saw the accused write the cheque, but a witness is familiar with the accused's handwriting and that witness is able to identify the writing and signature on the cheque as belonging to the accused, that is circumstantial evidence from which a judge or jury can draw the inference that the accused wrote the cheque.

Quite often, however, a document may be found in the possession of the accused that is incriminating in nature, but no one is able to say that they saw the accused prepare it and no one can identify his signature. Assume, for example, that the accused, a butcher, is charged with selling horsemeat that he fraudulently represented as beef. A search warrant is executed by the police at his home and they find invoices from a horse rancher in Texas indicating that certain horses were sold to the accused on a certain date. It is obvious that these invoices are relevant to the issue of whether the accused has been buying horses and selling them as beef. On the other hand, there is also the possibility that the documents are not relevant to the prosecution at all and simply indicate that the accused purchased some horses that he may still own or that he may have sold intact to someone else. It is also possible that the documents were fabricated by someone who wished to harm the accused.

Nevertheless, the courts have held that all documents found in the possession of an accused, which are relevant to an issue before the court, are admissible as evidence of the accused's knowledge of their contents, connection with, or complicity in, the transactions to which they relate, or his or her state of mind, and may be considered by the judge and jury on the issue of his or her guilt. The prosecution is not required to prove, as a condition of admissibility, that the accused has knowledge of the contents of the document.[147] However, the weight to be attached to those documents by the trier of fact will depend upon all of the circumstances of the case.

---

[146] *Bloomfield*, 1973 CarswellNB 1, 6 N.B.R. (2d) 5, 10 C.C.C. (2d) 398, 21 C.R.N.S. 97 (C.A.); *Emes*, 2001 CarswellOnt 2279, 157 C.C.C. (3d) 124 (C.A.).

[147] *Turlon*, 1989 CarswellOnt 96, 49 C.C.C. (3d) 186, 70 C.R. (3d) 376, 32 O.A.C. 396 (C.A.).

(b) Best Evidence Rule

The best evidence rule is a rule of evidence that requires the side that relies upon a document to produce the original of it, unless the original was destroyed or cannot be found, or it is impossible or impractical to produce. For example, it may be impossible or impractical to produce the original if it is in the possession of someone in another country since a Canadian court has no jurisdiction to order its production.

The rule dates back to the very early common law when witnesses did not testify before juries. It was connected to the doctrine of "profert" in pleading, which required a party relying upon a document as a ground of action or defence to produce it bodily to the court. As the law developed and witnesses were allowed to testify, the rule was justified on the basis that it prevented fraud. In other words, it was presumed that if the original document existed, then it was likely being withheld for some sinister motive. As well, there was a concern that a copy of a document, made by hand in those days, might be inaccurate.

Today, with modern technology, it is possible to produce a document that cannot be distinguished from the original and the best evidence rule is often relaxed. On the other hand, the same technology allows production of an authentic-looking "copy" that may actually be a forgery made up of several documents pasted together. Nevertheless, counsel will frequently admit that a particular document is a photocopy of the original and that it will not be necessary to comply with the best evidence rule. However, if the opposing side is not prepared to agree to the production of a photocopy, then the witness through whom the document is introduced must give some explanation as to why the original cannot be produced. He or she must, at least, be able to say that the copy is an exact reproduction of the original. In such instance, the court will generally admit it and the issue as to whether it is an exact copy of the original will go to the question of the weight of the evidence.

The *Canada Evidence Act* also permits the admissibility of certified copies of documents instead of the original where certain conditions are met. For example, section 29 authorizes the admission of a copy of any entry in any book or record maintained by a financial institution as defined by section 29(9), instead of the actual book or record, where the following is established: 1) the book or record must have been one of the ordinary books or records maintained by the financial institution when the entry was made; 2) the entry must have been made in the usual and ordinary course of business; 3) the book or record must have been in the control of the institution; and 4) the copy must be a true copy. The manager, accountant or any person employed by the institution who has knowledge of the book or record may give proof orally or by affidavit.

Sections 30 (business records and copies made in the usual and ordinary course of business) and 31 (a print from any photographic film of an entry in a book or record or of a negotiable instrument kept by any government or defined corporation that was destroyed, lost or delivered to a customer) also authorize the admission of a copy subject to the fulfillment of certain conditions.[148]

4. ARTICLES AND THINGS

Another form of evidence, in addition to oral and documentary evidence, may be an article or thing that is connected with the crime, such as a gun or a knife, or in the case of a stolen article, the thing itself. This is known as real evidence because it can be seen, heard or touched by the judge and jury. Where such evidence is being tendered, it is generally necessary for a witness to identify it and explain its relevancy to a fact in issue. It will then be made an exhibit (just as a document will be made an exhibit) so that if the verdict is appealed, it will be available for examination by the court of appeal.

There may be circumstances where it is impossible or inconvenient to produce the original article. For example, it would hardly add to the decorum of a trial to produce a stolen cow for inspection by the judge and jury, nor would it be practical to produce a stolen automobile. The usual practice is for the police to take a photograph of the particular article and to introduce the photograph in its place. Unless the other side agrees that the photograph is an accurate depiction of the article or object, the photographer who took the photograph or a witness present when the picture was taken must be called verify the accuracy of the photograph.

5. DEMONSTRATIVE EVIDENCE

Visual aids such as photographs, maps, diagrams or flow charts will often be admitted by the judge to assist the judge and jury in reaching their verdict. Whether the photograph, diagram, map, flow chart or any other item will assist the judge or jury will often depend on the facts of the particular case. A judge may also permit an experiment or demonstration in the courtroom. For example, in *Brooks*,[149] where the defence attacked the testimony of a police officer who said that he took a statement from the accused in eight minutes, the trial judge permitted defence counsel to conduct an ex-

---

[148] *Lemay*, 2004 CarswellBC 2823, 191 C.C.C. (3d) 497, 25 C.R. (6th) 17 (C.A.).
[149] 1993 CarswellOnt 797, 81 C.C.C. (3d) 428 (Gen. Div.).

periment and have the officer duplicate as far as possible the taking of the statement in an effort to discredit his evidence.

Sometimes opposing counsel will object to the introduction of a diagram or a map because it is not drawn to scale and may be misleading. In each case, the question of admissibility will depend upon whether the judge determines that the document will assist the jury in better understanding the evidence. If it is so distorted that it gives a wrong or a misleading impression, then the judge should refuse to admit it.[150] The most difficult question arises in the case of photographs. The first thing that must be established by the side that wishes to introduce a photograph is that the photograph is an accurate depiction of the scene or the subject and is being offered to assist the triers in determining the fact in issue before them. Often the main objection will be that the photograph, particularly of a victim, may inflame the jury and divert them from their main task or cause them to be prejudiced against the accused. For a long time, the main concern of the court was one of admissibility, not prejudice. Mr. Justice Masten pointed out over seventy years ago in *O'Donnell*:

> The only question to be considered is were they admissible under the rules of evidence. If they are the effect which they may have on the jury cannot interfere with their admission.[151]

However, with the development of judicial discretion has arisen the view that the trial judge has the right to exclude photographs if they are of minor assistance and their prejudicial effect far outweighs that assistance. On the other hand, the corollary of this is that, if the photograph will assist the judge and jury in understanding the evidence, it will generally be admitted, even it is inflammatory.[152] In each case, the judge must use his or her discretion to ensure that the accused receives a fair trial.[153]

---

[150] *Valley*, 1986 CarswellOnt 822, 26 C.C.C. (3d) 207, 13 O.A.C. 89 (C.A.); leave to appeal refused [1986] 1 S.C.R. xiii (note), 26 C.C.C. (3d) 207 (note), 67 N.R. 158 (note), 15 O.A.C. 240 (note).

[151] *O'Donnell*, 1936 CarswellOnt 259, 1936 CarswellOnt 269, 65 C.C.C. 299, [1936] 2 D.L.R. 517 (C.A.) at p. 383 [C.C.C.].

[152] *D. (No. 2)*, 1977 CarswellAlta 210, 3 A.R. 409, 35 C.C.C. (2d) 464, [1977] 4 W.W.R. 47 (C.A.); leave to appeal refused [1977] 1 S.C.R. vii.

[153] *Kendall*, 1987 CarswellOnt 93, 35 C.C.C. (3d) 105, 57 C.R. (3d) 249, 20 O.A.C. 134, [1987] O.J. No. 388 (C.A.); *Wade*, 1994 CarswellOnt 68, 18 O.R. (3d) 33, 89 C.C.C. (3d) 39, 29 C.R. (4th) 327, 69 O.A.C. 321 (C.A.); reversed in part 1995 CarswellOnt 123, 1995 CarswellOnt 527, [1995] 2 S.C.R. 737, 23 O.R. (3d) 415, 98 C.C.C. (3d) 97, 41 C.R. (4th) 100, 182 N.R. 387, 82 O.A.C. 182; *C. (R.)*, 2000 CarswellOnt 363, 31 C.R. (5th) 306 (S.C.J.).

With the rapid development of photographic equipment, the question arises whether the Crown or the defence should be permitted to use such equipment to re-enact its version of the events that are the subject of disputed issues. For example, a videotaped re-enactment of a crime may be of greater assistance to a jury in understanding the facts in issue than an oral recitation by a witness to the crime. On the other hand, a re-enactment video has the potential of unfairly influencing the jury. It will undoubtedly have an immediate visual impact, such that the jurors may be induced to give it more weight than it deserves.[154] It may also cause the jury to discount less compelling or less vivid evidence that may be more probative of the facts in issue. Here, the courts have been reluctant to lay down any rigid rules governing the admissibility of such evidence.[155] What has been said is that the overriding principle is whether the prejudicial effect of the video re-enactment outweighs its probative value having regard to its relevance, accuracy, and whether what it portrays can be verified under oath and the necessity of the evidence.

---

[154] *MacDonald*, 2000 CarswellOnt 2416, 49 O.R. (3d) 417, 146 C.C.C. (3d) 525, 35 C.R. (5th) 130, 134 O.A.C. 167 (C.A.).

[155] *MacDonald, ibid.* See also *Collins*, 2001 CarswellOnt 3462, 160 C.C.C. (3d) 85 (C.A.); *Nikitin*, 2003 CarswellOnt 2360, 176 C.C.C. (3d) 225 (C.A.); *Veinot*, 2011 CarswellNS 892, 280 C.C.C. (3d) 23 (C.A.)

PART B

Excluded Evidence

3
HEARSAY

1. THE ORTHODOX RULE

Probably no rule of evidence is more misunderstood than the rule against hearsay. It is misunderstood because it is commonly believed that the rule means that a witness is not allowed to repeat in court what he or she was told by someone else. Because this is only a partial explanation of the rule, it is important to start at the beginning.

The first question that must be asked whenever a possible hearsay problem arises is "what is the side calling the witness seeking to prove"? If the purpose in calling the witness is to prove the truth of what the witness was told by a third party to establish a fact in issue, then a hearsay problem arises. However, if the purpose of calling the witness is to prove only that a statement was made by the third party, not that the statement was true, then a hearsay problem does not arise. There is no potential hearsay problem because the fact in issue is not the truth of the statement, but whether the statement was made. If the witness is allowed to repeat in court what a third party said only to prove that he or she made a statement, then it is not hearsay. It is original evidence of the fact that the statement was made.

For example, assume the accused is charged with robbing a bank at five minutes after 12:00 noon and X saw the accused enter the bank at noon. Such evidence is offered, not as direct evidence that the accused robbed the bank, but rather as circumstantial evidence from which a jury can infer that the accused was in the bank at the time of the robbery. Together with other evidence, it may establish that the accused was the robber. The rule is that only X may be called to testify that he saw the accused enter the bank at noon. However, if X is unavailable to testify, but told Y that he saw the accused enter the bank at 12:00 noon, then a hearsay problem arises. Y will not be permitted to testify that X told him he saw the accused enter the bank at noon to prove that very fact.

Why do we prohibit hearsay evidence? Clearly, the fact that X saw the accused enter the bank at noon is logically probative of one of the three issues that the Crown must prove. Yet the rules of evidence do not permit Y to tell the court what X told him. The reason is that Y cannot be effectively cross-examined about what X told him. All Y can do is to repeat what X told him. There is no way that Y can assure the court that X's observation was reliable and his statement honest, when he told him that he saw the accused going into the bank at noon. Unless X is compelled to come to court, where his oath can be taken and his demeanour observed while his evidence is being tested by cross-examination, there is no way of ensuring the reliability and honesty of his evidence. Moreover, everyone knows that whenever information is passed from one person to the next, there is a risk that it may be misunderstood. Our system of justice recognizes that someone's life or liberty should not depend upon second-hand information.

Let us assume, however, that X also told Z that he saw the accused enter the bank at 2:00 p.m. and the defence wishes to call Z to say exactly what X told him. Is it hearsay? That will depend upon what the evidence is attempting to prove. Assume that the defence wishes to call the evidence to show that X should not be believed, or is confused about having seen the accused enter the bank at noon because X also told Z that he saw him enter the bank at 2:00 p.m. Here it is not being offered to prove that the accused entered the bank at 2:00 p.m., but to show that X was mistaken or lying when he testified that the accused entered the bank at noon. In such instance, it is admissible. It does not offend the hearsay rule. It is original or first-hand evidence because it is being offered to prove only that X *told* Z that the accused entered the bank at 2.00 p.m., not the fact that the accused entered the bank at 2.00 p.m.

What the law of evidence seeks to ensure is that only original or first-hand evidence is admitted to prove a fact in issue. Second-hand evidence will not suffice. On the other hand, where the fact in issue is whether a statement was made by a third party, the statement will be admitted because it bears directly on the issue to be proved. It is still original or first-hand evidence — not second-hand evidence.

Although the hearsay rule is relatively straightforward, its application often seems to create difficulties. For example, in *Ly*[1] at issue was the admissibility of a telephone conversation between an unidentified person and a police officer, in which the unidentified person made arrangements to deliver drugs to the police officer at a certain time and place. The trial judge had rejected the evidence as hearsay and acquitted the accused of possession for the purposes of trafficking because there was no evidence that the person who met the officer was the same person who spoke to the officer over the phone. The acquittal was set aside by the Alberta Court of Appeal who ordered a new trial. McClung J.A. for the Court held that the conversation was properly admissible as part of the narrative or the *res gestae* since it would have been impossible to understand the development of the later events without the evidence of the telephone conversation preceding them. Moreover, even if it was hearsay, the particulars of the telephone conversation were still admissible because it had the circumstantial guarantees of reliability, necessity and truthfulness.

Although the Supreme Court of Canada dismissed a further appeal by the accused, McLachlin J., delivering the judgment of the Court, felt that the statement was not hearsay at all. Rather, it was a statement of intention or a statement tendered to establish the alleged drug transaction, and hence not tendered for the truth of its contents. It was merely one of the circumstances which, combined with others, was capable of establishing that when the ac-

---

[1] 1997 CarswellAlta 942, 1997 CarswellAlta 943, [1997] 3 S.C.R. 698, 206 A.R. 309, 119 C.C.C. (3d) 479, 219 N.R. 237, 156 W.A.C. 309.

cused appeared at the time and place with drugs in his possession, he did so for the purpose of trafficking.

The first step in an analysis of whether the evidence was hearsay is whether the evidence was relevant to a fact in issue. If the drug dealer had spoken to the officer face to face and made arrangements to meet and deliver drugs, then what the drug dealer said would not only be relevant to a fact in issue, it would be admissible for its truth as an incriminating statement going towards the issue of intent. The difficulty here was that the identity of the drug dealer was unknown. Until his identity was known, the statement was not admissible against the accused for its truth.

What the Alberta Court of Appeal and the Supreme Court did not seem to consider was that the statement by the person who spoke to the officer had two aspects to it. The first was that he would meet the officer at a certain time and place. The second was that he would deliver drugs to the officer. The first aspect went to the issue of the identity of the person who offered to traffick in drugs; the second to his intention. The statement that he would meet the officer at a certain time and place, along with the fact that the accused met the police officer at the place and time stated, was circumstantial evidence from which it could be inferred, along with other evidence, if any, that the person who spoke to the officer over the telephone was the accused. Thus, the first aspect of the statement was admissible, not necessarily for the truth of its contents, but for the fact that it was made. It showed an intention by someone purporting to traffick in drugs to meet the officer. Once it was admitted for that purpose and the trier was satisfied that it was made by the accused, the issue of identity was satisfied.

However, there was a second aspect of the statement, namely, the intention to deliver drugs to the officer. Once the identity of the person was established, then surely the evidence was admissible for its truth as evidence of the accused's intention to traffick in drugs. Although hearsay, it constituted an incriminating admission by the accused and was receivable as one of the exceptions to the hearsay rule.

Baldree[2] presented a similar problem. At issue was whether the contents of a single telephone call on the cellphone of the accused seized by the police during his arrest on drug charges was hearsay and presumptively inadmissible, or circumstantial evidence from which the trial judge could conclude that the accused was a drug dealer. There the police had entered a residence suspected of a break and enter and found the accused who was brushing his teeth. The smell of freshly-burned marijuana was detected.

---

[2] 2012 ONCA 138, 2012 CarswellOnt 1741, 280 C.C.C. (3d) 191, 92 C.R. (6th) 331.

Seized by the police as an incident of arrest was cocaine, marijuana, a debt list and $230. The accused and others in the apartment were arrested and a cell phone seized from the accused. At the police station, a call was taken by an officer on the accused's cellphone asking for the accused and wanting one ounce of weed. The trial judge had admitted the evidence of the telephone call, not to prove the accused was trafficking in drugs, but as an item of circumstantial evidence of trafficking and, together with all of the other evidence, convicted the accused of trafficking. An appeal was allowed by the majority, all three judges delivering reasons.

Noting that Ontario cases were not consistent on the issue, Feldman J.A., delivering one of the majority decisions, relied on the majority decision of the House of Lords in *Kearley (No. 1)*,[3] where it was held that the police could not give evidence of the contents of the telephone calls or what the in-person purported purchasers said because those contents constituted implied hearsay and were therefore inadmissible. The implied hearsay was "the implicit statement of the caller who calls asking for drugs that he or she believes that the appellant sells drugs". Had the caller said directly, "I'm calling to purchase drugs because the appellant sells drugs", that would be a direct hearsay assertion of the same belief and presumptively inadmissible. Because the calls were requests for drugs rather than statements, the callers *were not asserting* but instead implying their belief that they could buy drugs from the appellant because he was a drug dealer and therefore the hearsay nature of the content was the same.[4] Feldman J.A. reasoned that where there are a number of calls, the reliability of the calls comes from the number of the calls and is therefore a necessity/reliability analysis of the calls. Where, however, there was a single call as here, "it is not circumstantial evidence from which an inference can be drawn that the accused is a drug dealer. The evidence gets its probative value from the belief of the callers, which may or may not be accurate".[5] Blair J.A. agreed with Feldman J.A holding that "(i)f the phone call evidence was hearsay, it ought to have been subjected to a necessity/reliability analysis, which, in his view would have failed. If, as the trial judge had concluded on the basis of the authorities he followed that it was not hearsay, he should nonetheless have subjected the phone call to a prejudice/probative value balancing exercise, which he did not do. Watt J.A. dissenting noted that the majority decision in *Kearley* had been repeatedly criticized and was statutorily overtaken by the enactment of the *Criminal Justice Act 2003* which abolished implied

---

[3] [1992] 2 All E.R. 345 (U.K. H.L.).

[4] *Supra* at para. 126.

[5] *Supra* at para. 141.

assertions as excluded hearsay.[6] He argued that if one looked out the window and saw people in the street opening their umbrellas, it would be reasonable to infer that it had started to rain. While accepting the logic of that argument, Feldman J.A. went on to point out that there was only one telephone call intercepted and "if only one or two people open their umbrellas while others do not, one could not reliably draw the inference of rain".[7]

2. WHEN IS HEARSAY ALLOWED?

Most legal historians believe that the hearsay rule, like all exclusionary rules, owes its origin to the jury system. The jury was only allowed to hear evidence that was given under oath and subjected to cross-examination. Some scholars argue that these two reasons have little substance today. For example, a witness who feels that his or her moral conscience cannot be bound by the oath is permitted to testify by affirmation. Moreover, juries today are sophisticated enough to know that the mere fact that a person takes an oath does not ensure the truth of the testimony. If anything does promote truth, it is the fear of a prosecution for perjury.

The second and real reason, today, why hearsay is still excluded is because it cannot be tested by cross-examination. The law requires a witness who has first-hand knowledge of the facts to come forward and to testify so that the reliability and honesty of the witness's evidence can be subjected to the scrutiny of cross-examination. As indicated earlier, a witness who has second-hand information cannot be effectively cross-examined to test the truth of the information given to him or her by a third party. All that the witness can say is that he or she was given information by a third party.

However, what if that person is dead or unavailable to testify or, if available, unable to communicate his or her evidence because of some mental or physical incapacity? Should the law, confronted with a choice of either accepting second-hand evidence or no evidence at all, choose the latter? No sooner was the exclusionary rule of hearsay invented in the late seventeenth century than judges began to realize that, unless certain types of hearsay were admitted, serious crimes might go unpunished or litigants denied justice. The result was that courts began to create a number of exceptions to

---

[6] *Singh (Alexander Sukadave)*, [2006] EWCA Crim 660; *Twist (Andrew Terence)*, [2011] EWCA Crim 1143 and *Lord Advocate's Reference (No.1 of 1992)*, 1992 S.C.C.R. 724 at p. 741.

[7] *Supra* at para.132.

the strict application of the hearsay rule where the declarant was dead. Professor Wigmore explained the rationale underlying the exceptions this way:

> The purpose and reason of the Hearsay rule is the key to the exceptions to it. The theory of the Hearsay rule is that many possible sources of inaccuracy and untrustworthiness which may lie underneath the bare untested assertion of a witness can best be brought to light and exposed, if they exist, by the test of cross-examination. But this test or security may in a given instance be superfluous; it may be sufficiently clear, in that instance, that the statement offered is free enough from the risk of inaccuracy and untrustworthiness, so that the test of cross-examination would be a work of supererogation. Moreover, the test may be impossible of employment — for example, by reason of the death of the declarant — so that, if his testimony is to be used at all, there is a necessity for taking it in the untested shape.[8]

For almost three centuries, these exceptions to the hearsay rule were applied strictly by the courts. So long as a hearsay statement fell within one of the recognized exceptions, the trial judge was obliged to admit it. However, in 1970 the Supreme Court of Canada delivered its landmark decision in *Ares v. Venner*,[9] a civil case. There the court permitted a plaintiff to introduce hospital records of his treatment for a broken leg as declarations made in the ordinary course of duty and as *"prima facie* proof of the facts stated therein" even though the nurses who had made the records were alive and were, in fact, waiting outside the courtroom to testify and available for cross-examination.

Unfortunately, *Ares v. Venner* lay dormant for another twenty years until another landmark decision of the Supreme Court of Canada, *Khan*.[10] This time the Court decided to strike out in a new direction. Instead of extending the old exceptions created centuries earlier, the Court adopted a new test — "necessity and reliability". The role of the trial judge was no longer restricted to determining whether the hearsay statement that counsel was seeking to introduce fell within one of the recognized exceptions. If it could be established that a declarant was unavailable or unable to give evidence and the statement had the indicia of reliability, the trial judge had the discretion to admit what the declarant had said through a third party.

---

[8] *Wigmore on Evidence* (3rd ed.), Vol. 5, (Boston: Little, Brown and Co., 1974) para. 1420, p. 202.

[9] 1970 CarswellAlta 80, 1970 CarswellAlta 142, [1970] S.C.R. 608, 14 D.L.R. (3d) 4, 73 W.W.R. 347, 12 C.R.N.S. 349.

[10] 1990 CarswellOnt 108, 1990 CarswellOnt 1001, [1990] 2 S.C.R. 531, 59 C.C.C. (3d) 92, 79 C.R. (3d) 1, 113 N.R. 53, 41 O.A.C. 353, [1990] S.C.J. No. 81.

In *Smith*,[11] Chief Justice Lamer characterized the *Khan* decision as signaling "an end to the categorical approach to the admission of hearsay evidence".[12] However, a year later, speaking for the majority of the Court in *B. (K.G.)*,[13] he was quick to affirm that the "new approach shares the same principled approach basis as the existing exceptions"[14] and some textbook writers[15] took this statement as affirming the continued existence of the traditional exceptions.

Ten years later in *Starr*,[16] Iacobbuci J., delivering the majority judgment of the Supreme Court, again reaffirmed that the traditional exceptions were not without merit.

> While the exceptions may need to be reexamined in light of the principled approach, their complete abolition is not the answer. Rather, the exceptions continue to play an important role under the principled approach. Our task therefore is to reconcile the traditional exceptions with the principled approach. [para 202]

He gave three reasons:

> [203] One important function that the hearsay exceptions have served has been to add predictability and certainty to the law of hearsay. In light of the exceptions, and regardless of how illogical or arbitrary they may be, litigants can be more or less certain when going into court of the types of issues that will be relevant in debating admissibility in a particular context, and of the likelihood that the evidence will indeed be admitted. This certainty has fostered greater efficiency in the use of court time both at trial and on appeal, and has facilitated the task of the too frequently overburdened trial judge who is called upon to rule on hearsay admissibility with speed and considerable regularity.

---

[11] 1992 CarswellOnt 997, 1992 CarswellOnt 103, [1992] 2 S.C.R. 915, 75 C.C.C. (3d) 257, 15 C.R. (4th) 133, 94 D.L.R. (4th) 590, 139 N.R. 323, 55 O.A.C. 321, [1992] S.C.J. No. 74.

[12] *Ibid.*, at p. 993 [S.C.R.].

[13] 1993 CarswellOnt 76, 1993 CarswellOnt 975, [1993] 1 S.C.R. 740, 79 C.C.C. (3d) 257, 19 C.R. (4th) 1, 148 N.R. 241, 61 O.A.C. 1, [1993] S.C.J. No. 22.

[14] *Ibid.*, at p. 798 [S.C.R.].

[15] See Sopinka, Lederman and Bryant, *The Law of Evidence in Canada*, 2nd ed., (Toronto: Butterworths, 1992) at p. 19 and Schiff, *Evidence in the Litigation Process*, 4th ed., (Toronto: Carswell, 1993).

[16] 2000 SCC 40, 2000 CarswellMan 449, 2000 CarswellMan 450, [2000] 2 S.C.R. 144, 147 C.C.C. (3d) 449, 36 C.R. (5th) 1, 190 D.L.R. (4th) 591, [2000] 11 W.W.R. 1, 148 Man. R. (2d) 161, 258 N.R. 250, 224 W.A.C. 161, [2000] S.C.J. No. 40.

[204] Second, in addition to serving the utilitarian goals of providing greater certainty and fostering judicial efficiency, the exceptions have served an explanatory or educative function, instructing litigants and judges about the relevant factors to consider in determining whether to admit a *particular type* of hearsay evidence, or whether to admit hearsay in a *particular factual context*. Different hearsay scenarios by their nature raise different reliability concerns, and different issues of necessity. The specific requirements of the individual exceptions have had the useful effect of focusing attention upon the peculiar factors that make it desirable, or undesirable, to admit a particular form of out-of-court statement.

[206] A third important function played by the traditional hearsay exceptions is that they teach us about the historical and contemporary rationale for admitting certain forms of hearsay. It has quite properly been noted that some hearsay exceptions allow for the admission of evidence that is unreliable, unnecessary, or both. In the interest of fairness for the litigant against whom it is used, unreliable hearsay evidence should never be admitted. Apart from that, a review of the traditional exceptions reveals that there are reasons beyond "pure" necessity why a court might wish to admit reliable hearsay evidence.

Nevertheless, it is clear that *Starr* has effectively delivered the quietus to the traditional exceptions. At issue was the admissibility of a traditional exception to the hearsay rule — the present intention exception. Delivering the majority judgment of the Court, Iacobucci J. held that, although historically, there has been no requirement for the trial judge to assess the reliability of a traditional exception to hearsay before admitting it, it was now necessary to do so. It was his opinion that the concern for reliability and necessity should be no less present when the hearsay is introduced under an established exception. It would compromise trial fairness and raise the spectre of wrongful convictions if the Crown were allowed to introduce unreliable hearsay against the accused, regardless of whether it happens to fall within an existing traditional exception.[17]

Before turning to the modern rule, it is important to discuss the traditional exceptions.

3. TRADITIONAL EXCEPTIONS TO THE HEARSAY RULE

(a) Dying Declarations

Should a victim of a homicide be allowed to identify his killer before he dies? A strict application of the hearsay rule would say "no" because his

---

[17] *Supra* at paras. 213-14.

identification evidence would have to be given second-hand by the person who overheard him. However, if such evidence was not admitted, a murderer might be able to escape punishment for his crime. On the other hand, there is always the danger that a person who is dying might try to settle a score with an enemy by falsely accusing him of murder.

Faced with these two policy considerations, the courts in the 19th century decided to opt in favour of admitting the evidence for what it was worth. It was argued that anyone going to his maker was unlikely to perjure his soul by dying with a lie on his lips. At the same time, the courts were anxious to ensure that there would be no danger of mistake or an attempt to settle old scores.[18] They did this by creating two conditions that must be satisfied before such evidence would be admitted.

The first was that a dying declaration could only be admitted in a trial for the murder or manslaughter of the victim who made the declaration. This rule was so strictly applied that, in one case, the court refused to accept the dying declaration of a woman on the trial of the person charged with procuring her abortion, even though it resulted in her death. The other condition was that the victim must have had a *settled hopeless expectation of impending death* at the time that he or she made the declaration. It was believed that a victim's apprehension of death when the declaration was made would ensure its trustworthiness. In other words, a person is unlikely to tell a deliberate lie when he knows that he is dying and has no hope of recovery.

Unfortunately, this latter condition has restricted the admissibility of a dying declaration because it cannot always be assumed that a person who is dying knows that he is dying. Moreover, it is unlikely that even the most seriously injured person can appreciate that his life is in danger or that he will be told this by anyone who comes to his aid. Indeed, it is more likely that he will be encouraged to "hang on" until help comes.

Nevertheless, these conditions were, and continue to be, strictly applied by the courts under this exception. A famous example where a dying declaration was not admitted is *Bedingfield*.[19] Bedingfield was charged with murdering a woman by cutting her throat. At his trial, a prosecution witness testified that she saw the victim running out of the house where she had just been with Bedingfield. Her throat was almost completely severed. Just before the victim died, she said, "Look what Bedingfield has done to me". However, Chief Justice Cockburn refused to permit the witness to repeat

---

[18] *Schwartzenhauer*, 1935 CarswellBC 84, [1935] S.C.R. 367, 64 C.C.C. 1, [1935] 3 D.L.R. 711.

[19] (1879), 14 Cox C.C. 341.

what she heard the victim say. The fact that the wound itself was very serious was not enough for the court to draw the inference that the victim knew that she was dying. Fortunately, Bedingfield was convicted on other evidence.

Kharsekin[20] is another strict application of this rule. Here the victim of a knife attack told a physician who was attending him that he had been wounded by the accused. An hour later, in response to an inquiry, the victim again identified the accused as his attacker. Two hours later, the victim died. It was held by the Newfoundland Court of Appeal that since the victim did not have a settled hopeless expectation of death at the time that he made his statement, the trial judge was correct in not admitting the statement under this exception. However, the Court went on to hold that the trial judge should have admitted the statement under the new *Khan* rule. Here, necessity arose because of the death of the victim. Reliability existed because the victim had a peculiar means of knowledge, there was little time to falsify and the medical evidence supported the position that the victim knew what he was saying.

Historically, not only have restrictive conditions been imposed on the admissibility of dying declarations, the courts have also imposed restrictions on what may be said if the declaration is admitted. The general rule has been that the dying declaration must be confined to the circumstances that led to the victim's death. On the other hand, a dying declaration is not only admissible against an accused, it is also admissible in the accused's favour. Under this exception, everything that occurred immediately before and after the incident is generally allowed into evidence. However, the courts have imposed some restrictions. For example, in *Buck*,[21] the accused was charged with manslaughter arising out of an illegal operation on a young girl. Although the court was prepared to allow the young girl's dying declaration as to what occurred at the time of the operation, it did not permit that part of her declaration that said that the accused attempted to procure an abortion on her some weeks before.

Although courts asked to admit dying declarations under the traditional rule may continue to apply the restrictive historical imperative, the decision

---

[20] 1992 CarswellNfld 147, (sub nom. *R. v. Kharsekin (No. 1)*) 99 Nfld. & P.E.I.R. 70, 74 C.C.C. (3d) 163, 315 A.P.R. 70 (T.D.); reversed 1994 CarswellNfld 17, 117 Nfld. & P.E.I.R. 89, 88 C.C.C. (3d) 193, 30 C.R. (4th) 252, 365 A.P.R. 89 (C.A.).

[21] (1940), 1940 CarswellOnt 32, [1940] O.R. 444, 74 C.C.C. 314, [1941] 1 D.L.R. 302 (C.A.).

in 2006 by the Supreme Court in *Khelawon*[22] (discussed below) has heralded a new liberal approach to the admissibility of all of the traditional exceptions to the hearsay rule that may eventually render the traditional exceptions obsolete. For example, in *Aziga*[23], the accused was charged with two counts of first degree murder and 13 counts of aggravated assault arising from allegations that he had unprotected sexual intercourse with 13 women without disclosing that he was HIV positive. The trial judge admitted videotaped statements of two complainants as dying declarations: one who gave her statement three weeks before her death and the other who gave her statement 18 days before her death. It was held that the statements were made by complainants whose illnesses were terminal and who had a settled, hopeless expectation of death. Notwithstanding the lengthy delay between making of the statement and the death of the complainants, the statements were clearly admissible under the modern requirements of necessity and reliability.

(b) Declarations Made in the Course of Duty

This exception to the hearsay rule allows the use of an oral or written record or statement made by a deceased person in the usual and ordinary course of his or her business. One rationale for this exception was that if an agent or servant routinely does something, it is likely to be accurate. Another was that an agent or servant has an interest in making an accurate record because an employer will probably check to see that the record is accurate, and fire the agent or servant if it is not.

One might seriously question whether these reasons are sound enough to support this exception to the hearsay rule. We all know that people do make errors when they are making reports, and there is no way of checking the accuracy of the record once it is admitted into evidence. There is also the possibility that an employee may be trying to cheat or defraud an employer. In such instance, an innocent accused might discover that he or she has no way of attacking the record's accuracy. However, error or deliberate fraud were considered to be such rare occurrences in comparison to usual or customary conduct, that it was felt to be in the public interest generally that the evidence be admitted.

Let us assume that Detective Jones sends out Officer Smith to make certain observations as to what is happening at the home of a suspect and to report to him. In due course, Officer Smith returns and reports his observa-

---

[22] 2006 CarswellOnt 7825, 2006 CarswellOnt 7826, 215 C.C.C. (3d) 161, 42 C.R. (6th) 1 (S.C.C.).

[23] 2006 CarswellOnt 7064, 42 C.R. (6th) 42 (S.C.J.).

tions in writing to Detective Jones. If Officer Smith dies before the case comes to trial, then Detective Jones would be entitled to repeat in court what was reported by Officer Smith, because it was a report made in the usual and ordinary course of business.

Are the notes prepared by a police officer admissible under this exception? It is well known that police officers, when conducting an investigation, are expected to make notes of everything that they observe in order to enable them to refresh their memories when called upon to testify days, weeks, months or even years after the event. We assume that an officer will try to be as accurate and as comprehensive as possible in the preparation of those notes. Are such notes admissible in evidence if the officer dies before the trial of the accused? It is arguable that the notes are made in the usual and ordinary course of business. However, the notes are for the officer's personal use. Unless the officer is required to file those notes with a superior officer who can check their accuracy, it cannot be said that it is unlikely that the notes will be false or inaccurate.

This common law exception must be distinguished from the provisions of sections 29 and 30 of the *Canada Evidence Act*. Those sections permit any financial record (s. 29) or business record (s. 30) made in the usual or ordinary course of business to be admitted whether the person who made them is dead or alive. A typical example involves a person's bank records. If Smith purchased a television set with a cheque that was returned N.S.F. and was charged with either false pretences or fraud, the prosecution would have to prove that Smith had insufficient funds in his account and that in the course of his dealings with the bank, Smith never did put in sufficient monies to honour the cheque. To prove this, the prosecution would have to produce his bank records. However, the bank records by themselves are hearsay. They are merely records made by bank employees who dealt with Smith. To comply with the no-hearsay rule, the prosecution would have to call every employee of the bank who ever dealt with Smith to show what he deposited in his account or withdrew from it.

Section 29 of the *Canada Evidence Act* allows the prosecution to introduce a copy of any entry in any book or record kept in any financial institution if it is established that, at the time of making the entry, the record was one of the ordinary records of the bank, that the entry was made in the usual and ordinary course of business, that the record was in the custody or control of the bank, and that the copy is a true copy of the entry. Proof of the entry may be given by the manager or accountant of the bank, either orally or by affidavit. Section 30 further permits the introduction of a business record made in the usual and ordinary course of business, provided that seven days' notice is given before its production.[24]

(c) Declarations against Interest

Another recognized exception to the hearsay rule is a declaration against penal, pecuniary or proprietary interest. What a person says that might affect his or her liberty, pocketbook, or right or interest to certain property will be admitted in evidence if that person dies before he or she can be called upon to give evidence at trial.

This was not always the rule. For a long time, only declarations affecting a person's pecuniary or proprietary interest, but not his penal interest, were admissible in court.[25] However, in 1977, the Supreme Court decided in *O'Brien*[26] that it was only logical and proper that it should extend to a penal interest. There Mr. Justice Dickson wrote:

> The effect of the rule in *The Sussex Peerage Case*, as it has been generally understood, is to render admissible the statement by a deceased that he received payment of a debt from another or that he held a parcel of land as a tenant and not an owner, but to render inadmissible a confession by a deceased that he and not someone else was the real perpetrator of the crime. The distinction is arbitrary and tenuous. There is little or no reason why declarations against penal interest and those against pecuniary or proprietary interests should not stand on the same footing. A person is as likely to speak the truth in a matter affecting his liberty as in a matter affecting his pocketbook. For these reasons and the ever-present possibility that a rule of absolute prohibition could lead to grave injustice I would hold that, in a proper case, a declaration against penal interest is admissible according to the law of Canada; the rule as to absolute exclusion of declarations against penal interest, established in *The Sussex Peerage case*, should not be followed.[27]

---

[24] *Bicknell*, 1988 CarswellBC 781, 41 C.C.C. (3d) 545 (C.A.).

[25] *Sussex Peerage Case* (1844), [1843–60] All E.R. Rep. 55, 8 E.R. 1034 (U.K. H.L.).

[26] (1977), 1977 CarswellBC 403, 1977 CarswellBC 494, [1978] 1 S.C.R. 591, 35 C.C.C. (2d) 209, 76 D.L.R. (3d) 513, [1977] 5 W.W.R. 400, 38 C.R.N.S. 325, 16 N.R. 271.

[27] *Ibid.*, at p. 214 [C.C.C.].

In the same year, the Supreme Court also endorsed the following test for determining what constituted a declaration against penal interest.[28]

> 1. The declaration must be made to a person in such circumstances that the declarant could be said to apprehend being vulnerable to penal consequences. For example, if someone says something to a member of his family, such as a parent or a spouse, or even a child, one does not expect that person to report him to the police and expose him to the risk of prosecution.
>
> 2. The declarant's vulnerability to penal consequences must not be too remote. In other words, one must be able to say that the person who hears the declaration will probably inform the police and expose the declarant to prosecution.
>
> 3. Not every declaration that appears to be against penal interest will be admitted. The court must look at the totality of the words spoken and conclude that the whole tenor of its weight is against the declarant's penal interest.
>
> 4. In a doubtful case, the court must look at all of the circumstances and consider whether or not there is any other evidence connecting the declarant with the crime, and whether there is evidence connecting the declarant and the accused.

It is of significance to note that the Court also said that the exception was not restricted only to declarants since deceased. The declaration was admissible if the declarant was alive but unavailable to testify by reason of insanity, grave illness that prevented the giving of testimony even from a bed, or absence in a jurisdiction where he could not be compelled by an order of the court to attend the accused's trial.

One can easily understand why the courts have carefully scrutinized declarations against penal interest. Just as a person who is about to die may wish to settle an old score with an enemy by accusing him of a crime, a person about to die may wish to save a member of his family or a friend from prosecution by falsely confessing to the crime. The law does not accept the former as evidence unless it is a dying declaration. The latter is accepted because the consequences are less severe. The possibility of convicting an innocent man based on a false accusation of guilt is far worse than the acquittal of a person who might be guilty.

---

[28] *Demeter* (1977), 1977 CarswellOnt 480F, 1977 CarswellOnt 15, [1978] 1 S.C.R. 538, 34 C.C.C. (2d) 137, 75 D.L.R. (3d) 251, 38 C.R.N.S. 317, 16 N.R. 46.

(d) Declarations as to Physical or Mental Condition

As was pointed out earlier, a statement is hearsay and excluded only when it is offered to prove a fact in issue. If, however, the statement is offered only to prove that the statement is made, it is not hearsay and is clearly admissible. This is what is known as original evidence. The failure to understand the difference between hearsay evidence and original evidence is a problem that frequently arises when one side seeks to call evidence of a statement or declaration made with respect to a physical or mental condition.

If X says to Y, "I am afraid because Z has threatened to kill me" and X is subsequently found dead, is the statement that X made to Y admissible against Z on a charge of murder? The first part of the statement — "I am afraid" — is a declaration as to a mental condition, namely, a fear. If the only purpose of admitting the statement is to show that X has a fear, then it would be clearly admissible. In that sense, it is original evidence. What is objectionable are the words "because Z has threatened to kill me." If admitted, these words would permit the jury to infer that X's fear of Z was justified. But without those added words, the declaration "I am afraid" standing alone would have no probative value.

The judge has three options. The first is to exclude the statement altogether. The second is to admit only the statement, "I am afraid." The third is to admit the entire statement and then to tell the jury that they are entitled to use it as evidence of X's fear, but not evidence that it was Z who was the cause of that fear.

Occasionally, the choices are not so straightforward. An example is the decision of the Privy Council in *Ratten*.[29] Ratten was charged with the murder of his wife by deliberately shooting her. His defence was that he shot her accidentally. Shortly before her death, Mrs. Ratten made a telephone call during which she said, "get me the police, please". Mr. Ratten denied that his wife ever made a telephone call. The trial judge allowed the telephone operator who had received that call to testify that she had received a telephone call from someone, that the voice on the other end was hysterical and sobbing, and what that person said. It was held by the Privy Council that the evidence was relevant to prove the state of mind or emotion of Mrs. Ratten and to rebut the defence of accident.

Another example is a Canadian case, *Wysochan*.[30] There the issue was whether a woman was killed by her husband or by the accused. Each blamed the other. About a half an hour after the woman had been shot, her

---

[29] (1971), [1972] A.C. 378, [1971] 3 All E.R. 801, [1971] 3 W.L.R. 930 (P.C.).
[30] 1930 CarswellSask 134, 54 C.C.C. 172 (C.A.).

husband appeared on the scene and the woman stretched out her arms to him and said, "Stanley, help me out because there is a bullet in my body", and later, "Stanley, help me. I am too hot." The Crown applied to have what she said admitted into evidence. The trial judge admitted her statements to show her state of mind. As he put it, "Would it not have been a most improbable thing had he (her husband) been the author of her death that night?"

One might ask — "What was the relevance of the statements in both cases?" In the *Ratten* case, the fact that the victim wanted the police was not relevant to the question of whether her death was deliberate or an accident, unless it was to infer that she wanted the police because her shooting was not an accident. In *Wysochan*, the fact that the victim wanted her husband to help her or that she was too hot was not relevant as to who shot her, unless it was to infer that she would not have asked for her husband (Staney) to help her if he had shot her. If the victim in each case had named her killer, then her statement would have been clearly hearsay and excluded unless it fell within one of the exceptions, such as a dying declaration or the *res gestae* (which will be discussed later). In both cases, the court held that it fell into neither exception.

In each case, the statement was admitted because it was a declaration as to the victim's physical or mental condition, even though her physical or mental condition was not a fact that the Crown was required to prove to establish its case against the accused. What the Crown had to establish was that a murder had been committed, that the accused had committed it and that he had the requisite mental intent. Because, in each case, the victim's statement was as to her physical or mental condition, the court said that it was original evidence as to that issue, not hearsay. However, by allowing the statement to be admitted as original evidence of the victim's state of mind, the court, in effect, also allowed it to be used for its hearsay content: in *Ratten*, to show that the killing was deliberate, not an accident; and, in *Wysochan*, to show that it was the accused and not the victim's husband who committed the murder.[31]

More recent cases appear to find no difficulty in permitting declarations as to state of mind if they are relevant to establish motive (and therefore intent), and meet the twin tests of necessity and reliability. For example, in *Walker*[32] the accused was charged with the murder of a woman who was

---

[31] See also *Collins*, 1997 CarswellBC 1800, 118 C.C.C. (3d) 514, 96 B.C.A.C. 49, 155 W.A.C. 49 (C.A.).

[32] 2002 CarswellBC 151, 163 C.C.C. (3d) 29 (C.A.); leave to appeal refused 2002 CarswellBC 3059, 2002 CarswellBC 3060, 169 C.C.C. (3d) vi (S.C.C.); see also

pregnant with his child. The accused conceded that he had killed the victim; the only issue being raised was his mental intent. The trial judge admitted evidence from the victim's friends and relatives that she had told them of threats by the accused as evidence of her state of mind, otherwise ". . . without the statements, the jury would be left with the impression that there was no dysfunction in the couple's relationship and thus, no full explanation of the circumstances under which the relationship ended". Again in *Foreman*,[33] evidence from friends of the victim that she said she was worried about the accused who had threatened to kill her was admitted against the accused charged with her murder. It was held that the victim's state of mind was relevant to prove motive on the part of the accused, and therefore intent.

(e) Declarations as to Intentions

If A says to B that he intends to go and visit C and is later found dead outside C's residence, the logical inference is that he was able to carry out his intention *to visit C*. This traditional exception to the hearsay rule permits B to tell the court what A told him as proof that A expressed an intention to visit C. However, what the exception forbids is the inference that A, in fact, met C where C is charged with causing the death of A, unless C was present when the statement was made.

One of the earliest cases dealing with this rule was an English case, *Wainwright*.[34] There Chief Justice Cockburn refused to admit a statement by the deceased victim that she intended to visit the accused. He ruled it out because "it was only a statement of intention which might or might not have been carried out". Although one might have thought that the Chief Justice should have been more concerned with the question of weight, rather than relevance, the view that such evidence is not admissible continues to influence Canadian authorities.

Some common law jurisdictions have rejected this restrictive view of such evidence. In *Walton*,[35] the High Court of Australia permitted evidence that the murder victim had stated that she intended to meet her husband (the

---

Mafi, 1998 CarswellBC 2129, 130 C.C.C. (3d) 329, 21 C.R. (5th) 139 (C.A.); leave to appeal refused (1999), 132 B.C.A.C. 117 (note) (S.C.C.).

[33] 2002 CarswellOnt 3848, 62 O.R. (3d) 204, 169 C.C.C. (3d) 489, 6 C.R. (6th) 201 (C.A.); leave to appeal refused 2003 CarswellOnt 3570, 2003 CarswellOnt 3571 (S.C.C.).

[34] (1875), 13 Cox C.C. 171.

[35] (1989), 166 C.L.R. 283, 38 A. Crim. R. 276, 63 A.L.J.R. 226, 84 A.L.R. 59 (H.C.).

accused) at the Town Centre, as evidence from which the jury could draw the inference that the two met at the appointed place. As Chief Justice Mason noted, ". . . her belief that she was to meet the applicant made it more probable that she travelled to the Town Centre".[36]

Over a century ago, the Supreme Court of the United States was prepared to permit inferences to be drawn from a declarant's intention. In *Mutual Life Insurance Co. of New York v. Hillmon*,[37] John Hillmon's wife had sued Mutual Life to recover on an insurance policy issued by them on the life of her husband whose body had been found in Kansas. The defence was that the body in the grave was not that of Hillmon, but of one, Walters, who had also disappeared and who had been killed by Hillmon to allow Mrs. Hillmon to collect on the policy. The Supreme Court held that letters written by Walters to his sister indicating an intention to accompany Hillmon on a trip out west were admissible as evidence of his intention to go with Hillmon, "which made it more probable both that he did go and that he went with Hillmon".

Canadian courts, however, have continued to apply the strict common law rule. In *Smith*,[38] the Supreme Court of Canada considered the *Hillmon* case but decided to reject it in favour of the English position.[39] In *Smith*, the victim of a murder had driven from Detroit to Canada with the accused where they spent the weekend together in a hotel. According to the theory of the Crown, the accused abandoned the victim at the hotel when she refused to take cocaine back to the United States. He then picked her up and drove her to a service station where he strangled her. To support this theory, the Crown relied upon four telephone calls made by the victim to her mother just before she was murdered discussing her association with the accused. On the first two occasions, the victim told her mother that she had been abandoned at a hotel by the accused and needed transportation home. On the third occasion, she called her mother and said that the accused had just returned and she would not need a ride home after all. On the fourth occasion, she called and told her mother that she was on her way home. She was later found dead near the service station where she made her last call.

The Ontario Court of Appeal held that the first two calls were admissible as statements of the victim's existing state of mind and of her intention to

---

[36] *Ibid.*, at p. 65 [A.L.R.].

[37] (1892), 36 L.Ed. 706, 12 S.Ct. 909, 145 U.S. 285 (Kan. S.C.).

[38] 1992 CarswellOnt 997, 1992 CarswellOnt 103, [1992] 2 S.C.R. 915, 75 C.C.C. (3d) 257, 15 C.R. (4th) 133, 94 D.L.R. (4th) 590, 139 N.R. 323, 55 O.A.C. 321, [1992] S.C.J. No. 74.

[39] *Kearley (No. 1)*, [1992] 2 All E.R. 345 (U.K. H.L.).

go home; they were not evidence that the accused left her at the hotel. Although it was argued that the third call was evidence of the victim's state of mind and her intention to leave with the accused, from which it could be inferred that she did go with the accused, the Court held that it was not admissible to prove that the accused picked her up. The fourth call was also held inadmissible for the same reason. A further appeal to the Supreme Court was dismissed. The Court agreed that a declaration of intention by the deceased could not be used to prove that someone other than the deceased probably acted in accordance with that intention. That rule was reaffirmed by the Supreme Court in *Starr*.[40]

As a matter of logic, evidence of a declarant's stated intention could, in some cases, have some evidentiary value when considered as part of a larger package of circumstantial evidence from which a jury might infer that the events referred to by the declarant actually occurred. However, the courts have continued to apply the traditional rule. For example, in *Maciel*,[41] identity was the central issue in the Crown's case against the accused in the shooting death of the victim in a pool hall. The Crown's theory was that the accused and his father had agreed to meet the victim at a pool hall and shoot him over a drug debt. The trial judge had admitted, as a declaration of intention, a statement by the victim to his mother that he was meeting the accused, his father and two others at the pool hall. On appeal, it was held that the judge instructions to the jury that the statement did not prove that the event took place or who was present, was correct.

In summary, Canadian authority does not permit B to tell the court that A told him that he was going to visit C for the purpose of drawing the inference that he probably met C. There is no prohibition, however, against B stating that A told him that he intended to visit C as evidence of his personal intention to visit C. If, for example, the fact in issue is whether C killed A, what is frowned upon is allowing B to tell the court that A told him that he intended to visit C for the purpose of inferring that A probably met C. The reason is that it would permit the trier to infer that A and C must have met and that C caused A's death. The difficulty is that once the evidence is introduced, it would be difficult for the jury not to draw that inference, even if they were instructed not to do so by the judge.

---

[40] 2000 SCC 40, 2000 CarswellMan 449, 2000 CarswellMan 450, [2000] 2 S.C.R. 144, 147 C.C.C. (3d) 449, 36 C.R. (5th) 1, 190 D.L.R. (4th) 591, [2000] 11 W.W.R. 1, 148 Man. R. (2d) 161, 258 N.R. 250, 224 W.A.C. 161, [2000] S.C.J. No. 40.

[41] 2007 CarswellOnt 1612, 219 C.C.C. (3d) 516, 47 C.R. (6th) 319 (C.A.); leave to appeal refused 2007 CarswellOnt 5637, 2007 CarswellOnt 5638, 220 C.C.C. (3d) vi (S.C.C.).

4. THE MODERN RULE

(a) History of the Modern Rule

As already noted, the traditional exceptions to the hearsay rule were only allowed where the speaker was dead and therefore unable to testify. However, in the 1970's the Supreme Court decided that the hearsay rule should be relaxed and hearsay statements admitted, even where the declarant was alive but was unable for some reason to come to the court to testify. One of the earliest cases where it was allowed was *O'Brien*.[42] There Chief Justice Dickson of the Supreme Court of Canada suggested that declarations against penal interest were admissible where the declarant was unavailable to testify by reason of insanity, grave illness or absence from the jurisdiction of Canadian courts.

The first Canadian decision to actually relax the rigidity of the hearsay rule was an Alberta civil case, *Ares v. Venner*,[43] dealing with declarations made in the course of duty. In that case, the plaintiff had fractured his leg while skiing and had sued the doctor who had reduced the fracture and applied a plaster cast for not removing the cast in time to prevent muscle necrosis from a lack of blood supply. The plaintiff's leg had to be amputated below the knee. The issue before the court was whether records kept by nurses at the hospital were admissible to show their observations of the pulse, temperature and condition of the plaintiff. Alberta at that time had no provision similar to that of other provinces, such as Ontario, allowing the admission of medical records of a patient. Although the nurses who made the records were alive and were, in fact, waiting outside the courtroom to testify, the plaintiff had not called them, but had been permitted by the trial judge to introduce the nurses' notes. The Supreme Court of Canada held that such records were admissible as declarations made in the ordinary course of duty and were *"prima facie* proof of the facts stated therein" even though the nurses were available to give oral testimony.

In reaching that conclusion, the Court rejected the reasoning of the House of Lords in *Myers v. Director of Public Prosecutions*,[44] where it was held that judges should not change the law to meet modern conditions, but should leave that responsibility to Parliament. Ironically, it was not really

---

[42] (1977), 1977 CarswellBC 403, 1977 CarswellBC 494, [1978] 1 S.C.R. 591, 35 C.C.C. (2d) 209, 76 D.L.R. (3d) 513, [1977] 5 W.W.R. 400, 38 C.R.N.S. 325, 16 N.R. 271.

[43] 1970 CarswellAlta 80, 1970 CarswellAlta 142, [1970] S.C.R. 608, 14 D.L.R. (3d) 4, 73 W.W.R. 347, 12 C.R.N.S. 349.

[44] (1964), [1965] A.C. 1001, [1964] 2 All E.R. 881, 48 Cr. App. R. 348, [1964] 3 W.L.R. 145 (U.K. H.L.).

necessary for the Supreme Court to have extended the rule at all. The issue in *Ares v. Venner* was whether the doctor was negligent in failing to remove the cast from the plaintiff's leg after he had read the nurses' notes describing the plaintiff's condition (*i.e.*, toes were swollen, numb, blue, *etc.*), not whether the contents of the notes were correct. In other words, had the nurses' notes been admitted, not as proof of the contents, but to show that the doctor should have been alerted by what he read in those notes to look at the plaintiff's leg, no hearsay problem would have arisen.

Twenty years later, the Supreme Court of Canada relied on *Ares v. Venner* to approve the reception of statements made by children to others about sexual abuse, provided that the twin requirements of "necessity" and "reliability" were met. In *Khan*,[45] Madam Justice McLachlin, delivering the judgment of the Court, noted that Canadian law was moving towards a more flexible attitude to the reception of the hearsay evidence of children, particularly where the statement concerned sexual abuse. She wrote:

> The hearsay rule has traditionally been regarded as an absolute rule, subject to various categories of exceptions, such as admissions, dying declarations, declarations against interest and spontaneous declarations. While this approach has provided a degree of certainty to the law on hearsay, it has frequently proved unduly inflexible in dealing with new situations and new needs in the law. This has resulted in courts in recent years on occasion adopting a more flexible approach, rooted in the principle and policy underlying the hearsay rule rather than the strictures of traditional exceptions.[46]

In *Khan*, a three-year-old girl had been examined privately in the office of Dr. Khan, a medical doctor. After the examination, the child's mother had noticed a wet spot on the sleeve of her daughter's clothing. About ten to fifteen minutes after the mother and daughter left Khan's office, they had a conversation about the visit and the child described an incident that could have amounted to a sexual assault. The trial judge had refused to permit the mother to testify as to what her daughter had told her because it was hearsay. McLachlin J. held that the judge should have admitted that evidence even though it was hearsay because it met the twin tests of necessity and reliability. The requirement of "necessity" had been met by the fact that, unless admitted, the child's evidence would be inadmissible and to require the child to testify would be traumatic to her. She found the requirement of "reliability" in the fact that the child had no motive to falsify her story which emerged naturally and without prompting, and the fact that she could not have knowledge of such sexual acts. McLachlin J. also noted that the

---

[45] 1990 CarswellOnt 108, 1990 CarswellOnt 1001, [1990] 2 S.C.R. 531, 59 C.C.C. (3d) 92, 79 C.R. (3d) 1, 113 N.R. 53, 41 O.A.C. 353, [1990] S.C.J. No. 81.
[46] *Ibid.*, at p. 540 [S.C.R.].

child's statement was corroborated by real evidence. Although some provincial appellate courts after *Khan* continued to strictly apply the traditional exceptions to the hearsay rule,[47] the Supreme Court suggested that courts should strike out into new territory and apply the twin tests of necessity and reliability whenever a hearsay problem arose.

Two years later in *Smith*,[48] the Supreme Court said that hearsay evidence of statements made by persons who are not available to give evidence at trial ought generally to be admissible where the circumstances under which the statements are made satisfy the twin tests of necessity and reliability set out in *Khan*, subject to the residual discretion of the trial judge to exclude the evidence where its probative value is slight and undue prejudice may result to the accused.

In *Kharsekin*,[49] the Newfoundland Court of Appeal followed *Khan*. There the victim of a knife attack told a physician who was attending him that he had been wounded by the accused. An hour later, in response to an inquiry, the victim again identified the accused as his attacker. Two hours later, the victim died. The trial judge refused to admit the statements to the physician as a dying declaration or as part of the *res gestae*. The Newfoundland Court of Appeal said that the trial judge was correct in not admitting the statements made to the physician under the old established exceptions but was wrong in not admitting the statements under the *Khan* exception. Necessity arose because of the death of the victim. Reliability existed because the victim had a peculiar means of knowledge of the identity of his attacker, there was little time to falsify the statements and the medical evidence supported the position that the victim knew what he was saying.

Similarly, in *Chahley*,[50] the accused, who was charged with murder by slitting the deceased's throat, had sought unsuccessfully at trial to adduce evidence of statements made by the deceased to his common law wife several days before his death to the effect that a black man had pulled a knife on him and he could not go downtown for a while. In fact, the deceased had remained in his apartment for several days until he received a telephone call

---

[47] *Crossley*, 1997 CarswellBC 1677, 117 C.C.C. (3d) 533, 95 B.C.A.C. 61, 154 W.A.C. 61 (C.A.) and *Collins*, 1997 CarswellBC 1800, 118 C.C.C. (3d) 514, 96 B.C.A.C. 49, 155 W.A.C. 49 (C.A.).

[48] *Supra*, note 38.

[49] 1992 CarswellNfld 147, (sub nom. *R. v. Kharsekin (No. 1)*) 99 Nfld. & P.E.I.R. 70, 74 C.C.C. (3d) 163, 315 A.P.R. 70 (T.D.); reversed 1994 CarswellNfld 17, 117 Nfld. & P.E.I.R. 89, 88 C.C.C. (3d) 193, 30 C.R. (4th) 252, 365 A.P.R. 89 (C.A.).

[50] 1992 CarswellBC 1094, 72 C.C.C. (3d) 193, 13 B.C.A.C. 213, 24 W.A.C. 213 (C.A.).

and had left telling his common law wife that — "everything's okay now". The British Columbia Court of Appeal decided that although the statements were not admissible as a dying declaration, they met the twin tests of necessity and reliability and should have been admitted as evidence for their truth to support the accused's defence that the murder had been committed, not by him, but by someone else. The test of necessity was satisfied because the declarant was dead. Reliability was met because the statements made by the declarant were not in favour of his interest, were made before dispute or litigation and the declarant had the peculiar means of knowledge not possessed in ordinary cases.

Any concern that the traditional exceptions had been abolished and replaced by a necessity/reliability test was quickly dispelled by the Supreme Court in *Starr*.[51] In *Starr*, it was decided that although the principled approach should play the primary role in determining whether to admit a hearsay statement, the traditional exceptions to the hearsay rule should also be maintained and continue to play an important role under the principled approach. Iacobbuci J., delivering the reasons of the Court, felt that while it was important to recognize the primacy of the principled approach,

>]202] . . . it is nevertheless important for a court to exercise a certain degree of caution when reconsidering the traditional exceptions. While the exceptions may need to be reexamined in light of the principled approach, their complete abolition is not the answer. Rather, the exceptions continue to play an important role under the principled approach. Our task therefore is to reconcile the traditional exceptions with the principled approach.

He advanced three reasons for the retention of the traditional exceptions. The first is that they,

> [203] . . . have served . . . to add predictability and certainty to the law of hearsay. In light of the exceptions, and regardless of how illogical or arbitrary they may be, litigants can be more or less certain when going into court of the types of issues that will be relevant in debating admissibility in a particular context, and of the likelihood that the evidence will indeed be admitted. This certainty has fostered greater efficiency in the use of court time both at trial and on appeal, and has facilitated the task of the too frequently overburdened trial judge who is called upon to rule on hearsay admissibility with speed and considerable regularity.

---

[51] 2000 SCC 40, 2000 CarswellMan 449, 2000 CarswellMan 450, [2000] 2 S.C.R. 144, 147 C.C.C. (3d) 449, 36 C.R. (5th) 1, 190 D.L.R. (4th) 591, [2000] 11 W.W.R. 1, 148 Man. R. (2d) 161, 258 N.R. 250, 224 W.A.C. 161, [2000] S.C.J. No. 40. Reaffirmed in *Mapara*, 2005 CarswellBC 963, 2005 CarswellBC 964, [2005] 1 S.C.R. 358, 195 C.C.C. (3d) 225, 28 C.R. (6th) 1.

The second is that,

> [204] ... in addition to serving the utilitarian goals of providing greater certainty and fostering judicial efficiency, the exceptions have served an explanatory or educative function, instructing litigants and judges about the relevant factors to consider in determining whether to admit a *particular type* of hearsay evidence, or whether to admit hearsay in a *particular factual context*. Different hearsay scenarios by their nature raise different reliability concerns, and different issues of necessity. The specific requirements of the individual exceptions have had the useful effect of focusing attention upon the peculiar factors that make it desirable, or undesirable, to admit a particular form of out-of-court statement.

And finally,

> [206] ... they teach us about the historical and contemporary rationale for admitting certain forms of hearsay ...

> The traditional exceptions are useful, therefore, because they are instructive as to the types of situations that may produce hearsay that is the best evidence in the circumstances.

In *Starr*, the Court went on to point out that although, historically, there has been no requirement for the trial judge to assess the reliability of a traditional exception to hearsay before admitting it, it was now necessary to do so. Reliability and necessity should be no less present when a hearsay statement is introduced under an established exception.

(b) The Requirement of Necessity

Following the *Khan* decision, it was naturally assumed by the trial courts that if the witness was competent and available to testify, then the element of necessity no longer existed and the hearsay declaration was not admissible through a third party. In fact, when Dr. Khan was re-tried, the victim was nine years old and found competent by the trial judge to testify. Since she was competent to testify, the trial judge held that her statement to her mother was now inadmissible because there was no longer any necessity for it.

In one of the earliest cases, *S. (K.O.)*,[52] Wetmore J. interpreted the word "necessity" in the context of the *Khan* case to have a two-fold meaning. The hearsay evidence, he said, had to be necessary in the sense of being crucial to the case. It also had to be "reasonably necessary" in the sense that direct evidence was not available.

Unfortunately, the second part of the test failed to consider that some children might have difficulty in expressing themselves fully and ade-

---

[52] 1991 CarswellBC 416, 63 C.C.C. (3d) 91, 4 C.R. (4th) 37 (S.C.).

quately in a courtroom setting. This was recognized by the Ontario Court of Appeal in *Khan v. College of Physicians & Surgeons (Ontario)*,[53] a case involving Dr. Khan's discipline proceedings before the Ontario College of Physicians. There the Court decided that it was "reasonably necessary" to admit an out-of-court statement, in addition to the direct evidence of the child, in order to obtain an accurate and frank rendition of the child's version of the events. The Court said that a child, though competent to testify, may be unable to express him or herself with frankness, accuracy, fullness or candidness. Unless the child's out-of-court statement was admitted, despite legal competency, the child's version of the events may not be adequately placed before the trier of fact. Mr. Justice Doherty delivering the judgment of the Court wrote:

> In my view, if that tribunal is satisfied that despite the viva voce evidence of the child, it is still "reasonably necessary" to admit the out-of-court statement in order to obtain an accurate and frank rendition of the child's version of the relevant events, then the necessity criterion set down in *Khan* is satisfied.[54]

That a mentally disabled person might be unable to express him or herself fully and accurately was recognized by the British Columbia Court of Appeal in *Pearson*.[55] There the issue was the identity of the perpetrator of a sexual assault upon an 18-year-old mentally disabled person. The trial judge had admitted statements made by the complainant to his mother shortly after the assault and several weeks later concerning the identity of his attacker. The Court of Appeal said that the trial judge was correct in admitting the evidence. Necessity arose from the fact that the complainant was unable, because of his mental disability, to give a full and coherent account of the assault and his credibility could not be assessed by applying the traditional tests of demeanour, consistency, perception and accuracy of recollection of other events. There was reliability in the circumstances in which it could be expected that a person in his position would tell the truth.

Similarly, in *Parkinson*,[56] a police officer was permitted to give evidence of what a 96-year-old victim of an assault in his own home told him about his assailant. Necessity was found in the fact that the victim's health was so fragile that there was a risk that he might have a stroke if called to testify.

---

[53] 1992 CarswellOnt 914, 9 O.R. (3d) 641, 11 Admin. L.R. (2d) 147, 76 C.C.C. (3d) 10, 94 D.L.R. (4th) 193, 57 O.A.C. 115, [1992] O.J. No. 1725 (C.A.).

[54] *Ibid.*, at p. 24 [C.C.C.].

[55] 1994 CarswellBC 597, 95 C.C.C. (3d) 365, 36 C.R. (4th) 343, 82 B.C.A.C. 1, 133 W.A.C. 1 (C.A.).

[56] (August 11, 1995) (Ont. Gen. Div.).

Necessity has been held to apply where the declarant is unavailable to testify at trial and where the party seeking to introduce a hearsay statement of a third party is unable to obtain evidence of a similar nature from another source. For example, in *Biscette*,[57] it was held that the trial judge properly admitted a witness's preliminary inquiry evidence for its truth when the witness recanted her testimony at trial, since the necessity arose out of the witness's recantation.

Similarly, in *Hawkins*,[58] unavailability was found in the fact that the spouse of the accused was incompetent to testify against him. There a woman, who had given evidence for the Crown at Hawkins' preliminary inquiry, subsequently married him before trial. Since the woman was now a spouse and incompetent to give testimony for the Crown against her husband and her evidence at the preliminary inquiry could not be read in at trial pursuant to section 715 of the *Criminal Code*, the Crown sought to introduce the evidence which she gave at the inquiry as a hearsay statement pursuant to the *Khan* rule. It was held by the Supreme Court that necessity arose because of her incompetency to give evidence as a spouse and was admissible provided that it also met the test of reliability.

One question that seems to have created difficulty for trial judges is the extent of the inquiry that must be conducted before hearsay testimony of a witness will be admitted. Is the trial judge entitled to rely on the fact that the witness of a tender age is probably unable to communicate his or her evidence fully or accurately or may be traumatized if required to give evidence in a courtroom, or should the trial judge first hold a *voir dire* and see what evidence the child may be able to give? Similarly, in the case of a person who may be mentally challenged and unable to communicate his or her testimony fully or accurately, should the trial judge first hear that witness in the absence of the jury before deciding whether to permit a hearsay statement of that witness from a third party? Should the Crown be required to call expert testimony on the witness's competence to testify or even be permitted to do so? In *Khan v. College of Physicians & Surgeons (Ontario)*,[59] the Ontario Court of Appeal was satisfied based on the age of the child that the child's hearsay statement should be admitted. Similarly, in

---

[57] 1995 CarswellAlta 1028, 169 A.R. 81, 99 C.C.C. (3d) 326, 31 C.R.R. (2d) 38, 97 W.A.C. 81 (C.A.); affirmed 1996 CarswellAlta 1113, 1996 CarswellAlta 1114, [1996] 3 S.C.R. 599, 187 A.R. 392, 110 C.C.C. (3d) 285, 39 C.R.R. (2d) 187, 203 N.R. 244, 127 W.A.C. 392.

[58] 1996 CarswellOnt 4063, 1996 CarswellOnt 4062, [1996] 3 S.C.R. 1043, 30 O.R. (3d) 641 (headnote only), 111 C.C.C. (3d) 129, 2 C.R. (5th) 245, 141 D.L.R. (4th) 193, 204 N.R. 241, 96 O.A.C. 81, [1996] S.C.J. No. 117.

[59] *Supra*, note 53.

Rockey,[60] the Supreme Court held that the trial judge had not erred in admitting the out-of-court statements of a two-and-a-half-year-old child on the basis of *Khan*. Although the child was five years old at the time of the trial, the Court was satisfied that the trial judge would have inevitably concluded that the child would have been traumatized by actually being called to give evidence, even though there was no evidence before the judge to that effect.[61]

In *F. (W.J.)*,[62] the Supreme Court said that an insistence on evidence to support necessity in every case cannot be reconciled with the values underlying the hearsay rule and the increasing difficulties children face when called upon to testify. Necessity may be established either on the basis of what has happened at trial or on the basis of evidence. If the circumstances reveal that the child cannot, for whatever reason, give evidence in a meaningful way, then the trial judge may conclude that it is self-evident or evident from the proceedings that the out-of-court statements are necessary if the court is to get the evidence and discover the truth of the matter. Lamer C.J.C., in a strong dissent, was concerned that this would place a heavy burden on trial judges who have no expertise in evaluating the risk of harm to a child witness giving evidence. He felt that it was incumbent on counsel seeking to introduce such evidence to make a reasonable attempt to establish such a foundation.

The rule, however, appears to be a different one where the complainant is an adult, even one who may suffer from a mental disability. In *Parrott*,[63] the accused was charged with offences in relation to a woman who suffered from Down's Syndrome. Although expert evidence before the trial judge had established that the woman had the mental development of a three-or-four-year-old child, the Supreme Court, in a majority decision, held that the

---

[60] 1996 CarswellOnt 4284, 1996 CarswellOnt 4285, [1996] 3 S.C.R. 829, 30 O.R. (3d) 577 (note), 110 C.C.C. (3d) 481, 2 C.R. (5th) 301, 140 D.L.R. (4th) 503, 204 N.R. 214, 95 O.A.C. 134.

[61] See also *P. (J.)*, 1992 CarswellQue 6, 1992 CarswellQue 2109, 74 C.C.C. (3d) 276, 13 C.R. (4th) 79, 150 N.R. 379, 54 Q.A.C. 82 (C.A.); affirmed 1993 CarswellQue 12, 1993 CarswellQue 2042, [1993] 1 S.C.R. 469, 20 C.R. (4th) 397, 150 N.R. 378, 54 Q.A.C. 81, where the Quebec Court of Appeal (2-1) came to a similar conclusion.

[62] 1999 CarswellSask 625, 1999 CarswellSask 626, [1999] 3 S.C.R. 569, 138 C.C.C. (3d) 1, 27 C.R. (5th) 169, 178 D.L.R. (4th) 53, [1999] 12 W.W.R. 587, 247 N.R. 62, 180 Sask. R. 161, 205 W.A.C. 161, [1999] S.C.J. No. 61.

[63] 2001 SCC 3, 2001 CarswellNfld 13, 2001 CarswellNfld 14, [2001] 1 S.C.R. 178, 198 Nfld. & P.E.I.R. 260, 150 C.C.C. (3d) 449, 39 C.R. (5th) 255, 194 D.L.R. (4th) 427, 595 A.P.R. 260, 265 N.R. 304, [2001] S.C.J. No. 4.

trial judge had erred in concluding that the witness was unable to communicate her evidence within the meaning of section 16 of the *Canada Evidence Act* on the basis of expert testimony. The majority said that if a witness is *physically* available to testify and there is no suggestion that he or she would suffer trauma by attempting to give evidence, that evidence should generally not be pre-empted by hearsay, unless the trial judge has first had an opportunity to hear the potential witness and form his or her own opinion as to testimonial competence. There is no automatic necessity for calling expert testimony on the issue of a mentally challenged person's competence to testify under section 16 of the Act. It was felt that trial judges are eminently qualified to assess such matters as "childlike mental condition" or "poor ability to sustain questioning" without expert evidence.

The dissenting members of the Court, however, felt that in cases involving young children or people with mental disabilities who are mentally assimilable to young children, there is no requirement for direct evidence of trauma or compulsory attendance of the witness to demonstrate it. The role of the trial judge should be to assess the whole condition of the witness and balance the potential value of the evidence that may result from *viva voce* testimony against the potential prejudice to the witness. Potential trauma or circumstances in which it would be harmful to the witness or serve no real purpose are instances where it should not be necessary to call the complainant to give direct testimony.

(c) The Requirement of Reliability

As Iacobbuci J. observed in *Starr*,[64]

> . . . a fundamental concern with reliability lies at the heart of the hearsay rule. By excluding evidence that might produce unfair verdicts, and by ensuring that litigants will generally have the opportunity to confront adverse witnesses, the hearsay rule serves as a cornerstone of a fair justice system.

A threshold test for establishing the requirement of "reliability" undoubtedly creates more difficulties than the "necessity" test. Critics of the modern rule argue that without the opportunity of cross-examination, the traditional method of testing the accuracy and truthfulness of a witness's testimony is lost. As Professor Wigmorehad noted:

> The theory of the Hearsay rule is that many possible sources of inaccuracy and untrustworthiness which may lie underneath the bare untested assertion

---

[64] 2000 SCC 40, 2000 CarswellMan 449, 2000 CarswellMan 450, [2000] 2 S.C.R. 144, 147 C.C.C. (3d) 449, 36 C.R. (5th) 1, 190 D.L.R. (4th) 591, [2000] 11 W.W.R. 1 at para. 199.

of a witness can best be brought to light and exposed, if they exist, by the test of cross-examination.

However, in the next sentence, Wigmore also went on to suggest:

But this test or security may in a given instance be superfluous; it may be sufficiently clear, in that instance, that the statement offered is free enough from the risk of inaccuracy and untrustworthiness, *so that the test of cross-examination would be a work of supererogation.* [Emphasis added.][65]

When would *the test of cross-examination be a work of supererogation?* In *Smith*,[66] Chief Justice Lamer, after referring to this passage, suggested that the trial judge, in determining whether the hearsay evidence is reliable, is required to conduct a search for alternative hypotheses (to the point of speculation) that might give an explanation for the hearsay statements inconsistent with their reliability. It was only where that search failed to the point that cross-examination, the traditional method of testing the accuracy and honesty of a witness's evidence, would be superfluous, that the evidence passed the threshold of reliability. In other words, to use the language of Gravely J. in *Cassidy*,[67] "the circumstances then will provide equivalence to the reliability normally insured by cross-examination".

In *Smith*,[68] the victim of a murder had driven from Detroit to Canada with the accused where they spent the weekend together in a hotel. According to the theory of the Crown, the accused abandoned the victim at a hotel when she refused to take cocaine back to the United States and then picked her up and drove her to a service station where he strangled her. To support this theory, the Crown relied upon four telephone calls made by the victim to her mother during which the victim discussed her association with the accused. On the first two occasions, the victim told her mother that she had been abandoned at a hotel by the accused and needed transportation home. On the third, she called her mother and said that the accused had just returned and she would not need a ride home after all. On the fourth occasion, she called and told her mother that she was on her way home. She was later found dead near the service station where she made her last call.

Lamer C.J.C. found that the first two calls had the necessary indicia of reliability because there was no known reason for the victim to lie. How-

---

[65] *Supra*, note 8, at p. 202.

[66] 1992 CarswellOnt 997, 1992 CarswellOnt 103, [1992] 2 S.C.R. 915, 75 C.C.C. (3d) 257, 15 C.R. (4th) 133, 94 D.L.R. (4th) 590, 139 N.R. 323, 55 O.A.C. 321, [1992] S.C.J. No. 74.

[67] 1993 CarswellOnt 139, 26 C.R. (4th) 252, [1993] O.J. No. 3231 (Gen. Div.) at (C.R.) p. 254.

[68] *Supra*, note 66.

ever, he rejected the third telephone call because *the circumstances under which it was made* were such that the victim might have been mistaken or might have intended to deceive her mother. His search for alternative hypotheses (to the point of speculation) that might give an explanation for the hearsay statements inconsistent with their reliability was in these words:

> I wish to emphasize that I do not advance these alternative hypotheses as accurate reconstructions of what occurred on the night of Ms. King's murder. I engage in such speculation only for the purpose of showing that the circumstances under which Ms. King made the third telephone call to her mother were not such as to provide that circumstantial guarantee of trustworthiness that would justify the admission of its contents by way of hearsay evidence, without the possibility of cross-examination. Indeed, at the highest, it can only be said that hearsay evidence of the third telephone call is equally consistent with the accuracy of Ms. King's statements, and also with a number of other hypotheses. *I cannot say that this evidence could not reasonably have been expected to have changed significantly had Ms. King been available to give evidence in person and subjected to cross-examination.* I conclude, therefore, that the hearsay evidence of the contents of the third telephone conversation did not satisfy the criterion of reliability set out in *Khan*, and therefore were not admissible on that basis.[69]

Following the decision in *Smith*, some trial courts looked at evidence unconnected to the making of the statement that could reinforce the reliability criterion. For example, in *Starr*,[70] the trial judge admitted the utterance of the deceased to her female friend that she intended to meet the accused for lunch. In considering the reliability of the statement, the trial judge noted that the accused denied any meeting to the police, but admitted to his wife and mother that he met the deceased for lunch. In *Parkinson*, discussed earlier, the trial judge considered other evidence connecting the accused to the victim's residence at the time of the assault as demonstrating sufficient reliability to admit the 96-year-old victim's statement to the police officer.

However, the Ontario Court of Appeal said that this approach was the wrong one. A trial judge was only entitled to look at *the circumstances surrounding the making of the statement* and not any confirmatory evidence that may arise after. For example, in *Merz*,[71] where the accused was charged with the murder of his former common-law spouse, at issue was

---

[69] *Ibid.*, at p. 151 [C.R.].

[70] [2000] 2 S.C.R. 144 (S.C.C.) at para. 217.

[71] 1999 CarswellOnt 3620, 46 O.R. (3d) 161, 140 C.C.C. (3d) 259, 30 C.R. (5th) 313, 127 O.A.C. 1, [1999] O.J. No. 4309 (C.A.); leave to appeal refused 2000 CarswellOnt 3925, 2000 CarswellOnt 3926, 147 C.C.C. (3d) vi (note), 263 N.R. 391 (note), 141 O.A.C. 398 (note) (S.C.C.).

whether the trial judge had erred in admitting three hearsay statements of the deceased for their truth. The first statement was the testimony of the deceased at an earlier trial of the accused on a charge of threatening her son to the effect that the accused had threatened her on January 31, 1993 and again on February 5, 1993. The second was her statement to a friend about the threat on January 31st. The third was her statement to her lawyer about the threat on February 5th. The Ontario Court of Appeal said that the trial judge should not have relied upon the second and third statements as confirmatory of the reliability of the deceased's evidence at the accused's trial for threatening her son. The Court noted that in *Smith*,[72] Lamer C.J.C. had said that in determining the reliability of a hearsay statement, the trial judge must *look at the circumstances under which the statement was made* to determine whether the circumstances "substantially negate the possibility that the statement was untruthful or mistaken".[73] This meant that the trial judge was not to rely on any other confirmatory evidence.

The British Columbia Court of Appeal, however, did not consider it necessary to impose that same stringent test on the issue of reliability. In *Misir*[74] the accused was charged with stabbing his wife to death. The trial judge had admitted evidence from various members of the victim's family and co-workers that the accused and the victim had a troubled marriage. This included evidence that the accused had physically and verbally abused the victim. The physical abuse included an incident of choking and forced intercourse. A good deal of the evidence came from conversations the victim had with family members and co-workers. Without referring to either *Smith* or *Merz*, it was held that although the evidence of the victim's family members must be treated with caution as it might be "coloured", the evidence of co-workers that supported the evidence of the victim's family which carried less suggestion that it was coloured provided support for the trustworthiness of all the victim's statements. The Court of Appeal did not consider it necessary to examine the circumstances under which the statements were made to determine whether the circumstances "substantially negate the possibility that the statement was untruthful or mistaken". Relying

---

[72] *Supra*, note 66.

[73] *Ibid.*, at p. 270 [C.C.C.].

[74] 2001 BCCA 202, 2001 CarswellBC 511, 86 B.C.L.R. (3d) 332, 153 C.C.C. (3d) 70, 150 B.C.A.C. 52, 245 W.A.C. 52; leave to appeal refused 2002 CarswellBC 531, 2002 CarswellBC 532 (S.C.C.). But see *Larsen*, 2001 CarswellBC 931, 42 C.R. (5th) 49 (S.C.) and *Nguyen*, 2001 CarswellAlta 526, 153 C.C.C. (3d) 495, 42 C.R. (5th) 35 (C.A.) where it was held that the surrounding circumstances must be examined to see if they provide sufficient guarantees of trustworthiness. See also *Starr* (2001), 147 C.C.C. (3d) 499 (S.C.C.) at para. 217.

upon *F. (W.J.)*[75] the Court seemed to be saying that so long as there is a sufficient indication of trustworthiness from all of the other evidence, the hearsay statements will meet the requisite threshold of reliability. In other words, the overwhelming evidence of complaints of abuse by the victim to family and friends was a sufficient indication of the reliability of her statements to them.

On the other hand, courts have taken a more relaxed view of the prerequisites to admissibility where the out-of-court statement is being tendered by the defence. The courts rationalized that although the rules of evidence generally applied equally to the Crown and the defence, a trial judge was entitled to relax those rules in favour of the defence where it was necessary to prevent a miscarriage of justice.[76] However, as Doherty J.A. observed in *Kimberley*,[77] they do not invite an abandonment of the threshold reliability inquiry altogether.

The strictness of the reliability criterion set out in *Smith*, was eventually abandoned by the Supreme Court in *Khelawon*[78] It was held that the trial judge should approach the issue of hearsay evidence as being presumptively inadmissible unless an exception to the hearsay rule applies. Hearsay evidence that did not fall under a traditional exception was still admissible under the principled approach if the indicia of necessity and reliability were established on a *voir dire*. The reliability requirement would generally be met by showing (1) that there is no real concern about whether the statement is true or not because of the circumstances in which it came about; or (2) that no real concern arises from the fact that the statement is presented

---

[75] *Supra*, note 62.

[76] *Williams*, 1985 CarswellOnt 86, 18 C.C.C. (3d) 356, 44 C.R. (3d) 351 (C.A.); leave to appeal refused (1985), 18 C.C.C. (3d) 356n, 44 C.R. (3d) 351n (S.C.C.); *Finta*, 1992 CarswellOnt 96, 73 C.C.C. (3d) 65, 14 C.R. (4th) 1 (C.A.) at pp. 200–203 [C.C.C.], ; affirmed 1994 CarswellOnt 61, 1994 CarswellOnt 1154, 88 C.C.C. (3d) 417, 28 C.R. (4th) 265 (S.C.C.) at pp. 527-28 [C.C.C.], ; reconsideration / rehearing refused (June 23, 1994), Doc. 23023, 23097 (S.C.C.); *F. (G.)*, 1999 CarswellOnt 129, 43 O.R. (3d) 290, 132 C.C.C. (3d) 14 (C.A.) at pp. 31-32 [C.C.C.].

[77] 2001 CarswellOnt 3161, 157 C.C.C. (3d) 129, 45 C.R. (5th) 273 (C.A.) at para. 80; leave to appeal refused 2002 CarswellOnt 1895, 2002 CarswellOnt 1896 (S.C.C.).

[78] 2006 CarswellOnt 7825, 2006 CarswellOnt 7826, 215 C.C.C. (3d) 161, 42 C.R. (6th) 1 (S.C.C.), adopting the dissenting reasons of Kennedy J. in *Idaho v. Wright*, 497 U.S. 805 (1990) and the comments of Professor David Paciocco, "The Hearsay Exceptions: A Game of 'Rock, Paper, Scissors'", in *Special Lectures of the Law Society of Upper Canada 2003: The Law of Evidence*.

in hearsay form because, in the circumstances, its truth and accuracy can nonetheless be sufficiently tested by means other than contemporaneous cross-examination. The trial judge acts as a gatekeeper in making the preliminary assessment of the threshold reliability of a hearsay statement and leaves the ultimate determination of its worth to the fact finder. The factors to be considered on the admissibility inquiry are not to be categorized in terms of threshold and ultimate reliability. All relevant factors are to be considered including, in appropriate cases, the presence of supporting or contradictory evidence.

Trial judges are now required to adopt a more functional approach focused on the particular dangers raised by the hearsay evidence sought to be introduced and on those attributes or circumstances relied upon by the proponent to overcome those dangers. Whether certain factors go only to ultimate reliability depends on the context.[79] Corroborating or conflicting evidence should now be considered in the admissibility inquiry in appropriate cases.[80] When the reliability requirement is met on the basis that the trier of fact has a sufficient basis to assess the statement's truth and accuracy, there is no need for the trial judge to inquire further into the likely truth of the statement. That question becomes one that is entirely left to the ultimate trier of fact and the trial judge exceeds his or her role by inquiring into the likely truth of the statement. However, when reliability is dependent on the inherent trustworthiness of the statement, the trial judge is required to inquire into those factors tending to show that the statement is true or not. In determining the question of threshold reliability, the trial judge has to be mindful that hearsay evidence is presumptively inadmissible. The judge's function is to guard against the admission of hearsay evidence which is unnecessary or the reliability of which is neither readily apparent from the trustworthiness of its contents nor capable of being meaningfully tested by the ultimate trier of fact. If the proponent of the evidence cannot meet the twin criteria of necessity and reliability, the general exclusionary rule prevails. In the context of a criminal case, the accused's inability to test the evidence may impact on the fairness of the trial, thereby giving the rule a constitutional dimension. As in all cases, the trial judge has a residual discretion to exclude admissible hearsay evidence where its prejudicial effect is out of proportion to its probative value.

---

[79] *Supra*, at para. 93.

[80] *Supra*, at para. 100.

(d) The Discretion to Exclude

The Courts have recognized that even where the criteria of necessity and reliability have been established, trial judges retain a residual discretion to exclude evidence.[81] This discretion should be exercised where the slight probative value of the hearsay statement is outweighed by the potential unfairness or undue prejudice to the accused.

5. ASSERTIONS OF LIVING PERSONS

(a) Co-conspirators

Where an accused is charged with the crime of conspiracy to commit an illegal act, proof that he or she agreed to commit the illegal act is sufficient to obtain a conviction. It is not necessary for the prosecution to prove that the accused also committed the illegal act which the conspirators are alleged to have planned to commit. Nor is it necessary for the accused to be aware of all of the details of the conspiracy, or of everyone who was involved or their respective roles. It is sufficient that the accused is aware of the general nature of the common design and agrees to adhere to it.[82]

But proving a conspiracy is generally very difficult, because such agreements are usually made in secret and the only witnesses present are the conspirators themselves. Thus, an exception to the hearsay rule has developed which allows the prosecution to prove the conspiracy by introducing evidence of the acts and declarations of fellow members of the conspiracy, performed and made in pursuance of the objects of the conspiracy. Some authorities have even held that the co-conspirators' exception extends beyond conspiracies to other crimes where there is a common criminal intent or design, or a common criminal enterprise.[83]

---

[81] *Hawkins*, 1996 CarswellOnt 4063, 1996 CarswellOnt 4062, 111 C.C.C. (3d) 129, 2 C.R. (5th) 245 (S.C.C.) at pp. 161-62; *M. (M.)*, 2001 CarswellOnt 2099, 156 C.C.C. (3d) 560 (C.A.).

[82] *Cotroni*, 1979 CarswellOnt 78, 1979 CarswellOnt 48, (sub nom. *Papalia v. R.*) [1979] 2 S.C.R. 256, 45 C.C.C. (2d) 1, 7 C.R. (3d) 185, 11 C.R. (3d) 150 at p. 276 [S.C.R.]; *Root*, 2008 CarswellOnt 7817, 241 C.C.C. (3d) 125, 62 C.R. (6th) 247 (C.A.) at para. 68; leave to appeal refused 2009 CarswellOnt 6604, 2009 CarswellOnt 6605 (S.C.C.); and *Khawaja*, 2006 CarswellOnt 6551, 214 C.C.C. (3d) 399, 42 C.R. (6th) 348 (S.C.J.) at para. 36; leave to appeal refused 2007 CarswellOnt 2154, 2007 CarswellOnt 2155 (S.C.C.).

[83] *Koufis*, 1941 CarswellNS 24, [1941] S.C.R. 481, 76 C.C.C. 161 at p. 488 [S.C.R.]; *Wilder*, 2003 CarswellBC 3126, [2003] B.C.J. No. 2884 (S.C.) at para. 649; affirmed 2006 CarswellBC 1, 204 C.C.C. (3d) 332, 36 C.R. (6th) 95 (C.A.); additional reasons 2006 CarswellBC 556 (C.A.); leave to appeal refused 2007

The exception to the hearsay rule is justified on the basis of necessity and reliability. Necessity arises from the combined effect of the non-compellability of a co-accused, the undesirability of trying co-conspirators separately, and the evidentiary value of contemporaneous declarations made in furtherance of a conspiracy. As has been argued,[84]

> It would become difficult and in many cases impossible to marshal the evidence of criminal conspiracy without the ability to use co-conspirators' statements of what was said in furtherance of the conspiracy against each other. To deprive the Crown of the right to use double hearsay evidence of co-conspirators as to what they variously said in furtherance of the conspiracy would mean that serious criminal conspiracies would often go unpunished.

Reliability is justified on the basis of the rule in *Carter*,[85] a two-step approach to admitting hearsay. This approach allows the trier to consider a co-conspirator's hearsay statement made in furtherance of the conspiracy *only* after the trier has found (1) beyond a reasonable doubt that the conspiracy existed, and (2) that the accused was *probably* a member of the conspiracy based only on direct evidence against him.[86] In other words, before the trier may consider hearsay statements by a co-conspirator against the accused, there must first be proof beyond a reasonable doubt of the existence of a conspiracy by direct evidence *other than hearsay evidence*. However, the initial proof of membership by the accused need only be made on a balance of probabilities. Once proof has been established, then the hearsay exception kicks in and the trier is allowed to consider evidence of acts and declarations of co-conspirators to prove beyond a reasonable doubt the accused's membership in the conspiracy.The *Carter* approach, it has been said, does not simply amount to corroborating the statement in issue but provides circumstantial indicators of reliability.[87]

CarswellBC 366, 2007 CarswellBC 367 (S.C.C.); *Samuels*, 2007 CarswellOnt 5530, [2007] O.J. No. 3320 (C.A.).

[84] *Mapara*, 2005 SCC 23, 2005 CarswellBC 963, 2005 CarswellBC 964, [2005] 1 S.C.R. 358, 195 C.C.C. (3d) 225, 28 C.R. (6th) 1 per McLachlin C.J.C. at para. 29; *Chang*, 2003 CarswellOnt 1007, 173 C.C.C. (3d) 397, 9 C.R. (6th) 304 (C.A.) at para. 105.

[85] 1982 CarswellNB 13, 1982 CarswellNB 55, [1982] 1 S.C.R. 938, 67 C.C.C. (2d) 568, 31 C.R. (3d) 97 at pp. 102–106 [C.C.C.].

[86] *Mapara*, 2005 SCC 23, 2005 CarswellBC 963, 2005 CarswellBC 964, [2005] 1 S.C.R. 358, 195 C.C.C. (3d) 225, 28 C.R. (6th) 1.

[87] *Mapara*, *supra*, at para. 27.

In practice what happens is that all of the evidence (including the hearsay) is admitted and, at the conclusion of the case, the trial judge is required to instruct the jury (or himself where trial is by judge alone) that they must conduct their deliberations in three stages. At the first stage, the judge must instruct the jury whether on all of the evidence they are satisfied beyond a reasonable doubt that the conspiracy charged in the indictment existed. If they are not satisfied, then the accused charged with participation in the conspiracy must be acquitted. If they conclude that a conspiracy as alleged existed, they must (the second stage) review the evidence and decide whether, on the basis of the evidence directly receivable against the accused, a probability is raised that he was a member of the conspiracy.[88] In doing so, they must look at only the direct evidence of membership and determine whether the accused is *probably* a member of the conspiracy. If they are satisfied that he is probably a member of the conspiracy, then and only then (the final stage) are they allowed to consider the hearsay evidence of the acts and declarations of other conspirators in furtherance of the objects of the conspiracy in determining whether the guilt of the accused has been established beyond a reasonable doubt. Before doing so, the trial judge must first decide whether there is some evidence upon which a jury could find that the acts or declarations were made in furtherance of the conspiracy.

Since it is not necessary that only the directly admissible evidence be introduced first and a determination whether a conspiracy exists before any hearsay evidence of co-conspirators is received, there is a serious risk that a jury may confuse the hearsay evidence with the direct evidence and rely on the hearsay evidence in deciding whether there was a conspiracy and whether the accused was probably a member of it. However, the *Carter* approach is justified on the basis that the exigencies of the trial would make a chronological separation of the evidence impossible. It is argued that it avoids the delays and difficulties in trial procedure that would arise if, with respect to admissibility, the necessity and reliability of particular pieces of hearsay evidence were to be decided on a case-by-case basis.

The confusion for a jury in following these instructions must be obvious. Moreover, it must be even more confusing for the jury where there are only two members of the alleged conspiracy, as the Ontario Court of Appeal observed in *Bogiatzis*.[89] The difficulty posed by the first stage of the *Carter* analysis in a two-person conspiracy is the risk that the jury will have found the accused guilty at the first stage by using all of the evidence, including

---

[88] *Collins*, 1999 CarswellNfld 43, 133 C.C.C. (3d) 8, 22 C.R. (5th) 269 (C.A.).
[89] 2010 ONCA 902, 2010 CarswellOnt 9789, 285 C.C.C. (3d) 437.

hearsay statements from the co-conspirator that may not be properly admissible against the accused. If the jury has found an agreement and there are only two people involved, it follows that both must be guilty, otherwise there could be no agreement. However, the Court of Appeal has said that it was not open for a trial judge to abandon the *Carter* test in a two-person conspiracy until the Supreme Court holds otherwise.

Although the co-conspirator's rule permitting the admission of acts and declarations of co-conspirators has been based traditionally on principles of agency, it is still an exception to the hearsay rule. The courts have said that it must be interpreted in a manner consistent with the principled approach to the hearsay rule.[90] Since the non-compellability of a co-accused declarant being tried with the accused is one justification for admitting his hearsay statement, this raises the question whether there is an obligation upon the Crown to call a co-conspirator who has had the charges against him resolved and is available to testify as to his declaration. In other words, does the availability of the co-conspirator to testify require that evidence of his or her declaration be adduced through the co-conspirator's testimony and not his hearsay declaration? This would give the accused the opportunity to cross-examine him on his evidence.

In *Simpson*,[91] LaForme J.A. held that the Crown should be required to do so where the statements are made by a co-conspirator to an undercover officer and are recorded later-on. Such statements are "potentially less reliable than the direct communication between two actual co-conspirators whose conversation is recorded contemporaneously". However, he recognized that out-of-court declarations are presumptively admissible and may apply even where the declarant is available to testify. As he said,[92] ". . . the availability of the declarant, *in some circumstances*, can support the "rare exception" in which the *Carter* test *might yield* to that required by *Starr*".

---

[90] *Chang*, 2003 CarswellOnt 1007, 173 C.C.C. (3d) 397, 9 C.R. (6th) 304 (C.A.); *Connolly*, 2001 CarswellNfld 370, 176 C.C.C. (3d) 292 (C.A.); *Mapara*, 2005 CarswellBC 963, 2005 CarswellBC 964, [2005] 1 S.C.R. 358, 195 C.C.C. (3d) 225, 28 C.R. (6th) 1.

[91] 2007 CarswellOnt 7519, 230 C.C.C. (3d) 542, 53 C.R. (6th) 1 (C.A.) at para. 32; leave to appeal refused 2008 CarswellOnt 3693, 2008 CarswellOnt 3694 (S.C.C.). See Lisa Dufraimont, R. v. Marpara: Preserving the Co-Conspirators Exception to the Hearsay Rule, 2006, 51 CLQ 169.

[92] *Supra*, at para. 36.

On the other hand, the Supreme Court of the United States has held that there is no obligation upon the state to call the available co-conspirator.[93] The Court noted that,[94]

> Conspirators are likely to speak differently when talking to each other in furtherance of their illegal aims than when testifying on the witness stand. Even when the declarant takes the stand, his in-court testimony seldom will reproduce a significant portion of the evidentiary value of his statements during the course of the conspiracy.

Marshall J., who dissented, would have required the state to establish the unavailability of the declarants before admitting their hearsay statements. He argued,[95]

> But the Framers, had they the prescience, would surely have been as apprehensive of the spectacle of a defendant's conviction upon the testimony of a handful of surveillance technicians and a very large box of tapes recording the boasts, faulty recollections, and coded or ambiguous utterances of outlaws.

(b) Identification Parades

Where a fact in issue is the identity of the perpetrator of the crime, it will be necessary for the prosecutor to ask a witness, who is able to identify the person, to point him out to the jury. A typical question is "Do you see the person who . . . in this courtroom"? In such instances, it is usually not very difficult for the witness to identify the accused because the accused will be sitting by himself (or with a co-accused) in the prisoner's dock.

However, those involved in the administration of justice know from experience that the identification of an accused for the first time in the prisoner's dock is notoriously suspect and can lead to a miscarriage of justice.[96] The ordinary juror on the other hand may not be aware of this. For this reason, a rule has developed which permits police officers, or anyone else who is present when a prior identification is made by a witness, to give evidence not only that the witness identified the accused but also of the surrounding circumstances of that identification. Although such evidence is hearsay, it is permitted for the truth of the assertion.

---

[93] *United States v. Inadi*, 475 U.S. 387 (1986).

[94] At p. 395.

[95] At p. 411.

[96] *Browne*, 1951 CarswellBC 25, 99 C.C.C. 141, 11 C.R. 297, 1 W.W.R. (N.S.) 449 (C.A.); *Hibbert*, 2002 CarswellBC 847, 2002 CarswellBC 848, [2002] 2 S.C.R. 445, 163 C.C.C. (3d) 129, 50 C.R. (5th) 209 at para. 50; *Tebo*, 2003 CarswellOnt 1749, 175 C.C.C. (3d) 116, 13 C.R. (6th) 308, 172 O.A.C. 148 (C.A.) at para. 19.

For example, an officer who was present during an identification parade (a lineup) or when a witness was shown a photo-lineup, or when a composite drawing was prepared, is entitled to give evidence that the witness identified a particular person in the lineup or the composite drawing, whether or not the witness hesitated before making the identification, what words the witness used in making the identification, etc. Such evidence will give the trier of fact a complete picture of all of the surrounding circumstances which led to the accused's ultimate identification in the prisoner's dock and will enable the trier to properly assess the value of that identification.[97]

Some text writers[98] and authorities[99] have suggested that evidence by a police officer of a prior identification by a witness is hearsay and the rule which allows such evidence is an exception to the hearsay rule. It is submitted that it is really an exception to the rule which prohibits a witness from giving evidence of a prior consistent statement.[100] It is not hearsay because the evidence is not tendered to prove the truth of what the identifying witness has said: simply the fact that it was said. The officers are not saying that the accused committed the crime, only that the witness said that the accused is the person who committed the crime. As such, the evidence is offered only to prove that the witness has identified the accused as the person who committed the crime, not that the identification is necessarily a correct one. In other words, it may be used only to assess the value of the witness's evidence at trial "by showing that the witness identified the accused before the sharpness of his recollection was dimmed by time".[101] It provides no independent substantive evidence of identity.[102] Such evidence is thus original or first-hand evidence of identification by the witness; it is not second hand or hearsay evidence that the accused committed the

---

[97] *Langille*, 1990 CarswellOnt 2730, 75 O.R. (2d) 65, 59 C.C.C. (3d) 544, 40 O.A.C. 355 (C.A.); *McCay* (1990), 91 Cr. App. R. 84 (Eng. C.A.).

[98] Sopinka, Lederman and Byrant, *The Law of Evidence* (Toronto: Butterworths, 1992) at pp. 313-14; Paciocco, Steusser, *The Law of Evidence* (1996) at 76–78; Cross and Tapper on *Evidence*, 8th ed. (1996) at p.587.

[99] *T. (W.P.)*, 1993 CarswellOnt 1056, 14 O.R. (3d) 225, 83 C.C.C. (3d) 5, 16 C.R.R. (2d) 49, 63 O.A.C. 321 (C.A.); *Starr*, 2000 CarswellMan 449, 2000 CarswellMan 450, [2000] 2 S.C.R. 144, 147 C.C.C. (3d) 449, 36 C.R. (5th) 1 at para. 222.

[100] *Langille, ibid.*; *Tat*, 1997 CarswellOnt 5434, 35 O.R. (3d) 641, 117 C.C.C. (3d) 481, 14 C.R. (5th) 116, (sub nom. *R. v. T.T.*) 103 O.A.C. 15 (C.A.).

[101] Libling, *Evidence of Past Identification*, [1977] Crim.L.R. 268 at pp. 271-72.

[102] *Campbell*, 2006 CarswellBC 502, 207 C.C.C. (3d) 18 (C.A.); *Crate*, 2011 CarswellBC 3281, 288 C.C.C. (3d) 38, 90 C.R. (6th) 388 (C.A.)

crime.[103] Nevertheless, because of the concern that the trier may infer from the officer's testimony that the witness must have picked out the right person, the trial judge is required to instruct the jury as to the limited use of such evidence.

Since in-court identification evidence of an accused is inherently suspect because of the risk of error and has no probative value standing alone, the "probative force of identification evidence is best measured by a consideration of the entire identification process which culminates with an in-court identification".[104] As Doherty J.A. noted in *Tat*[105]

> If a witness identifies an accused at trial, evidence of previous identifications made and descriptions given is admissible to allow the trier of fact to make an informed determination of the probative value of the purported identification. The trier of fact will consider the entirety of the identification process as revealed by the evidence before deciding what weight should be given to the identification made by the identifying witness. Evidence of the circumstances surrounding any prior identifications and the details of prior descriptions given will be central to that assessment.

If a witness, who has made an out-of-court identification, is not asked at trial to identify the accused, then it would follow that police officers should not be permitted to give evidence of that prior positive identification by the witness. Moreover, any evidence of what the witness told the officers as to the circumstances underlying the prior identification is hearsay, although it may have some probative value. This was pointed out by the Supreme Court in *Starr*.[106] There two murder victims had given witness B a ride home in their car shortly before they were murdered in a gang-related execution. Soon after the murders, B was shown three photos by two police officers and pointed to one of them and said the person (who was the accused) looked familiar. At trial, B was not asked by the prosecutor to identify the accused, why the person in the photo looked familiar, where she had seen the person or whether she had seen the accused on the night of the murder. However, police officers were permitted to give evidence that when B identified a photo (of the accused) shortly after the murders, she stated

---

[103] *Starr*, 2000 CarswellMan 449, 2000 CarswellMan 450, [2000] 2 S.C.R. 144, 147 C.C.C. (3d) 449, 36 C.R. (5th) 1 at para. 222.

[104] *Tat*, 1997 CarswellOnt 5434, 35 O.R. (3d) 641, 117 C.C.C. (3d) 481, 14 C.R. (5th) 116 (C.A.).

[105] *Supra*, at p. 656.

[106] 2000 SCC 40, 2000 CarswellMan 449, 2000 CarswellMan 450, [2000] 2 S.C.R. 144, 147 C.C.C. (3d) 449, 36 C.R. (5th) 1, 190 D.L.R. (4th) 591, [2000] 11 W.W.R. 1, 148 Man. R. (2d) 161, 258 N.R. 250, 224 W.A.C. 161, [2000] S.C.J. No. 40.

that it looked like the man she had seen at the gas station talking to one of the deceased and who was also probably driving the other car. It was held by the Supreme Court that the trial judge had erred in admitting the officer's evidence of identification by B.

Iacobucci J., delivering the judgment of the majority, held that what B told the officers was hearsay and inadmissible unless reliable and necessary, because the Crown sought to use the statements to show that the accused was present at the gas station, thus creating an inference that he followed the victims from the gas station and was driving the car B saw when she was let off at her home. The issue, as he saw it, was whether the prior identification exception to the hearsay rule permitted the reception of an out-of-court identification by a witness, where the witness does not testify at trial that she made the identification. If she had testified that she previously gave an accurate description or made an accurate identification, the out-of-court identification by the officers would have been permitted, *even if she was unable to identify the accused at trial*.[107] His rationale for the distinction was this:

> If the witness can at least testify that at some point she made an accurate identification, then a police officer's testimony that he or she observed the identifying witness in the act of identification is *original evidence* that the identifying witness did indeed select a particular person, and that that person is the accused. However, for this rationale to apply, the identifying witness must confirm that the person he or she identified in the police officer's presence was the person who committed an act that is relevant in the immediate proceedings.[108]

The same problem will arise if the witness called to identify the accused at trial has no recollection of identifying the accused or denies identifying the accused at a photo-lineup. If the purpose of the hearsay out-of-court identification is to allow the trier of fact to make an informed determination of the probative value of the in-court identification, then it would make any cross-examination on the circumstances meaningless. This was pointed out by Doherty J.A. in *Tat*,[109]

> [82] [T]he absence of contemporary cross-examination, is said to be the most important of the dangers associated with the admission of hearsay evidence. . . . If the proffered hearsay consists of a previous statement made by a person who testifies, that danger will usually be alleviated by the ability to

---

[107] See *Tat, supra*, note 100.

[108] *Ibid.*, at para. 222.

[109] *Tat*, 1997 CarswellOnt 5434, 35 O.R. (3d) 641, 117 C.C.C. (3d) 481, 14 C.R. (5th) 116 (C.A.) at p. 669 [O.R.]. See also *James*, 2011 ONCA 839, 2011 CarswellOnt 15037, 283 C.C.C. (3d) 212 at para. 45.

cross-examine that witness at trial. . . . If, however, the prior statement is one of identification and the witness denies making the identification, special problems arise and cross-examination at trial may not provide a suitable substitute for contemporaneous cross-examination.

[83] Cross-examination of the maker of the statement at trial will certainly assist in assessing the credibility of the witness, but may not assist in testing the reliability of the out-of-court statement.

As he pointed out, "a bald in-court identification of an accused from a photo array carries no circumstantial guarantees of trustworthiness" to satisfy the reliability requirement.[110]

(c) Past Memory Recorded

In Chapter 2, dealing with "Refreshing The Witness's Memory", it was noted that the present rule is that a witness may refresh his or her memory while in the witness box from any record of the event that he or she has brought, provided, (a) that he or she made the note of the event or, if it was made by another person, he or she verified the accuracy of the other person's note, and (b) the note was personally written, or the record of another person was verified by the witness when the facts were fresh in his or her memory.[111] The question was also asked — what happens if the witness has no recollection of the events at all?

At the foundation of the common law adversarial system is the notion that a witness will have a memory of the events that he or she is relating to the court and that the other side will be allowed to test the accuracy or reliability of that memory and the truth of that testimony by cross-examination. Is the testimony of that witness lost forever, even though the witness may have made notes of the event? Can the written word ever replace the lost memory?

Professor Wigmore recognized that total memory loss did not necessarily result in lost testimony where certain conditions were met.[112] He called it "past recollection recorded". Those conditions were:

1. The past recollection must have been recorded in some reliable way.

---

[110] *Supra, James* at para. 49. However, it is suggested that it might be admissible if shown to be necessary and reliable.

[111] *B. (K.G.)*, 1998 CarswellOnt 1914, 125 C.C.C. (3d) 61, 109 O.A.C. 138, [1998] O.J. No. 1859 (C.A.); *Coffin*, 1956 CarswellQue 1, [1956] S.C.R. 191, 114 C.C.C. 1, 23 C.R. 1; *Shergill*, 1997 CarswellOnt 5225, 13 C.R. (5th) 160, 23 O.T.C. 218 (Gen. Div.).

[112] *Wigmore on Evidence* (Chadbourn rev. 1970), Vol. 3, c. 28, para. 744.

2. At the time, it must have been sufficiently fresh and vivid to be probably accurate.

3. The witness must be able now to assert that the record accurately represented his knowledge and recollection at the time, The usual phrase requires the witness to affirm that "he knew it to be true at the time".

4. The original record itself must be used, if procurable.

In other words, the notes or record made at the time replaces the memory of the witness and becomes "past memory recorded".

The admissibility of "past memory recorded" is, in effect, an exception to the hearsay rule. It is an exception because the original record is admissible as proof of the truth of the contents, even though the recorder of the note cannot be tested as to the accuracy or truth of the note. The note is considered to have a substantial guarantee of trustworthiness or reliability because it was made by the recorder when it was sufficiently fresh in the recorder's mind to be probably accurate. It is necessary because the recorder of the note has no memory of the event.[113] Nevertheless, it is important that the trier recognize the potential risk of error because of the inability to cross-examine the maker of the note.

6. RES GESTAE

The term *"res gestae"* is a Latin phrase that is too often used and misused by judges and lawyers. Professor Wigmore called it useless "because every rule of Evidence to which it has ever been applied exists as a part of some other well established principle and can be explained in the terms of that principle".[114] He also called it harmful "because by its ambiguity it invites the confusion of one rule with another and thus creates uncertainty as to the limitations of both". He suggested that it should be wholly repudiated. Regrettably, judges and lawyers continue to use it more than ever.

The rule has been expressed this way.[115]

> Acts, declarations, and incidents which constitute, or accompany and explain, the fact or transaction in issue, are admissible, for or against either party, as forming part of the *res gestae*.

---

[113] See E.M. Morgan "Hearsay and Preserved Memory", (1926) 40 Harv. L.R. 712.

[114] *Supra*, note 112, Vol. 6, para. 1767.

[115] *Phipson on Evidence*, (11th ed.), para. 171.

In *Teper*,[116] Lord Normand attempted to justify the reception of evidence that forms part of the *res gestae* this way:

> It appears to rest ultimately on two propositions, that human utterance is both a fact and a means of communication, and that human action may be so interwoven with words that the significance of the action cannot be understood without the correlative words, and the dissociation of the words from the action would impede the discovery of truth.

The above passages suggest that the term *res gestae* refers to words that give significance to or explain conduct or action. In *Bedingfield*,[117] the victim, who was Bedingfield's mistress, came out of a room where Bedingfield was subsequently found, pointed to her throat which was cut and said to one of her assistants "see what Harry has done". She died ten minutes later. Bedingfield's first name was Harry. The trial judge, Chief Justice Cockburn, would not permit the statement to be admitted in evidence because the transaction, that is the cutting of her throat, was over and completed when she made the statement. Later decisions accepted this restriction and argued that a statement or declaration could not be admitted as part of the *res gestae* unless it accompanied the act and explained it.

Professor Wigmore strongly criticized this restriction. He argued that it arose out of a failure to understand the distinction between what may be described as a verbal act and a spontaneous exclamation. A verbal act is simply words that accompany an act and explain it. As Wigmore pointed out:

> Without the words, the act as a whole may be incomplete; and until the words are taken into consideration, the desired significance cannot be attributed to the wordless conduct.[118]

Without the accompanying words, the act has no significance. The words explain the act. This means that when a witness who has seen the act and heard the accompanying words testifies as to what he or she has seen and heard, the witness is giving first-hand or original evidence, not second-hand or hearsay evidence. Thus, in a strict sense, *res gestae* is not really an exception to the hearsay rule because it allows the admission of a statement that would otherwise be hearsay as first-hand or original evidence to explain conduct or actions that might otherwise be ambiguous.

---

[116] [1952] A.C. 480, [1952] 2 All E.R. 447, 68 L.Q.R. 433 (British Guyana P.C.) at p. 449 [All E.R.].

[117] (1879), 14 Cox C.C. 341.

[118] *Supra*, note 112, at Vol. 6, para. 1772.

Professor Wigmore, however, argued that spontaneous exclamations ought to be admitted as an exception to the hearsay rule. His reasons were these:

> Under certain external circumstances of physical shock, a stress of nervous excitement may be produced which stills the reflective faculties and removes their control, so that the utterance which then occurs is a spontaneous and sincere response to the actual sensations and perceptions already produced by the external shock. Since this utterance is made under the immediate and uncontrolled domination of the senses, and during the brief period when considerations of self-interest could not have been brought fully to bear by reasoned reflection, the utterance may be taken as particularly trustworthy, (or, at least, as lacking the usual grounds of untrustworthiness), and thus as expressing the real tenor of the speaker's belief as to the facts just observed by him; and may therefore be received as testimony to those facts.[119]

Using the *Bedingfield* case as an example, Professor Wigmore would argue that Bedingfield's mistress's exclamation as to "what Harry has done" was "a spontaneous and sincere response to the actual sensations and perceptions already produced by the external shock" of having her throat cut. It was also made "during the brief period when considerations of self-interest could not have been brought fully to bear by reasoned reflection". Thus, he would argue that the utterance should be taken as particularly trustworthy and should be admitted as an exception to the hearsay rule.

For almost seventy years, *Bedingfield* was religiously followed by Canadian and English courts. In 1950, there was some attempt to introduce the concept of "spontaneous exclamation" in an Ontario case, but it was quickly rejected. In *Leland*[120] the accused and her husband were jointly charged with manslaughter arising out of the stabbing of one Monteith, in whose house both were residing as roomers. During a quarrel between Monteith and the accused's husband, all of the lights in the house were turned off. When the lights were turned on again, Monteith was heard to say to his wife, "Rose, she stabbed me". He died a few minutes later. Monteith's wife's name was Rose. The trial judge admitted the statement without specifically referring to it as a "spontaneous exclamation". However, the Ontario Court of Appeal said that the judge was wrong to do so because "our rules of evidence do not seem to extend to cover a case of spontaneous exclamation, in the broad terms stated by Wigmore". Nor was the Court prepared to admit it as part of the *res gestae* because, "[t]he fight had

---

[119] *Ibid.*, at para. 1747.
[120] (1950), 1950 CarswellOnt 21, [1951] O.R. 12, 98 C.C.C. 337, 11 C.R. 152 (C.A.).

ceased. No one was pursuing the deceased or seeking to continue the struggle".

However, in 1972, the House of Lords in *Ratten*[121] concluded that the *Bedingfield* rule was too restrictive. In *Ratten*, the Crown sought to introduce the evidence of a telephone operator who had received a telephone call from the deceased's home ten minutes before she was shot. The call came from a woman who sounded hysterical and who said, "get me the police, please", and gave her address but, before a connection was made, hung up. The trial judge admitted the statement. Lord Wilberforce, delivering the judgment of the House, said that the judge was correct in doing so. It was his view that the admissibility of such statements did not depend on there being exact contemporaneity with the act to be explained.

> . . . hearsay evidence may be admitted of the statement providing it is made in such conditions (always being those of approximate but not exact contemporaneity) of involvement or pressure as to exclude the possibility of concoction or distortion to the advantage of the maker or the disadvantage of the accused.[121]

The test that the trial judge had to apply was whether there was the possibility of concoction or fabrication, not whether the statement was part of the event or transaction. Lord Wilberforce had said earlier,

> . . . if the drama, leading up to the climax, has commenced and assumed such intensity and pressure that the utterance can safely be regarded as a true reflection of what was unrolling or actually happening, it ought to be received.[122]

Ratten was re-affirmed 14 years later by the House of Lords in *Blastland*[123] and again, a year later, by the House of Lords in *Andrews*.[124] In *Andrews*, *Bedingfield* was specifically overruled.

The concept of "spontaneous exclamation" espoused by Wigmore and the relaxation of the narrow "exact contemporaneity" test of *Bedingfield* was finally accepted by the Ontario Court of Appeal in *Clark*,[125] There it was held that the evidence of a witness that she heard the victim yell, "Help! Help! I've been murdered! I've been stabbed!" was admissible as a sponta-

---

[121] (1971), [1972] A.C. 378, [1971] 3 All E.R. 801, [1971] 3 W.L.R. 930 (P.C.).

[122] *Ibid.*, at p. 390 [A.C.].

[123] (1985), [1986] 1 A.C. 41, [1985] 2 All E.R. 1095, 81 Cr. App. R. 266, Crim. L.R. 727 (U.K. H.L.).

[124] [1987] A.C. 281, [1987] 1 All E.R. 513, [1987] 2 W.L.R. 413 (U.K. H.L.).

[125] 1983 CarswellOnt 96, 42 O.R. (2d) 609, 7 C.C.C. (3d) 46, 35 C.R. (3d) 357, 1 D.L.R. (4th) 46 (C.A.); leave to appeal refused (1983), 42 O.R. (2d) 609 (note), 7 C.C.C. (3d) 46 (note), 39 C.R. (3d) xxvii, 1 D.L.R. (4th) 46 (note).

neous statement made in such circumstances as to exclude the possibility of concoction or distortion. The statements were contemporaneous with the unfolding events even though they did not accompany the actual stabbing.

However, in *Khan*,[126] the Supreme Court of Canada cast doubt upon the correctness of *Clark* by re-affirming that the traditional tests of contemporaneity and pressure or emotional intensity must exist before a hearsay statement will be admitted under this exception. In *Khan*, a three-and-one-half year-old girl had been examined privately by Dr. Khan, a medical doctor. About 15 minutes after the child and her mother had left Khan's office, the child described to her mother an incident that took place in his office that could amount to a sexual assault. The mother was not allowed by the trial judge to repeat what her daughter told her because it was not, in his opinion, a spontaneous utterance. The Court of Appeal, however, disagreed.[127]

Mr. Justice Robins delivering the judgment of the Court wrote:

> The time that may elapse before a statement following an event capable of rendering it spontaneous is rendered inadmissible will depend on a variety of factors. These include, for instance, the nature and circumstances of the act or event, the nature and circumstances of the statement, the place where the event occurred or the statement was made, the possible influence of intervening events, and the condition and age of the declarant. Each case must depend on its own circumstances; no two cases are identical, and the exact length of time is not subject to mathematical measurement. In any given case, the ultimate question is whether the statement relating to the alleged startling event was made near enough in time to the event to exclude any realistic opportunity for fabrication or concoction.[128]

However, on further appeal to the Supreme Court, McLachlin J., delivering the judgment of the Court,[129] held that the trial judge was correct in rejecting the statement as a spontaneous utterance because it was neither contemporaneous nor made under pressure or emotional intensity. She was not prepared to relax the strict requirements as to the admissibility of a spontaneous utterance, as had been done in the United States, particularly in cases of sex offences against children. It was her concern that admissibility under this exception to the hearsay rule did not impose the twin tests of

---

[126] 1990 CarswellOnt 108, 1990 CarswellOnt 1001, [1990] 2 S.C.R. 531, 59 C.C.C. (3d) 92, 79 C.R. (3d) 1, 113 N.R. 53, 41 O.A.C. 353, [1990] S.C.J. No. 81.

[127] 1988 CarswellOnt 69, 42 C.C.C. (3d) 197, 64 C.R. 281, 64 C.R. (3d) 281, 27 O.A.C. 142 (C.A.); affirmed 1990 CarswellOnt 108, 1990 CarswellOnt 1001, 59 C.C.C. (3d) 92, 79 C.R. (3d) 1 (S.C.C.).

[128] *Ibid.*, at p. 210 [C.C.C.].

[129] *Supra*, note 127.

necessity and reliability before such utterances could be received. She preferred to admit such utterances only where they met those requirements that
had been earlier imposed by the Supreme Court in *Ares v. Venner*.[130]

7. STATUTORY EXCEPTIONS

(a) Generally

As noted earlier, some statutes permit the introduction of hearsay evidence by affidavit or certificate where it would be inconvenient or even
impossible to call the witness who is able to give direct evidence of the fact
in issue. Although the evidence is hearsay, once admitted, the evidence becomes admissible for the truth of the contents.

For example, if what has to be established is that X made certain deposits
and withdrawals from his account at the Bank of Montreal, a strict application of the hearsay rule would require each bank teller who dealt with X to
come forward and give evidence of that specific transaction so that he or
she could be subjected to the test of cross-examination. But we know that it
would be unlikely that any of the tellers would remember the details of
those transactions.

Section 29(1) of the *Canada Evidence Act*, however, authorizes either the
Crown or the defence to introduce proof of those transactions by production
of "a copy of any entry in any book or record kept in any financial institution" notwithstanding that the copy of the entry, or even the actual entry
itself is, in a strict sense, hearsay. But before a copy of the entry is admitted,
section 29(2) requires that certain conditions be established. Those conditions are considered crucial to the twin tests of necessity and reliability or
trustworthiness discussed earlier. They include the requirement that the
book or record be one of the ordinary books or records of the financial institution, that the entry was made in the usual and ordinary course of business,
that the book or record be in the custody or control of the financial institution and that the copy be a true copy of the book or record. When these
conditions are established, proof of the entry may be given by the bank
manager or the accountant, either orally or by affidavit. Similar provisions
are contained in section 26 of the Act dealing with Government of Canada
records and in section 30 with respect to business records.

Another common exception to the hearsay rule is section 50 of the *Controlled Drugs and Substances Act*.[131] Section 50(1) permits the results of

---

[130] 1970 CarswellAlta 80, 1970 CarswellAlta 142, [1970] S.C.R. 608, 14 D.L.R.
(3d) 4, 73 W.W.R. 347, 12 C.R.N.S. 349: see discussion under heading 3 "The
Modern Rule".

[131] S.C. 1996, c. 19.

the analysis of a controlled substance to be given by a certificate or report purporting to be signed by a qualified analyst, provided that the other side has been given reasonable notice of the intention to rely on certificate evidence together with a copy of the certificate or report. Section (2) does, however, give the court the right to order the attendance of the analyst for the purpose of cross-examination.

(b) Videotaped Evidence of a Complainant or Victim or Witness Who has a Disability

Section 715.1 of the *Criminal Code* permits an out-of-court statement to be admitted *in any proceeding against an accused*[132] if,

1. the complainant was under the age of eighteen years at the time the offence is alleged to have been committed;

2. a videotape of the complainant's statement was made within a reasonable time after the alleged offence;

3. the complainant in the videotape describes *the acts complained of*; and

4. the complainant, while testifying, *adopts* the contents of the videotape.

The judge may exclude the video recording if its admission would interfere with the administration of justice.

Section 715.2 also permits the admission of a video recording of a victim or other witness who is able to communicate evidence but mat have difficulty doing so because of a mental or physical disability. As in the case of a complainant under the age of eighteen years, the video must describe the acts complained of, the contents must be adopted by the witness while testifying and the video must have been made within a reasonable time after the alleged offence. Again, the judge may exclude the video recording if its admission would interfere with the administration of justice.

Following the enactment of section 715.1, one issue that the courts were asked to consider was the meaning of the phrase "adopts the contents of the videotape". This required the courts to determine the nature of a videotaped statement. In *Meddoui*,[133] the Alberta Court of Appeal said that section 715.1 was a statutory exception to one of the conditions for the past recol-

---

[132] Although s. 715.1 was initially restricted to certain enumerated offences, the restriction was removed on January 2, 2006.

[133] (1990), 1990 CarswellAlta 187, 111 A.R. 295, 77 Alta. L.R. (2d) 97, 61 C.C.C. (3d) 345, 2 C.R. (4th) 316, [1991] 2 W.W.R. 289, 5 C.R.R. (2d) 294 (C.A.); leave to appeal refused (1991), [1991] 3 S.C.R. ix, 82 Alta. L.R. (2d) lxv (note),

lection recorded exception to the hearsay rule. Therefore, in order to be admitted as past recollection recorded at the time the witness testifies, the witness must have had no recollection of the events recorded. The Court reasoned that this meant that it was not necessary for the complainant to be able, based on a present memory of the events referred to in the videotape, to verify the accuracy and contents of the statement, so long as she recalls giving the statement and her attempt then to be truthful. The Court went further and argued that, if the complainant had a present memory of the events, then her videotape evidence was not necessary because it added nothing to her evidence and would infringe the rule against the admission of prior consistent statements.

In *T. (W.P.)*,[134] the Ontario Court of Appeal disagreed with that reasoning. The Court was of the view that section 715.1 is a statutorily created exception to the rule prohibiting the admission of a prior consistent statement. It could not agree that a witness who has no recollection of the events referred to in a prior statement can be said to *adopt* that statement. The Court, understandably, was concerned that a complainant who has no recollection of the events, and who was only required to *vouch* for the accuracy of the videotaped statement, could not be cross-examined about the actual events because he or she has no memory of those events. The requirement that the complainant while testifying, "adopt(s) the contents of the videotape", meant that she must not only acknowledge making the statement but also be able, *based on a present memory of the events referred to in the statement*, to verify the accuracy of the contents of the statement. This did not mean that the admission of the videotaped statement adds nothing to the testimony. The videotaped statement may communicate additional information to the trier of fact that could assist in determining the truth of the allegations.

However, in *F. (C.)*,[135] the Supreme Court disagreed with the reasoning in both cases. Cory J. for the Court said that section 715.1 is a statutory exception to the hearsay rule. "(i)t permits an out-of-court statement to be admitted for the truth of its contents, provided that certain conditions are

---

69 C.C.C. (3d) vi, [1992] 1 W.W.R. lxv (note), 6 C.R.R. (2d) 192 (note), 137 N.R. 389 (note).

[134] 1993 CarswellOnt 1056, 14 O.R. (3d) 225, 83 C.C.C. (3d) 5, 16 C.R.R. (2d) 49, 63 O.A.C. 321 (C.A.).

[135] 1997 CarswellOnt 4448, 1997 CarswellOnt 4449, (sub nom. *R. v. F. (C.C.)*) [1997] 3 S.C.R. 1183, 120 C.C.C. (3d) 225, 11 C.R. (5th) 209, 154 D.L.R. (4th) 13, 220 N.R. 362, 104 O.A.C. 321, [1997] S.C.J. No. 89.

met".[136] Nevertheless, he did approve the interpretation of "adopts" in *Meddoui* and said that the complainant need not have a present memory of the events referred to in the statement, so long as she is able to recall giving the statement and her attempt then to be truthful. He felt that since children, particularly younger ones, are prone to forget details of an event with the passage of time, it was precisely in this situation that a videotaped statement is needed. It was his view that a videotaped statement made shortly after the event is more likely to be accurate than a child's *viva voce* testimony, given months later, at trial.

He also rejected the view expressed in *Meddoui* that the videotaped evidence added nothing to the testimony when the complainant has an independent *present* memory of the events. He concluded that *the adopted videotaped statement, together with the viva voce evidence given at trial, will comprise the whole of the evidence in chief of the complainant.*

On closer analysis, it would appear that section 715.1 is probably a statutory exception to both the hearsay rule and the rule that prohibits introduction of a prior consistent statement. In other words, when the complainant has no recollection of the events and the evidence is admitted as past recollection recorded, then it is a statutory exception to the rule rendering hearsay inadmissible. On the other hand, when the complainant has an independent present memory of the events, then the admissibility of the videotape is a statutory exception to the rule prohibiting a prior consistent statement.

Can the videotaped statement be used to corroborate or bolster the testimony of a complainant who also gives *viva voce* evidence? The British Columbia Court of Appeal has said *no*.[137] Unless there is an allegation of recent fabrication, the statement is nothing more than a prior consistent statement. The purpose of the statement is to provide a fuller account from the complainant of the relevant events along with the opportunity to assess the complainant's demeanour.

Another condition requires that the videotape of the complainant's statement be made within *a reasonable time after the alleged offence.* The purpose of the condition is to preserve an early account of the complaint in order to assist in the discovery of the truth. The cases, however, suggest that what is a reasonable time after the alleged offence will often depend on the nature of the offence, the age of the complainant and the effect that the

---

[136] *Ibid.*, at p. 232 [C.C.C.].

[137] *Aksidan*, 2006 CarswellBC 1273, 209 C.C.C. (3d) 423, 38 C.R. (6th) 270 (C.A.); followed in *S. (K.P.)*, 2007 CarswellBC 1730, 224 C.C.C. (3d) 62 (C.A.); leave to appeal refused 2007 CarswellBC 3067, 2007 CarswellBC 3068 (S.C.C.).

offence may have had on the complainant. For example, in *L. (S.J.)*,[138] it was held that two videos of a child complainant made almost four years after the event did not comply with the section. On the other hand, in *G. (S.)*,[139] it was held that a three year delay of a 13 year old's videotaped statement was admitted, and understandable, given the complainant's fear of the accused and her mother's failure to take action once the complainant told her of the incident. The trial judge reasoned that the complainant was not of such an age that the three-year delay would raise obvious concerns about her ability to recall the incidents. Finally, where the accused is alleged to have committed sexual offences over a period of time, it has been held that the operative date must be the last incident of abuse, not when the first abuse occurred.[140]

---

[138] 2001 CarswellBC 1140, 155 C.C.C. (3d) 338, 44 C.R. (5th) 380 (C.A.).

[139] 2007 CarswellOnt 3570, 221 C.C.C. (3d) 439 (S.C.J.).

[140] *Archer*, 2005 CarswellOnt 4964, 202 C.C.C. (3d) 60, 34 C.R. (6th) 271 (C.A.).

4
PREVIOUS CONSISTENT STATEMENTS

1. THE RULE

The general rule at common law is that a witness may not be asked in chief whether he previously made a statement consistent with his present testimony. For example, the prosecutor is not entitled to ask the victim of an assault whether she made a statement to the police consistent with her present testimony; nor may any other prosecution witness be permitted to repeat the victim's prior consistent statement. When it comes to the defence, there are two aspects of this rule. The first is that the defence is not allowed to call the accused or any other witness to testify that the accused made a statement before trial declaring his innocence. Secondly, the defence is not allowed to ask a prosecution witness during cross-examination about any statement made by the accused declaring his innocence.[1]

---

[1] *Campbell*, 1977 CarswellOnt 5, 17 O.R. (2d) 673, 38 C.C.C. (2d) 6, 1 C.R. (3d) 309 (C.A.); varied 1977 CarswellOnt 6, 17 O.R. (2d) 673 at 699, 38 C.C.C. (2d) 6 at 32, 1 C.R. (3d) S-49 (C.A.).

The rule, often called the rule against self-serving evidence, explains one of the reasons for it. It is to prevent witnesses, particularly an accused, from manufacturing or inventing evidence that serves his or her interests. It is only human nature for a jury to believe that because a victim previously declared the accused's guilt or an accused protested his innocence before trial, their previous statements must be true. Another purpose of the rule is to avoid opening the trial process to the time-consuming and confusing consideration of a collateral issue. It also prevents the jury from being swayed by this side issue.

A good example of the application of this rule against an accused is in *Roberts*.[2] Roberts was charged with the murder of his girlfriend. His defence at trial was that he had shot her accidently while they were making up after a quarrel. Two days after the shooting, he told his father that his defence was that the shooting had been an accident. His father was not permitted to give evidence of that conversation because it was self-serving.

Evidence from an accused that he offered to take a polygraph test to demonstrate his innocence is another example of a self-serving statement which is not admissible, even where his offer is refused by the police.[3] Although the probative value of such evidence is to enable the defence to argue that the accused was prepared to do something which a guilty person would not do, it is generally rejected because the results are inadmissible and, accordingly, the accused risks nothing.[4] On the other hand, such an offer might have probative value if the accused honestly believed that a negative test could be used against him.[5]

Another reason for the rule, particularly where it affects the defence, is to prevent an accused from avoiding the witness box by having someone else advance his or her defence. An accused who wishes to tell what happened must do so by entering the witness box where he or she will be required to testify under oath and be subjected to cross-examination.

However, the rule will not apply where the prosecution chooses to make the accused's explanation part of its case. For example, if the Crown de-

---

2 [1942] 1 All E.R. 187, 28 Cr. App. R. 102, 86 Sol. Jo. 98, 58 T.L.R. 138 (C.A.).

3 *Béland*, 1987 CarswellQue 14, 1987 CarswellQue 96, [1987] 2 S.C.R. 398, 36 C.C.C. (3d) 481, 60 C.R. (3d) 1, (sub nom. *Béland v. R.)* 43 D.L.R. (4th) 641, 79 N.R. 263, 9 Q.A.C. 293; *Richards*, 1997 CarswellBC 272, 6 C.R. (5th) 154, 87 B.C.A.C. 21, 143 W.A.C. 21, [1997] B.C.J. No. 339 (C.A.); leave to appeal refused 2003 CarswellBC 1322, 2003 CarswellBC 1323 (S.C.C.); *B. (S.C.),* 1997 CarswellOnt 3907, 36 O.R. (3d) 516, 119 C.C.C. (3d) 530, 10 C.R. (5th) 302, 104 O.A.C. 81, [1997] O.J. No. 4183 (C.A.).

4 *Béland, ibid.,* at pp. 494-95 [C.C.C.].

5 *B.(S.C.), supra,* note 3 at p. 310 [C.R.].

cides, for whatever reason, to introduce an accused's exculpatory statement at trial, it will be admissible, even if it is self-serving. Once the Crown chooses to introduce the accused's self-serving statement as part of its case, then the Crown must accept the consequences of its decision.

The strict application of the rule is not without its critics, particularly where it is applied to the evidence of children. In *B. (D.C.)*,[6] the Manitoba Court of Appeal felt that the common law rule should be changed in cases of sexual abuse of children because it fails to recognize the difficulty of obtaining a full account from the child of the events in question. The Court noted that the rule ignores the fact that credibility may more readily be judged in the case of a child by considering the circumstances in which a complaint was first made. For example, evidence of a spontaneous account of abuse by a child may be highly relevant to the difficult task which a judge or jury has in assessing the credibility of that child. The prior consistent statement may tend to confirm the consistency of the testimony of a young victim who is required to recall and recount dramatic events in an intimidating and hostile courtroom environment. It was the Court's view that a new rule of admissibility would ensure that, in appropriate cases, and for a limited purpose, this kind of evidence should not be excluded from the court's truth-seeking process. It was suggested that the evidence should be received subject to such safeguards as the judge may consider necessary and subject always to considerations affecting the weight that should be accorded to the evidence.

2. EXCEPTIONS TO THE RULE

(a) To Rebut the Suggestion of Recent Fabrication

There are undoubtedly instances where a prior consistent statement should be admitted. The first is where the defence suggests that the complainant is testifying to events that one would have expected the complainant to have mentioned at an earlier time, or where the prosecution suggests that the defence was recently invented or contrived. Here, it is only fair that the Crown or the defence be allowed to rebut the suggestion of recent fabrication by leading evidence that the complainant's evidence or the accused's defence has been consistent throughout.[7] At the same time, the

---

6 1994 CarswellMan 150, 91 C.C.C. (3d) 357, 32 C.R. (4th) 91, [1994] 7 W.W.R. 727, 95 Man. R. (2d) 220, 70 W.A.C. 220, [1994] M.J. No. 403 (C.A.). But see *Aksidan*, 2006 CarswellBC 1273, 209 C.C.C. (3d) 423, 38 C.R. (6th) 270 (C.A.), *contra*.

7 *Garofoli*, 1988 CarswellOnt 68, 41 C.C.C. (3d) 97, 64 C.R. (3d) 193, 43 C.R.R. 252, 27 O.A.C. 1 (C.A.); reversed 1990 CarswellOnt 119, 1990 CarswellOnt

judge must remind the jury (or him or herself) of the limited use of such evidence. It can only be used to rebut the suggestion of recent fabrication or concoction. It must not be used as proof of its contents or to confirm or show the consistency in the testimony of the witness being impeached.[8]

As a practical matter, the suggestion by the Crown that the defence was recently invented or contrived will not arise very often because of an accused's right to remain silent. It would be very unfortunate if police officers were required to warn an accused of his or her right to remain silent and then be allowed to use that silence to complain of recent fabrication when the defence is revealed for the first time at trial. However, an exception will arise where the defence is alibi. Here, it is necessary for the defence to give to the prosecution particulars of that alibi at the earliest opportunity.[9] The failure to do so at a time that is early enough to allow the Crown to investigate the alibi will permit the trier to draw an adverse inference against an alibi defence.[10]

The usual time that the defence will suggest that a victim recently fabricated a complaint against the accused is during the course of the cross-examination of that witness. However, the suggestion need not be raised only at that time. In *Campbell*, the Ontario Court of Appeal noted that:

> . . . an express allegation of recent fabrication in cross-examination is not necessary before the exception, with respect to rebutting an allegation of recent fabrication, becomes operative, and that a suggestion that the accused's story has been recently contrived may also arise implicitly from the whole circumstances of the case, the evidence of the witnesses who have been called and the conduct of the trial.[11]

However, it has also been recognized that a prior consistent statement should not be admitted under the guise of rebutting an allegation of recent

---

1006, [1990] 2 S.C.R. 1421, 60 C.C.C. (3d) 161, 80 C.R. (3d) 317, 50 C.R.R. 206, 116 N.R. 241, 43 O.A.C. 1, 36 Q.A.C. 161; *Campbell, supra,* note 1.

[8] *Collins,* 1991 CarswellOnt 126, 9 C.R. (4th) 377 (C.A.); *F. (J.E.),* 1993 CarswellOnt 137, 16 O.R. (3d) 1, 85 C.C.C. (3d) 457, 26 C.R. (4th) 220, 67 O.A.C. 251, [1993] O.J. No. 2589 (C.A.).

[9] *Robertson,* 1975 CarswellOnt 6, 21 C.C.C. (2d) 385, 29 C.R.N.S. 141 (C.A.); leave to appeal refused (1975), 21 C.C.C. (2d) 385 (note) (S.C.C.).

[10] *Cleghorn,* 1995 CarswellOnt 126, 1995 CarswellOnt 802, [1995] 3 S.C.R. 175, 100 C.C.C. (3d) 393, 41 C.R. (4th) 282, 32 C.R.R. (2d) 41, 186 N.R. 49, 85 O.A.C. 129.

[11] *Supra,* note 1 at p. 325 [C.R.]. But see *Hunter,* 2004 CarswellOnt 486, 182 C.C.C. (3d) 121 (C.A.)

fabrication unless the door is clearly opened.[12] But it may be opened through cross-examination of the complainant or other Crown witnesses, or by the allegation of recent fabrication becoming implicit from the defence's conduct of the case or by an opening statement of the defence.

Once the suggestion of recent fabrication is raised, the Crown is required to apply to the court to be allowed to lead the evidence. If the trial judge is satisfied, after hearing submissions from both sides, that there has been a clear suggestion of recent fabrication by the defence, then the Crown will be entitled to lead the evidence through its witnesses. The same procedure will apply where the Crown has made a similar suggestion about the defence.

(b) To Show Consistency of Identification

The rule preventing the admissibility of a prior consistent statement is regularly breached in cases where the identification of the accused is in dispute. Evidence by a witness that the person standing in the prisoner's dock "is the man" is generally regarded as valueless, because it is open to "honest mistake and self-deception".[13]

Therefore, if the prosecution is relying on eyewitness identification, the police will usually attempt, in the initial stages of the investigation, to have the witness view a series of photographs or attend a lineup. The purpose is to see if the witness is able to pick out the suspect from photographs or from a lineup without any suggestion by the police. At trial, the witness will be allowed to testify that he or she was shown a series of photographs or attended a lineup and was able to pick out the accused without prompting.

Where the witness gives such evidence at trial, the witness is, in effect, giving evidence of his or her own prior consistent statement. Similarly, police officers present at the out-of-court identification are regularly allowed to testify that the witness viewed a series of photographs or attended a lineup and picked out the accused. This is also evidence of a prior consistent statement. Although it has been suggested by some text writers that the evidence of the police officers is an exception to the hearsay rule because

---

[12] *Owens*, 1986 CarswellOnt 145, 33 C.C.C. (3d) 275, 55 C.R. (3d) 386, 18 O.A.C. 125 (C.A.).

[13] *Browne*, 1951 CarswellBC 25, 99 C.C.C. 141, 11 C.R. 297, 1 W.W.R. (N.S.) 449 (C.A.); *Hibbert*, 2002 CarswellBC 847, 2002 CarswellBC 848, [2002] 2 S.C.R. 445, 163 C.C.C. (3d) 129, 50 C.R. (5th) 209 at para. 50; *Tebo*, 2003 CarswellOnt 1749, 175 C.C.C. (3d) 116, 13 C.R. (6th) 308, 172 O.A.C. 148 (C.A.) at para. 19.

they are telling the court what the witness said,[14] such evidence is not really hearsay. The officers are giving original evidence, not hearsay evidence.[15] The evidence is being tendered not to prove that the witness correctly identified the accused as the person who committed the offence, only the fact that the identification was made by the witness. In other words, when the officer repeats in court that the witness said — "that is the man" — the officer is not verifying the accuracy of the identification. That would be hearsay. He is only verifying or confirming as to the fact of an identification by the witness.[16] That is not hearsay; it is original or first-hand evidence.

When a police officer is permitted to give evidence that the witness identified the accused, the evidence is offered, as one writer has said, only to prove that the "witness identified the accused before the sharpness of his recollection was dimmed by time".[17] Its purpose is to strengthen the value of the identification evidence given in court by the witness. It is not to prove that the witness identified the right person, which would be hearsay.[18] However, even where a warning to the jury is given that such evidence does not amount to independent identification of the accused, there is always the risk that the jury will use the confirming evidence of identification as actual evidence of identification.

If the purpose of such evidence is to prove only that the witness has made an out-of-court identification, but not necessarily the correct one, then it would logically follow that such evidence should not be admissible if the witness denies at trial that he made the previous identification or says that the accused is not the person who committed the offence.[19] If the officer's

---

[14] McWilliams, *Canadian Criminal Evidence*, 3rd ed., para. 10130; Sopinka, Lederman and Byrant, *The Law of Evidence* (Toronto: Butterworths, 1992) at pp. 313-14; Paciocco, Steusser, *The Law of Evidence* (1996) at 76–78; Cross and Tapper on *Evidence*, 8th ed. (1996) at p.587.

[15] *Starr*, 2000 CarswellMan 449, 2000 CarswellMan 450, [2000] 2 S.C.R. 144, 147 C.C.C. (3d) 449, 36 C.R. (5th) 1 at per Iacobbuci J. at para. 222; *Langille*, 1990 CarswellOnt 2730, 75 O.R. (2d) 65, 59 C.C.C. (3d) 544, 40 O.A.C. 355 (C.A.); *Tat*, 1997 CarswellOnt 5434, 35 O.R. (3d) 641, 117 C.C.C. (3d) 481, 14 C.R. (5th) 116, (sub nom. *R. v. T.T.*) 103 O.A.C. 15 (C.A.).

[16] *T. (W.P.)*, 1993 CarswellOnt 1056, 14 O.R. (3d) 225, 83 C.C.C. (3d) 5, 16 C.R.R. (2d) 49, 63 O.A.C. 321 (C.A.) at p. 27 [C.C.C.].

[17] See Libling, "Evidence of Past Identification", [1977] Crim L.R. 268 at pp. 271-72.

[18] *Alexander* (1981), 145 C.L.R. 395, 55 A.L.J.R. 355, 34 A.L.R. 289 (H.C.) at p. 407 [C.L.R.]

[19] *McGuire*, 1975 CarswellBC 98, 23 C.C.C. (2d) 385, [1975] 4 W.W.R. 124, 29 C.R.N.S. 282 (C.A.); *Tat, supra*, note 15.

evidence is admitted as original evidence only for the purpose of strengthening the witness's earlier out-of-court identification, then the foundation for the officer's evidence would not exist. There would be nothing to strengthen or confirm. An exception might arise where the prior out-of-court identification was held to be admissible under the rule in *B.(K.G.)*.[20] Under that rule, a prior statement made by the witness and not adopted at trial as true could, in some circumstances, be received as original (not hearsay) evidence for its truth. Once admitted for its truth, then there would be a foundation for the confirmatory or strengthening evidence of the officer present at the out-of-court identification.

What happens if the witness is able to identify the accused at trial, but cannot recall identifying the accused out-of-court? Alternatively, what happens if the witness can recall making an accurate identification out-of-court, but is unable to identify the accused in court or cannot positively do so? In the first situation, it has been held that the police officer's evidence of a prior identification by the witness is admissible.[21] Such evidence is admissible to allow the jury to make an informed assessment of the witness's identification of the accused at trial. In other words, the fact that the witness identified the accused as the offender on an earlier date, even though the witness does not remember doing so, will strengthen and confirm the witness's identification of the accused at trial. In the second situation, evidence by the police officer of the prior identification of the witness is also admissible as original evidence, even though the witness is unable or cannot positively identify the accused at trial.[22]

Where the witness has identified the accused on a previous occasion but is unable or cannot positively identify the accused at trial, independent evidence of identity by a police officer is permitted even though there is no in-court testimony of the witness to confirm.[23] The rationale underlying the admissibility of such evidence as independent evidence of identity is that the earlier identification has greater probative value than an identification

---

[20] 1993 CarswellOnt 76, 1993 CarswellOnt 975, [1993] 1 S.C.R. 740, 79 C.C.C. (3d) 257, 19 C.R. (4th) 1, 148 N.R. 241, 61 O.A.C. 1, [1993] S.C.J. No. 22.

[21] *Tat, supra,* note 15; *Starr,* 2000 CarswellMan 449, 2000 CarswellMan 450, [2000] 2 S.C.R. 144, 147 C.C.C. (3d) 449, 36 C.R. (5th) 1 per Iacobbuci J. at para.222.

[22] *Tat, supra* note 15, *Starr, ibid; Swanston,* 1982 CarswellBC 12, 33 B.C.L.R. 391, 65 C.C.C. (2d) 453, 25 C.R. (3d) 385, [1982] 2 W.W.R. 546 (C.A.); overruling *McGuire, supra,* note 19; *Osbourne,* [1973] 1 All E.R. 649, 57 Cr. App. R. 297, [1973] 1 Q.B. 678 (C.A.).

[23] *Swanston, ibid.,* following *People v. Gould* (1960), 7 Cal. Rptr. 273, 354 P.2d 865 (U.S. Cal. Sup. Ct.).

made in the courtroom "after the suggestions of others and the circumstances of the trial may have intervened to create a fancied recognition in the witness' mind . . .".[24] This view is not without its difficulties, since it precludes effective cross-examination of the witness by the defence. If the witness is unable to identify the accused at trial, then it would difficult to probe what led the witness to make the original identification. Because of the concern that the trier may infer from the officer's testimony that the witness must have picked out the right person, there is an obligation upon the trial judge to warn the jury to consider the possibility of error that might have been made in the original out-of court identification.

The rationale underlying the admission of an officer's testimony *as independent evidence of identification* would render the officer's testimony inadmissible where the witness is, for some reason, unavailable to testify or is not asked to make an identification at trial. Since the purpose of the officers evidence is only to confirm the out-of-court identification of the witness, then, in the absence of testimony by the witness, there would be nothing to strengthen or confirm.[25] There would be the danger that the jury might use the evidence to infer that the witness correctly identified the accused, even though the purpose of the evidence would be only to confirm that the witness on an earlier occasion said — "that is the man". In the absence of admissible evidence by the witness that he or she identified the accused on a prior occasion as the perpetrator, there would be nothing to confirm or strengthen.

As Iacobbuci J. observed in *Starr*,[26]

> If the witness can at least testify that at some point she made an accurate identification, then a police officer's testimony that he or she observed the identifying witness in the act of identification is *original evidence* that the identifying witness did indeed select a particular person, and that that person is the accused. However, for this rationale to apply, the identifying witness must confirm that the person he or she identified in the police officer's presence was the person who committed an act that is relevant in the immediate proceedings

[24] *People v. Gould, ibid., per* Traynor J. at (P.2d) p. 867.

[25] *Timm*, 1981 CarswellAlta 180, 1981 CarswellAlta 281, [1981] 2 S.C.R. 315, 29 A.R. 509, 59 C.C.C. (2d) 396, 21 C.R. (3d) 209 (Eng.), 28 C.R. (3d) 133 (Fr.), 124 D.L.R. (3d) 582, [1981] 5 W.W.R. 577, 37 N.R. 204.

[26] 2000 SCC 40, 2000 CarswellMan 449, 2000 CarswellMan 450, [2000] 2 S.C.R. 144, 147 C.C.C. (3d) 449, 36 C.R. (5th) 1, 190 D.L.R. (4th) 591, [2000] 11 W.W.R. 1, 148 Man. R. (2d) 161, 258 N.R. 250, 224 W.A.C. 161, [2000] S.C.J. No. 40 at para. 222.

Where evidence of prior identification is admitted, the officers are not restricted to merely testifying that the witness identified a particular person or photograph. They are also entitled to give evidence with respect to all of the relevant circumstances surrounding the identification. On the other hand, the defence will usually wish to cross-examine the officers on the circumstances surrounding the identification. By showing that the witness may have hesitated before making the identification or was uncertain about it, the defence will wish to submit to the trier of fact that not much weight should be given to the evidence.

(c) As Part of the Res Gestae

Although *res gestae*, discussed in Chapter 3, is commonly linked with the hearsay rule, it has also been regarded as an exception to the rule against previous consistent statements. Thus an exculpatory statement that is part of the *res gestae* may be admitted, even though it is self-serving. The theory is that a self-serving statement which is uttered contemporaneously with, and is explanatory of, the act is unlikely to be contrived or manufactured.[27]

An explanation given by an accused to the police when first found in possession of stolen property or narcotics is regularly admitted, at the instance of the defence, as part of the *res gestae*. Such evidence is admitted even if the accused does not choose to go into the witness box and give any evidence at trial.[28]

One rationale for this exception to the rule against the admission of a prior consistent statement is that an explanation given spontaneously at the moment of discovery is unlikely to be given upon reflection and therefore contrived.[29] If the accused chooses to go into the witness box and give the same explanation that he gave immediately upon discovery, that will be strong proof of the consistency of the accused's evidence.

Another rationale for this exception in possession of stolen property cases probably lies in the *inference* that may be drawn from the unexplained possession of recently stolen property. The doctrine of recent possession provides that the unexplained possession of recently stolen goods entitles the

---

[27] *Slugoski*, 1985 CarswellBC 438, 17 C.C.C. (3d) 212, 43 C.R. (3d) 369 (C.A.).

[28] *Graham* (1972), 1972 CarswellBC 123, 1972 CarswellBC 321, [1974] S.C.R. 206, 7 C.C.C. (2d) 93, (sub nom. *R. v. McKenzie)* 26 D.L.R. (3d) 579, [1972] 4 W.W.R. 488, 19 C.R.N.S. 117; *Risby*, 1976 CarswellBC 395, 32 C.C.C. (2d) 242 (C.A.); affirmed 1978 CarswellBC 563, 1978 CarswellBC 563F, [1978] 2 S.C.R. 139, 39 C.C.C. (2d) 567.

[29] *Crossley*, 1997 CarswellBC 1677, 117 C.C.C. (3d) 533, 95 B.C.A.C. 61, 154 W.A.C. 61 (C.A.).

trier of fact to draw the inference that the possessor stole the goods.[30] If a contemporaneous explanation of possession by the possessor of the goods was not admissible, then the trier of fact, unaware that an innocent explanation had been given, could well draw the inference that the accused had the requisite knowledge.[31]

(d) To Rebut the Presumption of Consent in Sexual Assaults

At common law, the fact that a complaint was made by the victim of a sexual assault, but not what she actually said, was admissible at the trial of her attacker to show consistency in the victim's testimony. This rule developed from the ancient requirement that the victim of an attack should raise the "hue and cry" if a prosecution of rape were to succeed. It was based on the belief and the legal presumption that a woman who did not complain of rape at the earliest opportunity must have consented to intercourse. The judge was required to instruct the jury and the jury was entitled to infer that a woman who failed to complain at the earliest opportunity must have consented. The fact of the complaint, so long as it was made at the earliest opportunity, was admitted to show that the victim acted as one would normally expect her to do after a sexual attack and thereby rebut the inference of consent. It allowed the judge and jury to infer that her consistency in repeating the same story at trial that she did after her attack was because she was a credible person.

Initially, the rule only allowed the fact of the complaint to be admitted, but not what the victim actually said. Eventually, in *Lillyman*,[32] what the victim actually said was admitted, although the jury was instructed that it was only relevant to show that her conduct in complaining was consistent with her testimony in the witness box denying that she consented. In other words, although the particulars of the complaint were now admissible, the emphasis was still on the fact of the complaint rather than the details of it. The jury was not entitled to infer that because the details of the complaint and her testimony were the same, the witness must be credible. That would infringe the rule prohibiting the admission of a prior consistent statement.

---

[30] *Newton* (1976), 1976 CarswellBC 148, 1976 CarswellBC 315, [1977] 1 S.C.R. 399, 28 C.C.C. (2d) 286, 66 D.L.R. (3d) 639, [1976] 3 W.W.R. 199, 34 C.R.N.S. 161, 8 N.R. 431.

[31] *Kowlyk*, 1988 CarswellMan 162, 1988 CarswellMan 259, [1988] 2 S.C.R. 59, 43 C.C.C. (3d) 1, 65 C.R. (3d) 97, [1988] 6 W.W.R. 607, 55 Man. R. (2d) 1, 86 N.R. 195; *Crossley, supra*, note 29.

[32] (1896), [1895–99] All E.R. Rep. 586, [1896] 2 Q.B. 167 (C.C.R.).

The details could only be used to show consistency in conduct, not in credibility.

Not surprisingly, this archaic rule was finally abrogated by Parliament in 1983. Its abolition does not mean that a complaint by a victim of a sexual assault is no longer ever admissible. It only means that there is no longer a presumption of consent by the victim that the Crown must attempt to rebut by leading evidence-in-chief of a recent complaint.

The abolition of the rule has raised a number of difficult issues for trial judges. One is whether the defence should now be allowed to cross-examine a complainant as to the timeliness of her complaint. Where consent is in issue, the defence may wish to suggest to the complainant that she delayed making a complaint, or made no complaint at all, because she really consented to sexual activity with the accused and later changed her mind. Some courts have refused to permit the defence to cross-examine the complainant as to the timeliness of her complaint because it evokes the stereotypical response that a woman who has not promptly complained must have consented.[33]

That view, however, has been rejected by the Ontario Court of Appeal.[34] In *H. (J.)*, the Court said that a delayed complaint is different from prior sexual conduct, as it relates to the timing of the disclosure of the very accusations that are before the court. There may be a number of reasons why a complainant has not complained promptly or at all. Although the assumption that all victims of sexual aggression will promptly report the acts against them is stereotypical and flawed, that does not mean that exploring the issue of the timeliness of a complaint should be foreclosed. On the contrary, the timeliness of the complaint should be an issue that both the Crown and the defence can explore. It will be for the trier of fact to determine what to make of the explanation.

If there is no longer any presumption of consent and thus no necessity for the Crown to lead any evidence-in-chief of a complaint, then it would seem to follow that evidence-in-chief of a prior complaint, in the absence of a suggestion by the defence of recent concoction, would breach the rule

---

[33] *James*, 1993 CarswellOnt 123, 24 C.R. (4th) 229, 18 C.R.R. (2d) 128 (Gen. Div.).

[34] *H. (J.)*, 1996 CarswellOnt 2601, 29 O.R. (3d) 740, 108 C.C.C. (3d) 97, 92 O.A.C. 94 (C.A.); additional reasons 1996 CarswellOnt 3663, 29 O.R. (3d) 740 at 751, 110 C.C.C. (3d) 533, 94 O.A.C. 68 (C.A.), *over ruling* James and approving *Ross*, 1996 CarswellOnt 1306, [1996] O.J. No. 1366 (Gen. Div.).

against admitting a prior consistent statement. That reasoning was accepted by Finlayson J.A. in *F. (J.E.)*.[35] There he wrote:

> Now what is the effect of the abrogation of this exception to the rule against past consistent statements? Since the exception was only applicable in sexual offences, and only to the case-in-chief for the Crown, surely the consequences of abrogation must be that evidence of recent complaint by the complainant is no longer admissible as part of the Crown's case when the sexual offences enumerated in the present s. 275 of the Code are alleged. This is a result which was probably not anticipated by the proponents of the abrogation of the rule against recent complaint because it has resulted in the Crown being unable to lead this evidence, where it exists, to show consistency on the part of the complainant and rebut the possible adverse inference . . . that her allegations were true.[36]

However, Mr. Justice Finlayson went on to conclude that evidence of recent complaint could still be admissible in some instances as part of the narrative "in the sense that it advances the story from offence to prosecution". To put it another way, the Crown was entitled to lead evidence that the alleged victim complained to someone that she had been sexually assaulted by the accused in order to show the sequence of events leading up to the charge against the accused, even though that evidence might also infringe the rule against self-serving evidence.

That view was also echoed by Mr. Justice Wood in *Ay*.[37]

> If the full purpose underlying Parliament's abrogation of this particular rule relating to evidence of recent complaint is to be achieved, then evidence of when a complaint was first made, why it was not made at the first available opportunity if that was the case, and what it was that precipitated the complaint eventually made, *must be receivable as part of the narrative*, in order to ensure that the jury have all of the evidence of the complainant's conduct necessary to enable them to draw the right inference with respect to her credibility.[38]

Wood J.A. then went on to summarize what he understood to be the law:

> . . . the fact that a prior complaint was made, when it was made, and why it was or was not made in a timely fashion, are all matters relevant and admissible to establish the conduct of the complainant in a criminal case, from

---

[35] 1993 CarswellOnt 137, 16 O.R. (3d) 1, 85 C.C.C. (3d) 457, 26 C.R. (4th) 220, 67 O.A.C. 251, [1993] O.J. No. 2589 (C.A.); see also *Jones*, 1988 CarswellOnt 84, 44 C.C.C. (3d) 248, 66 C.R. (3d) 54, 29 O.A.C. 219 (C.A.).

[36] *F. (J.E.)*, *ibid.*, at p. 469 [C.C.C.].

[37] 1994 CarswellBC 1112, 93 C.C.C. (3d) 456, 59 B.C.A.C. 161, 98 W.A.C. 161, [1994] B.C.J. No. 2024 (C.A.).

[38] *Ibid.*, at p. 470 [C.C.C.].

which conduct the trier of fact is entitled to draw inferences relative to the credibility of that complainant's evidence. However, the content of any prior statement cannot be used to demonstrate its consistency with, and therefore, the probable truthfulness of, the complainant's evidence at trial, and thus, such content is inadmissible unless relevant for some other purpose such as providing necessary context for other probative evidence.[39]

What Wood J.A. seemed to be saying is that evidence of the fact of a complaint, but not the full particulars of what the complainant said, is still admissible. It is admissible as part of the Crown's case-in-chief to show the sequence of events leading up to the charge against the accused. It is admitted, not as recent complaint, but as part of the narrative of those events. As part of the narrative, only evidence of the fact of the complaint is admissible, not the particulars of that complaint. As part of the narrative, it is admissible to show the credibility of the complainant in the sense that her conduct was credible. However, it cannot be used by the Crown to show that her evidence at trial is consistent with her earlier complaint. In fact, the jury must be instructed to that effect by the trial judge.[40]

Unfortunately, in sexual offences, the credibility of the complainant is usually the central issue and consistency is regarded as a hallmark of credibility. Thus the distinction between use of a prior complaint as part of the narrative for the purpose of assessing her conduct, but not for consistency in her testimony at trial, may be difficult for a jury to grasp. It is difficult to understand how the jury is able to distinguish between conduct and consistency. An instruction less confusing to a jury might focus on the use of the evidence as part of the narrative and avoids any reference to the question of the complainant's credible conduct. In other words, an instruction more consistent with the purpose of the evidence would tell the jury that the prior complaint is only admissible to show the sequence of events that brought this matter to court and not to show consistency in the complainant's testimony.

(e) As Part of the Narrative

At common law, victims of an offence were routinely permitted to give evidence that they complained to the police. Similarly, the police were permitted to say that the victim made a complaint to them about a certain matter and they proceeded to investigate the complaint. Such evidence is tech-

---

[39] *Ibid.*, at p. 471.

[40] *Ay* was followed in *Le*, 2003 CarswellBC 1590, 177 C.C.C. (3d) 300, 16 C.R. (6th) 375 (C.A.) and *Hughes*, 2001 CarswellBC 1284, 156 C.C.C. (3d) 206, 43 C.R. (5th) 325 (C.A.). In *Le*, Hall, J.A., observed that this area of the law is not simple.

nically a prior consistent statement, but is admitted as an exception to the rule, not to show a consistency of conduct, but simply as part of the narrative. To put it another way, it is admitted by the court to show the sequence of events leading up to how the police became involved in the investigation.

In the past, the admission of a complaint by a victim under this exception was not necessarily restricted to a complaint to the police. Nevertheless, where the prior complaint was made to someone other than a police officer, such as a member of the family or a social worker, it was only admitted "if it was so inextricably interwoven with their (the complainant's) evidence that the case could not have been properly presented to the court without admitting this evidence".[41] Allowing a complaint to be admitted simply as part of the sequence of events leading up to the arrest of the accused without the condition that it be "inextricably interwoven" with the complainant's evidence was considered a breach of the general rule prohibiting the admission of a prior consistent statement.

An example of where the evidence was "inextricably interwoven" is *George*.[42] There, a 14-year-old girl complained to her grandmother and her parents that her cousin had sexual intercourse with her without her consent. The cousin was then confronted with the allegation and admitted that it was true and that he was sorry. When the defence suggested to the girl in cross-examination that she had consented but changed her mind overnight, the trial judge permitted the Crown to call her grandmother, the girl's father and a doctor who had examined her, to repeat what she had told them about what had happened.

MacFarlane J.A., who delivered the judgment of the British Columbia Court of Appeal, said that the fact of the complaint, but not the contents, was admissible not to show consistency in conduct, but as part of the narrative. In other words, it was to show the sequence of events beginning with the complaint to the grandmother, who in turn confronted the accused with the allegation. A similar view was expressed by the same Court in *Beliveau*.[43]

However, in *F. (J.E.)*,[44] the complainant, who was 16, testified that her stepfather had sexually assaulted her over a period of three years, commencing when she was nine. The trial judge had permitted the Crown to lead evidence from the complainant and from other witnesses that the com-

---

[41] *Per* Martin J.A. in *Cassibo*, 1982 CarswellOnt 850, 39 O.R. (2d) 288, 70 C.C.C. (2d) 498 (C.A.).

[42] 1985 CarswellBC 714, 23 C.C.C. (3d) 42 (C.A.).

[43] 1986 CarswellBC 665, 30 C.C.C. (3d) 193 (C.A.).

[44] *Supra*, note 35.

plainant had told a number of persons over the years that the accused was hurting her. The complainant was also permitted to testify that after she had left the province and had gone to Saskatchewan, she had told her teacher, a friend at school and a social worker that the accused had sexually assaulted her. The Ontario Court of Appeal said that the statements of abuse made to the school friend and teacher should not have been admitted because they "neither advance nor enlarge upon the narrative." However, the balance of the statements was held to be admissible.

Finlayson J.A. for the Court wrote:

> The story that unfolds in this case is that of a vulnerable child who has been sexually abused, has been physically abused as a disciplinary matter, has seen her mother assaulted by her tormentor, and has been threatened with injury if she complains about the sexual assaults. She had every reason to believe that the appellant would carry out his threats. This explains her early silence. After her mother separated from the appellant and she returned to the west and her father, we have her account of how she had trouble dealing with the knowledge of what she had been subjected to and had difficulty in discussing the matter with her father from whom she had been estranged. With a proper limiting instruction to the jury, I think that this evidence was properly admissible as part of the unfolding of events from the alleged offences to the inception of this prosecution.[45]

Apparently, Mr. Justice Finlayson did not feel that it was necessary that the complaint be "inextricably interwoven" with the events leading up to the arrest of the accused. All that was necessary was that the complaint be "part of the unfolding of events from the alleged offences to the inception of this prosecution".

Similarly, in *F. (H.P.)*,[46] evidence of a written complaint of sexual abuse given by an 11-year-old complainant to her mother two weeks after the alleged offence was admitted as part of the narrative, even though the formal complaint to the police was not lodged until 18 months later. The accused was the 33-year-old common law husband of the complainant's mother. Both the complainant and her mother were permitted by the trial judge to testify that, two weeks after the alleged offence, the complainant had given her mother a written complaint of the sexual abuse. Gibbs J.A., for the British Columbia Court of Appeal, held that the evidence was properly admitted as part of the narrative.

As in the case of the other exceptions to the rule against prior consistent statements, the trial judge is required to explain to the jury about the limited

---

[45] *Ibid.*, at p. 475 [C.C.C.].
[46] 1995 CarswellBC 90, 39 C.R. (4th) 80, 59 B.C.A.C. 24, 98 W.A.C. 24, [1995] B.C.J. No. 831 (C.A.).

value of the evidence. Arguably, if the evidence is admitted simply "to show the sequence of events leading up to how the police became involved in the investigation", then the judge's charge to the jury should be limited to that instruction, with an added instruction that it may not be used by the jury as evidence of the consistency of the complainant's testimony. However, in *F. (J.E.)*,[47] Finlayson J.A. noted that the trial judge was obliged to instruct the jury as to the limited value of the evidence and then, surprisingly, went on to add:

> The fact that the statement was made is admissible to assist the jury as to the sequence of events from the alleged offence to the prosecution *so that they can understand the conduct of the complainant and assess her truthfulness.*[48]

As already noted, Wood J.A. expressed the same view in *Ay*,[49]

The rule drawn from *F. (J.E.)* and *Ay* seems to be that although the *content* of any statement made by the complainant to the witnesses may not be used to demonstrate its consistency with, and therefore the truthfulness of the complainant's evidence at trial, the jury are entitled to look at the *fact* that the statement was made to draw inferences relative to the credibility of the complainant. However, the distinction between a permitted use of the fact of a complaint to show credibility but not the *content* of the complaint may be difficult for the jury to grasp. As one legal scholar has written, "surely, the trier must appreciate the contents of the complaint for the complaint to have any meaning".[50]

(f) Answers of an Accused When Taxed with the Situation

If the reason for excluding a prior consistent statement of an accused is to prevent the accused from manufacturing or inventing a defence, one might ask why a statement by an accused when taxed with the situation either by a policeman or someone else is not admissible, if it is made spontaneously and without time for reflection? In England, such an exception to the rule has been recognized and is not limited to a statement made on the first encounter with the police.[51]

---

[47] *Supra*, note 35.

[48] *Ibid.*, at p. 241 [C.R.].

[49] *Supra*, note 37, at p. 470 [C.C.C.]. See also *Hughes*, 2001 CarswellBC 1284, 156 C.C.C. (3d) 206, 43 C.R. (5th) 325 (C.A.).

[50] Professor Ron Delisle 43 C.R. (5th) 351 at p. 352.

[51] *Pearce* (1979), 69 Cr. App. R. 365 (Eng. C.A.).

The rationale underlying this exception was discussed in *McCarthy*.[52]
There the accused, charged with robbery, was arrested three days after the
offence and questioned by the police. He denied the charge and gave details
of an alibi orally and in writing. The trial judge refused to admit the statement. In holding that the trial judge had erred, the English Court of Appeal
wrote:

> One of the best pieces of evidence that an innocent man can produce is his
> reaction to an accusation of a crime. If he has been told, as the appellant
> was told, that he was suspected of having committed a particular crime at a
> particular time and place and says at once, "That cannot be right, because I
> was elsewhere" and gives details of where he was, that is something which
> the jury can take into account.[53]

Admissibility of a statement under this exception will usually depend
upon whether the statement was given spontaneously or after "careful reflection". A good example of the distinction is another English case,
Tooke.[54] There, the accused was charged with unlawful wounding. He had
been involved in an altercation in the lavatory of a public house during
which he and the victim were injured. The bar manager gave evidence that,
immediately after the incident, the two men blamed each other. The accused
then went voluntarily to the police station and made a statement setting out
his version of the events. The bar manager had been permitted to tell the
court what the accused had said, but the trial judge had refused to allow
defence counsel to elicit from the officer what the accused had said at the
police station. The English Court of Appeal said that his ruling was correct.
The statement to the bar manager was spontaneous and showed the accused's reaction shortly after the incident. Although the statement at the
police station was also spontaneous, it would add nothing to his reaction to
the suggestion that he had committed the assault. Lord Chief Justice Lane,
delivering the judgment of the Court, laid down a threefold test for admissibility — spontaneity, relevance and whether the statement which is sought
to be admitted added any weight to the other testimony which had been
given in the case.

Until the decision of the Ontario Court of Appeal in *Edgar*,[55] Canadian
courts were generally reluctant to recognize such an exception unless it

---

[52] *McCarthy* (1980), 71 Cr. App. R. 142 (Eng. C.A.).

[53] *Ibid.*, at p. 145.

[54] (1990), 90 Cr. App. R. 417 (Eng. C.A.).

[55] 2010 ONCA 529, 2010 CarswellOnt 5380, 260 C.C.C. (3d) 1, 78 C.R. (6th) 106;
leave to appeal refused 2011 CarswellOnt 2153, 2011 CarswellOnt 2154
(S.C.C.).

formed part of the *res gestae*. Although in *Lucas*,[56] Chief Justice Kerwin of the Supreme Court of Canada had no difficulty in accepting that "it was open to the defence to obtain evidence from the appellant to the effect that he had made a statement to the police, following his arrest, which was similar to the evidence which he had given at trial",[57] in *Pappin*,[58] Chief Justice Gale of the Ontario Court of Appeal was of the view that the trial judge was correct in refusing to permit the accused to testify concerning statements made by him to the police at the police station after his arrest, as to his knowledge of what was in a package taken from him, because the statements were self-serving. Similarly, in *Keeler*,[59] the Alberta Court of Appeal refused to acknowledge that such an exception to the rule against admitting a prior consistent statement existed unless it was part of the *res gestae*.

However, in *Edgar*,[60] the Ontario Court of Appeal finally accepted that there was a limited exception to the rule. There the accused, who was charged with the stabbing and murder of his girlfriend, had made three statements to the police shortly after his arrest and later during the morning. The first two statements were partially exculpatory, but largely aberrant and incoherent. The third statement made about four hours after his arrest was coherent and entirely exculpatory. At his first trial, the trial judge excluded all three statements. On appeal from his conviction, the accused took the position that the edited versions of the first two statements containing aberrant utterances about bikers and police trying to kill him were relevant to the issue of his state of mind and capacity to form a criminal intent. The accused also argued that the third statement was admissible to rebut the Crown's allegation of recent fabrication. The Court of Appeal accepted the first submission and ruled that the edited portions of the first two statements bearing upon the appellant's state of mind were properly admissible as an exception to the rule against the admissibility of prior consistent statements. It rejected the second argument on the ground that the Crown had not alleged recent fabrication. At his second trial, the accused urged the trial judge to admit all three of his post-arrest statements in their entirety. The trial judge refused to do so and admitted only the edited versions of the

---

[56] (1962), 1962 CarswellOnt 26, [1963] 1 C.C.C. 1, 39 C.R. 101 (S.C.C.).

[57] *Ibid.*, at pp. 10-11 [C.C.C.].

[58] 1970 CarswellOnt 34, 12 C.R.N.S. 287 (C.A.).

[59] 1977 CarswellAlta 230, 4 A.R. 449, 36 C.C.C. (2d) 8, [1977] 5 W.W.R. 410 (C.A.).

[60] 2010 ONCA 529, 2010 CarswellOnt 5380, 260 C.C.C. (3d) 1, 78 C.R. (6th) 106; leave to appeal refused 2011 CarswellOnt 2153, 2011 CarswellOnt 2154 (S.C.C.).

statements found to be admissible by the Court of Appeal from the first trial.

On appeal of his conviction on the second trial, it was submitted that the time had come to reassess the general exclusion of an accused person's post-arrest exculpatory utterances as prior consistent statements. It was argued that under certain conditions, prior consistent statements of an accused person do have probative value and therefore should not be excluded. The Court agreed holding that the spontaneous exculpatory statements made by an accused person upon or shortly after arrest may be admitted as an exception to the general rule excluding prior consistent statements for the purpose of showing the reaction of the accused when first confronted with the accusation and as proof of consistency, *provided the accused testifies and thereby exposes him or herself to cross-examination.* However, the accused had asked the trial judge to rule that he should be allowed to adduce evidence of the prior consistent statements before taking the stand, on the basis of defence counsel's undertaking to call the appellant as a witness in his own defence. It was held that the trial judge did not err in refusing to so rule at that point in the trial. Since the issue of admissibility was not revisited by defence counsel after the accused took the stand, and the probative value of the statement was low, there was no reasonable possibility that a different verdict would have ensued and the appeal was dismissed.

Sharpe J.A. delivering the judgment of the Court noted, in a thoughtful judgment, that Lawton L.J. in *McCarthy* had held that such a statement should be admitted *even where the accused does not testify* but had added,[61] that in that event, the trial judge "is entitled to invite the jury's attention to the failure in direct terms, provided of course that he does not suggest that the failure amounts to any evidence upon which the prosecution can rely".[62] But Sharpe J.A. was not prepared to go that far. He also reaffirmed that the statement of the accused was not strictly evidence of the truth of what was said (subject to being admissible under the principled approach to hearsay evidence) but was evidence of the reaction of the accused, which is relevant to the credibility of the accused and as circumstantial evidence that may have a bearing on guilt or innocence.

Although there appears to be a close connection between an exception to the rule based on "answers given by an accused as part of the *res gestae*" and "answers given by an accused when taxed with the situation", the distinction appears to be only in the language used. Both exceptions restrict admissibility to the situation where the accused has not had time to reflect

---

[61] *Edgar, ibid.,* at para. 146.

[62] *Ibid.*

upon an explanation. However, Canadian courts have only allowed an exception to the rule where the statement has been a spontaneous reaction by the accused, made contemporaneously with discovery by the police of incriminating evidence in the accused's possession. English courts, on the other hand, have not always applied such a strict test, permitting the admission of a statement made by the accused when questioned by a police officer, provided that it is a spontaneous response to the officer's inquiry.[63]

(g) Where the Allegations may Provide Important Context for Assessing Credibility

More recently, the Supreme Court has said that although a prior inconsistent statement cannot be used to confirm credibility, it may be used if a complainant has difficulty situating events in time, is easily confused, and lies on occasion. In *Dinardo*,[64] a mildly mentally challenged complainant alleged that she had been assaulted by the accused while a passenger in his taxi. Although in her evidence at trial, she provided essentially consistent answers on the central parts of her allegations, she gave contradictory answers on many points, much as she had done on her *voir dire* testimony to determine whether she was competent to testify. She also gave conflicting testimony about inventing the allegations. The accused had testified and denied the allegations. In convicting the accused, the trial judge had held that the complainant's evidence at trial was corroborated by her out-of-court statements made shortly after the alleged incident. The Supreme Court ordered a new trial on the basis that the trial judge had erred by failing to explain how he reconciled the inconsistencies in the complainant's testimony, particularly, on the issue of whether she had invented the allegations.

The Court, however, went on to deal with the admissibility of a prior inconsistent statement. It reaffirmed that prior inconsistent statements cannot be used to confirm in-court testimony. It agreed that when a prior inconsistent statement is admitted as part of the narrative, the statements may be used for the limited purpose of helping the trier of fact to understand how the complainant's story was initially disclosed. It also accepted that the challenge is to distinguish between "using narrative evidence for the impermissible purpose of 'confirm[ing] the truthfulness of the sworn allegation'" and "using narrative evidence for the permissible purpose of showing the fact and timing of a complaint, which may then *assist the trier of fact in the*

---

[63] *Storey* (1968), 52 Cr. App. R. 334, 112 Sol. Jo. 417 (Eng. C.A.) *per* Widgery C.J at pp. 337-38 [Cr. App. R.].

[64] 2008 CarswellQue 3451, 2008 CarswellQue 3452, 231 C.C.C. (3d) 177, 57 C.R. (6th) 48 (S.C.C.),

assessment of truthfulness or credibility" However, relying upon a decision of the Ontario Court of Appeal in *C. (G.)*,[65] it was held that prior consistent statements of a complainant may assist the court *in assessing the complainant's likely truthfulness*, particularly in cases involving allegations of sexual assault against children. Its rationale was that the spontaneous nature of the initial complaint and the complainant's repetition of the essential elements of the allegations may provide important context for assessing her credibility.

Has the Supreme Court created a new exception or has it merely extended the narrative exception to allow a prior consistent complaint to be used to assess the credibility of children or persons who are mentally challenged? It is unfortunate that the Court did not go on to explain its rationale for the exception, only that it was relying upon the Ontario Court of Appeal.

---

[65] 2006 CarswellOnt 3413, *(sub nom. R. v. G.C.)* [2006] O.J. No. 2245 (C.A.).

5
CHARACTER EVIDENCE

1. THE RULE

One of the most important rules of evidence is that the prosecution is generally not allowed to lead evidence of an accused's bad character or previous convictions to show that he or she probably committed the offence charged. An exception to that rule is section 360 of the *Criminal Code*.[1] It contains an unusual provision that allows the Crown, in prosecutions for possession of stolen property or stolen mail, to introduce evidence of an accused's prior convictions for theft or possession of stolen property within the previous five years for the purpose of proving that he or she knew that the property was unlawfully obtained.

The general rule excluding evidence of the accused's bad character is unique to the common law system of criminal justice. In many countries

---

[1] R.S.C. 1985, c. C-46.

with a civil law system, evidence of an accused's character is not only admissible, it is the first to be adduced at trial. It is believed that a person's previous history and conduct are relevant to the issue of whether he or she may be guilty of the charge the person is now facing.

In *B. (F.F.)*[2] Chief Justice Lamer summarized the potential harmful effects of leading evidence of the character of the accused:

> . . . there are three possible effects of such evidence upon a jury; first, the jury may convict based on propensity; second, the jury might convict to punish for past acts; and third, the jury might become confused and substitute a verdict with respect to the past acts for a verdict on the charges in issue.

Arguably, there is a great deal of merit in that view. As a matter of common sense, people usually take into account the history and character of someone with whom they are dealing. The common law, however, has historically rejected the view that the disposition of a person is relevant to his or her guilt. The common law rule does not purport to be based on common sense, but rather on a number of policy considerations. The first consideration is one of fairness. It is obviously fairer to compel the prosecution to try a person on the facts of the particular case than on that person's whole life. The second is that it allows the trier to focus on the particular issues to be proved, rather than be sidetracked by what the accused may have done on other occasions. There is always the risk, particularly in trials by jury where jurors have no legal training or experience, that the jury may be unduly influenced by the accused's previous conduct. The jury may conclude that because of the accused's previous criminal habits, he or she is probably guilty of the offence. As one judge said almost 150 years ago:

> The evidence is relevant to the issue, but is excluded for reasons of policy and humanity; because although by admitting it you may arrive at justice in one case out of a hundred, you would probably do injustice in the other ninety-nine.[3]

The general rule prohibiting evidence of an accused's bad character was stated by Lord Herschell L.C. in *Makin v. Attorney General for New South Wales*:

> It is undoubtedly not competent for the prosecution to adduce evidence tending to show that the accused has been guilty of criminal acts other than those covered by the indictment, for the purpose of leading to the conclusion that the accused is a person likely from his criminal conduct or charac-

---

[2] 1993 CarswellNS 271, 1993 CarswellNS 13, [1993] 1 S.C.R. 697, 79 C.C.C. (3d) 112, 18 C.R. (4th) 261 at p. 708 [S.C.R.].

[3] *Rowton* (1865), L.& C. 520, *per* Willes J., at p. 541.

ter to have committed the offence for which he is being tried. On the other hand, the mere fact that the evidence adduced tends to show the commission of other crimes does not render it inadmissible if it be relevant to an issue before the jury, and it may be so relevant if it bears upon the question whether the acts alleged to constitute the crime charged in the indictment were designed or accidental, or to rebut a defence which would otherwise be open to the accused. The statement of these general principles is easy, but it is obvious that it may often be very difficult to draw the line and to decide whether a particular piece of evidence is on one side or the other.[4]

However, as Lord Herschell also pointed out, the court will not automatically exclude evidence of the accused's bad character, even though it may show the accused's disposition or propensity to commit the offence, if the evidence is also relevant to an issue at trial. For example, in *Lepage*,[5] three persons were living in a house in which drugs were found. At issue was which of them was in possession of the drugs. The Supreme Court of Canada could find nothing wrong with the trial judge allowing one of three persons to testify that the drugs were not his and that the accused was in the business of dealing in drugs, so that the inference could be drawn that it was more likely that the accused was the owner of the drugs. Such evidence was admissible against the accused, even though incidentally it was evidence of the accused's propensity to traffic in narcotics.

Evidence of the accused's bad character has also been held to be admissible where it is necessary to the development of Crown's case or provides background. For example, in *Lamirande*,[6] the accused was charged with and convicted of manslaughter and robbery. Documents seized from the accused that demonstrated her connection to the robbery and other accused who were members of a gang were admitted by the trial judge to make the narrative easier to understand. On appeal, it was held that the evidence was properly admitted. Moreover, the judge's charge to the jury that the evidence could only be used as background and narrative, and not for any other purpose, was adequate.

The policy rule prohibiting evidence of the accused's bad character, however, has no application where a co-accused seeks to lead evidence of an

---

[4] (1893), [1894] A.C. 57, [1891–94] All E.R. Rep. 24, 17 Cox C.C. 704, 58 J.P. 148, 63 L.J.P.C. 41, 69 L.T. 778, 6 R. 373, 10 T.L.R. 155 (New South Wales P.C.) at p. 65 [A.C.].

[5] 1995 CarswellOnt 3, 1995 CarswellOnt 517, [1995] 1 S.C.R. 654, 95 C.C.C. (3d) 385, 36 C.R. (4th) 145, 178 N.R. 81, 79 O.A.C. 191.

[6] 2002 CarswellMan 151, 164 C.C.C. (3d) 299 (C.A.); leave to appeal refused 2003 CarswellMan 21, 2003 CarswellMan 22 (S.C.C.); leave to appeal refused 2003 CarswellMan 19, 2003 CarswellMan 20 (S.C.C.).

accused's propensity for violence in order to show that it was more likely that it was the accused, not he, who committed the offence.[7] Even in such instance, the trial judge is required to minimize the prejudice to the accused by explaining to the jury in clear terms the reason why the evidence has been permitted.

The rule prohibiting bad character evidence of an accused does not necessarily apply in the case of an ordinary witness. The reason is that there is no danger of a wrongful conviction.[8] So long as it is relevant and not excluded by a rule of evidence, evidence of the bad character of a Crown witness can be adduced by the defence even if it only refers to one event.[9]

There are four well-established exceptions to the rule.

2. EXCEPTIONS TO THE RULE

(a) When the Accused Puts His or Her Character in Issue

Although the rule is that the Crown may not adduce evidence of the character of the accused, that rule applies only to the prosecution. An accused is always entitled to introduce evidence of his or her good character. Indeed, the fact that the accused may have lived a good and honest life to date may be the only defence that the accused has to the offence charged. Evidence of good character may be considered by the trier in determining the credibility of the accused and whether the accused is the kind of person who would likely have committed the offence.[10]

On the other hand, the weight that the courts attach to evidence of good character will usually depend upon the nature of the offence and the age of the victim. For example, in a case involving the sexual assault of children, evidence of good character will not, as a matter of common sense, have very much weight. Since sexual misconduct upon young children usually occurs in private, it will not be reflected in the reputation of a person in the

---

[7] *Valentini*, 1999 CarswellOnt 271, 43 O.R. (3d) 178, 132 C.C.C. (3d) 262, 118 O.A.C. 1, [1999] O.J. No. 251 (C.A.).

[8] *Arcangioli*, 1994 CarswellOnt 1151, 1994 CarswellOnt 51, [1994] 1 S.C.R. 129, 87 C.C.C. (3d) 289, 27 C.R. (4th) 1.

[9] *Kendall*, 1987 CarswellOnt 93, 35 C.C.C. (3d) 105, 57 C.R. (3d) 249 (C.A.).

[10] *McMillan*, 1975 CarswellOnt 7, 7 O.R. (2d) 750, 23 C.C.C. (2d) 160, 29 C.R.N.S. 191 (C.A.); affirmed 1977 CarswellOnt 474, 1977 CarswellOnt 474F, [1977] 2 S.C.R. 824, 33 C.C.C. (2d) 360, 73 D.L.R. (3d) 759, 15 N.R. 20; *Molnar*, 1990 CarswellOnt 91, 55 C.C.C. (3d) 446, 76 C.R. (3d) 125, 38 O.A.C. 62, [1990] O.J. No. 339 (C.A.).

community.[11] Yet, even in cases of sexual misconduct involving children, trial judges are required to tell the jury that they must not ignore character evidence altogether; it is simply not entitled to the same weight as it would have with other offences.[12]

An accused may lead evidence of character in one of three ways. The first is by leading evidence of good character through the cross-examination of Crown witnesses. The second is by going into the witness stand and testifying, not only that he or she did not commit the crime, but that he or she is not *the kind of person* who would commit such a crime. For example, in *Farrant*,[13] where the charge was second degree murder, the accused, during examination-in-chief testified, "It's not my character to be violent, you know, use violence or a rifle, you know, to get my own way. That's not my character". It was held by Dickson J. that the accused had put his non-violent character in issue.

On the other hand, the accused's mere denial of guilt and repudiation of the allegations against him or her alone or by giving an explanation on matters which are essential to his defence will not amount to placing his character in issue.[14] Nor do introductory routine questions as to education, marital status and religious affiliation have the effect of putting the accused's character in issue.[15] Similarly, an admission by the accused in his evidence in-chief that he has a criminal record is not an assertion of good character, although having brought out his record, it is the fair subject of cross-examination.[16]

---

[11] *Profit*, 1993 CarswellOnt 993, 1993 CarswellOnt 126, [1993] 3 S.C.R. 637, 15 O.R. (3d) 803, 85 C.C.C. (3d) 232 at 248, 24 C.R. (4th) 279, 159 N.R. 395, 68 O.A.C. 37.

[12] *Norman*, 1993 CarswellOnt 140, 16 O.R. (3d) 295, 87 C.C.C. (3d) 153, 26 C.R. (4th) 256, 68 O.A.C. 22, [1993] O.J. No. 2802 (C.A.).

[13] 1983 CarswellSask 132, 1983 CarswellSask 235, [1983] 1 S.C.R. 124, 4 C.C.C. (3d) 354, 32 C.R. (3d) 289, 147 D.L.R. (3d) 511, [1983] 3 W.W.R. 171, 46 N.R. 337, 21 Sask. R. 271.

[14] *Shortreed*, 1990 CarswellOnt 83, 54 C.C.C. (3d) 292, 75 C.R. (3d) 306, 37 O.A.C. 144 (C.A.).

[15] *McNamara (No. 1)*, 1981 CarswellOnt 1243, 56 C.C.C. (2d) 193 (C.A.); leave to appeal refused [1981] 1 S.C.R. xi; affirmed 1985 CarswellOnt 939, 1985 CarswellOnt 96, (sub nom. *R. v. Canadian Dredge & Dock Co.)* [1985] 1 S.C.R. 662, 19 C.C.C. (3d) 1, 45 C.R. (3d) 289, 19 D.L.R. (4th) 314, 59 N.R. 241, 9 O.A.C. 321.

[16] *Bricker*, 1994 CarswellOnt 921, 90 C.C.C. (3d) 268, 71 O.A.C. 383 (C.A.); leave to appeal refused (1994), 92 C.C.C. (3d) vi (note), 180 N.R. 399 (note), 82 O.A.C. 400 (note).

It should also be stressed that the evidence of good character must come from the accused while giving testimony. The Crown is not permitted to lead evidence of out-of-court statements of good character made by the accused to the police and then argue that the accused has put his or her character in issue.[17]

Finally, the accused may put character in issue by calling witnesses to attest to that good character. The Crown, however, is not entitled by clever cross-examination of the accused or a witness called by the defence to claim that the accused has put his or her character in issue. For example, in *A. (W.A.)*,[18] the accused's wife was asked by the Crown why she supported the accused and she replied, "because I know my husband". In the circumstances in which that response was elicited, it would have been clearly unfair to allow the Crown to lead evidence of the accused's bad character. It was held by the Manitoba Court of Appeal that the character of an accused is not put in issue where a witness for defence gives evidence of character during cross-examination by Crown counsel. The Court said that evidence of defence witnesses can only put the accused's character in issue through examination-in-chief. In this latter respect, the Court probably went a little too far. It would hardly be fair to the Crown if a defence witness gratuitously volunteered evidence of the accused's good character during cross-examination, precluding the Crown from leading evidence of the accused's bad character.

Where witnesses are called by the accused to attest to the accused's good character, the witnesses are not allowed to give their personal opinion of the accused's good character. Nor are they permitted to point out specific incidents of good character or citizenship, such as the fact that the accused may have saved the life of a child or returned a wallet found in the street (although this rule is not always strictly enforced). The rule is that a character witness for an accused can only swear to the general reputation of the accused in the community and not give his or her personal opinion. In this respect, the courts have not confined the "community" to the actual community where the accused lives. In *Levasseur*,[19] the Alberta Court of Appeal said that evidence of the accused's reputation in the business commu-

---

[17] *Wilson*, 1999 CarswellMan 243, 136 C.C.C. (3d) 252, [1999] 10 W.W.R. 334, 138 Man. R. (2d) 139, 202 W.A.C. 139 (C.A.); leave to appeal refused (1999), 139 C.C.C. (3d) vi (note), 148 Man. R. (2d) 158 (note), 252 N.R. 193 (note), 224 W.A.C. 158 (note).

[18] (1996), 1996 CarswellMan 535, 112 C.C.C. (3d) 83, 3 C.R. (5th) 388, [1997] 2 W.W.R. 305, 113 Man. R. (2d) 153, 131 W.A.C. 153 (C.A.).

[19] 1987 CarswellAlta 75, 77 A.R. 241, 51 Alta. L.R. (2d) 226, 35 C.C.C. (3d) 136, 56 C.R. (3d) 335 (C.A.).

nity is admissible because it reflects the modern metropolitan reality in which frequently not even neighbours' names are known let alone their general reputation.

Evidence of a person's character is generally handled in the following manner. The witness will be asked whether he or she knows the accused's reputation for honesty (where the crime is one of dishonesty) or peacefulness (where the crime is one of violence), *etc.*, in the community. If the witness answers in the affirmative, the witness will then be asked, "What is that reputation?" and the witness will be allowed to give evidence of the community's view.

Once the accused calls evidence of his or her good character, that character is put in issue. In such instance, it is considered only fair that the prosecution be allowed the right to answer that evidence by calling evidence of the accused's bad character. Evidence of the accused's bad character must be led in the same way, that is, by witnesses who disagree with the witnesses for the accused and who testify as to the accused's bad reputation in the community. The Crown is not permitted to lead evidence of specific acts of bad conduct, unless it is of acts that would also constitute evidence of similar facts. (See (d) "When the Evidence is of Similar Facts", *post*). The Crown is limited to leading evidence of general reputation.[20] Section 666 of the *Criminal Code* also gives the Crown the right to call evidence of the accused's bad character by introducing evidence of the accused's previous convictions for offences. Section 667 of the *Code* sets out the method by which such previous convictions may be proved. If the accused gives evidence in his defence, he or she may also be cross-examined with respect to specific acts of previous misconduct or previous convictions (see (c) "When the Accused Testifies", *post*).

Although the general rule is that the cross-examination of an accused on a prior criminal record is restricted to the nature of the offence, the date and place of the conviction and the penalty imposed, the same restrictions do not apply where the accused puts his character in issue.[21] If the accused puts his character in issue, the Crown is entitled to cross-examine the accused on prior acts of discreditable conduct, including details of prior con-

---

[20] *Brown*, 1999 CarswellOnt 2443, 137 C.C.C. (3d) 400, 27 C.R. (5th) 151, 177 D.L.R. (4th) 170, 123 O.A.C. 258, [1999] O.J. No. 2983 (C.A.).

[21] *W. (L.K.)*, 1999 CarswellOnt 3014, 138 C.C.C. (3d) 449, 126 O.A.C. 39 (C.A.); leave to appeal refused 2000 CarswellOnt 4252, 2000 CarswellOnt 4253, 264 N.R. 393 (note) (S.C.C.).

victions,[22] subject to the right of the trial judge to exclude such evidence where its prejudicial effect outweighs its probative value.

Finally, it should be noted that where the Crown is permitted to adduce evidence of an accused's bad character to rebut evidence of good character and that evidence does not constitute similar fact evidence, the jury must be instructed that the reply evidence can only be used to neutralize the evidence of good character and to assess the accused's credibility. It must not be used as affirmative evidence of the accused's disposition to commit the offence charged.[23]

(b) Where the Accused Puts the Victim's or a Third Party's Character in Issue

The general rule is that a victim's character is not admissible on the issue of whether the accused committed the offence. Even bad people are entitled to protection from having crimes committed against them. However, there may be instances where the character of the victim is relevant to the defence of the accused. For example, if the accused is charged with a crime of violence, such as murder, manslaughter or assault and claims self-defence, the victim's disposition for violence may be relevant to the issue of who was the aggressor.[24] Similarly, if the defence says that it was not the accused who committed the offence, but his or her co-accused or a third party, evidence of the co-accused or third party's character for violence would have probative value provided that the co-accused or third party had the propensity to commit the type of act in question and was connected with the circumstances surrounding the charge.[25] Evidence of a co-accused or third party's character or violent disposition has been held to be admissible even if it refers only to one event.[26]

The admissibility of the deceased's or the victim's disposition for violence is not restricted only to those instances where the accused claims that

---

[22] *McNamara (No. 1)*, *supra*, note 15; *Farrant*, 1983 CarswellSask 132, 1983 CarswellSask 235, [1983] 1 S.C.R. 124, 4 C.C.C. (3d) 354, 32 C.R. (3d) 289, 147 D.L.R. (3d) 511, [1983] 3 W.W.R. 171, 46 N.R. 337, 21 Sask. R. 271.

[23] *Brown*, *supra*, note 20.

[24] *Scopelliti*, 1981 CarswellOnt 814, 34 O.R. (2d) 524, 63 C.C.C. (2d) 481 (C.A.).

[25] *Arcangioli*, 1994 CarswellOnt 1151, 1994 CarswellOnt 51, [1994] 1 S.C.R. 129, 87 C.C.C. (3d) 289, 27 C.R. (4th) 1, 111 D.L.R. (4th) 48, 162 N.R. 280, 69 O.A.C. 26.

[26] *Yaeck*, 1991 CarswellOnt 65, 6 O.R. (3d) 293, 68 C.C.C. (3d) 545, 10 C.R. (4th) 1, 50 O.A.C. 29 (C.A.) at p. 563 [C.C.C.], ; leave to appeal refused [1992] 1 S.C.R. xii, 71 C.C.C. (3d) vii, 139 N.R. 240n.

he or she acted in self-defence. It may, in some instances, be led where the defence advanced is accident. For example, in *Sims*,[27] the defence was that the deceased was killed when he lunged at the accused with a knife during an altercation and was accidently stabbed by the accused during a struggle to prevent the deceased from using the knife. It was held that evidence of the deceased's disposition for violence was admissible because, if accepted by the jury, it tended to support the accused's evidence that it was the deceased who produced the knife and attacked him.

Evidence of the victim's disposition for violence may be elicited through the cross-examination of Crown witnesses or by the defence calling evidence of the victim's general reputation in the community for violence. In such instance, it is only fair that the prosecution be allowed, by way of reply, to establish that the accused also has a propensity for violence and that it was he, not the victim, who was the aggressor. The prosecution is also entitled to lead reputation evidence by way of reply as to the peaceable disposition of the victim or the third party. The Crown, however, is not entitled to lead such evidence in chief in anticipation of the defence. The Crown must wait until the defence first leads evidence of the violent disposition of the victim or the third party.[28]

Evidence of the disposition of a co-accused for violence will not automatically be admissible. In deciding whether to admit evidence of a co-accused's disposition for violence on behalf of one accused, the trial judge is required to balance the fair rights of the two accused. Where the Crown seeks to adduce character evidence of an accused, the Crown must establish that its probative value outweighs its prejudicial value. The balancing is different where one accused seeks to introduce character evidence of a co-accused. Here, the power to exclude relevant evidence is substantially narrower. The rule is that the evidence is admissible unless its prejudicial effect *substantially* outweighs its probative value.[29] If the trial judge con-

---

[27] 1994 CarswellBC 574, 87 C.C.C. (3d) 402, 28 C.R. (4th) 231 (C.A.).

[28] *Dejong*, 1998 CarswellBC 1208, 125 C.C.C. (3d) 302, 16 C.R. (5th) 372, 108 B.C.A.C. 126, 176 W.A.C. 126 (C.A.). But see *K. (H.W.)*, 2000 BCCA 209, 2000 CarswellBC 661, 32 C.R. (5th) 359; leave to appeal refused 2000 CarswellBC 2173, 2000 CarswellBC 2174, 263 N.R. 396 (note) (S.C.C.), a murder case, where it was held that the trial judge did not err in permitting the Crown to lead evidence-in-chief regarding the absence of paedophilic propensities of the deceased, where the defence was that the accused said that "he lost it" after the deceased expressed paedophilic intentions towards his son.

[29] *Pollock*, 2004 CarswellOnt 2576, 187 C.C.C. (3d) 213, 23 C.R. (6th) 98 (C.A.); leave to appeal refused 2005 CarswellOnt 276, 2005 CarswellOnt 277 (S.C.C.); leave to appeal refused 2005 CarswellOnt 278, 2005 CarswellOnt 279 (S.C.C.).

cludes that a fair balance cannot be struck within the confines of a single trial, it may be necessary to order a severance of the trial.

Courts have been generally reluctant to permit the Crown to lead evidence in-chief of the victim's peaceable disposition in the absence of an attack by the defence on the victim's general character for violence. This has raised the question of whether the Crown should be entitled to introduce evidence of the victim's peaceful disposition where the defence raised is one of self-defence. Since self-defence by necessary implication involves an allegation that the victim was the aggressor, it would seem to follow, logically, that the Crown should be entitled to lead evidence of the victim's peaceful disposition. Indeed, that was the opinion expressed in the "Report of the Federal/Provincial Task Force on Uniform Rules of Evidence" (1982). The Report noted:

> In homicide cases the victim will not be there to deny it, and reputation evidence as to his peaceable nature is therefore an important factor in determining what weight to be given to the evidence of the accused.[30]

Courts, however, have not been prepared to lay down a clear rule dealing with the evidence of the peaceful disposition of a victim. Rather, the preferred rule has been to deal with the issue on a case-by-case basis, assessing the relevance of the disposition evidence to the issues raised.[31] As Rowles J.A. observed in *Dejong*:

> Having an inflexible rule governing the admissibility of such evidence would eliminate the discretion to excluded evidence where its probative value is outweighed by its prejudicial value.[32]

In England, the accused is protected from questions about his previous criminal convictions or questions tending to show previous bad character unless he puts his own character in issue or attacks the character of the Crown witnesses. The English rule is essentially a "tit-for-tat" rule. So long as the defence does not attack the prosecution, the prosecution is not entitled to attack the defence. This rule is contained in the *Criminal Evidence Act of 1898*.

Canada has no similar provision. A suggestion by the defence that a Crown witness may not be telling the truth does not give the prosecution, under Canadian law, the right to attack the accused by leading evidence of bad character. As already noted, the only recognized exception arises where

---

[30] At p. 91.

[31] *Soares*, 1987 CarswellOnt 1058, 34 C.C.C. (3d) 403, 19 O.A.C. 97 (C.A.); *Diu*, 2000 CarswellOnt 1727, 49 O.R. (3d) 40, 144 C.C.C. (3d) 481, 33 C.R. (5th) 203, 133 O.A.C. 201, [2000] O.J. No. 1770 (C.A.).

[32] *Supra*, note 28 at p. 323 [C.C.C.].

the defence is one of self-defence, and possibly accident.[33] Here the Crown is only allowed to call evidence of the accused's disposition for violence by way of reply to the defence's suggestion that it was the victim who was the aggressor.

(c) When the Accused Testifies

At common law, an accused was not allowed to give evidence in his or her defence. This rule was based on the civil practice that prohibited persons from testifying in a case that affected their interest. In Canada, the right of an accused to testify on his or her own behalf was first recognized in 1886 with respect to some offences, and later in 1893 by the *Canada Evidence Act*[34] with respect to all offences. Sections 3 and 4(1) of the *Canada Evidence Act*[35] provide that:

> 3. A person is not incompetent to give evidence by reason of interest or crime.

> 4. (1) Every person charged with an offence and, except as otherwise provided in this section, the wife or husband, as the case may be, of the person so charged, is a competent witness for the defence whether the person so charged is charged solely or jointly with any other person.

This means that although an accused has the right to give evidence on his or her own behalf, the accused cannot be forced to go into the witness box if he or she does not wish to do so. Nor can an accused be forced to do so by a co-accused where they are jointly charged. However, once an accused chooses to testify on his or her own behalf, the accused is in the same position as any other witness. Whenever an accused testifies, he or she puts themselves forward as a credible person and asks the jury to take their word. The accused's credibility becomes relevant to the truth and accuracy of the testimony. An accused's credibility is thus subject to attack by cross-examination, as any other witness's credibility would be.

Nevertheless, it has been recognized that the right of the Crown to attack the credibility of an accused is not superior to the policy rule that protects an accused against an attack upon his character. This means that although an accused, like any ordinary witness, is generally open to cross-examination at large as to credibility, he may not be cross-examined by the prosecution as to previous misconduct or discreditable associations for the purpose of attacking his credibility, unless such cross-examination is relevant to

---

[33] *Sims, supra*, note 27.
[34] S.C. 1893, c. 31.
[35] R.S.C. 1985, c. C-5.

prove the falsity of his own evidence.[36] That protection, however, does not extend to the case of an accused who gives damning evidence against a co-accused. In such instance, it is open for the co-accused to ask the accused questions about his character to show that the accused is a disreputable person not worthy of belief.[37] The policy of the law is that the right of an accused to full answer and defence does not allow him to hide under that umbrella of protection thereby impairing the right of his co-accused to full answer and defence by asking questions pertinent to his defence.

The criminal record of a witness or the accused stands on a different level. Section 12(1) and (1.1) of the *Canada Evidence Act* provides:

> 12. (1) A witness may be questioned as to whether the witness has been convicted of any offence, excluding any offence designated as a contravention under the *Contraventions Act*, but including such an offence where the conviction was entered after a trial on an indictment.
>
> (1.1) If the witness either denies the fact or refuses to answer, the opposite party may prove the conviction.

In England, section 1(f) of the *Criminal Evidence Act, 1898* forbids cross-examination of an accused on his record unless it is relevant to a fact in issue; the accused leads evidence of his own good character; the defence impugns the character of the prosecutor or a Crown witness; or the accused gives evidence against a co-accused. In Canada, there is no such protection. Section 12(1) of the *Canada Evidence Act* permits the Crown to cross-examine an accused on his criminal record even if the defence does not attack the Crown witnesses or lead evidence of the accused's good character. The rationale for section 12 is that a prior conviction is a relevant factor in assessing the credibility or reliability of the witness. In other words, there is no reason why the jury should not be informed of what sort of person is asking them to accept his word, particularly one who has shown contempt of the law by a previous violation of it.

For a long time, it was believed that a trial judge had a general discretion to exclude evidence of an accused's prior convictions where revealing those

---

[36] *Davison*, 1974 CarswellOnt 559, 6 O.R. (2d) 103, 20 C.C.C. (2d) 424 (C.A.); leave to appeal refused [1974] S.C.R. viii, 6 O.R. (2d) 103n, 20 C.C.C. (2d) 424n.

[37] *Jackson*, 1991 CarswellOnt 119, 68 C.C.C. (3d) 385, 9 C.R. (4th) 57, 51 O.A.C. 92 (C.A.); affirmed 1993 CarswellOnt 997, 1993 CarswellOnt 136, [1993] 4 S.C.R. 573, 86 C.C.C. (3d) 385, 26 C.R. (4th) 178, 109 D.L.R. (4th) 318, 162 N.R. 113, 68 O.A.C. 161.

convictions would prejudice him in the eyes of the jury.[38] However, four years before the enactment of the *Charter of Rights and Freedoms*,[39] the Ontario Court of Appeal decided that a trial judge had no discretion to prevent the Crown from cross-examining the accused as to prior convictions for any offence.[40] That Court also held that the word "any offence" in section 12(1) included convictions for offences committed outside of Canada provided that the process of adjudication of guilt constituted a conviction under Canadian law.[41] In an earlier case, that Court had also decided that a "conviction" included the sentence so that the accused could be cross-examined on the penalty imposed.[42]

In 1988, the Supreme Court of Canada decided that section 12(1) was not so absolute in its terms. In *Corbett*,[43] the Supreme Court said that a trial judge did have the discretion to exclude evidence of previous convictions in those cases where a mechanical application of section 12 would undermine the right to a fair trial as guaranteed by the *Charter*. The Court also accepted, "as a useful catalogue of factors", certain criteria which La Forest J. felt should be considered by the trial judge in determining how his discretion was to be exercised.

La Forest J. acknowledged that it was impossible to provide an exhaustive catalogue of the factors that are relevant in assessing the probative value or prejudice of the accused's prior criminal record. Nevertheless, he felt that among the most important factors is the nature of the previous conviction, its similarity to the conduct for which the accused is on trial and the remoteness or nearness of the prior conviction to the charge before the court. He reasoned that if the purpose of permitting cross-examination on a prior conviction is to test credibility, then a conviction which involves an act of deceit, fraud, cheating or stealing is more probative of a person's credibility than an act of violence which had little or no direct bearing on a

---

[38] *Powell*, 1977 CarswellOnt 1171, 37 C.C.C. (2d) 117 (Gen. Div.); *Skehan*, 1978 CarswellOnt 1337, 39 C.C.C. (2d) 196 (H.C.).

[39] Part 1 of the *Constitution Act, 1982*, being schedule B to the Canada Act 1982 (U.K.), 1982, c. 11.

[40] *Stratton*, 1978 CarswellOnt 29, 21 O.R. (2d) 258, 42 C.C.C. (2d) 449, 3 C.R. (3d) 289, 90 D.L.R. (3d) 420.

[41] *Stratton, ibid.*

[42] *Boyce*, 1974 CarswellOnt 46, 7 O.R. (2d) 561, 23 C.C.C. (2d) 16, 28 C.R.N.S. 336 (C.A.).

[43] 1988 CarswellBC 756, 1988 CarswellBC 252, [1988] 1 S.C.R. 670, 28 B.C.L.R. (2d) 145, 41 C.C.C. (3d) 385, 64 C.R. (3d) 1, [1988] 4 W.W.R. 481, 34 C.R.R. 54, 85 N.R. 81.

person's veracity or integrity. As far as he was concerned, the similarity of the prior conviction to the charge before the court created a potential for prejudice, unless the evidence met the stringent test for admitting similar fact evidence.[44] He also felt that a conviction, even one which involved an act of dishonesty, which occurred long before and was followed by a legally blameless life, should generally be excluded on the ground of remoteness.

As noted previously, section 1(f) of the English *Criminal Evidence Act, 1898* forbids cross-examination of an accused on his record unless it is relevant to a fact in issue, the accused leads evidence of his own good character, the defence impugns the character of the prosecutor or a Crown witness, or the accused gives evidence against a co-accused. In *Corbett*, Mr. Justice La Forest observed that Canada had no similar rule and acknowledged the potential unfairness to the Crown of prohibiting the cross-examination of the accused on prior convictions where the defence has made a deliberate attack upon the credibility of a Crown witness, particularly where the case boils down to a credibility contest between the accused and that witness.[45] He recognized that in such instance, the jury was entitled to have before it the record of the accused attacking the character of the Crown witness in order to determine whether the accused was any more worthy of belief than the person attacked and avoid a distorted picture being presented to the jury. Nevertheless, he felt that this was not a factor that should override the concern for a fair trial. In other words, cross-examination of an accused on his record should only be permitted "where to do so would render the trial more, and not less, fair".[46]

The general rule is that cross-examination of an accused on a criminal record is restricted to the nature of the offence, the date and place of the conviction, and the penalty imposed.[47] Since the purpose of allowing cross-

---

[44] See also *P. (G.F.)*, 1994 CarswellOnt 67, 18 O.R. (3d) 1, 89 C.C.C. (3d) 176, 29 C.R. (4th) 315, 70 O.A.C. 350 (C.A.); *Trudel*, 1994 CarswellQue 167, 1994 CarswellQue 2492, [1994] R.J.Q. 678, 90 C.C.C. (3d) 318, 60 Q.A.C. 138, [1994] A.Q. No. 114 (C.A.); *Brooks*, 1998 CarswellOnt 3866, 41 O.R. (3d) 661, 129 C.C.C. (3d) 227, 20 C.R. (5th) 116, 113 O.A.C. 201, [1998] O.J. No. 3913 (C.A.); reversed 2000 SCC 11, 2000 CarswellOnt 292, 2000 CarswellOnt 293, [2000] 1 S.C.R. 237, 46 O.R. (3d) 640 (headnote only), 141 C.C.C. (3d) 321, 30 C.R. (5th) 201, 182 D.L.R. (4th) 513, 250 N.R. 103, 129 O.A.C. 205, [2000] S.C.J. No. 12.

[45] *Supra* note 43, at paras. 138–145.

[46] See the judgment of Weiler J.A. in *Brooks, ibid.*

[47] *Laurier*, 1983 CarswellOnt 825, 1 O.A.C. 128 (C.A.); *W. (L.K.)*, 1999 CarswellOnt 3014, 138 C.C.C. (3d) 449, 126 O.A.C. 39 (C.A.); leave to appeal refused 2000 CarswellOnt 4252, 2000 CarswellOnt 4253, 264 N.R. 393 (note) (S.C.C.).

examination on a record is to test the credibility of the accused, the details surrounding the commission of the offences are irrelevant. Where, however, the accused puts his or her character in issue, the same restrictions do not apply. Details of the prior convictions are relevant to the accused's character. Here, it is permissible for the Crown to cross-examine the accused, not only on the details of the prior convictions, but on prior acts of discreditable conduct.[48] Nevertheless, the trial judge does have the right and the duty to exclude such evidence where its prejudicial effect outweighs its probative value.[49]

(d) When the Evidence is of Similar Facts

(i) The Rule

At the outset of this chapter, it was pointed out that although, as a matter of common sense, the disposition of an accused may be relevant to the accused's guilt or innocence, such evidence is excluded because the law considers it unfair to allow the prosecution to try a person on his or her whole life, rather than on the facts of the case. Another reason is to ensure that the jury's attention is not diverted from the central issue in the case. On the other hand, there may be instances where evidence of a person's bad character or disposition is so probative of the particular issues in the case that it should be admitted. As Lord Herschell L.C. pointed out in the second part of his classic statement of the rule in *Makin v. Attorney General for New South Wales*:

> On the other hand, the mere fact that the evidence adduced tends to show the commission of other crimes does not render it inadmissible if it be relevant to an issue before the jury, and it *may be so relevant if it bears upon the question whether the acts alleged to constitute the crime charged in the indictment were designed or accidental, or to rebut a defence which would otherwise be open to the accused.* The statement of these general principles is easy, but it is obvious that it may often be very difficult to draw the line

---

[48] *McNamara (No. 1)*, 1981 CarswellOnt 1243, 56 C.C.C. (2d) 193 (C.A.); leave to appeal refused [1981] 1 S.C.R. xi; affirmed 1985 CarswellOnt 939, 1985 CarswellOnt 96, (sub nom. *R. v. Canadian Dredge & Dock Co.*) [1985] 1 S.C.R. 662, 19 C.C.C. (3d) 1, 45 C.R. (3d) 289, 19 D.L.R. (4th) 314, 59 N.R. 241, 9 O.A.C. 321 at p. 350 [C.C.C.].

[49] See *McNamara (No. 1)*, *ibid.*, at p. 352 [C.C.C.]; *Farrant*, 1983 CarswellSask 132, 1983 CarswellSask 235, [1983] 1 S.C.R. 124, 4 C.C.C. (3d) 354, 32 C.R. (3d) 289, 147 D.L.R. (3d) 511, [1983] 3 W.W.R. 171, 46 N.R. 337, 21 Sask. R. 271.

and to decide whether a particular piece of evidence is on the one side or the other. [Emphasis added.][50]

In the years that followed Lord Herschell's classic statement of the rule, judges, lawyers and legal scholars attempted "to draw the line" in an effort to make some sense of the rule. Judges approached their task by creating categories of relevance in an effort to place each case in a particular pigeon-hole. Evidence was admitted if the prosecution was able to show that the evidence went "to prove intent" or "to prove a system" or "to prove a plan" or "to show malice" or "to rebut the defence of accident or mistake" or "to prove identity" or "to rebut the defence of innocent association". However, in 1975, the House of Lords in *Boardman v. Director of Public Prosecutions*,[51] decided that although the categories were useful illustrations of the similar fact rule, they were no longer an automatic ticket to admissibility.

Boardman, the headmaster of a boarding school for boys, had been accused of buggery and attempted buggery by two of the students. His defence was that the boys had made up the story because he had threatened to discipline them; in other words, that no offences had been committed. The House of Lords said that the proper approach to be followed in the future was for the trial judge to balance the probative value of the evidence against the prejudice that the accused might suffer if the evidence was admitted. In one of the speeches, Lord Wilberforce said:

> The basic principle must be that the admission of similar fact evidence . . . is exceptional and requires a strong degree of probative force. This probative force is derived, if at all, from the circumstances that the facts testified to by the several witness bear to each other such a striking similarity that they must, when judged by experience and common sense, either all be true, or have arisen from a common cause to the witnesses or from pure coincidence. The jury may, therefore, properly be asked to judge whether the right conclusion is that all are true, so that each story is supported by the other.[52]

[50][1894] A.C. 57, 17 Cox C.C. 704 (New South Wales P.C.).
[51](1974), [1975] A.C. 421, [1974] 3 All E.R. 887, 60 Cr. App. R. 165 (U.K. H.L.).
[52]*Ibid.*, at p. 175 [Cr. App. R.].

Three years later, the *Boardman* approach was adopted by the Supreme Court of Canada in *Guay*,[53] and reaffirmed by the Court in *Sweitzer*.[54] In *B. (C.R.)*,[55] Madam Justice McLachlin, writing for the majority, added:

> The judge must consider such factors as the degree of distinctiveness or uniqueness between the similar fact evidence and the offences alleged against the accused, as well as the connection, if any, of the evidence *to issues other than propensity*, to the end of determining whether, in the context of the case before him, the probative value of the evidence outweighs its potential prejudice and justifies its reception.[56]

In 2002, the Supreme Court reaffirmed the *B. (C.R.)* test in *Handy*[57] as stating the law in Canada. Binnie J., delivering the judgment of the Court, explained,

> [55] Similar fact evidence is thus presumptively inadmissible. The onus is on the prosecution to satisfy the trial judge on a balance of probabilities that in the context of the particular case the probative value of the evidence in relation to a particular issue outweighs its potential prejudice and thereby justifies its reception.

In *Handy*, the Court provided a number of useful principles for trial judges to apply in determining whether to admit similar fact evidence. The first was that the issue which the Crown seeks to establish should be identified:

> [74] The issues in question derive from the facts alleged in the charge and the defences advanced or reasonably anticipated. It is therefore incumbent on the Crown to identify the live issue in the trial to which the evidence of disposition is said to relate. If the issue has ceased to be in dispute, as for example when the fact is admitted by the accused, then the evidence is irrelevant and it must be excluded . . . The relative importance of the issue in the particular trial may also have a bearing on the weighing up of factors for and against admissibility. Similar fact evidence that is virtually conclusive of a minor issue may still be excluded for reasons of overall prejudice.

---

[53] (1978), 1978 CarswellQue 39, 1978 CarswellQue 147, [1979] 1 S.C.R. 18, 42 C.C.C. (2d) 536, 6 C.R. (3d) 130, 89 D.L.R. (3d) 532, 23 N.R. 451.

[54] 1982 CarswellAlta 552, 1982 CarswellAlta 132, [1982] 1 S.C.R. 949, 37 A.R. 294, 21 Alta. L.R. (2d) 97, 68 C.C.C. (2d) 193, 29 C.R. (3d) 97, 137 D.L.R. (3d) 702, [1982] 5 W.W.R. 555, 42 N.R. 550.

[55] 1990 CarswellAlta 35, 1990 CarswellAlta 650, [1990] 1 S.C.R. 717, 109 A.R. 81, 73 Alta. L.R. (2d) 1, 55 C.C.C. (3d) 1, 76 C.R. (3d) 1, [1990] 3 W.W.R. 385, 107 N.R. 241.

[56] *Ibid.*, at p. 25 [C.R.].

[57] 2002 CarswellOnt 1968, 2002 CarswellOnt 1969, 164 C.C.C. (3d) 481, 1 C.R. (6th) 203 (S.C.C.) at para. 54.

The next issue will be the identification of the required degree of similarity. This will depend upon the issues in the particular case, the purpose for which the evidence is sought to be introduced and the other evidence. The judge must then identify the connecting factors and ask whether the similar fact evidence is appropriately connected to the facts alleged in the charge. As the Court said,

> [81] The decided cases suggest need to pay close attention to similarities in character, proximity in time and frequency of occurrence

Admissible from inadmissible propensity evidence must also be differentiated. Finally, the judge, in deciding whether to admit the similar fact evidence, must remember that it need not be conclusive. As the Court noted, "the "conclusiveness" test takes the trial judge's "gatekeeper" function too far into the domain of the trier of fact".[58]

(ii) Identifying the Fact in Issue

Before a trial judge can begin to weigh the probative value of the evidence versus its potential prejudice, the judge must first identify the fact in issue that the evidence is adduced to prove. In Chapter 1, it was pointed out that in every criminal trial, there are three factual issues which the Crown must prove for a successful prosecution: the act, that is, whether a crime was committed; the identity of the perpetrator; and the intent of the perpetrator. Whenever the Crown seeks to have similar fact evidence admitted, the judge should be told by the prosecution of the issue or issues towards which the evidence is directed. In some instances, the similar fact evidence will be relevant to a single issue; in others, it may be relevant to all three issues. Whatever the issue or issues, the trial judge is required to instruct the jury that they may use the evidence in relation to that issue or issues, and not otherwise.

However, the Crown may be foreclosed in proving a particular issue by similar fact evidence where the defence is prepared to admit that issue, or where it seeks to rebut a defence that on the evidence is not realistically open to the accused.[59] In *Thompson*,[60] Lord Sumner observed:

> The prosecution cannot credit the accused with fancy defences in order to rebut them at the outset with some damning piece of evidence.[61]

---

[58] *Ibid.*, at para. 97.

[59] *Handy, supra* at para. 74.

[60] [1918] A.C. 221, 13 Cr. App. R. 61 (U.K. H.L.); *Handy*, 2002 CarswellOnt 1968, 2002 CarswellOnt 1969, 164 C.C.C. (3d) 481, 1 C.R. (6th) 203 (S.C.C.).

[61] *Ibid.*, at p. 78 [Cr. App. R.].

Mr. Justice Martin echoed the same view in his Law Society of Upper Canada lecture on "Similar Fact Evidence" in 1984:

> The Crown ought not, however, to be permitted to introduce evidence of similar facts to the prejudice of the accused under the guise of rebutting a defence, which on the evidence is not realistically open to the accused, and upon which he has given no indication that he intends to rely. To permit the Crown to introduce similar fact evidence to rebut a possible defence in those circumstances would gravely undermine the accused's right to a fair trial. If a defence is raised by the accused which could not reasonably be anticipated, and which is properly rebutted by similar fact evidence, the evidence is admissible in reply.[62]

The *Makin*[63] case is a good example of where the court permitted the admission of similar fact evidence to prove all three issues. Makin and his wife were charged with the murder of a child whose body had been found in their back garden. The Makins had agreed to look after the child and had received a very small amount of money from the child's mother. The bodies of eleven other infants who had been entrusted to the care of the Makins for a very small amount of money were also found buried in the gardens of houses occupied by them at various times. Although no one had seen the Makins kill any of the children, it was held that such evidence was admissible to show that the children had died, not from natural causes or by accident, but by design. The evidence was tendered to show that the only natural or irresistible inference that the jury could draw was that the child had died by design (the act) and that it was the Makins who had killed him (identity) and that they intended to do so (intent).

On the other hand, in the famous "Brides in the Bath" case, *Smith*,[64] similar fact evidence was admitted to prove that a crime had been committed. Smith had married successively three women all of whom had drowned, supposedly accidentally, in a bath that he had arranged to have installed. In each case, Smith benefited financially from their deaths. He was charged with the murder of his first wife and the prosecution was granted the right to call evidence as to the circumstances surrounding the deaths of his second and third wives. The English Court of Criminal Appeal held that the evidence was admissible to rebut the defence of accident, that is, whether it was a crime at all. Although there was no evidence directly establishing that the deaths of Smith's three wives were not accidental, the court held that it

---

[62] (1984) at p. 16.

[63] *Supra*, note 50.

[64] (1915), 11 Cr. App. R. 229 (Eng. C.A.).

was highly unlikely that all three could have died by accident. The trial judge, Scrutton J., charged the jury this way:

> If you find an accident which benefits a person and you find that the person has been sufficiently fortunate to have that accident happen to him a number of times, benefiting him each time, you draw a very strong, frequently an irresistible inference, that the occurrence of so many accidents benefiting him is such a coincidence that it cannot have happened unless it was designed.

Although *Makin* and *Smith* are often regarded as straightforward examples of the application of the similar fact evidence exception, it is significant to note that in both cases the similar acts were not evidence of criminal acts on their face. They only became evidence of crimes when the jury inferred, because of the similarity and number of incidents, that the death of the victims was as a result of the deliberate act of the accused.

The importance of identifying the fact in issue which the similar fact evidence is being sought to prove cannot be overemphasized in determining whether to admit the evidence. As McIntyre J. emphasized in *Sweitzer*, "whether or not probative value exceeds prejudicial effect can only be determined in light of the purpose for which the evidence is proffered".[65]

(iii) The Link between the Accused and the Similar Fact Evidence

Once the fact in issue is identified by the Crown, the next question which must be considered is whether there is a link between the accused and the similar fact evidence. This issue becomes particularly important in cases where the issue is the identity of the offender. Canadian authorities have required the Crown to lead, on the threshold question of admissibility, some evidence directly linking or connecting the accused with the similar fact evidence before it will be admitted. For example, in *Sweitzer*,[66] the accused was originally charged in an indictment containing fifteen counts of sexual assault on women. Before the trial began, the trial judge severed the various counts. The prosecution then elected to proceed on the first count and was permitted by the judge to lead evidence of the other fourteen assaults as similar fact evidence. Although there was some direct evidence identifying Sweitzer as the assailant in four of the assaults, the victims in the eleven other assaults were unable to identify their assailant. Mr. Justice McIntyre, delivering the judgment of the Supreme Court, held that although there was

---

[65] 1982 CarswellAlta 552, 1982 CarswellAlta 132, [1982] 1 S.C.R. 949, 68 C.C.C. (2d) 193, 29 C.R. (3d) 97 at p. 953 [S.C.R.].

[66] *Supra*, note 54.

some similarity between the conduct of the assailant in those four episodes with the conduct of the assailant in the eleven episodes where he could not be identified, the trial judge had erred in admitting evidence of the eleven episodes. Since the eleven episodes were not shown to be connected to Sweitzer, they were not admissible. The admissibility of such evidence had to be confined to cases where there was some evidentiary link, direct or circumstantial, with the accused. He wrote:

> . . . there must be some evidence upon which the trier of fact can make a proper finding that the similar facts to be relied upon were in fact the acts of the accused for it is clear that if they were not his own but those of another they have no relevance to the matters at issue under the indictment . . .[67]

Where the issue is identity, the next threshold issue of admissibility for the trial judge is the degree of distinctiveness that the evidence must bear to the charges against the accused to be regarded as a similar fact. Earlier English and Canadian authorities had suggested that to be admissible, the similar acts had to be strikingly similar to the alleged charges against the accused. However in *Arp*,[68] the Supreme Court said that the striking similarity test was only necessary where *identity* was in issue. In such instance, the jury is asked to infer from the distinctiveness or uniqueness that exists between the manner in which the crime under consideration was committed and the similar act that the accused is the very person who committed the crime. This inference is made possible only if the high degree of similarity between the acts renders the likelihood of coincidence objectively improbable. Similarity between the acts may consist of a unique trademark or signature on a series of significant similarities.

In *Arp*, the Court stressed that in assessing the similarity of the acts, the trial judge should only consider the manner in which the acts were committed and not the evidence as to the accused's involvement in each act. Once the trial judge concludes that the similar acts were *likely* committed by one person and there is evidence linking the accused to those acts, it is not necessary to conclude that the acts were *likely* committed by the accused. This question was a matter to be decided by the trier of fact on the basis of all the evidence relating to the acts.

Another area of difficulty for the trial judge in deciding whether the similar acts have passed the threshold test of admissibility occurs when the ac-

---

[67] *Ibid.*, at p. 197 [C.C.C.].

[68] (1998), 1998 CarswellBC 2545, 1998 CarswellBC 2546, [1998] 3 S.C.R. 339, 58 B.C.L.R. (3d) 18, 129 C.C.C. (3d) 321, 20 C.R. (5th) 1, 166 D.L.R. (4th) 296, [1999] 5 W.W.R. 545, 114 B.C.A.C. 1, 232 N.R. 317, 186 W.A.C. 1, [1998] S.C.J. No. 82.

cused is a member of a group with the same propensities as the perpetrator of a crime. At one time, the courts considered that evidence of a man's homosexuality was admissible on a charge of indecent assault to rebut the defence of innocent association[69] or to prove identity.[70] However, that view was rejected by the House of Lords in *Boardman* and later by the Supreme Court of Canada in *Morin*.[71] In *Morin*, Mr. Justice Sopinka said that there also had to be some further distinguishing feature.

> Accordingly, if the crime was committed by someone with homosexual tendencies, it is not sufficient to establish that the accused is a practising homosexual, or indeed is engaged in numerous homosexual acts. The tendered evidence must tend to show that there was some striking similarity between the manner in which the perpetrator committed the criminal act and such evidence.[72]

In those instances where the issue is not the identity of the perpetrator, but rather the credibility of the complainant, the concern in admitting similar discreditable conduct is that the trier will be persuaded of the guilt of the accused because of the similar incidents. Identifying the issue merely as credibility risks admitting evidence of nothing more than general disposition. In *Handy*,[73] the Supreme Court accepted that while propensity evidence is presumptively inadmissible, evidence which demonstrated propensity was sometimes admissible if its probative valued outweighed its prejudicial effect. The principal driver of probative value was the connectedness of the evidence to the alleged offences. The onus is on the prosecution to show on a balance of probabilities that the probative value of the similar fact evidence outweighs its potential for prejudice. The Court pointed out that factors that may support admission of such evidence include the proximity in time of the similar acts, similarity in detail, the number of occurrences of similar acts, similarities of circumstances, and any distinctive features. Exclusionary factors include the inflammatory nature of the similar acts, whether the Crown can prove its point with less prejudicial evidence, the potential for distraction, and whether admitting the evidence will consume undue time.

---

[69] *King (Dennis Arthur)* (1966), (1967) 51 Cr. App. R. 46.

[70] *Glynn* (1971), 1971 CarswellOnt 15, [1972] 1 O.R. 403, 5 C.C.C. (2d) 364, 15 C.R.N.S. 343 (C.A.).

[71] 1988 CarswellOnt 82, 1988 CarswellOnt 967, [1988] 2 S.C.R. 345, 44 C.C.C. (3d) 193, 66 C.R. (3d) 1, 88 N.R. 161, 30 O.A.C. 81.

[72] *Ibid.*, at p. 23 [C.R.].

[73] 2002 CarswellOnt 1968, 2002 CarswellOnt 1969, 164 C.C.C. (3d) 481, 1 C.R. (6th) 203 (S.C.C.).

(iv) The Onus of Proof

Until the decision of the Supreme Court of Canada in *Arp*,[74] trial judges struggled with the degree of proof that the Crown is required to establish to the satisfaction of the jury before they may use the similar fact in relation to the charge against the accused. Before *Arp*, the weight of authority suggested that the onus was not proof beyond a reasonable doubt, but something akin to the civil onus. Juries were customarily told that they could use similar fact evidence to assist them in deciding whether the accused committed the offence charged "if they believe it".[75]

That view, however, was difficult to reconcile with authorities which said that if an accused had been acquitted of a previous incident in another trial, evidence of that previous incident could not be used as similar fact evidence against him.[76] Those authorities reasoned that since an acquittal is considered the equivalent of a finding of innocence,[77] such similar fact evidence could not be used by the trier of fact because another court has found that the accused did not commit the offence. Indeed, the Ontario Court of Appeal went so far as to say that if the trial judge admitted evidence of a similar act that was later prosecuted resulting in an acquittal, then any conviction based on evidence of that similar act resulted in a new trial.[78]

---

[74] *Supra*, note 68.

[75] *Simpson*, 1977 CarswellOnt 1048, 16 O.R. (2d) 129, 35 C.C.C. (2d) 337, 77 D.L.R. (3d) 507, 2 L.M.Q. 40 (C.A.); *Lawson*, 1971 CarswellAlta 51, 3 C.C.C. (2d) 372, [1971] 4 W.W.R. 350, 14 C.R.N.S. 377 (C.A.); *Arp, ibid.*

[76] *Cullen*, 1989 CarswellOnt 853, 52 C.C.C. (3d) 459, 36 O.A.C. 195 (C.A.); *M. (R.A.)* (1994), 1994 CarswellMan 174, 94 C.C.C. (3d) 459, [1995] 1 W.W.R. 509, 97 Man. R. (2d) 70, 79 W.A.C. 70 (C.A.); leave to appeal refused 1995 CarswellMan 754, 1995 CarswellMan 755 (S.C.C.); *Verney*, 1993 CarswellOnt 1157, 87 C.C.C. (3d) 363, 67 O.A.C. 279 (C.A.); *Merdsoy*, 1994 CarswellNfld 131, 121 Nfld. & P.E.I.R. 181, 91 C.C.C. (3d) 517, 377 A.P.R. 181 (C.A.) and *N. (R.S.)*, 1995 CarswellAlta 263, 169 A.R. 378, 31 Alta. L.R. (3d) 424, 97 W.A.C. 378 (C.A.).

[77] *Grdic*, 1985 CarswellBC 737, 1985 CarswellBC 2382, [1985] 1 S.C.R. 810, 19 C.C.C. (3d) 289, 46 C.R. (3d) 1, 19 D.L.R. (4th) 385, [1985] 4 W.W.R. 437, 59 N.R. 61, [1985] S.C.J. No. 41; *Grant*, 1991 CarswellPEI 12, 1991 CarswellPEI 98, [1991] 3 S.C.R. 139, 93 Nfld. & P.E.I.R. 181, 67 C.C.C. (3d) 268, 7 C.R. (4th) 388, 31 M.V.R. (2d) 309, 292 A.P.R. 181, 5 C.R.R. (2d) 193, 130 N.R. 250, [1991] S.C.J. No. 78.

[78] *G. (K.R.)*, 1991 CarswellOnt 727, 5 O.R. (3d) 406, 68 C.C.C. (3d) 268, 51 O.A.C. 294 (C.A.).

For example, in *G. (K.R.),*[79] the accused was charged with sexually assaulting two children and an adult. The Crown was allowed to introduce, as
similar fact evidence, the testimony of a child who said that he was also
sexually assaulted by the accused. The accused was convicted. He was then
tried on a charge of sexually assaulting that child, based on the evidence
that had been introduced as similar fact evidence and acquitted of the
charge. On the appeal of his conviction, the accused applied to introduce as
fresh evidence the fact of his acquittal on the similar fact evidence charge
and the Court granted the application. It was held that if the accused had
been tried and acquitted of the charge of sexual assault upon the child
before the trial which gave rise to the appeal, that child's evidence would
not have been admissible as similar fact evidence.[80] The Court also noted
the well-established principle that an acquittal is the equivalent of a finding
of innocence.[81] Therefore, it had to be assumed that the accused was innocent of the allegations made against him by the child.

In *Arp*, the Supreme Court decided that the proper standard to apply to
the primary inference drawn from the similar fact evidence is proof on a
balance of probabilities. Cory J., delivering the judgment of the Court, reasoned that since the probative value of similar fact evidence, as circumstantial evidence, lies in the unlikelihood of coincidence, it simply did not make
sense to require one of the allegations to be proved beyond a reasonable
doubt as a prerequisite to the trier's consideration of it. Although the similar
fact evidence, standing alone, may fall short of proof beyond a reasonable
doubt, it can be relied upon to assist in proving another allegation beyond a
reasonable doubt. In other words, the correct approach to a consideration of
similar fact evidence is the pooling or cumulative approach.

(v) Evidence Possibly Tainted by Collusion

In those instances where the accused is charged with more than one offence involving more than one alleged victim, such as in a case of sexual
assault, the defence may suggest that the victims have conspired or collabo-
rated to bring false charges against the accused. This has raised the question
whether there should be an onus upon the Crown, before similar fact evidence is admitted, to negate any suggestion of collaboration or conspiracy.
In *Boardman*, Lord Wilberforce suggested that before the evidence was admitted, the trial judge should find "absence of proved conspiracy . . . if this

---

[79] *Ibid.*

[80] *Cullen, supra,* note 76.

[81] *Grant, supra,* note 77.

evidence is to be allowed". In *B. (C.R.)*,[82] Sopinka J., delivering the minor-ity judgment of the Court, adopted that view, although the majority ex-pressed no opinion on the point. However, in *Director of Public Prosecutions v. P.*,[83] the House of Lords changed their opinion and held that the possibility of collusion among complainants was an issue that should be left for the jury to decide. In *Burke*,[84] Sopinka J., now delivering the majority judgment of the Supreme Court, opted for this approach and held that it should be left to the jury to determine the reliability of the evi-dence having regard to all of the circumstances, including the opportunities for collusion or collaboration to concoct the evidence.

It is now settled that where the Crown seeks to lead evidence of similar facts and there is some evidence of actual collusion, or at least an "air of reality" to the allegations, the Crown is required to satisfy the trial judge, on a balance of probabilities, that the evidence of similar facts is not tainted with collusion. Mere opportunity for contact is insufficient to give rise to an "air of reality" to the allegation of collusion. The issue is "concoction or collaboration, not contact".[85] It would then be for the jury to make the ulti-mate determination of its worth. If the Crown is unable to satisfy the trial judge on a balance of probabilities that the evidence is not tainted by collu-sion and the judge finds actual collusion among complainants, he or she must exercise their gatekeeper function and deny the similar fact applica-tion. If the evidence of collusion amounts to no more than opportunity to collude, the issue is best left to the jury. If the trial judge admits the evi-dence, he or she must still warn the jury that they should assess the evi-dence carefully and consider whether it is reliable, given the possibility of deliberate or accidental tainting by collusion among the witnesses.[86]

---

[82] 1990 CarswellAlta 35, 1990 CarswellAlta 650, [1990] 1 S.C.R. 717, 109 A.R. 81, 73 Alta. L.R. (2d) 1, 55 C.C.C. (3d) 1, 76 C.R. (3d) 1, [1990] 3 W.W.R. 385, 107 N.R. 241.

[83] (1990), 93 Cr. App. R. 267 (C.A.); reversed [1991] 2 A.C. 447, 93 Cr. App. R. 267 (H.L.) at p. 272 (Cr. App. R.).

[84] 1996 CarswellNfld 85, 1996 CarswellNfld 85F, [1996] 1 S.C.R. 474, (sub nom. *R. v. Burke (No. 3)*) 139 Nfld. & P.E.I.R. 147, 105 C.C.C. (3d) 205, 46 C.R. (4th) 195, 433 A.P.R. 147, 194 N.R. 247, [1996] S.C.J. No. 27; reconsideration / re-hearing refused (May 23, 1996), Doc. 24071 (S.C.C.).

[85] *Handy*, 2002 CarswellOnt 1968, 2002 CarswellOnt 1969, [2002] 2 S.C.R. 908, 164 C.C.C. (3d) 481, 1 C.R. (6th) 203 at para. 111.

[86] *Handy, ibid.*; *Shearing*, 2002 CarswellBC 1661, 2002 CarswellBC 1662, 165 C.C.C. (3d) 225, 2 C.R. (6th) 213 (S.C.C.); *F. (J.)*, 2003 CarswellOnt 3135, 177 C.C.C. (3d) 1, 16 C.R. (6th) 317 (C.A.); *Dorsey*, 2012 CarswellOnt 3846, 288 C.C.C. (3d) 62, 93 C.R. (6th) 65 (C.A.).

6
OPINION EVIDENCE

1. THE RULE

The general rule is that a witness is not allowed to express personal beliefs or give an opinion about a fact in issue unless the matter calls for his or her special skill or knowledge, and the witness is an expert in such matters. This rule is based upon the notion that a distinction must be drawn between a fact in issue and the inference to be drawn from that fact. Witnesses are supposed to testify as to matters which they have observed through their senses, that is, the eyes, ears, nose, or what they felt or did. It is for the jury or judge (in trials by judge alone) to decide what is the proper inference to be drawn from the facts established by the witness.

The difficulty with the rule is that it is not always easy to draw a line between a fact and an opinion. For example, when a witness says that "the car was going very fast" or that "the accused was angry" or that "the girl was very pretty" or "the person is very old", the witness is really expressing a personal opinion based on his or her own experience and view of matters. Yet, such evidence is routinely given in court without objection. Indeed, in

German,[1] an Ontario case decided over 60 years ago, a witness was allowed to give evidence that the accused was intoxicated. Chief Justice Robertson justified the reception of that evidence this way:

> No doubt, the general rule is that it is only persons who are qualified by some special skill, training or experience who can be asked their opinion upon a matter in issue. The rule is not, however, an absolute one. There are a number of matters in respect of which a person of ordinary intelligence may be permitted to give evidence of his opinion upon a matter of which he has personal knowledge. Such matters as the identity of individuals, the apparent age of a person, the speed of a vehicle, are among the matters upon which witnesses have been allowed to express an opinion, notwithstanding that they have no special qualifications, other than the fact they have personal knowledge of the subject matter, to enable them to form an opinion.

Not all courts have adopted this liberal approach to the general rule. For example in *Browne*,[2] the question was whether a witness could identify a person as the perpetrator of a crime. O'Halloran J.A. argued:

> A positive statement 'that is the man', when rationalized, is found to be an opinion and not a statement of single fact. All a witness can say is, that because of this or that he remembers about a person, he is of opinion that person is 'the man'. A witness recognizes a person because of a certain personality that person has acquired in the eyes of the witness. That personality is reflected by characteristics of the person, which, when associated with something in the mind of the witness, causes the latter to remember that person in a way the witness does not remember any other person.

> Unless the witness is able to testify with confidence what characteristics and what 'something' has stirred and clarified his memory or recognition, then an identification confined to 'that is the man', standing by itself, cannot be more than a vague general description and is untrustworthy in any sphere of life where certitude is essential.

Nevertheless, the courts have continued to allow an ordinary witness to give evidence on a "subject about which most people should be able to express an opinion from their ordinary day-to-day experience of life". These include such matters as disputed handwriting, if the witness has acquired previous knowledge of the handwriting of a person whose handwriting is in dispute,[3] the age of another person, his own mental or physical condition, whether a person is intoxicated or impaired by alcohol, the degree of intoxi-

---

[1] 1947 CarswellOnt 15, [1947] O.R. 395, 89 C.C.C. 90, 3 C.R. 516, [1947] 4 D.L.R. 68 (C.A.).

[2] 1951 CarswellBC 25, 99 C.C.C. 141, 11 C.R. 297, 1 W.W.R. (N.S.) 449 (C.A.).

[3] *Derrick (Alfred Ernest)* (1910), 5 Cr. App. R. 162.

cation, and whether the person's ability to drive is impaired,[4] and estimates of such things as speed, distance, size, *etc.*

2. EXPERT OPINION

(a) The Rule

An exception to the rule exists in favour of witnesses who are classified as experts. The theory underlying expert testimony is that experts, because of their knowledge, training and experience, are able to form better opinions on a given state of facts than opinions formed by those not so well equipped, such as ordinary jurors. Their opinions are admitted in evidence to aid the jury to understand questions which uninformed and inexperienced persons are not likely to decide correctly without such assistance. However, if the subject is one of common knowledge and the facts can be intelligibly described to the jury, and they can form a reasonable opinion for themselves, the opinion of an expert will be rejected. An expert is therefore someone who is qualified by study or experience to form a definite opinion respecting a division of science, branch of art or department of trade, which persons having no particular training or special study are incapable of accurately forming. It is not a university degree that makes a person an expert; it is special knowledge acquired through study or practical experience. The expert, however, is not required to have had some experience as a clinician or to have written articles with respect to his or her particular area of expertise before he or she may be qualified and allowed to testify as an expert.[5]

On the other hand, the fact that a witness may have knowledge about a subject, or understand it better than the judge or jury, does not necessarily justify receiving his or her evidence. If the judge or jury can become sufficiently informed about the subject during the trial, so that they can reach an accurate conclusion, there is really no basis for the expert opinion. As Dickson J. (as he then was) wrote in *Abbey*,[6]

> With respect to matters calling for special knowledge, an expert in the field may draw inferences and state his opinion. An expert's function is precisely this: to provide the judge and jury with a ready-made inference which the judge and jury, due to the technical nature of the facts, are unable to formu-

---

4   *Graat*, 1982 CarswellOnt 101, 1982 CarswellOnt 745, [1982] 2 S.C.R. 819, 2 C.C.C. (3d) 365, 31 C.R. (3d) 289, 144 D.L.R. (3d) 267, 18 M.V.R. 287, 45 N.R. 451.

5   *R. (W.D.)*, 1994 CarswellOnt 121, 95 C.C.C. (3d) 190, 35 C.R. (4th) 343, 77 O.A.C. 59, [1994] O.J. No. 2934 (C.A.).

6   1982 CarswellBC 230, 1982 CarswellBC 740, [1982] 2 S.C.R. 24, 68 C.C.C. (2d) 394, 29 C.R. (3d) 193 at p. 42 [S.C.R.].

late. "An expert's opinion is admissible to furnish the Court with scientific information which is likely to be outside the experience and knowledge of a judge or jury. If on the proven facts a judge or jury can form their own conclusions without help, then the opinion of the expert is unnecessary". (Turner (1974), 60 Crim. App. R. 80, at p. 83, per Lawton L.J.)

For a long time, courts were only prepared to accept expert evidence that was "generally accepted" within its field.[7] The courts cautioned against opening the door too quickly to the admission of expert evidence that was "novel science". The concern was that a jury might be unduly influenced by the expert's opinion simply because the witness was an expert. In *Mohan*,[8] Sopinka J. explained,

> There is a danger that expert evidence will be misused and will distort the fact-finding process. Dressed up in scientific language which the jury does not easily understand and submitted through a witness of impressive antecedents, this evidence is apt to be accepted by the jury as being virtually infallible and as having more weight than it deserves.

He was also concerned that,

> ... in the application of this criterion that experts not be permitted to usurp the functions of the trier of fact. Too liberal an approach could result in a trial's becoming nothing more than a contest of experts with the trier of fact acting as referee in deciding which expert to accept.[9]

Similar concerns were expressed by Finlayson J.A. in *McIntosh*,[10]

> In my respectful opinion, the courts are overly eager to abdicate their fact-finding responsibilities to 'experts' in the field of behavioural sciences. We are too quick to say that a particular witness possesses special knowledge and experience going beyond that of the trier of fact without engaging in an analysis of the subject-matter of the expertise ... simply because one has lectured and written extensively on a subject that is of interest to him or her does not constitute him or her an expert for the purpose of testifying in a court of law on the subject of that specialty. It seems to me that before we even get to the point of examining the witness's expertise, we must ask ourselves if the subject-matter of his testimony admits of expert testimony.[11]

---

[7] *Frye v. United States*, 293 F. 1013 (D.C. Cir., 1923).

[8] 1994 CarswellOnt 1155, 1994 CarswellOnt 66, [1994] 2 S.C.R. 9, 89 C.C.C. (3d) 402, 29 C.R. (4th) 243.

[9] *Ibid.* at p. 24.

[10] 1997 CarswellOnt 2682, 35 O.R. (3d) 97, 117 C.C.C. (3d) 385, 102 O.A.C. 210, [1997] O.J. No. 3172 (C.A.); leave to appeal refused (1998), (sub nom. *R. v. McCarthy*) 227 N.R. 279 (note), 111 O.A.C. 395 (note) (S.C.C.).

[11] *Ibid.*, at p. 392 [C.C.C.].

The courts, he felt, should,

> ... scrutinize the nature of the subject-matter of the expert testimony. Any natural or unnatural phenomenon may become the subject of an investigation conducted according to the scientific method. The scientific method requires the formation of a hypothesis, the testing of the hypothesis using reliable methodology, the examination of the results (usually with statistical analysis) and the formation of a conclusion. However, the fact that the testimony recites the application of the scientific method does not necessarily render the original object of study a matter requiring opinion evidence at trial.[12]

In *Mohan*,[13] the Supreme Court indicated that it was prepared to open the door to "novel science" provided that it met four criteria: relevance; necessity in assisting the trier of fact; absence of any exclusionary rule; and a properly qualified expert. The relevance criteria had two aspects to it. The first was logical relevance. Relevance was a threshold question to be decided by the judge as a matter of law. The second was "a cost benefit" analysis. Logically relevant evidence was to be excluded if its probative value was overborne by its prejudicial effect, if the time required was not commensurate with its value, or if it could influence the trier of fact out of proportion to its reliability. The reliability versus effect factor had special significance in assessing the admissibility of expert evidence. Expert evidence was not to be admitted where there was a danger that it would be misused or would distort the fact-finding process, or confuse the jury.

To be necessary, the evidence had to be outside the experience and knowledge of a judge or jury and had to be assessed in light of its potential to distort the fact-finding process. However, necessity was not to be judged by too strict a standard. The possibility that evidence would overwhelm the jury and distract them from their task could often be offset by proper instructions. Experts, however, were not to be permitted to usurp the functions of the trier of fact causing a trial to degenerate into a contest of experts. The evidence had to be necessary to enable the trier of fact to appreciate the matters in issue due to their technical nature. Compliance, however, did not ensure the admissibility of expert evidence if it fell afoul of an exclusionary rule of evidence separate and apart from the opinion rule itself. Finally, the evidence had to be given by a witness who was shown to have acquired special or peculiar knowledge through study or experience in respect of the matters on which he or she undertakes to testify.

The Court decided that expert evidence which was advancing a novel scientific theory or technique was to be subjected to "special scrutiny to deter-

---

[12] *Ibid.*, at pp. 393-94.

[13] *Supra*, note 8.

mine whether it meets a basic threshold of reliability and whether it is essential in the sense that the trier of fact would be unable to come to a satisfactory conclusion without the assistance of the expert". The closer the evidence approached an opinion on an ultimate issue, the stricter was the application of this principle. The trial judge had the duty to act as gatekeeper and carefully scrutinize the admissibility of the proposed expert testimony.[14]

In *Mohan*, the accused, a practising pediatrician, was charged with four counts of sexual assault on four female patients, aged 13 to 16, during medical examinations conducted in his office. At issue on appeal was whether the trial judge had erred in refusing to allow a psychiatrist to testify that the perpetrator of the alleged offences would be part of a limited and unusual group of individuals and that accused did not fall within that narrow class because he did not possess the characteristics belonging to that group. In dismissing the appeal, the Supreme Court said that nothing in the record supported a finding that the profile of a paedophile or psychopath has been standardized to the extent that it could be said that it matched the supposed profile of the offender depicted in the charges. The expert's group profiles were not seen as sufficiently reliable to be considered helpful. In the absence of these indicia of reliability, it could not be said that the evidence would be necessary in the sense of usefully clarifying a matter otherwise inaccessible, or that any value it may have had would not be outweighed by its potential for misleading or diverting the jury.

The *Mohan* criteria were considered again six years later in *J. (J.-L.)*.[15] There the accused was charged with sexual offences involving two young boys who were between three and five years old. The Crown alleged anal penetration. The defence sought unsuccessfully to call expert evidence from a psychiatrist to establish that in all probability a serious deviant had inflicted anal intercourse on two children of that age, and that no such deviant personality traits were disclosed in the psychiatrist's testing of the accused. It was held by the Supreme Court that the trial judge had not erred in excluding the psychiatrist's evidence.

Although the Supreme Court was prepared to accept that psychiatric evidence of disposition is admissible where the particular disposition in issue is characteristic of a distinctive group and the characteristics fell within the expertise of the psychiatrist — that alone did not establish admissibility.

---

[14] *Ibid.*, [1994] 2 S.C.R. at p. 25.

[15] 2000 SCC 51, 2000 CarswellQue 2310, 2000 CarswellQue 2311, [2000] 2 S.C.R. 600, (sub nom. *R. v. J. (J-L.)*) 148 C.C.C. (3d) 487, 37 C.R. (5th) 203, 192 D.L.R. (4th) 416, 261 N.R. 111.

The changing nature of scientific knowledge required that novel science be evaluated on a case-by-case basis. As it had said in *Mohan*, novel science was subject to "special scrutiny", especially where the psychiatrist's opinion was close to the ultimate issue of guilt or innocence. Where the crime could only, or in all probability would only, be committed by a person having identifiable peculiarities that the accused did not possess, the personality profile of the perpetrator group had to be sufficiently complete to identify distinctive psychological elements that were in all probability present and operating in the perpetrator at the time of the offence. In other words, what exactly differentiated or distinguished the perpetrator class from the rest of the population had to be clearly identified, *i.e.*, a standard profile. The Court noted that the range and distinctiveness of personality traits attributable to perpetrators of different offences vary greatly. The issue for the trial judge was whether the profile is sufficient for the expert to identify and describe with workable precision what exactly distinguishes the distinctive or deviant perpetrator from other people.

The Court suggested the *reliable foundation* test adopted by the U.S. Supreme Court in *Daubert v. Merrell Dow Pharmaceuticals Inc.*[16] could be helpful to the trial judge in evaluating the soundness of novel science. The test listed a number of factors such as:

1. whether the theory or technique can be tested;

2. whether it has been subjected to peer review and publication;

3. the known or potential rate of error or existence of standards; and

4. whether the theory or technique used has been generally accepted.

(b) Admissibility

Before a witness is permitted to give expert evidence, the side that calls the witness must properly qualify the witness as an expert in all the areas in which the expert is to give opinion evidence.[17] The witness must also be accepted by the court as an expert in the particular field about which the witness is to testify. Although the other side will often admit the witness's qualifications, there is still an obligation upon the trial judge to be satisfied that the expert's testimony meets the four *Mohan* criteria.

Once qualified and accepted by the court to give expert testimony, the witness may be permitted to express an opinion with respect to the conclusion that should be drawn from certain facts. The expert may have personal

---

[16](1993), 125 L.Ed.2d 469, 113 SCt. 2786, 509 U.S. 579 (Cal. Sup. Ct.).

[17]*Marquard*, 1993 CarswellOnt 995, 1993 CarswellOnt 127, [1993] 4 S.C.R. 223, 85 C.C.C. (3d) 193, 25 C.R. (4th) 1.

knowledge of the facts; but more often than not, the witness will have to rely on information received from others. In this latter instance, the expert may be asked to give an opinion on what is called a hypothesis or a hypothetical question. The witness will be asked to assume certain facts that will be outlined and will then be asked for an opinion on the conclusion that should be drawn from those facts. However, the opinion expressed must only relate to the facts. The expert is not entitled to give an answer that amounts to a conclusion of law.

If the opinion of an expert is premised upon the truth of facts that he or she has assumed hypothetically, those assumed facts must be established by evidence in the usual way, otherwise, the foundation for the expert's opinion collapses.[18] Indeed, the judge must warn the jury (or instruct him or herself in trials by judge alone) that before the opinion can be considered, they must be satisfied as to the truth of the facts upon which the expert is relying. Thus an attack on the facts assumed by the expert is usually one of the ways a cross-examiner will attempt to discredit the expert's opinion.

For example, it is the usual practice for a psychiatrist who is called upon to give an opinion as to the mental state of an accused to rely upon interviews with the accused and with others, all of which form part of the accused's psychiatric history. The fact that the expert's opinion is dependent upon the truth of statements made by the accused and others will not affect the admissibility of the opinion, although it is a factor in assessing the weight of the opinion.[19] The trial judge must be careful to warn the jury that in considering the weight of the opinion, they must be satisfied of the truth of the statements relied upon by the psychiatrist.

On the other hand, if the psychiatrist (or any other expert) is present during the course of the trial and is asked at the conclusion to give an opinion based on the evidence he or she has heard, such evidence is not admissible. The reason is that what the expert is being asked to do is to pass on the truthfulness of the witnesses who have testified and that is within the exclusive jurisdiction of the trier of fact.[20]

---

[18] *Abbey*, 1982 CarswellBC 230, 1982 CarswellBC 740, 68 C.C.C. (2d) 394, 29 C.R. (3d) 193 (S.C.C.). Although Wilson J. in *Lavallee*, 1990 CarswellMan 198, 1990 CarswellMan 377, 55 C.C.C. (3d) 97, 76 C.R. (3d) 329 (S.C.C.) suggested that it is wrong to assume the *Abbey* case suggested otherwise.

[19] *Swietlinski*, 1978 CarswellOnt 52, 22 O.R. (2d) 604, 44 C.C.C. (2d) 267, 5 C.R. (3d) 324, 94 D.L.R. (3d) 218 (C.A.) at p. 301 [C.C.C.], ; affirmed 1980 CarswellOnt 59, 1980 CarswellOnt 648, [1980] 2 S.C.R. 956, 55 C.C.C. (2d) 481, 18 C.R. (3d) 231, 117 D.L.R. (3d) 285, 34 N.R. 569.

[20] *Bleta* (1964), 1964 CarswellOnt 17, [1964] S.C.R. 561, [1965] 1 C.C.C. 1, 44 C.R. 193, 48 D.L.R. (2d) 139.

OPINION EVIDENCE

A common complaint about expert evidence is that the expert may give an opinion on the very issue which the jury must decide and thus usurp their function. Whether the evidence is simply opinion to assist the jury in deciding the ultimate issue or evidence of the very issue itself, is not often easy to determine. For example, if the issue is whether the accused was criminally responsible for an act committed while suffering from a mental disorder, a psychiatrist called as an expert will be asked to give his or her opinion about whether the accused was capable of *appreciating the nature and quality of his acts* or of *knowing that his acts were wrong* in accordance with section 16 of the *Criminal Code*. Such evidence is regularly received even though it would appear to be on the very issue which the judge or jury must decide.

The courts have always had difficulty with the application of the ultimate issue rule. For example, in *Lupien*,[21] the accused was charged with gross indecency. His defence was that he thought that the male person with whom he was found was, in fact, a female, and attempted to introduce psychiatric evidence to show that he had a strong aversion to homosexual practices and therefore would not knowingly engage in homosexual acts. The Supreme Court of Canada was divided on the issue.

The dissenting judges felt that the psychiatric opinion ought not to be admitted because it came too close to the very question that the jury had to decide on the whole of the evidence. The majority, however, decided that the expert testimony was admissible on the question of whether or not the man was "homosexually inclined or otherwise sexually perverted". Mr. Justice Hall gave these reasons:

> That type of evidence is very close, if not identical, to the conclusion the jury must come to in such a case if it is to find that the accused was not guilty because he did not have intent necessary to support conviction. The weight to be given the opinion of the expert is entirely for the jury, and it is the function of the trial judge to instruct the jury that the responsibility for weighing the evidence is theirs and theirs alone.[22]

The real difficulty for a jury will arise where there are two experts expressing diametrically opposed views. This means that their decision will turn not so much on which facts are proved in evidence, but on which expert the jury or judge accepts. In other words, their decision will often depend on which expert they find more credible, rather than on whose opinion is the correct one. In criminal cases, however, the difficulty for the trier may

---

[21] *Lupien* (1964), 1969 CarswellBC 258, 1969 CarswellBC 185, [1970] S.C.R. 263, [1970] 2 C.C.C. 193, 9 D.L.R. (3d) 1, 71 W.W.R. 110, 9 C.R.N.S. 165.

[22] *Ibid.*, [1970] S.C.R. at pp. 280.

be more apparent than real. The rule is that before the judge and jury are entitled to accept the opinion of the prosecution expert over the defence expert, they must be satisfied that it is the correct one.[23]

3. OPINION AS TO THE CREDIBILITY OF A WITNESS

(a) Generally

Where the central issue at trial is whether a certain event occurred (such as a sexual assault) and the only two persons present at the event are the complainant and the accused, the trier is faced with the difficult question of determining who is telling the truth. This raises the question of whether a witness should be allowed to give evidence that one of the witnesses to the event is or is not a credible witness. Historically, opinion evidence as to the credibility of a witness, called "oath-helping", was not allowed, although evidence in the form of character evidence of the witness's reputation in the community for lack of credibility was always allowed. In other words, while a witness could not be called to say that a witness had a good reputation in the community for truthfulness, the witness was allowed to given evidence that a witness had a reputation in the community for lack of credibility.

The reason why opinion evidence as to the truthfulness of a witness was not allowed was because of the reluctance of allowing evidence on the very issue that the trier was required to decide. Another concern was that it might prolong the trial unduly by creating confusion and a multiplicity of issues. McLachlin J. described the rule this way:[24]

> The rule against oath-helping holds that evidence adduced solely for the purpose of proving that a witness is truthful is inadmissible: *R. v. Marquard, supra*. The rule finds its origins in the medieval practice of oath-helping; the accused in a criminal case or the defendant in a civil case could prove his innocence by providing a certain number of compurgators to swear to the truth of his oath: see *R. v. Béland, supra, per* Wilson J. at pp. 419-20. In modern times, it is defended on the ground that determinations of credibility are for the trier of fact, and that the judge or jurors are in as good a position to determine credibility as another witness. Therefore the fundamental requirement for expert evidence — that it assist the judge or jury on a technical or scientific matter which might otherwise not be appar-

---

[23] *Molnar*, 1990 CarswellOnt 91, 55 C.C.C. (3d) 446, 76 C.R. (3d) 125, 38 O.A.C. 62, [1990] O.J. No. 339 (C.A.); *Laverty*, 1979 CarswellOnt 88, 47 C.C.C. (2d) 60, 9 C.R. (3d) 288 (C.A.) at p. 62 [C.C.C.].

[24] *B. (R.H.)*, 1994 CarswellBC 1237, 1994 CarswellBC 576, [1994] 1 S.C.R. 656, 89 C.C.C. (3d) 193, 29 C.R. (4th) 113 at p. 667 [S.C.R.].

ent — is not met. The rule, as Iacobucci J. noted in *B. (F.F.)*, [1993] 1 S.C.R. 697 at p. 729, goes to evidence "that would tend to prove the truthfulness of the witness, rather than the truth of the witness' statements".

The rule is that a witness is not allowed to testify that another witness is credible and worthy of belief. It is the function of the trier of fact, the judge or the jury, to make that decision. For example in *Khan*,[25] the accused was charged with and convicted of murdering and conspiring to murder a woman who was pregnant with his child. The Crown relied on the evidence of two unsavoury witnesses who said that the accused had enlisted them to kill the deceased. A parole officer had been allowed to testify that the unsavoury witnesses were generally forthcoming and honest in their dealings with her. An appeal was allowed and a new trial ordered. It was held that the testimony of the parole officer constituted impermissible oath-helping.

The same rule, however, does not apply where a witness is called to testify that another witness should not be believed. Fifty years ago in *Gunewardene*,[26] the English Court of Criminal Appeal accepted that an impeaching witness should no longer be confined to expressing an opinion simply as to the *lack of veracity of a prosecution witness* based upon that witness's general reputation in the community. The impeaching witness was now entitled to state that from his or her knowledge of the witness, the witness was unworthy of credit. But in *Gunewardene*, the Court would not let the impeaching witness detail his reasons for that opinion, even though he was a medical witness. It took another thirteen years before that restriction was overruled. In *Toohey v. Metropolitan Police Commissioner*,[27] the House of Lords decided that a medical witness could give his reasons why the witness should not be believed. For example, the witness was allowed to say that the witness suffered from a mental defect or abnormality that made his or her evidence unreliable. That view was finally accepted by the Ontario Court of Appeal in *Gonzague*.[28]

Three years later, the Ontario Court of Appeal went further and removed the restrictions upon a lay person giving reasons why a witness should not be believed. In *T. (S.)*,[29] it was held that the opinions of the defence witnesses in a sexual trial that the complainant ought not to be believed, and the basis of their belief, were receivable. The Court also said that reply evi-

---

[25] 2011 CarswellBC 2584, 282 C.C.C. (3d) 396, 89 C.R. (6th) 321 (C.A.).

[26] [1951] 2 All E.R. 290, 35 Cr. App. R. 80, [1951] 2 K.B. 600 (Ct. of Crim. App.).

[27] [1965] A.C. 595, [1965] 1 All E.R. 506, 49 Cr. App. R. 148 (U.K. H.L.).

[28] 1983 CarswellOnt 81, 4 C.C.C. (3d) 505, 34 C.R. (3d) 169 (C.A.).

[29] 1986 CarswellOnt 144, 57 O.R. (2d) 737, 31 C.C.C. (3d) 1, 55 C.R. (3d) 321, 18 O.A.C. 219 (C.A.).

dence was admissible to reduce the impact of that impeaching evidence. But it was stressed that the jury should also be told that the reply evidence must not be used to bolster the credibility of the complainants.

The way in which a character witness is entitled to question the testimony of a witness who has given evidence is by the following questions:

1. Do you know the reputation of (the witness) as to truth and veracity in the community in which he (or she) resides?

If the answer is "yes", then the witness may be asked:

2. Is that reputation good or bad?

If the answer is "bad", the following question is permitted:

3. From that reputation, would you believe that witness on oath?

The rule in *Gonzague* and *T. (S.)* was eventually reconsidered by the Ontario Court of Appeal in *Clarke*.[30] Rosenberg J.A., delivering the judgment of the Court, questioned the usefulness of permitting a character witness, who has not heard the evidence in the case, to predict whether another witness had told the truth under oath. He noted that a witness who is sworn to tell the truth is subject to prosecution for lying under oath, the testimony takes place before a judge and sometimes a jury, and the witness knows that he or she is subject to cross-examination. Thus, the circumstances in which a person may be willing to lie under oath are probably considerably different from the circumstances in which he or she would likely lie to an acquaintance or even acquire a reputation for lack of veracity. As far as he was concerned, counsel did not have the absolute right to ask the third question and a judge would be justified in refusing to permit it.

Although opinion evidence *discrediting* a witness's testimony is receivable, the authorities are clear that evidence *bolstering* a witness's testimony is generally not receivable, even if it is expert testimony. For example, in *Kyselka*,[31] the Crown had called a psychiatrist who had testified that the complainant, a retarded girl who had alleged that she had been raped, was likely to be a truthful witness because of her mental retardation. The Ontario Court of Appeal, however, held that evidence bolstering the testimony of a witness was not admissible because it amounted to "oath helping".[32]

---

[30] 1998 CarswellOnt 3447, 129 C.C.C. (3d) 1, 18 C.R. (5th) 219, 112 O.A.C. 233, [1998] O.J. No. 3521 (C.A.).

[31] 1962 CarswellOnt 13, 133 C.C.C. 103, 37 C.R. 391, [1962] O.W.N. 160 (C.A.).

[32] See also *Burkart* (1964), 1964 CarswellSask 75, [1965] 3 C.C.C. 210, 45 C.R. 383, 50 W.W.R. 515 (C.A.).

(b) Child Abuse Cases

In child abuse cases, the Crown may seek to have expert evidence admitted to the effect that certain behavioural patterns exhibited by a child complainant are consistent with sexual or other abuse. The purpose of such evidence is to persuade the trier of fact that the allegations of abuse by the complainant against the accused are probably true. It then becomes the responsibility of the trial judge, as gatekeeper, to ensure that such evidence does not cross the fine line and tread upon the oath-helping rule that prohibits opinion as to the credibility of the witness.

Although the rule is clear that evidence *bolstering* a witness's testimony is generally not receivable, even if it is expert testimony, the courts in recent years have come under increasing pressure to admit medical or psychiatric evidence of the credibility of a complainant in sexual assault cases. That pressure has been strong, particularly where the complainant is a child or is mentally infirm, because of the ease with which their evidence can be attacked by the defence and the fear that such victims are not receiving the kind of protection from the courts that they need and deserve. Although the courts have continued to apply the rule prohibiting direct comment by an expert on the credibility of the complainant, such evidence has been not been rejected if it only *inferentially* bolsters the complainant's credibility.

For example, in *Beliveau*,[33] MacFarlane J.A. admitted the testimony of a paediatrician that the complainant, because of her age, was unlikely to have a motive to lie only because,

> These questions were necessary in assessing the validity of his opinion on an issue in the case, and not to establish that the child was a truthful witness.

In *B. (G.)*,[34] the Supreme Court was prepared to go even further. There, three young offenders were charged with the sexual assault of a seven-year-old child. A psychologist specializing in the treatment of victims of sexual abuse had testified that the changes noted in the victim's behaviour, such as bed-wetting and nightmares, were characteristic of behaviour noted in victims of this type of sexual abuse. It was held that evidence of an expert as to the psychological and physical conditions that frequently arise as a result of sexual abuse of a child was admissible because it provided assistance to the trier of fact in concluding whether an assault had occurred. Since the defence was that there had been no assault, the admissibility of that evidence

---

[33] 1986 CarswellBC 665, 30 C.C.C. (3d) 193 (C.A.).
[34] 1990 CarswellSask 20, 1990 CarswellSask 410, [1990] 2 S.C.R. 30, 56 C.C.C. (3d) 200, 77 C.R. (3d) 347, (sub nom. *R. v. B. (G.) (No. 2)*) 111 N.R. 31, 86 Sask. R. 111, [1990] S.C.J. No. 58.

inferentially bolstered the complainant's credibility on that particular issue. Nevertheless, Madam Justice Wilson delivering the judgment of the Court, warned that:

> ... the expert evidence should not be used to bolster the credibility of witnesses or indicate that they should be believed since credibility is a matter exclusively reserved for the trier of fact.[35]

Unfortunately what amounts to a direct comment on a complainant's credibility and an inferential bolstering of that testimony is not always easy to determine.

One issue that frequently arises in child abuse cases is why there was a delay between the alleged assault and the complaint. In such instance, the Crown may seek to adduce expert evidence to explain why a child has delayed making a complaint of abuse, particularly where there has been an unusually long delay between the occurrence of the alleged assault and the complaint by the child. Here the courts have been generally reluctant to admit such evidence. For example, in *R. (S.)*,[36] evidence was admitted on behalf of the Crown to explain why there was a delay of several months between the time that the child first complained of sexual abuse and the date when the charges were laid. The explanation was that a social worker believed her, but the investigating officer did not. To resolve the issue, a psychologist was called in to conduct an assessment of the child's credibility and the charges were laid. Both the social worker and the psychologist were allowed to give evidence, before the child testified, that they believed her. In allowing an appeal from a conviction, the Ontario Court of Appeal said that the effective purpose of the evidence was to bolster the credibility of the complainant and it was therefore not admissible. The better way to deal with the question of delay between the report and the charges was to simply tell the jury that they should not speculate about the delay, because it was not a matter that concerned them.

The question of delayed reporting was also considered by the Supreme Court in *D. (D.)*.[37] There it was held that delay was the proper subject for a simple jury instruction by the trial judge that there was no inviolable rule as to how victims of trauma, like a sexual assault, will behave. Some will make an immediate complaint, some will delay in exposing abuse and some will never disclose abuse. Reasons are many and include embarrassment,

---

[35] *Ibid.*, at p. 207 [C.C.C.].

[36] 1992 CarswellOnt 101, 8 O.R. (3d) 679, 73 C.C.C. (3d) 225, 15 C.R. (4th) 102, 56 O.A.C. 1 (C.A.).

[37] 2000 CarswellOnt 3255, 2000 CarswellOnt 3256, 148 C.C.C. (3d) 41, 36 C.R. (5th) 261 (S.C.C.).

fear, guilt or lack of understanding or knowledge. On the other hand in *Talbot*,[38] it was held that while the timing of delay, standing alone, signifies nothing and therefore expert evidence is not needed, expert evidence with respect to patterns of disclosure among sexual abuse victims that include not only delays in disclosure but also inconsistencies in disclosure and recantation is admissible to help the jury make an appropriate and informed determination of the complainant's credibility.

Nevertheless, the Supreme Court has been prepared to accept that expert evidence of human conduct in the psychological and physical factors that may lead to certain behaviour relevant to credibility is admissible, *provided the testimony goes beyond the ordinary experience of the trier of fact.* In *Marquard*,[39] the accused was charged with the aggravated assault of her three-and-a-half-year-old granddaughter. It was alleged that she had put the child's face against a hot stove door in order to discipline her. The child's unsworn testimony was that her "nana" had put her in (or on) the stove. Both the accused and her husband had testified that they discovered the child early in the morning, screaming, after she had burned herself trying to light a cigarette with a butane lighter. Among the expert testimony called by both the Crown and the defence was a witness who commented on the child's credibility. The Court said that the testimony of an expert as to why children may lie to hospital staff about the cause of their injuries was clearly admissible because the witness was an expert in child behaviour. A lay jury needed expert evidence to understand the full implication of the witness's change in story. However, the Court said that when the expert testified that she personally did not believe the child's first story, preferring the second version which the child told at trial, she crossed the line between expert testimony and human behaviour and assessment of credibility of the witness herself.

Similarly, in *B. (R.H.)*,[40] the Supreme Court re-affirmed that the use of experts to explain human behaviour is now clearly admissible to furnish the court with scientific information likely to be outside the experience and knowledge of the judge and jury. The Court said that the behaviour of a person who has been systematically abused is an example of a matter on which experts may assist. Moreover, the fact that such evidence is inadmis-

---

[38] 2002 CarswellOnt 63, 161 C.C.C. (3d) 256, 1 C.R. (6th) 396 (C.A.); see also *Tayebi*, 2001 CarswellBC 2731, 161 C.C.C. (3d) 197, 48 C.R. (5th) 354 (C.A.).

[39] 1993 CarswellOnt 995, 1993 CarswellOnt 127, [1993] 4 S.C.R. 223, 85 C.C.C. (3d) 193, 25 C.R. (4th) 1, 108 D.L.R. (4th) 47, 159 N.R. 81, 66 O.A.C. 161, [1993] S.C.J. No. 119.

[40] 1994 CarswellBC 1237, 1994 CarswellBC 576, [1994] 1 S.C.R. 656, 89 C.C.C. (3d) 193, 29 C.R. (4th) 113, 42 B.C.A.C. 161, 165 N.R. 374, 67 W.A.C. 161.

sible for one purpose (*i.e.*, to show the truthfulness of a witness) does not automatically prevent it being received for another legitimate purpose (*i.e.*, to show whether the complainant was sexually abused). Here, B. was charged with indecently assaulting the complainant when she was nine and sexually assaulting her when she was 16. The charges came to light when the complainant, herself, was convicted of sexually abusing young boys that she was babysitting and ordered to take counselling. At that time, the complainant revealed that she had been sexually abused as a child. At trial, the complainant said that she did not reveal the assaults when they occurred because B. was a good friend of her father. She feared that she would be disbelieved and would lose her father. Her psychiatrist testified as to her condition as a consequence of what she had undergone, giving a picture of why she reacted as she did. On appeal, the accused's counsel argued that the psychiatrist's evidence went to the very root of the issue before the judge — that she had been sexually abused by the accused — which the court had to decide and usurped the function of the trial judge. The Supreme Court disagreed. The Court said that the fact that such testimony was admissible to explain human behaviour did not render it inadmissible just because it also violated the rule against oath helping.

Again, in *W. (A.)*,[41] the Ontario Court of Appeal held that the testimony of an abuse expert that young children do not have the motivation or sophistication, nor the mental capacity, to be elaborately deceptive and to manufacture a complex fabrication to achieve an ulterior purpose was properly received by the trial judge. Although this opinion supported the credibility of the complainant, it was not excluded by the rule prohibiting a witness, expert or otherwise, from simply asserting his or her belief in the truthfulness of a particular child in support of that child's credibility. However, the Court did say that the opinion expressed by another expert psychologist, who had examined the complainant, to the effect that she did not believe that the complainant could have fabricated the allegations, was not proper evidence for the witness to give because it went directly to an opinion as to the credibility of the witness.

The courts, however, are more reluctant to admit expert testimony of the behavioural characteristics of child sexual abusers. Here the characteristics must be of such distinctiveness that a comparison of one with the other will be of material assistance in determining guilt or innocence. For example, in

---

[41] 1994 CarswellOnt 1211, 94 C.C.C. (3d) 441, 44 C.R. (4th) 319, (sub nom. *R. v. W.*) 75 O.A.C. 130 (C.A.); reversed 1995 CarswellOnt 957, 1995 CarswellOnt 1181, [1995] 4 S.C.R. 51, 102 C.C.C. (3d) 96, 44 C.R. (4th) 317, (sub nom. *R. v. W.*) 206 N.R. 161, 96 O.A.C. 244.

A. (G.R.),[42] a charge of sexual assault, the Ontario Court of Appeal rejected the evidence of a psychologist that certain characteristics were usually found in child sexual abusers, namely, that abusers will be members of the family or close friends and will use bribes or threats to have the victim remain silent. The Court said that the opinion did not have that distinctiveness which would permit its use as evidence.

4. OPINION AS TO THE CREDIBILITY OF THE ACCUSED

The general rule is that the Crown is not entitled to call either experts or lay persons to give opinion evidence that the accused is not a credible witness, unless the accused puts his or her character in issue, in which case only character evidence may be called in reply. Nor is the Crown allowed to lead in-chief expert opinion about the accused's disposition to commit a crime unless it is relevant to an issue and is not being used merely as evidence of disposition.[43] The same rule applies to prevent an accused from calling experts and laymen to give their opinion that he or she is a credible witness. However, in the last twenty-five years, some authorities have allowed experts to testify as to the disposition or propensity of the accused to commit or not commit certain acts where they are relevant to a fact in issue. Unfortunately, the principles governing the admission of such evidence have not been clearly stated.

For example, in *Lupien,*[44] the Supreme Court of Canada said that an expert could testify that an accused lacked homosexual propensities to support the accused's evidence that he did not know that his companion, who was dressed as a woman was, in fact, a man. Similarly, in *McMillan,*[45] an accused charged with the murder of his child was allowed to call an expert to testify that his wife had the disposition to commit the murder. A closer examination of both these cases reveals that the evidence was admitted more to demonstrate lack of propensity of the accused, rather than to support his

---

[42] 1994 CarswellOnt 120, 35 C.R. (4th) 340, [1994] O.J. No. 2930 (C.A.).

[43] *Mohan,* 1994 CarswellOnt 1155, 1994 CarswellOnt 66, [1994] 2 S.C.R. 9, 18 O.R. (3d) 160 (note), 89 C.C.C. (3d) 402, 29 C.R. (4th) 243, 114 D.L.R. (4th) 419, 166 N.R. 245, 71 O.A.C. 241.

[44] (1969), 1969 CarswellBC 258, 1969 CarswellBC 185, [1970] S.C.R. 263, [1970] 2 C.C.C. 193, 9 D.L.R. (3d) 1, 71 W.W.R. 110, 9 C.R.N.S. 165.

[45] 1975 CarswellOnt 7, 7 O.R. (2d) 750, 23 C.C.C. (2d) 160, 29 C.R.N.S. 191 (C.A.); affirmed 1977 CarswellOnt 474, 1977 CarswellOnt 474F, [1977] 2 S.C.R. 824, 33 C.C.C. (2d) 360, 73 D.L.R. (3d) 759, 15 N.R. 20.

credibility. Again, in *Dietrich*,[46] the Ontario Court of Appeal, relying on the authority of *Lupien*, permitted an expert to testify that the accused had a psychopathic personality with a propensity for confessing to things that he did not do and should be believed when he testified that his confession was false. Although *Dietrich* is authority that an expert may give evidence bolstering the credibility of an accused, the evidence really went to establish that Dietrich had the propensity and time to confess to things that he did not do.

However, in *Mohan*,[47] the Supreme Court of Canada stressed that evidence of an expert witness that the accused, by reason of his or her mental make-up or condition of the mind, would be incapable of committing or disposed to commit the crime is limited in scope. The Court noted that although the exception has been applied to abnormal behaviour connoting sexual deviance, its underlying rationale was based on distinctiveness.

Sopinka J., delivering the judgment of the Court, said that before an expert's opinion as to disposition may be admitted as evidence, the trial judge must be satisfied, as a matter of law, that either the perpetrator of the crime or the accused has distinctive behavioural characteristics such that a comparison of one with the other will be of material assistance in determining innocence or guilt. Although the judge's decision should be on the basis of common sense and experience, it must not be made in a vacuum. The judge must determine whether the expert is merely expressing a personal opinion or whether the behavioural profile which the expert is putting forward is in common use as a reliable indicator of membership in a distinctive group. A finding that the scientific community has developed a standard profile for the offender who commits this type of crime will satisfy the criteria of relevance and necessity. The evidence will qualify as an exception to the exclusionary rule relating to character evidence, provided the trial judge is satisfied that the proposed evidence is within the field of expertise of the expert witness.

In *Mohan*, the defence of the accused, a doctor charged with sexually assaulting four female patients aged 13 to 16, was that what the patients said was not true. The trial judge had refused to allow the defence to call a psychiatrist who would say that the offences had unusual features that would indicate that a physician who committed them was a member of one or the other of an unusual and limited class and, that in his opinion, the

---

[46] 1970 CarswellOnt 12, [1970] 3 O.R. 725, 1 C.C.C. (2d) 49, 11 C.R.N.S. 22 (C.A.); leave to appeal refused [1970] S.C.R. xi, [1970] 3 O.R. 744n, 1 C.C.C. (2d) 68n.

[47] *Supra*, note 43.

accused was not a member of either class. It was held that the trial judge was correct in not allowing the admission of such evidence. There was no body of evidence that doctors who commit sexual assaults fall into a distinctive class with identifiable characteristics.

7

ADMISSIONS AND CONFESSIONS

1. THE RULE

A confession is defined as a statement either in writing or given orally by a person accused of a crime that shows or tends to show that he is guilty of the crime with which he is charged. An admission is said to be distinguishable from a confession because it is only an acknowledgment of a material fact that may form a link in the chain of proof against the accused. Unlike a confession, an admission need not necessarily be in writing or made orally; it can also include conduct that could reasonably be taken to be intended as an assertion.[1] The simplest example of an admission by conduct is when a police officer asks the accused if the murder weapon belongs to him and the accused nods his head affirmatively. No words have been spoken, but his

---

[1] *St. Lawrence*, 1949 CarswellOnt 4, [1949] O.R. 215, 93 C.C.C. 376, 7 C.R. 464 (H.C.).

221

conduct is sufficient to constitute an admission that the weapon belongs to him.

Some legal scholars regard admissions and confessions as exceptions to the hearsay rule; others say they are not because they are not offered to prove a fact in issue, but only to impeach the credibility of the accused. The first view is probably correct. Admissions and confessions are exceptions to the hearsay rule because it is only logical to assume that what a person says against his or her own interest is probably true.

The distinction between a confession and an admission is not important when it comes to the rule relating to their admissibility. Both are governed by the same rule, which was stated almost 100 years ago by Lord Sumner in *Ibrahim*,[2] and judicially endorsed in 1949 in Canada by the Supreme Court in *Boudreau*:[3]

> It has long been established as a positive rule of English criminal law, that no statement by an accused is admissible in evidence against him unless it is shown by the prosecution to have been a voluntary statement, in the sense that it has not been obtained from him either by fear of prejudice or hope of advantage exercised or held out by a person in authority. The principle is as old as Lord Hale.

There are three reasons for this rule. The first is the concern that a confession obtained as a result of a threat or an inducement may be false; only a confession freely made should be considered reliable. The second reason is a more emotional one. Until the middle of the seventeenth century, it was a common practice of the Ecclesiastical Courts to compel anyone suspected of committing a crime against the security of the state to attend before a government official and to require him to take an oath, called the *ex officio* oath, to tell the truth to all questions that might be put to him. He was not told of the specific crime or the names of the witnesses for the Crown. If he told the truth, he might find himself charged with a crime that would put his life in peril. If he lied, he was charged with perjury and imprisoned. If he said nothing, he was arrested, tortured and incarcerated. It was not until the famous *Lilburne* case in 1641[4] that the *ex officio* oath was abolished and it was recognized that no man should be required to incriminate himself — *nemo tenetur prodere se ipsum* or *nemo tenetur prodere accusare*.

---

[2] (1914), [1914] A.C. 599, [1914-15] All E.R. Rep. 874, 24 Cox C.C. 174 (Hong Kong P.C.).

[3] 1949 CarswellQue 3, [1949] S.C.R. 262, 94 C.C.C. 1, 7 C.R. 427, [1949] 3 D.L.R. 81.

[4] (1641) (3 State Tr. 1316).

There is a third reason why the courts will reject a confession that has been obtained under circumstances indicating that it is not voluntary. It is important that the public have confidence in the way that the police carry out their duties to investigate crime. Unless the court is satisfied that the confession of an accused is free and voluntary, there is the concern that the public will believe that oppressive tactics are regularly used by the police. This will result in a loss of support and respect by the community for the criminal justice system.

Thus no statement made by an accused is admissible against him unless it is found to be voluntary "in the sense that it has not been obtained from him either by fear of prejudice or hope of advantage exercised or held out by a person in authority". The onus is upon the Crown to prove that the statement is voluntary before the trial judge is authorized to allow the jury to hear it. To pass this threshold test, the Crown must satisfy the trial judge beyond a reasonable doubt that the statement was a voluntary one.

2. FORMAL ADMISSIONS

At common law, an accused was not permitted to make a formal admission where he was charged with a felony; nor is it certain that he could even do so where the charge was a misdemeanour. Section 655 of the *Criminal Code*[5] has altered that rule. It permits an accused charged with an indictable offence to "admit *any fact* alleged against him for the purpose of dispensing with proof thereof".

Does section 655 permit the defence to admit the voluntariness of a confession? The voluntariness of a confession is a question of law and is, strictly speaking, not something that can be admitted because section 655 only permits admissions of fact. However, trial judges usually get around this problem by having the accused admit that all of the facts leading up to the taking of the statement are consistent with it being voluntary.

Although the admission is characterized as a factual one, it does have legal consequences. In *Park*,[6] the Supreme Court went so far as to suggest that the defence has the right to waive the usual *voir dire* held to consider the voluntariness of the statement, and the trial judge has a wide discretion to accept that waiver if he or she is satisfied that the statement is voluntary.

---

[5] R.S.C. 1985, c. C-46.

[6] 1981 CarswellOnt 100, 1981 CarswellOnt 52, [1981] 2 S.C.R. 64, 59 C.C.C. (2d) 385, 21 C.R. (3d) 182 (Eng.), 26 C.R. (3d) 164 (Fr.), 122 D.L.R. (3d) 1, 37 N.R. 501.

3. ADMISSIONS BY CONDUCT

If we can assume that what a person says against his or her own interest is probably true and should be admitted, it follows that how a suspect reacts when an incriminating statement is made in the suspect's presence should be admissible against that person if the suspect's actions or conduct is indicative of guilt.

For example, if Constable Jones, who is investigating a charge of assault, confronts the accused Brown and tells him that he has reasonable grounds to believe that he has just assaulted Smith and Brown responds by punching the officer and running away, it would be natural to assume that his conduct is indicative of guilt and should be admissible against him. However, if Brown responds by denying the charge, as one would expect an innocent person to do, then his denial is not admissible at the instance of the defence because it is self-serving. This contradiction is often difficult to understand.

The Ontario Court of Appeal has correctly warned that the probative value of demeanour evidence is in many circumstances more apparent than real for two reasons.[7] First of all, it assumes that there is a "normal" range of reaction to highly stressful situations that is applicable to all individuals. The second is that demeanour evidence assumes that outward appearance accurately reflects an individual's state of mind or emotional state. Unfortunately, demeanour evidence has been routinely admitted without recognizing that there may be cultural responses to stressful situations that may not be necessarily consistent with the expected norm.

Silence of the accused in the face of an accusation by the police creates another problem. Although generally silence might cause one to ask why an innocent person has not denied his guilt, the law does not permit the Crown to lead evidence of the accused's silence in the face of an accusation. The reason is that an accused's right to silence is a constitutional guarantee under the *Charter of Rights and Freedoms*. It is unfair for the police to caution an accused that he has the right to remain silent and then use that silence in the face of a question that suggests his guilt.[8]

---

[7] *Trotta*, 2004 CarswellOnt 4363, 190 C.C.C. (3d) 199 (C.A.); reversed 2007 CarswellOnt 7160, 2007 CarswellOnt 7161, 225 C.C.C. (3d) 97, 50 C.R. (6th) 273 (S.C.C.).

[8] *Chambers*, 1990 CarswellBC 217, 1990 CarswellBC 761, [1990] 2 S.C.R. 1293, 49 B.C.L.R. (2d) 299, 59 C.C.C. (3d) 321, 80 C.R. (3d) 235, [1990] 6 W.W.R. 554, (sub nom. *R. v. Chambers (No. 2)*) 119 N.R. 321; *Turcotte*, 2005 CarswellBC 2209, 2005 CarswellBC 2210, 200 C.C.C. (3d) 289, 31 C.R. (6th) 197 (S.C.C.).

On the other hand, silence in the face of an accusation by someone other than the police will permit an inference that the accused assented to the accusation.[9] This will depend upon whether the accused's lack of response to the accusation, in the circumstances in which it is made, is reasonable.

A denial of an accusation might in some circumstances also amount to an acknowledgment of its truth.[10] In *Baron*, Mr. Justice Martin explained that:

> A denial by an accused of an incriminating statement in his or her presence does not necessarily preclude a jury from concluding that the accused has assented to the truth of the facts contained in the statement. The denial may be so equivocal or evasive as to permit an inference that the accused by his words or conduct has assented to it. However, mere disbelief of an unequivocal denial by an accused cannot have the effect of converting such a denial into an adoption of the facts contained in such statement, in the absence of additional circumstances warranting such an inference.[11]

Understandably, the courts have always been concerned that the jury may draw an unwarranted inference from such evidence. This has imposed on the trial judge the duty of determining in advance whether there is sufficient evidence from which a jury might reasonably conclude that the accused's conduct amounted to an acknowledgment of responsibility.[12] As Chief Justice MacKeigan observed in *Thompson*:[13]

> Where an accused has denied a statement such as this, it is for the trial Judge on the *voir dire* to consider whether there is any evidence in the accused's words, conduct or demeanour from which a jury could conclude that the accused, despite words of denial, really acknowledged or admitted the truth of statement. If there is no such evidence, the statement so denied should not go to the jury.

The real difficulty arises where the accused's response is ambiguous and open to interpretation. Should the trial judge refuse to admit the accused's response, or should he admit it and leave it to the jury to draw their own

---

[9] *Baron*, 1976 CarswellOnt 530, 14 O.R. (2d) 173, 31 C.C.C. (2d) 525, 73 D.L.R. (3d) 213 (C.A.).

[10] *Christie*, [1914] A.C. 545, 24 Cox C.C. 249 (U.K. H.L.).

[11] *Supra*, note 9, at p. 538 [C.C.C.].

[12] *Hebert*, 1990 CarswellYukon 4, 1990 CarswellYukon 7, [1990] 2 S.C.R. 151, 47 B.C.L.R. (2d) 1, 57 C.C.C. (3d) 1, 77 C.R. (3d) 145, [1990] 5 W.W.R. 1, 49 C.R.R. 114, 110 N.R. 1 and *Warner*, 1994 CarswellOnt 159, 21 O.R. (3d) 136, 94 C.C.C. (3d) 540, 75 O.A.C. 288 (C.A.); *Tanasichuk*, 2007 CarswellNB 532, 2007 CarswellNB 565, 227 C.C.C. (3d) 446 (C.A.); leave to appeal refused 2009 CarswellNB 68, 2009 CarswellNB 69 (S.C.C.).

[13] 1974 CarswellNS 5, 16 C.C.C. (2d) 374, 26 C.R.N.S. 144 (C.A.) at p. 380 [C.C.C.].

conclusions? One of the earliest decisions of the Ontario Court of Appeal in *Fargnoli*[14] demonstrates how even judges view a suspect's responses differently. There the accused was arrested for indecently assaulting his daughter and, when asked whether he wished to say anything, replied, "You got it all there . . . there is nothing more for me to say about it". Two members of the Ontario Court of Appeal held that the response amounted to an acceptance of the facts while the third dissented, holding that the response was ambiguous and ought not to have been admitted.

Nevertheless, it seems to be now accepted that it is the responsibility of the trial judge to determine whether, as a matter of law, the response of an accused to an accusation of guilt could reasonably be interpreted as an admission of guilt. If it could, then the judge must leave the issue to be decided by the jury. On the other hand, if there is some concern that its probative force is greatly outweighed by its prejudicial character, then such evidence should not be admitted.[15]

4. THE MEANING OF VOLUNTARY

A strict application of the *Ibrahim* rule means that no statement can be admitted if it was obtained as a result of either fear of prejudice induced (threat) or hope of advantage held out (promise of favour) by a person in authority. The test that the trial judge must apply is an objective one. What must be decided is the effect that the threat or promise of favour by the police, viewed objectively, could be expected to have on the ordinary citizen if he or she were accused of an offence.

The authorities do not require that the threat be made openly. Words or conduct which would lead an accused to believe that, unless a confession is made, violence will be used will amount to a threat. Even a veiled promise of punishment will amount to a threat. Indeed, threats or promises need not be aimed directly at the suspect for them to have a coercive effect.[16] However, they must be of such a nature that when considered in the light of the relationship between the person in authority and the accused, and all of the

---

[14] 1957 CarswellOnt 3, (sub nom. *Fargnoli v. R.*) 117 C.C.C. 359, 25 C.R. 310 (S.C.C.).

[15] *Moore*, 1984 CarswellOnt 1178, 15 C.C.C. (3d) 541, 5 O.A.C. 51 (C.A.); leave to appeal refused (sub nom. *Moore v. R.*) [1985] 1 S.C.R. x, 15 C.C.C. (3d) 541 (note), 7 O.A.C. 320 (note).

[16] *Oickle*, 2000 SCC 38, 2000 CarswellNS 257, 2000 CarswellNS 258, [2000] 2 S.C.R. 3, 187 N.S.R. (2d) 201, 147 C.C.C. (3d) 321, 36 C.R. (5th) 129, 190 D.L.R. (4th) 257, 585 A.P.R. 201, 259 N.R. 227, [2000] S.C.J. No. 38.

surrounding circumstances of the confession, it would tend to induce an accused to make an untrue statement. Thus, in considering the effect of the words or conduct of the person in authority on the accused, the trial judge must examine all of the surrounding circumstances that led to the making of the statement.

Historically words such as "it would be better for you if you told us what happened", or "you will be arrested if you do not tell us where the stolen goods are", or "you had better tell us the truth", or "it is necessary to give an explanation" have been held to be a threat; whereas words such as "be sure to tell the truth" and "be a good girl and tell the truth" have been held not to constitute a threat. The reason is that the first group of words is considered an expression of compulsion or obligation to speak, whereas the second is not. The dividing line, however, is often difficult to draw.[17] Subtle veiled threats, although implying that dire consequences may flow from a refusal to talk, do not automatically require exclusion.[18] The trial judge is required to examine carefully the entire context in which the specific words are used and ask whether there is a reasonable doubt that the resulting confession was voluntary.

The background of the accused may also be a relevant factor. Someone who has never been involved with the police before may be so terrified by the predicament in which he finds himself that he may be more influenced by suggestions made by a police officer than an experienced criminal would be.

A promise of favour or an inducement is anything that gives the accused some hope or expectation with respect to the charge or contemplated charge, or some other matter. That "some other matter" could be another charge against the accused or a charge against someone whom the accused might wish to help, such as his wife or child, or a close friend.[19] A promise of favour or inducement could result, not only from the police officer's words, but also from a combination of his words and those of the accused. For example, a police officer's affirmative reply to a question by an accused whether he would be released "if I give a statement" could constitute an inducement. Indeed, any explicit offer of assistance by a police officer to procure lenient treatment in return for a confession will usually warrant exclusion in all but exceptional cases.[20] Similarly, an offer of psychiatric as-

---

[17] See *S. (S.L.)*, 1999 CarswellAlta 88, 228 A.R. 361, 132 C.C.C. (3d) 146, 22 C.R. (5th) 71, 188 W.A.C. 361, [1999] A.J. No. 69 (C.A.).

[18] *Oickle, supra,* note 16.

[19] *Ibid.*

[20] *Ibid.*

sistance or other counselling for the suspect in exchange for a confession is clearly an inducement, although not as strong as an offer of leniency, and may be excluded. However, the officer must be in a position to deliver on the offer. Thus, moral or spiritual inducements that produce a confession will generally not be excluded since the inducement offered is not in the control of the officer. Similarly, a statement by the officer that convinces the suspect that he will feel better if he confesses will not be excluded since the officer has not offered anything.[21]

For forty years after *Ibrahim*, the courts applied the rule so strictly that exclusion occurred only where there was an actual threat or inducement. However, in 1956, the Supreme Court of Canada in *Fitton*,[22] finally recognized the role which compulsion or oppression could play in causing someone to make a confession. Mr. Justice Rand expressed it this way:

> The rule on the admission of confession . . . at times presents difficulty of application because its terms tend to conceal underlying considerations material to a determination. The cases of torture, actual or threatened, or of unabashed promises are clear; perplexity arises when more subtle elements must be evaluated. The strength of mind and will of the accused, the influence of custody or its surroundings, the effect of questions or of conversation, all call for delicacy in appreciation of the part they have played behind the admission, and to enable a court to decide whether what was said was freely and voluntarily said, that is, was free from the influence of hope or fear aroused by them.[23]

Oppressive conditions can sap a person's free will, which is a necessary element of a voluntary confession, and cause the suspect to confess in order to escape those conditions. Oppressive conditions can also overbear a suspect's will to the point that he or she comes to doubt their own memory, believe the relentless accusations made by the police and give an induced confession.[24] Since each individual has a unique psychological make-up, the court must closely examine all of the circumstances surrounding the taking of the statement, such as the length of the period of questioning, the length of time intervening between periods of questioning, whether the ac-

---

[21] *Ibid.*

[22] 1956 CarswellOnt 26, [1956] S.C.R. 958, 116 C.C.C. 1, 24 C.R. 371, 6 D.L.R. (2d) 529.

[23] *Ibid.*, at p. 5 [C.C.C.].

[24] *Oickle, supra,* note 16.

cused was given proper refreshment, and the individual characteristics of the accused.[25]

> What may be oppressive as regards a child, an invalid or an old man or somebody inexperienced in the ways of this world may turn out not to be oppressive when one finds that the accused person is a tough character and an experienced man of the world.[26]

It is important to observe at this stage that the focus of the traditional *Ibrahim* Rule was not on any conscious choice of an accused whether to speak or not to speak to the police; his or her rights could be viewed only negatively in the sense that there was a right not to be tortured or coerced into making a statement by threats or promises held out by a person who was, and whom the accused believed, was a person in authority. In 1979, however, the Supreme Court of Canada recognized for the first time that the focus should also be on the accused's state of mind. In *Ward*,[27] Mr. Justice Spence wrote:

> In my view, there is a further investigation of whether the statements were freely and voluntarily made even if no hope of advantage or fear of prejudice could be found in consideration of the mental condition of the accused at the time he made the statements *to determine whether or not the statements represented the operating mind of the accused.*[28]

Ward, who had been involved in a single car collision, was found lying unconscious outside his vehicle. His lady friend was found dead beside him. After being revived by mouth-to-mouth resuscitation at the scene of the accident, Ward was questioned by police officers but denied driving the vehicle. Thirty minutes later and again some five or six hours later at the hospital, he was questioned again and this time admitted driving the vehicle. He was charged with criminal negligence.

On the *voir dire*, Ward said that he could not remember anything from the time that he was in a hotel some hours before the accident until the afternoon or evening following the accident. His doctor testified that he could answer simple questions but was unable to tell them what happened. The Court held that the trial judge was correct in excluding Ward's answers to the police officers because they did not represent his "operating mind".

---

[25] *Hoilett*, 1999 CarswellOnt 1886, 136 C.C.C. (3d) 449, 26 C.R. (5th) 332, 121 O.A.C. 391 (C.A.).

[26] Note to *Priestley* (1966), 51 Cr. App. R. 1 (Eng. C.A.).

[27] 1979 CarswellAlta 192, 1979 CarswellAlta 164, [1979] 2 S.C.R. 30, 14 A.R. 412, 44 C.C.C. (2d) 498, 7 C.R. (3d) 153 (Eng.), 10 C.R. (3d) 289 (Fr.), 94 D.L.R. (3d) 18, [1979] 2 W.W.R. 193, 25 N.R. 514.

[28] *Ibid.*, at p. 506 [C.C.C.].

A similar result was reached in *Horvath*.[29] Horvath, a youth of 17, was charged with the murder of his mother. On the evening of his arrest, he was interrogated and cross-examined by two police officers for two and one-half hours, but the statement he gave contained nothing inculpatory. The next day, he was interviewed by another officer, a skilled interrogator, for four hours except for three brief intervals. Horvath, who was left alone during those three intervals, was observed by the officer reflecting aloud in what were called "monologues" or "soliloquies". During the second monologue, he admitted killing his mother and repeated the confession to the officer. In the third monologue, he asked his mother's forgiveness for having disclosed the incident. He then signed a confession.

The trial judge rejected the confession after accepting the opinion of a psychiatrist that Horvath had been in a hypnotic state for a large part of the interview before he signed the confession. In a split decision, the Supreme Court held that the confession, which had followed directly from the earlier statement, and which was made while under hypnosis, was not voluntary because it had been induced by conditions created earlier.

In 1986, the importance of the accused's subjective state of mind was expanded into a further consideration: whether the accused was aware of what was at stake in making any statement. In *Clarkson*,[30] the accused, while intoxicated, had confessed to the police to murdering her husband. The trial judge had excluded the statement because he was not satisfied that the accused was "aware of the consequences" of making the statement. The Supreme Court agreed that the judge was correct in excluding the confession, but only two of the seven members of the Court agreed with his reasons. Although the rest found that the accused had been deprived of her right to counsel, none specifically rejected the "awareness of the consequences" test. They held that it was up to the trial judge, in his or her unique position of hearing all of the witnesses, to decide that issue by balancing the probative value of the evidence in the light of the possible prejudice to the accused.

The "awareness of the consequences" test means that a statement made by an accused is not admissible if the accused is not aware that he or she is making a statement that may be used against him or her. *Clarkson* was a straightforward case involving an intoxicated accused, who, because of her

---

[29] 1979 CarswellBC 667, 1979 CarswellBC 758, [1979] 2 S.C.R. 376, 44 C.C.C. (2d) 385, 7 C.R. (3d) 97, 11 C.R. (3d) 206, 93 D.L.R. (3d) 1, [1979] 3 W.W.R. 1, 25 N.R. 537.

[30] 1986 CarswellNB 14, 1986 CarswellNB 104, [1986] 1 S.C.R. 383, 69 N.B.R. (2d) 40, (sub nom. *Clarkson v. R.*) 25 C.C.C. (3d) 207, 50 C.R. (3d) 289, 26 D.L.R. (4th) 493, 177 A.P.R. 40, 19 C.R.R. 209, 66 N.R. 114.

condition, was found by the trial judge not to be aware of the consequences of making a statement. Should the rule be limited to persons in similar situations, such as the intoxicated or the mentally challenged; or should it be extended to persons of limited cognitive ability who may not appreciate the consequences of speaking to the police?

In a series of cases that followed *Clarkson*, the Supreme Court said that the "awareness of the consequences" test should only be extended to persons of limited cognitive ability. The first, *Hebert*,[31] involved an accused who had refused to give a statement to the police after he had consulted counsel, but who later unknowingly confessed to an undercover police officer who had been placed in his cell. McLachlin J. (as she then was), delivering the majority judgment of the Court, held that the confession to the undercover officer should be excluded because the accused's right to counsel had been infringed. In other words, by placing an undercover officer in his cell, the accused's right to remain silent, which is protected as a fundamental principle of justice under section 7 of the *Canadian Charter of Rights and Freedoms*, had been breached. This was because "the guarantee of the right to counsel confirms that the essence of the right is the accused's freedom to choose whether to make a statement or not".

McLachlin J., however, went on to stress that:

> I should not be taken as suggesting that the right to make an informed choice whether to speak to the authorities or to remain silent necessitates *a particular state of knowledge on the suspect's part over and above the basic requirement that he possess an operating mind.* The Charter does not place on the authorities and the courts *the impossible task of subjectively gauging whether the suspect appreciates the situation and the alternatives.* Rather, it seeks to ensure that the suspect is in a position to make an informed choice by giving him the right to counsel. The guarantee of the right to counsel in the Charter suggests that the suspect must have the right to choose whether to speak to the police or not, but it equally suggests that the test for whether that choice has been violated is essentially objective. [Emphasis added.][32]

In other words, the mental element required by an accused before a confession will be accepted is that of an "operating mind", the *Horvath* and *Ward* test. The test is essentially an objective one with a limited subjective element. The *Clarkson* case was only referred to in her judgment in the context of the waiver of the right to silence.

---

[31] 1990 CarswellYukon 4, 1990 CarswellYukon 7, [1990] 2 S.C.R. 151, 47 B.C.L.R. (2d) 1, 57 C.C.C. (3d) 1, 77 C.R. (3d) 145, [1990] 5 W.W.R. 1, 49 C.R.R. 114, 110 N.R. 1.

[32] *Ibid.*, at p. 183 [C.R.].

The second case, *Evans*,[33] reaffirmed that distinction. The *Evans* case involved a youth of subnormal intelligence who was charged with the brutal murder of two women. The police had suspected that the accused's older brother was involved in the killings and had arrested the accused on a charge of trafficking in marijuana in the hope that he would be able to provide evidence against his brother. When advised of his right to counsel and asked if he understood his rights, the accused said "no". During the course of his interrogation by the police, the accused became the prime suspect in the murders, but was not told that he was being detained for murder; nor was he advised again of his right to counsel. The Court found that the statements taken from the accused had been improperly admitted by the trial judge because the accused's right to counsel had been infringed. McLachlin J., who again delivered the majority view, this time said:

> In view of the appellant's subnormal mental capacity and the circumstances surrounding his arrest — the fact that no attempt was made to explain his rights to him after he indicated that he did not understand them, as well as the fact that he was subjected to a day of aggressive and at times deceptive interrogation which apparently left him feeling as if he had "no choice" but to confess — *I am not satisfied that he appreciated the consequences of making the written statement and thereby waiving his right to counsel* or, to put it another way, that he waived his right "with full knowledge of the rights the procedure was enacted to protect and of the effect the waiver will have on those rights in the process. [Emphasis added.][34]

In other words, because of his subnormal mental capacity, the test was "an appreciation of the consequences of making the statement". This time, the *Clarkson* case was cited as authority.

In *Hebert* and *Evans*, the Supreme Court drew a distinction between a person with normal mental faculties and a person who is mentally incapacitated because of an inherited condition or because of alcohol (and possibly drugs). In the former, the threshold test for voluntariness is an operating mind, that is, one who understands what he or she is saying. In the latter, the threshold test appears to be higher. It includes not only one who understands what he or she is saying, but one who also appreciates that what he or she is saying may be used against them.

---

[33] 1991 CarswellBC 918, 1991 CarswellBC 417, [1991] 1 S.C.R. 869, 63 C.C.C. (3d) 289, 4 C.R. (4th) 144, 3 C.R.R. (2d) 315, 124 N.R. 278.
[34] *Ibid.*, at p. 164 [C.R.].

In *Whittle*,[35] the Supreme Court re-affirmed its earlier decision in *Hebert*. It adopted a dual test in determining whether a confession should be admitted. The first test requires a focus on the cognitive ability of the accused. This required no more than "an operating mind". The "operating mind" test includes,[36]

> ... a limited mental component which requires that the accused have sufficient cognitive capacity to understand what he or she is saying and what is said. This includes the ability to understand a caution that the evidence can be used against the accused.

The same standard applies with respect to the right to silence in determining whether the accused has the mental capacity to make an active choice.

> In exercising the right to counsel or waiving the right, the accused must possess the limited cognitive capacity required for fitness to stand trial. The accused must be capable of communicating with counsel to instruct counsel, and understand the function of counsel and that he or she can dispense with counsel even if this is not in the accused's best interests. It is not necessary that the accused possess analytical ability. The level of cognitive ability is the same as that required with respect to the confession rule and the right to silence. The accused must have the mental capacity of an operating mind as outlined above.

The judge is not required to determine whether the accused is capable of making a good or a wise choice, or one that is in his best interests when he chooses to speak. In other words, there is no requirement that the accused be capable of understanding the consequences of making a statement.[37]

The Court said that once the subjective mental capacity of the accused is established, the trial judge must turn his or her attention to the second part of the test: the effect of police conduct on the accused's decision to speak. Here the issue for the judge is whether the actions of the police deprived the accused of making an effective choice by reason of threats or inducement, oppression or coercion, trickery or misinformation, or lack of information. If the judge has any doubt on the point, then the statement should not be admitted.

This raises the issue of how far the police are entitled to go in aggressive questioning of an accused that will constitute an "atmosphere of oppression" depriving the accused of the effective choice whether or not to speak.

---

[35] 1994 CarswellOnt 1163, 1994 CarswellOnt 91, [1994] 2 S.C.R. 914, 92 C.C.C. (3d) 11, 32 C.R. (4th) 1, 116 D.L.R. (4th) 416, 23 C.R.R. (2d) 6, 170 N.R. 16, 73 O.A.C. 201.

[36] *Ibid.*, [1994] 2 S.C.R. at 934.

[37] *Oickle, supra,* note 16.

In *Paternak*,[38] the trial judge had excluded statements made by the accused because of aggressive questioning by the police. In allowing an appeal by the Crown from the trial judge's decision, Mr. Justice Kerans of the Alberta Court of Appeal was of the view that the existence of an atmosphere of oppression by the police does not, *of itself*, create a loss of effective choice. As far as he was concerned, there could be an atmosphere of oppression and yet no loss of cognitive ability.

> For an otherwise healthy and mature human to be deprived of an effective choice, I am inclined to the view that the influence must be so overbearing that it can be said that the detainee has lost any meaningfully independent ability to choose to remain silent, and has become a mere tool in the hands of the police. That can happen, of course. And sometimes a judge will have a doubt whether it happened, and shall refuse to admit the statement.[39]

On further appeal, the Supreme Court[40] restored the trial judge's decision excluding the statement on the basis that the accused's rights had been violated when the police failed to re-warn him concerning his right to counsel when there was a substantial change in his jeopardy. The Court did not deal with the question of aggressive questioning by the police.

In *Oickle*,[41] the Supreme Court decided that threats or promises, oppression, the operating mind requirement and police trickery were at the core of the confessions rule. The Court said that although a threat need not be aimed directly at the suspect to have a coercive effect, it had to be of such a nature that when considered in the light of the relationship between the interrogator and the accused, and all the surrounding circumstances, it would tend to induce the accused to make an *untrue* statement. An explicit offer to procure lenient treatment in return for a confession would warrant exclusion in all but exceptional cases; an offer of psychiatric or other assistance in exchange for a confession was not as strong as leniency, while moral or spiritual inducements would generally not produce an involuntary confession. Persistent and often accusatorial questioning *that was not hostile ag-*

---

[38] 1995 CarswellAlta 281, 174 A.R. 129, 33 Alta. L.R. (3d) 71, 101 C.C.C. (3d) 452, 42 C.R. (4th) 292, 102 W.A.C. 129, [1995] A.J. No. 795 (C.A.); reversed 1996 CarswellAlta 948, 1996 CarswellAlta 949, 110 C.C.C. (3d) 382, 2 C.R. (5th) 119 (S.C.C.).

[39] *Ibid.*, at p. 301 [C.R.].

[40] 1996 CarswellAlta 948, 1996 CarswellAlta 949, [1996] 3 S.C.R. 607, 187 A.R. 395, 44 Alta. L.R. (3d) 201, 110 C.C.C. (3d) 382, 2 C.R. (5th) 119, 203 N.R. 250, 127 W.A.C. 395.

[41] 2000 CarswellNS 257, 2000 CarswellNS 258, 147 C.C.C. (3d) 321, 36 C.R. (5th) 129 (S.C.C.).

gressive or intimidating and did not hold out any implied threat or promise would not of itself render a confession involuntary. The Court stressed that the application of the confessions rule was, of necessity, contextual. When reviewing a confession, a trial judge had to consider all of the relevant factors together: threats or promises, oppression and the operating mind requirement. Only police trickery was a discrete inquiry. While police trickery was still related to voluntariness, its more specific objective was maintaining the integrity of the criminal justice system.

In *Spencer*, the *Paternak* test was applied by the trial judge and the accused's statement was admitted on the basis that "nowhere is there an indication of a threat or a quid pro quo".[42] The British Columbia Court of Appeal,[43] however, allowed the appeal, specifically rejecting the *Paternak* test because it required a high degree of domination over the will of the accused, lessening the burden on the Crown to prove voluntariness, and substituted volition as the key element instead of the element of a *quid pro quo*. A majority (5-2) panel of the Supreme Court, however, restored the trial judge's decision. The Court said that while a *quid pro quo* is an important factor in establishing the existence of a threat or promise, it was not, *by itself*, determinative. The proper test, the Court said, was the contextual test set out in *Oickle*. The trial judge was required to consider all of the relevant factors when reviewing a confession.

The *Spencer* decision was followed in the same year by *Singh*.[44] In *Singh*, the accused was advised of his right to counsel and privately consulted with counsel. However, during the course of two subsequent interviews with the police, he asserted his right to remain silent on 18 occasions and was ignored by his interrogator. The trial judge ruled, after reviewing all of the circumstances surrounding the interrogation and the making of an incriminating admission, that the admission came freely and did not result from the police systematically breaking down his operating mind or undermining his right to silence. In split (5-4) decision, the majority surprisingly said this did not amount to either an involuntary confession or a violation of the right to remain silent. The majority felt that it was not appropriate to impose a rigid requirement that police refrain from questioning a detainee who states that he or she does not wish to speak to police. Such an approach

---

[42] 2003 CarswellBC 760, [2003] B.C.J. No. 751 (S.C.); reversed in part 2006 CarswellBC 407, 207 C.C.C. (3d) 47 (C.A.); reversed 2007 CarswellBC 479, 2007 CarswellBC 480, 217 C.C.C. (3d) 353, 44 C.R. (6th) 199 (S.C.C.).

[43] 2006 CarswellBC 407, 207 C.C.C. (3d) 47 (C.A.); reversed 2007 CarswellBC 479, 2007 CarswellBC 480, 217 C.C.C. (3d) 353, 44 C.R. (6th) 199 (S.C.C.).

[44] 2007 SCC 48, 2007 CarswellBC 2588, 2007 CarswellBC 2589, [2007] 3 S.C.R. 405, 225 C.C.C. (3d) 103, 51 C.R. (6th) 199.

would overshoot the protection afforded to the individual's freedom of choice both at common law and under the *Charter, and ignored the state interest in the effective investigation of crime.* The minority strongly disagreed. They argued that while detainees who have asserted their right to silence are entitled to change their minds, they cannot be compelled to do so by the persistent disregard of that asserted choice. The right to silence, like the right to counsel, is a constitutional promise that must be kept. Moreover, there was no evidence to support the majority proposition that the ability of the police to investigate crime in Canada would be unduly impaired by the effective exercise of the pre-trial right to silence or would have a "devastating impact" on criminal investigations anywhere in Canada.

Although the majority in *Singh* was not prepared to impose a rigid requirement that the police refrain from questioning a detainee who stated that he or she did not wish to speak to them, it was not suggested that persistent questioning would ever preclude a claim by a detainee that his or her answers to the questions were not voluntary. Indeed, the majority recognized that under both the common law and *Charter* rules, police persistence in continuing an interview, despite repeated assertions by the detainee that he or she wishes to remain silent, may well raise a strong argument that the subsequently obtained statement was not the product of a free will to speak to authorities.[45] Thus, the law now seems to be reasonably clear that questions by the police that are designed to influence the accused to speak freely about his or her possible involvement in the crime are not prohibited, so long as they are not obtained as a result of threats or promises, oppression, or police trickery that would shock the community.

5. THE DERIVATIVE CONFESSION

At common law, the admissibility of a confession which had been preceded by an involuntary confession required an examination of the circumstances under which the prior statement was obtained to ascertain the degree of connection between the two statements. However, as Laskin C.J. pointed out in *Hobbins*,[46]

> There can be no hard and fast rule that merely because a prior statement is ruled inadmissible a second statement taken by the same interrogating officers must be equally vulnerable. Factual considerations must govern, in-

---

[45] *Singh*, at para. 47.
[46] 1982 CarswellOnt 70, 1982 CarswellOnt 724, [1982] 1 S.C.R. 553, 66 C.C.C. (2d) 289, 27 C.R. (3d) 289 at p. 558 [S.C.R.].

cluding similarity of circumstances and of police conduct and the lapse of time between the obtaining of the two statements.

Nevertheless, the common law recognized that a subsequent confession might be excluded if the prior statement had been ruled involuntary and its admissibility was affected by the grounds for exclusion of the first statement.[47] A subsequent confession would be considered involuntary if either the tainting features which disqualified the first confession continued to be present, or if the fact that the first statement was made was a substantial factor contributing to the making of the second statement. Sopinka J. in *I. (L.R.) and T. (E.)*,[48] explained that the tainting features or substantial factors contributing to the second statement, include

... the time span between the statements, advertence to the previous statement during questioning, the discovery of additional incriminating evidence subsequent to the first statement, the presence of the same police officers at both interrogations and other similarities between the two circumstances.

On the other hand, a *Charter* breach, such as a breach of the right to counsel, which has resulted in the exclusion of the prior statement will not necessarily result in the tainting of a second confession. The reason is that a *Charter* breach requires a determination of whether that evidence was obtained "in a manner that infringed or denied any rights or freedoms guaranteed by the *Charter*" and its admissibility would bring the administration of justice into disrepute pursuant to section 24(2). The fact that there has been a *Charter* breach resulting in the exclusion of a prior confession under section 24, will not necessarily have a causative effect on the making of the subsequent confession.[49] As Sopinka J. pointed out,

If a statement is followed by a further statement which in and of itself involves no Charter breach, its admissibility will be resolved under s. 24(2) of the Charter.

However, a later statement following a *Charter* breach cannot be considered in isolation from the first. For example in *G.(B.)*,[50] the accused went to a police station and, after he was cautioned and his constitutional rights were read, made a statement to the police in which he admitted to engaging in various acts of a sexual nature with his young cousin. The accused was

[47] *I. (L.R.)*, 1993 CarswellBC 1273, 1993 CarswellBC 513, [1993] 4 S.C.R. 504, (sub nom. *R. v. T. (E.)*) 86 C.C.C. (3d) 289, 26 C.R. (4th) 119. See also *G. (B.)*, 1999 CarswellQue 1204, 1999 CarswellQue 1205, [1999] 2 S.C.R. 475, (sub nom. *R. v. G. (B.)*) 135 C.C.C. (3d) 303, 24 C.R. (5th) 266 at para. 21.
[48] *Ibid.*, [1993] 4 S.C.R. at 528.
[49] *I. (L.R.) and T. (E.)*, *supra*, note 47.
[50] *Supra*, note 47.

subsequently charged, and a court ordered an assessment of his mental condition under section 672.11(a) and (b) of the *Criminal Code*. During this assessment, the accused made an incriminating admission (the "protected statement") to the psychiatrist when the latter asked him to explain the out-of-court statement he had made to the police. The defence requested a second assessment. Both psychiatrists' reports noted the accused's limited mental capacity, but nevertheless concluded that he was fit to stand trial. The reports also indicated that the accused was very accommodating toward those in authority and that his answers were unreliable in an anxiety-producing situation. At trial, following the victim's testimony, the Crown sought to introduce the accused's out-of-court statement. Based on the psychiatric assessments, the trial judge ruled it inadmissible.

In a majority decision (6-3), the Supreme Court held that since the first confession to the police was inadmissible, the second statement was also inadmissible because the degree of connection between the two statements was sufficient for the second to have been contaminated by the first. This interpretation met the requirements of section 7 of the *Charter*, which entrenched certain aspects of the confessions rule. A confession found to be inadmissible could not be introduced indirectly without affecting the right to silence and the principle against self-incrimination. The second statement was inadmissible because of its degree of connection with the prior inadmissible confession. The admission to the psychiatrist resulted directly from the confrontation of the accused with his previous statement. No additional information was obtained. Since the second statement existed only because of the first, it was unnecessary to consider here whether the tainting factors continued to exist, although in this case they were still present to some extent.

Similarly, in *Plaha*,[51] the accused, who was charged with second degree murder, had been interrogated by the police over a 14-hour period during which he had made five statements. The first three and the fifth statements were excluded by the trial judge. He was not advised of his right to counsel until after the third statement when he told the police that he wished to consult a lawyer and was allowed to exercise that right. The trial judge found that the fourth statement was not obtained in a manner that infringed the accused's rights and not tainted by the earlier statements. On appeal it was held that the trial judge had erred in admitting the fourth statement. The connection between the breach and the obtaining of evidence may be temporal, contextual, causal, or a combination of all three. Here the entire chain of events from the arrest of the accused to the end of his interrogation, some

---

[51] 2004 CarswellOnt 3424, 188 C.C.C. (3d) 289, 24 C.R. (6th) 360 (C.A.).

14 hours had to be considered. Here all of the statements and the breaches were part of the same interrogation and the police had made no effort to sever any connection between the earlier statements, which they should have known would not be admissible, and the fourth statement. The fourth statement was closely connected, both temporally and contextually, to the earlier breaches of the right to counsel and was obtained in a manner that infringed his right to counsel.

6. PERSONS IN AUTHORITY

The *Ibrahim* rule said that a confession of an accused is not admissible unless it is voluntary in the sense that it was not obtained by a threat or promise held out by "a person in authority". The underlying rationale of the person in authority prohibition is to avoid the unfairness and unreliability of admitting statements when the accused believes him or herself to be under pressure from the uniquely coercive power of the state.[52] If the person is not someone in authority, then the rule does not apply and the confession will be admissible.[53]

The general rule is that a person in authority includes anyone who has authority or control over the accused or over the proceedings or prosecution against him.[54] In the past, people such as police officers, jailers or guards, magistrates or judges, prosecutors, informants, employers and complainants have been regarded as persons in authority.

In *B. (A.)*,[55] Mr. Justice Cory reviewed a number of authorities and set out the following principles:

> 1. As a general rule, a person in authority is someone engaged in the *arrest, detention, examination or prosecution* of the accused; the word

---

[52] *Grandinetti*, 2005 CarswellAlta 81, 2005 CarswellAlta 82, 191 C.C.C. (3d) 449, 25 C.R. (6th) 1 (S.C.C.).

[53] In *T. (S.G.)*, 2008 CarswellSask 600, 237 C.C.C. (3d) 55, 61 C.R. (6th) 302 (C.A.); reversed 2010 CarswellSask 304, 2010 CarswellSask 305, 255 C.C.C. (3d) 1, 74 C.R. (6th) 217 (S.C.C.), it was held that the trial judge does have a residual discretion to exclude a confession not made to a person in authority made after an admissible confession if the factors tainting the previous confession continue to apply or if the inadmissible confession precipitated the subsequent confession.

[54] *Todd*, 1901 CarswellMan 4, 4 C.C.C. 514, 13 Man. R. 364 (K.B.).

[55] 1986 CarswellOnt 100, 26 C.C.C. (3d) 17, 50 C.R. (3d) 247, 13 O.A.C. 68 (C.A.); leave to appeal refused [1986] 1 S.C.R. v, 26 C.C.C. (3d) 17n, 50 C.R. (3d) xxv.

"examination" refers to interrogation by police officers, detention or security guards and members of the Crown Attorney's office.

2. In some circumstances, the complainant in a criminal prosecution may be considered to be a person in authority.

3. The parent of an infant who is the injured party or a complainant in a criminal prosecution may be a person in authority, depending upon the factual background.[56]

4. An inducement given by one who is not a person in authority, but made in the presence of persons in authority, may be deemed to have been given by a person in authority; in other words, a person not in authority is clothed with that authority by the presence of those in authority.

On the other hand, persons such as physicians, surgeons and psychiatrists, the father or wife of the accused, or a friend, have been held not to be persons in authority. Nevertheless, in some instances, someone such as a doctor or a psychiatrist who is called in by the Crown to examine the accused may be considered a person in authority if he or she pursues an active role in questioning the accused for the purpose of obtaining an admission or confession. Similarly, section 672.21(2) of the *Criminal Code* dealing with an accused in respect of whom a verdict of not criminally responsible on account of mental disorder has been rendered, gives an accused protection from admission into evidence of any statement made by the accused "during the course and for the purpose of an assessment or treatment directed by a disposition, to the person specified in the assessment order or disposition, or to anyone acting under that person's direction".[57]

For a long time, a perplexing question was whether a subjective or an objective test should be used in determining if the person was someone "in authority". In other words, was it enough that the person was someone in authority or was it necessary for the accused to believe as well that he or she was a person in authority? One would have thought that the answer was self-evident, at least in the case of an inducement. How can a person be affected by an inducement unless he or she believes that the person has the ability to make good on a promise? However, the case of a threat or a beat-

---

[56] See *Wells* (1998), 1998 CarswellBC 1932, 1998 CarswellBC 1931, [1998] 2 S.C.R. 517, 57 B.C.L.R. (3d) 104, 127 C.C.C. (3d) 500, 18 C.R. (5th) 181, 163 D.L.R. (4th) 628, [1999] 5 W.W.R. 331, 112 B.C.A.C. 101, 230 N.R. 183, 182 W.A.C. 101.

[57] *G. (B.)*, 1999 CarswellQue 1204, 1999 CarswellQue 1205, [1999] 2 S.C.R. 475, (sub nom. *R. v. G. (B.)*) 135 C.C.C. (3d) 303, 24 C.R. (5th) 266, 174 D.L.R. (4th) 301, 63 C.R.R. (2d) 272, 240 N.R. 260, [1999] S.C.J. No. 29.

ing would be another matter. Here a confession would be rejected by a trial judge in the exercise of his or her discretionary power to prevent the administration of justice from being brought into disrepute, rather than from the rules relating to persons in authority.

Nevertheless, that question was never settled until the decision of the Supreme Court of Canada in *Rothman*.[58] There the court held that the test was a subjective one. The real issue was whether the accused thought that the person to whom he confessed could either make good his promise or carry out his threats. Thus, if the accused confessed to someone such as an undercover officer, then that officer was not a person in authority even though he might be, from a purely objective point of view, considered to be in a position of undoubted authority.

The rule is that if a statement is made to someone who is not ordinarily engaged in the arrest, detention, examination or prosecution of an accused person, there is a duty upon the defence to raise before the trial judge the issue of the legal admissibility of a confession to that person and request a *voir dire*. In other words, in the absence of a conventional authority figure at the time when the inculpatory statement was made, the trial judge is not required to hold a *voir dire*. The defence must put the judge on notice and request a *voir dire*.[59]

On the *voir dire*, the accused will have the evidential burden of demonstrating that there is a valid issue for consideration. If the accused meets the burden, the Crown will then have the persuasive burden of demonstrating beyond a reasonable doubt that the receiver of the statement was not a person in authority. If the trial judge finds that the receiver of the statement was a person in authority, then the Crown will be required to establish beyond a reasonable doubt that the statement was made voluntarily.[60]

Generally, it is only the accused who can know that the statement was made to someone regarded by the accused as a person in authority. However, if the evidence viewed objectively indicates that the issue should be explored on a *voir dire*, then the trial judge has the duty to raise the matter and direct a *voir dire*.[61] Evidence that indicates a close connection between the receiver of the statement and the authorities should alert the trial judge

---

[58] 1981 CarswellOnt 43, 1981 CarswellOnt 93, [1981] 1 S.C.R. 640, 59 C.C.C. (2d) 30, 20 C.R. (3d) 97, 121 D.L.R. (3d) 578, 35 N.R. 485.

[59] *Hodgson*, 1998 CarswellOnt 3417, 1998 CarswellOnt 3418, [1998] 2 S.C.R. 449, 127 C.C.C. (3d) 449, 18 C.R. (5th) 135, 163 D.L.R. (4th) 577, (sub nom. *R. v. M.C.H.*) 230 N.R. 1, 113 O.A.C. 97, [1998] S.C.J. No. 66; *Wells, supra,* note 56.

[60] *Hodgson, ibid.*

[61] *Hodgson, ibid.; Wells, supra,* note 56.

of the need to hold a *voir dire*. In such instance, the trial judge is required to inquire of the defence whether it is prepared to discharge its evidential burden on the person in authority issue or whether it waives a *voir dire*.

7. THE RIGHT TO COUNSEL

Section 7 of the *Charter of Rights and Freedoms* protects the right to remain silent in the face of questioning by the agents of the state. It provides:

> Everyone has the right to life, liberty and security of the person and the right not to be deprived thereof except in accordance with the principles of fundamental justice.

> Section 10 also guarantees everyone the right . . . on arrest or detention:

> (a) to be informed promptly of the reasons therefore;

> (b) to retain and instruct counsel without delay and be informed of that right . . .

Whenever a person is detained or arrested, that person must be informed of his or her right to retain and instruct counsel. The Supreme Court has said that the phrase "without delay" in section 10(b) must be interpreted as "immediately".[62] The immediacy of this obligation is only subject to concerns for officer or public safety, or to reasonable limitations that are prescribed by law and justified under s. 1 of the *Charter*. However, except in the case of a youthful offender, the mentally or physically infirm, and possibly someone who has had no experience with the police, that duty is simply to advise the detainee of his or her right to counsel and to provide the opportunity to contact a lawyer if requested. The police are not required to satisfy the trial judge that the detainee understood his or her rights, unless there are circumstances that would lead the detainee to believe otherwise. It is generally presumed that a person understands the meaning of the right to counsel unless that person can establish otherwise.[63]

Nevertheless, the police must advise the detainee in language that the detainee can understand exactly what the right to counsel means. In other words, there is an obligation on the arresting officer to advise the detainee of the right to counsel in language that makes that right meaningful and

---

[62] *Suberu*, 2009 CarswellOnt 4106, 2009 CarswellOnt 4107, [2009] 2 S.C.R. 460, 245 C.C.C. (3d) 112, 66 C.R. (6th) 127.

[63] *Anderson*, 1984 CarswellOnt 45, 45 O.R. (2d) 225, 10 C.C.C. (3d) 417, 39 C.R. (3d) 193, 7 D.L.R. (4th) 306, 9 C.R.R. 161, 2 O.A.C. 258 (C.A.).

comprehensible to him.[64] Moreover, the detainee should be advised of the right to counsel when he or she is capable of understanding and appreciating that right. For example, if the detainee is ill or intoxicated, then the officer has an obligation to wait until the detainee is feeling better or has sobered up.[65] However, it is only where the lack of understanding is apparent that the police must take such additional measures.

Once a person, who has been advised of his right to counsel, indicates that he or she wishes to exercise that right, all questioning must stop until that request is fulfilled.[66] There is also an obligation on the police to assist the detainee to contact counsel so that he or she can exercise that right. This includes the duty to inform the detainee of the existence and availability of duty counsel and legal aid in the jurisdiction, particularly if the detainee expresses a concern that his or her inability to afford a lawyer is an impediment to the exercise of the right to counsel.[67] Since duty counsel and legal aid are an intrinsic part of the practice of criminal law in Canada, this duty requires the police to provide information about access to counsel free of charge where an accused meets the prescribed financial criteria set by provincial Legal Aid. It also requires the police to provide information about access to duty counsel providing immediate, although temporary, legal advice, irrespective of financial status, as to services actually available within

---

[64] *Vanstaceghem*, 1987 CarswellOnt 100, 36 C.C.C. (3d) 142, 58 C.R. (3d) 121, 48 M.V.R. 311, 21 O.A.C. 210 (C.A.).

[65] *Clarkson*, 1986 CarswellNB 14, 1986 CarswellNB 104, [1986] 1 S.C.R. 383, 69 N.B.R. (2d) 40, (sub nom. *Clarkson v. R.)* 25 C.C.C. (3d) 207, 50 C.R. (3d) 289, 26 D.L.R. (4th) 493, 177 A.P.R. 40, 19 C.R.R. 209, 66 N.R. 114.

[66] *Manninen*, 1987 CarswellOnt 967, 1987 CarswellOnt 99, [1987] 1 S.C.R. 1233, 61 O.R. (2d) 736 (note), 34 C.C.C. (3d) 385, 58 C.R. (3d) 97, 41 D.L.R. (4th) 301, 38 C.R.R. 37, 76 N.R. 198, 21 O.A.C. 192.

[67] *Brydges*, 1990 CarswellAlta 3, 1990 CarswellAlta 648, [1990] 1 S.C.R. 190, 104 A.R. 124, 71 Alta. L.R. (2d) 145, 53 C.C.C. (3d) 330, 74 C.R. (3d) 129, [1990] 2 W.W.R. 220, 46 C.R.R. 236, 103 N.R. 282.

the jurisdiction.[68] However, there is no constitutional obligation for provinces to establish legal aid and duty counsel services.[69]

Although a detainee must be given a reasonable opportunity to exercise the right to counsel, that right is not an absolute one. It must be exercised with reasonable diligence.[70] An accused who requests the right to contact counsel cannot indefinitely delay consulting with counsel. The detainee must take reasonable steps to try to contact his or her counsel to obtain advice.[71] If the detainee fails to do so, then the police may proceed to question him.[72]

A person may waive the right to counsel and that waiver need not be in writing. However, the onus of establishing that the detainee waived the right to counsel, with full knowledge of the consequences of doing so, lies upon the prosecution. That may in some instances be onerous if it appears that the detainee does not have full mental faculties, such as a detainee who

[68] *Prosper*, 1994 CarswellNS 438, 1994 CarswellNS 25, [1994] 3 S.C.R. 236, 133 N.S.R. (2d) 321, 92 C.C.C. (3d) 353, 92 C.C.C. (3d) 358, 33 C.R. (4th) 85, 118 D.L.R. (4th) 154, 6 M.V.R. (3d) 181, 380 A.P.R. 321, 23 C.R.R. (2d) 239, 172 N.R. 161; *Harper*, 1994 CarswellMan 8, 1994 CarswellMan 381, [1994] 3 S.C.R. 343, 92 C.C.C. (3d) 423, 33 C.R. (4th) 61, 118 D.L.R. (4th) 312, 6 M.V.R. (3d) 138, 23 C.R.R. (2d) 291, 97 Man. R. (2d) 1, 172 N.R. 91, 79 W.A.C. 1; *Pozniak*, 1994 CarswellOnt 1165, 1994 CarswellOnt 101, [1994] 3 S.C.R. 310, 19 O.R. (3d) 802 (note), 92 C.C.C. (3d) 472, 33 C.R. (4th) 49, 118 D.L.R. (4th) 205, 6 M.V.R. (3d) 113, 23 C.R.R. (2d) 303, 172 N.R. 72, 74 O.A.C. 232.

[69] *Prosper, ibid.*

[70] *Leclair*, 1989 CarswellOnt 67, 1989 CarswellOnt 953, (sub nom. *R. v. Ross*) [1989] 1 S.C.R. 3, 46 C.C.C. (3d) 129, 67 C.R. (3d) 209, 37 C.R.R. 369, 91 N.R. 81, 31 O.A.C. 321.

[71] *Bartle*, 1994 CarswellOnt 1164, 1994 CarswellOnt 100, [1994] 3 S.C.R. 173, 19 O.R. (3d) 802 (note), 92 C.C.C. (3d) 289, 33 C.R. (4th) 1, 118 D.L.R. (4th) 83, 6 M.V.R. (3d) 1, 23 C.R.R. (2d) 193, 172 N.R. 1, 74 O.A.C. 161, [1994] S.C.J. No. 74.

[72] *Tremblay*, 1987 CarswellOnt 111, 1987 CarswellOnt 972, [1987] 2 S.C.R. 435, 37 C.C.C. (3d) 565, 60 C.R. (3d) 59, 45 D.L.R. (4th) 445, 2 M.V.R. (2d) 289, 32 C.R.R. 381, 79 N.R. 153, 25 O.A.C. 93.

may be mentally ill, or is under the influence of drugs or alcohol.[73] In *Clarkson*, the Supreme Court of Canada held:

> While this constitutional guarantee cannot be forced upon an unwilling accused, any voluntary waiver in order to be valid and effective must be premised on a true appreciation of the consequences of giving up the right.[74]

The Supreme Court, however, seems to have drawn a distinction between mental illness or drunkenness that deprives a person of the ability to appreciate the consequences of giving up the right to counsel and a person who simply has limited cognitive ability. In *Whittle*,[75] the Court said that there is no obligation upon the Crown to prove that an accused, who has the limited cognitive capacity to understand the legal process that he or she is facing and the right to communicate with counsel, is capable of making a rational decision that is personally beneficial:

> . . . provided the accused possesses this limited capacity, it is not necessary that he or she be capable of exercising analytical reasoning in making a choice to accept the advice of counsel in coming to a decision that best serves her interests.[76]

The Court said that,

> In exercising the right to counsel or waiving the right, the accused must possess the limited cognitive capacity required for fitness to stand trial. The accused must be capable of communicating with counsel to instruct counsel, and understand the function of counsel and that he or she can dispense with counsel even if this is not in the accused's best interests. It is not necessary that the accused possess analytical ability. The level of cognitive ability is the same as that required with respect to the confession rule and the right to silence. The accused must have the mental capacity of an operating mind as outlined above.[77]

The police are not required to stop all questioning of an accused after he or she has consulted with counsel. The police may question an accused provided that he or she is willing to be questioned.[78] Nor are they required to advise the accused's counsel that they are about to question the accused;

---

[73] *Clarkson, supra*, note 65.

[74] *Ibid.*, at p. 303 [C.R.].

[75] 1994 CarswellOnt 1163, 1994 CarswellOnt 91, [1994] 2 S.C.R. 914, 92 C.C.C. (3d) 11, 32 C.R. (4th) 1, 116 D.L.R. (4th) 416, 23 C.R.R. (2d) 6, 170 N.R. 16, 73 O.A.C. 201.

[76] *Ibid.*, at p. 16 [C.R.].

[77] *Ibid.*, at p. 21 [C.R.].

[78] *Hebert*, 1990 CarswellYukon 4, 1990 CarswellYukon 7, [1990] 2 S.C.R. 151, 47 B.C.L.R. (2d) 1, 57 C.C.C. (3d) 1, 77 C.R. (3d) 145, [1990] 5 W.W.R. 1, 49

presumably, if the accused has consulted with counsel, counsel has advised the accused of the right to remain silent. If an accused consents to being questioned after consulting a lawyer, then there is nothing objectionable about the police doing so. However, the prosecution will be required to establish, as in any case where the right to counsel has been waived, that the accused agreed to the interrogation without the presence of counsel.

The *Charter* does not give a detainee the right to have counsel present during a custodial interrogation as that right exists in the United States for detainees.[79] Section 10(b) only gives a detainee the right "to retain and instruct counsel without delay and be informed of that right". The Supreme Court of Canada has said that in the context of a custodial interrogation, the purpose of section 10(b) is to support a detainee's right to choose whether to cooperate with the police investigation or not by giving the detainee access to legal advice regarding the situation he or she is facing.[80] This is achieved by requiring that the detainee be informed of the right to consult counsel and, if the detainee so requests, be given an opportunity to consult with counsel. Achieving this purpose may require that the detainee be given an opportunity to re-consult counsel where developments make this necessary. However, the right to counsel *does not demand the continued presence of counsel throughout the interview process*, although there is nothing to prevent counsel from being present at an interrogation where all sides consent. The police remain free to facilitate such an arrangement *if they so choose, and the detainee may wish to make counsel's presence a precondition of giving a statement.* A request to consult counsel, without more, is not sufficient to re-trigger the section 10(b) right. What is required is a *change in circumstances that suggests that the choice faced by the detainee has been significantly altered*, requiring further advice on the new situation in order to fulfill the purpose of section 10(b). Police tactics short of such a change may result in the Crown being unable to prove beyond a reasonable doubt that a subsequent statement was voluntary, rendering it inadmissible; but it does not follow that the procedural rights granted by section 10(b) have been breached.

C.R.R. 114, 110 N.R. 1; *Singh*, 2007 SCC 48, 2007 CarswellBC 2588, 2007 CarswellBC 2589, [2007] 3 S.C.R. 405, 225 C.C.C. (3d) 103, 51 C.R. (6th) 199.

[79] *Miranda v. Arizona*, 384 U.S. 436 (1966); affirmed 385 U.S. 890 (U.S. Sup. Ct.); *Michigan v. Mosley*, 423 U.S. 96 (1975).

[80] *Sinclair*, 2010 SCC 35, 2010 CarswellBC 2664, 2010 CarswellBC 2679, [2010] 2 S.C.R. 310, 259 C.C.C. (3d) 443, 77 C.R. (6th) 203.

In *Sinclair*[81] the Supreme Court cautioned that this interpretation of section 10(b) does not give *carte blanche* to the police who must still conduct an interview in strict conformity with the confessions rule. Nevertheless, in defining the contours of the section 7 right to silence and related *Charter* rights, the Court said that consideration must also be given to the societal interest in the investigation and solving of crimes. Any suggestion that the questioning of a suspect, in and of itself, runs counter to the presumption of innocence and the protection against self-incrimination is clearly contrary to settled authority and practice. The police are charged with the duty to investigate alleged crimes. In performing this duty, they necessarily have to make inquiries from relevant sources of information, including persons suspected of, or even charged with, committing the alleged crime. It was stressed that while the police must be respectful of an individual's *Charter* rights, a rule that would require the police to automatically retreat upon a detainee stating that he or she has nothing to say would not strike the proper balance between the public interest in the investigation of crimes and the suspect's interest in being left alone.

The issue of persistent or aggressive questioning by the police has been discussed earlier.[82] In *Singh*,[83] a majority (5-4) panel of the Supreme Court said that it was not appropriate to impose a rigid requirement that police refrain from questioning a detainee who states that he or she does not wish to speak to police after the detainee has consulted with counsel. Such an approach, they felt, would overshoot the protection afforded to the individual's freedom of choice both at common law and under the *Charter*, and ignore the state interest in the effective investigation of crime. It was argued unsuccessfully by the minority that while detainees who have asserted their right to silence are entitled to change their minds, they should not be compelled to do so by the persistent disregard of that asserted choice. The right to silence, like the right to counsel, is a constitutional promise that must be kept. Moreover, there was no evidence to support the proposition, as the majority argued, that requiring the police to respect a detainee's right of silence, once it has been unequivocally asserted, would impair the ability of the police to investigate crime in Canada.

When questioning an accused, the police must not belittle the accused's counsel with the express goal or effect of undermining the accused's confi-

---

[81] *Ibid.*

[82] (4. The Meaning of Voluntary).

[83] 2007 SCC 48, 2007 CarswellBC 2588, 2007 CarswellBC 2589, [2007] 3 S.C.R. 405, 225 C.C.C. (3d) 103, 51 C.R. (6th) 199.

dence in that counsel.[84] Nor can the police enter into a plea bargain without the participation of counsel unless the accused expressly waives that right.[85] Any plea bargain must be offered either to the accused's counsel, or to the accused while in the presence of his or her counsel, unless the accused has expressly waived the right to counsel. In *Burlingham*, Iacobucci J. for the majority of the Supreme Court noted that section 10(b) of the *Charter* mandates:

> [23] . . . to the extent that the plea bargain is an integral element of the Canadian criminal process, the Crown and its officers engaged in the plea bargaining process must act honourably and forthrightly.[86]

Finally, the police are required to re-advise an accused of the right to counsel whenever there is a fundamental and discrete change in the purpose of the investigation. This will arise where the police seek to question the accused about a different and unrelated offence, or a significantly more serious offence than the one contemplated at the time of the warning.[87] The rationale underlying this rule is that an accused cannot exercise the right to counsel in a meaningful way unless he or she knows the extent of the risk of self-incrimination.[88] That obligation will arise even where it is the accused, rather than the police, who initiates the shift in focus of the investigation. However, the obligation to re-advise of the right to counsel will only arise if the officer questioning the accused has knowledge of the other offence and is investigating it. If the officer has no knowledge of the other offence, the officer is entitled to ask exploratory questions to elicit some further information before deciding whether an investigation of the other offence should be undertaken. Once the officer has a realistic indication that the accused might incriminate him or herself in a different and unrelated offence and that an investigation is warranted, the accused must be re-advised of the right to counsel before pursuing further questioning of that offence.

---

[84] *Burlingham*, 1995 CarswellBC 71, 1995 CarswellBC 639, [1995] 2 S.C.R. 206, 97 C.C.C. (3d) 385, 38 C.R. (4th) 265, 124 D.L.R. (4th) 7, 58 B.C.A.C. 161, 28 C.R.R. (2d) 244, 181 N.R. 1, 96 W.A.C. 161 at p. 280 [C.R.].

[85] *Burlingham*, *ibid.*, at p. 282 [C.R.].

[86] *Ibid.*

[87] *Evans*, 1991 CarswellBC 918, 1991 CarswellBC 417, [1991] 1 S.C.R. 869, 63 C.C.C. (3d) 289, 4 C.R. (4th) 144, 3 C.R.R. (2d) 315, 124 N.R. 278.

[88] *Sawatsky*, 1997 CarswellOnt 2994, 35 O.R. (3d) 767, 118 C.C.C. (3d) 17, 9 C.R. (5th) 23, 150 D.L.R. (4th) 750, 47 C.R.R. (2d) 360, 103 O.A.C. 68, [1997] O.J. No. 3561 (C.A.).

8. THE RIGHT TO REMAIN SILENT

The right to remain silent is rooted in an abhorrence of the interrogation practised by the old Ecclesiastical courts and the Star Chamber which required everyone to submit to an *ex officio* oath and answer questions when he had never been charged with any offence. The objection that "no man should be required to incriminate himself — *nemo tenetur prodere se ipsum* or *nemo tenetur prodere accusare*, first raised in the Ecclesiastical Courts in the early 17th century, was soon heard in the common law courts.[89] By the end of the 17th century, it became firmly established in all courts.[90] In Canada, the right to remain silent has been given constitutional recognition in sections 7, 11(c) and 13 of the *Charter of Rights and Freedoms.*

Section 7 provides,

> Everyone has the right to life, liberty and security of the person and the right not to be deprived thereof except in accordance with the principles of fundamental justice.

Section 11(c) provides,

> Any person charged with an offence has the right,

> > (c) not to be compelled to be a witness in proceedings against that person in respect of the offence;

Section 13 provides,

> A witness who testifies in any proceedings has the right not to have any incriminating evidence so given used to incriminate that person in any other proceedings, except in a prosecution for perjury or for the giving of contradictory evidence.

The first thing that must be noted is that sections 11(c) and 13 only protect a person from compulsion to speak or from prior testimony in proceedings against that person. Neither section nor any other section of the *Charter* specifically provides any protection of the right to remain silent when an accused is detain or arrested. Although section 7 does not specifically protect the right to remain silent, as we shall see in the discussion that follows, it has been interpreted only as a guarantee of the right to choose whether or not to make a statement when detained by the authorities.[91]

---

[89] *Lilburne* (1637), 3 State Tr. 1316.

[90] Salhany, Roger E. The Origin of Rights; Levy, Leonard W. Origins of the Fifth Amendment.

[91] *Hebert,* 1990 CarswellYukon 4, 1990 CarswellYukon 7, [1990] 2 S.C.R. 151, 47 B.C.L.R. (2d) 1, 57 C.C.C. (3d) 1, 77 C.R. (3d) 145, [1990] 5 W.W.R. 1, 49

As cases emanating from the *Charter* wended their way to the Supreme Court following the enactment of the *Charter* in April 1982, the Supreme Court of Canada was faced with the question whether the rights guaranteed by the *Charter* were to be cast in the straightjacket of the common law as it existed in 1982 or given an expanded meaning. In 1985, Le Dain J. in *Therens*,[92] observed that,

> ... the premise that the framers of the *Charter* must be presumed to have intended that the words used by it should be given the meaning which had been given to them by judicial decisions at the time the *Charter* was enacted is not a reliable guide to its interpretation and application. By its very nature a constitutional charter of rights and freedoms must use general language which is capable of development and adaptation by the courts.

In the same year, Dickson J. (as he then was) also agreed that a *Charter* right "is not to be determined solely by the degree to which that right was enjoyed by Canadians prior to the proclamation of the Charter". The interpretation, he said, to be given is "a generous rather than a legalistic [interpretation] one, aimed at fulfilling the purpose of the guarantee and securing for individuals the full benefit of the *Charter*'s protection".[93]

However, that expectation did not bear fruit. In *Hebert*,[94] the Supreme Court decided to tether the right to remain silent in its common law straightjacket. McLachlin J, speaking for seven members of the Court noted that section 7 and section 10(b), (the right to consult with counsel upon arrest or detention) meant,

> ... the drafters of the *Charter* viewed the ambit of the right to silence embodied in s. 7 as extending beyond the narrow formulation of the confessions rule, comprehending not only the negative right to be free of coercion induced by threats, promises or violence, but a positive right to make a free choice as to whether to remain silent or speak to the authorities.[95]

C.R.R. 114, 110 N.R. 1; *Broyles*, 1991 CarswellAlta 212, 1991 CarswellAlta 560, [1991] 3 S.C.R. 595, 68 C.C.C. (3d) 308, 9 C.R. (4th) 1.

[92] 1985 CarswellSask 851, 1985 CarswellSask 368, [1985] 1 S.C.R. 613, 18 C.C.C. (3d) 481, 45 C.R. (3d) 97 at p. 638 [S.C.R.].

[93] *Big M Drug Mart Ltd.*, 1985 CarswellAlta 316, 1985 CarswellAlta 609, [1985] 1 S.C.R. 295, 18 C.C.C. (3d) 385 at p. 344 [S.C.R.].

[94] 1990 CarswellYukon 4, 1990 CarswellYukon 7, [1990] 2 S.C.R. 151, 47 B.C.L.R. (2d) 1, 57 C.C.C. (3d) 1, 77 C.R. (3d) 145, [1990] 5 W.W.R. 1, 49 C.R.R. 114, 110 N.R. 1.

[95] *Ibid.*, [1990] 2 S.C.R. at p. 177.

However,

> The *Charter* does not place on the authorities and the courts the impossible task of subjectively gauging whether the suspect appreciates the situation and the alternatives. Rather, it seeks to ensure that the suspect is in a position to make an informed choice by giving him the right to counsel. The guarantee of the right to counsel in the *Charter* suggests that the suspect must have the right to choose whether to speak to the police or not, but it equally suggests that the test for whether that choice has been violated is essentially objective. Was the suspect accorded his or her right to consult counsel? By extension, was there other police conduct which effectively deprived the suspect of the right to choose to remain silent, thus negating the purpose of the right to counsel?[96]

As she pointed out, the historical common law right to remain silent existed in two instances: the first was where an accused *was detained* by the authorities for questioning. Here the common law confession rule kicked in to ensure that any statement or admission made by the accused to the authorities was free and voluntary. *The right to silence did not exist outside the police station.* The second was where an accused was being tried for an offence. Here there was no obligation upon an accused to speak at his trial. It was her view that the *Charter* did not expand the right to silence beyond what existed at common law.

> The common law rules related to the right to silence suggest that the scope of the right in the pre-trial detention period must be based on the fundamental concept of the suspect's right to choose whether to speak to the authorities or remain silent. Any doubt on the question is resolved by consideration of related rights protected by the *Charter*, by the *Charter*'s approach to the question of improperly obtained evidence, and by the fundamental purpose of the right to silence and related procedural guarantees. In keeping with the approach inaugurated by the *Charter*, our courts must adopt an approach to pre-trial interrogation which emphasizes the right of the detained person to make a meaningful choice and permits the rejection of statements which have been obtained unfairly in circumstances that violate that right of choice.[97]

In other words, section 7 did not create an absolute right to silence capable of being discharged only by waiver. She found "nothing in the rules underpinning the section 7 right to silence or other provisions of the *Charter* that suggests that the scope of the right to silence should be extended this far". She was of the view that a new rule should be adopted permitting consideration of an accused's informed choice, as well as fairness to the

---

[96] *Ibid.*, at p. 177.
[97] *Ibid.*, at p. 181.

accused and the repute of the administration of justice. This change struck a proper and justifiable balance between the interest of the state in law enforcement and the interest of the suspect. It permitted the courts to correct abuses of power against the individual, while allowing them to nevertheless admit evidence under section 24(2) where, despite a *Charter* violation, the admission would not bring the administration of justice into disrepute. Retaining an objective, rather than a subjective, approach to confessions would permit the rule to be subject to the following limits.

> First, there is nothing in the rule to prohibit the police from questioning the accused in the absence of counsel after the accused has retained counsel. Police persuasion, short of denying the suspect the right to choose or depriving him of an operating mind, does not breach the right to silence.
>
> Second, the *Charter* does not extend the right to counsel to pre-detention investigations. There is no need to protect an individual from an undercover operation prior to detention since the individual is not in the control of the state. After detention, the state takes control and assumes the responsibility of ensuring that the detainee's rights are respected.
>
> Third, the right to silence predicated on the suspect's right to choose freely whether to speak to the police or to remain silent does not affect voluntary statements made to fellow cell mates. The violation of the suspect's rights occurs only when the Crown acts to subvert the suspect's constitutional right to choose not to make a statement to the authorities.
>
> Fourth, a distinction must be made between the use of undercover agents to observe the suspect, and the use of undercover agents to actively elicit information in violation of the suspect's choice to remain silent. When the police use subterfuge to interrogate an accused after he has advised them that he does not wish to speak to them, they are improperly eliciting information that they were unable to obtain by respecting the suspect's constitutional right to silence. In the absence of eliciting behaviour on the part of the police, there is no violation of the accused's right to choose whether or not to speak to the police. If the suspect speaks, it is by his or her own choice, and he or she must be taken to have accepted the risk that the recipient may inform the police.[98]

The *Hebert* case was concerned with the right to silence of an accused in police custody. What about the right to silence in the face of police inquiries? In *Rothman*,[99] a pre-*Charter* case, Lamer J. noted that the right to si-

---

[98] *Ibid.*, at p. 184.
[99] 1981 CarswellOnt 43, 1981 CarswellOnt 93, [1981] 1 S.C.R. 640, 59 C.C.C. (2d) 30, 20 C.R. (3d) 97 at p. 683 [S.C.R.].

lence existed at all times whether or not the person asserting it was within the power or control of the state.

> In Canada the right of a suspect not to say anything to the police . . . is merely the exercise by him of the general right enjoyed in this country by anyone to do whatever one pleases, saying what one pleases or choosing not to say certain things, unless obliged to do otherwise by law. It is because no law says that a suspect, save in certain circumstances, must say anything to the police that we say that he has the right to remain silent, which is a positive way of explaining that there is on his part no legal obligation to do otherwise.

Moreover, silence in the face of questioning could not be used as a snare for anyone exercising it. It would be an illusory right if the decision not to speak to the police could be used by the Crown as evidence of guilt. As Cory J. explained in *Chambers*[100] where the trial judge failed to instruct the jury that the accused's silence could not be used as evidence of guilt:

> It has as well been recognized that since there is a right to silence, it would be a snare and a delusion to caution the accused that he need not say anything in response to a police officer's question but nonetheless put in evidence that the accused clearly exercised his right and remained silent in the face of a question which suggested his guilt.

9. ONUS OF PROOF

If the prosecution seeks to introduce a confession or admission, the trial judge must conduct a *voir dire* in the absence of the jury. The *voir dire* may be waived where the defence admits that the statement is voluntary or does not apply to have it excluded on the basis that the accused was denied his or her right to counsel.

The onus of proof will be different depending on whether the issue is the voluntariness of the statement or the breach of the accused's right to counsel. Where the issue is the voluntariness of the statement, the onus is upon the Crown to prove that the statement was given voluntarily by the accused and proof is beyond a reasonable doubt. Where, however, the issue is whether the accused has been denied his or her constitutional right to counsel under the *Charter*, the onus is upon the defence to show firstly, that there was a *right to counsel Charter* breach, and secondly, that the admission of the statement would bring the administration of justice into disrepute. That onus, however, is not as onerous as the one upon the Crown to

---

[100] 1990 CarswellBC 217, 1990 CarswellBC 761, [1990] 2 S.C.R. 1293, 59 C.C.C. (3d) 321, 80 C.R. (3d) 235 at p. 1316 [S.C.R.].

prove that the accused's statement was given voluntarily; the defence need only establish both requirements upon a balance of probabilities.

Where the issue is the voluntariness of the statement, the prosecution will be required, on the *voir dire*, to lead evidence on that issue. The defence is entitled to cross-examine the prosecution witnesses and to call witnesses on behalf of the defence, including the accused who may, in turn, be cross-examined by the prosecution. After hearing arguments from both sides, the judge will decide whether the Crown has satisfied the onus of proving beyond a reasonable doubt that the statement was made voluntarily.

If the accused elects to testify on the *voir dire*, he or she may be cross-examined on the particular issue in dispute, that is, whether the statement is voluntary. In *DeClercq*,[101] the Supreme Court held that the right to cross-examine the accused includes the right to ask him or her whether the confession is true because the answer to that question goes to the issue of credibility. This decision, however, has been strongly criticized because it does "under the guise of 'credibility' . . . transmute what is initially an inquiry as to 'admissibility' of the confession into an inquisition of an accused".[102]

The argument that the prosecution should be allowed to test an accused's credibility by asking him or her on a *voir dire* whether the confession is true is really a double-edged sword. If the accused denies the truth of the statement, is the accused to be disbelieved simply because he or she contradicts the testimony of the police? On the other hand, if the accused admits that the confession is true, is the accused to be disbelieved when he or she says that it was obtained by threats or inducement? Logically, an accused who admits that the confession is true is more likely to be telling the truth when he or she says that the police used threats or inducements to obtain the statement. Moreover, if the accused does admit that the confession was true, the trial judge is put in the unenviable position of having to decide whether to exclude an important piece of evidence obtained under circumstances which the administration of justice does not condone, even though the judge knows that the confession is an important piece of evidence with respect to the guilt of the accused.

Where the issue is the voluntariness of a statement, the onus upon the Crown is not established simply by calling the interrogating officers to say that the confession was preceded by the usual caution or warning, and then

---

[101] (1968), 1968 CarswellOnt 15, [1968] S.C.R. 902, [1969] 1 C.C.C. 197, 70 D.L.R. (2d) 530, 4 C.R.N.S. 205.

[102] *Hnedish*, 1958 CarswellSask 46, 29 C.R. 347 (Q.B.) at pp. 349-50 [C.R.]. See also *Tessier*, 2001 CarswellNB 120, 153 C.C.C. (3d) 361, 41 C.R. (5th) 242 (C.A.); reversed 2002 CarswellNB 5, 2002 CarswellNB 6, 162 C.C.C. (3d) 478 (S.C.C.).

have the officers who took the statement say that it was made freely and voluntary.[103] The officers' opinion as to whether the statement was made freely and voluntarily is irrelevant; it is the trial judge who must decide that issue. This means that all of the surrounding circumstances must be examined by the Court to ensure that the statement was made freely and voluntarily. This imposes an obligation upon the Crown to call as witnesses everyone who had anything to do with the accused while he or she was detained and during the accused's interrogation, or at least make them available for cross-examination.[104]

It is not enough, in order to prove that a statement is voluntary, for a police officer to relate to the court the recorded questions and answers which the officer considered important and relevant to the prosecution. Some authorities have rejected a confession where the police officer who questioned the accused failed to keep a proper record of all of the questions which were put to the accused and the answers given.[105] The rationale underlying the exclusion of such statements is that, although the record need not necessarily be verbatim, it should be detailed enough to enable the court to assess all of the circumstances in which the statement was taken. In other words, where the police have editorialized the statement, the court cannot be satisfied that it is the full and correct statement of the accused, and that it was given voluntarily. However, this is not a firm and fast rule, and whether the confession will be excluded will depend on all of the surrounding circumstances.[106]

In Canada today, video and audio recording equipment are readily available to most police authorities. Although the Supreme Court said in *Oickle*[107] that *unrecorded statements are not inherently suspect*, the Ontario Court of Appeal has decided that the failure of the police to make a reliable record of a confession by an accused in custody, *where recording*

---

[103] *Sankey*, 1927 CarswellBC 104, [1927] S.C.R. 436, 48 C.C.C. 97, [1927] 4 D.L.R. 245; *Koszulap*, 1974 CarswellOnt 30, 20 C.C.C. (2d) 193, 27 C.R.N.S. 226 (C.A.).

[104] *Thiffault*, 1933 CarswellQue 40, [1933] S.C.R. 509, 60 C.C.C. 97, [1933] 3 D.L.R. 591; *Magnowski*, 2011 CarswellBC 1916, 277 C.C.C. (3d) 282 (S.C.).

[105] *Belanger*, 1978 CarswellOnt 1350, 40 C.C.C. (2d) 335 (H.C.); *Smith*, 1981 CarswellQue 228, 1981 CarswellQue 1190, 60 C.C.C. (2d) 327, 125 D.L.R. (3d) 181 (S.C.); *Stefiuk*, 1981 CarswellMan 297, 11 Man. R. (2d) 411 (Co. Ct.).

[106] *Arkell*, 1980 CarswellBC 659, 54 C.C.C. (2d) 266 (B.C. C.A.).

[107] *Supra*, note 41.

equipment is available, will render a confession suspect.[108] That Court has said that where a confession of a person in custody is not recorded, the trial judge is required to determine whether there is a sufficient substitute for a recording to satisfy the heavy onus on the Crown to prove voluntariness beyond a reasonable doubt.[109] However, the Court has also said that the recording requirement will depend upon the circumstances in which the interrogation takes place. If the police do not set out to interrogate the accused, giving no thought to the making of a reliable recording, a confession will not necessarily be considered suspect.[110] The Manitoba Court of Appeal, on the other hand, has said that while the recording of confessions, either by video or audio taping, is a desirable practice, it has not been legally mandated by Parliament or the courts.[111]

There is no requirement that a confession be admitted only after a *voir dire* where the Crown has established the voluntariness of the statement beyond a reasonable doubt. In *Park*,[112] the Supreme Court of Canada recognized that an accused or his counsel is entitled to waive or dispense with the holding of a *voir dire* where the voluntariness of a confession is not in dispute. The decision whether or not to hold a *voir dire* lies with the trial judge. The judge may, if satisfied that no objection is taken to the admission of the statement without a *voir dire* and that voluntariness is not in issue, admit the statement without a *voir dire*.

As indicated earlier, where the issue is the denial of the right to counsel, the onus is upon the defence to establish on a balance of probabilities that the statement was obtained in breach of the *Charter*. Once the *Charter* breach is shown, then the defence must go on to establish under section 24(2) of the *Charter* that, "having regard to all the circumstances, the ad-

---

[108] *Moore-McFarlane*, 2001 CarswellOnt 4242, 56 O.R. (3d) 737, 160 C.C.C. (3d) 493, 47 C.R. (5th) 203 (C.A.); *Sabri*, 2002 CarswellOnt 1842, 166 C.C.C. (3d) 179, 4 C.R. (6th) 349 (C.A.); *Holmes*, 2002 CarswellOnt 3614, 62 O.R. (3d) 146, 169 C.C.C. (3d) 344, 7 C.R. (6th) 287 (C.A.); leave to appeal refused 2003 CarswellOnt 1381, 2003 CarswellOnt 1382 (S.C.C.); *Ahmed*, 2002 CarswellOnt 4075, 170 C.C.C. (3d) 27, 7 C.R. (6th) 308 (C.A.).

[109] *White*, 2003 CarswellOnt 2330, 176 C.C.C. (3d) 1, 16 C.R. (6th) 162 (C.A.).

[110] *Backhouse*, 2005 CarswellOnt 761, 194 C.C.C. (3d) 1, 28 C.R. (6th) 31 (C.A.); *Swanek*, 2005 CarswellOnt 506, 28 C.R. (6th) 93 (C.A.).

[111] *Ducharme*, 2004 CarswellMan 66, 182 C.C.C. (3d) 243, 20 C.R. (6th) 332 (C.A.); leave to appeal refused 2004 CarswellMan 219, 2004 CarswellMan 220 (S.C.C.).

[112] 1981 CarswellOnt 100, 1981 CarswellOnt 52, [1981] 2 S.C.R. 64, 59 C.C.C. (2d) 385, 21 C.R. (3d) 182 (Eng.), 26 C.R. (3d) 164 (Fr.), 122 D.L.R. (3d) 1, 37 N.R. 501.

mission of it (the statement) in the proceedings would bring the administration of justice into disrepute". In 1987 in *Collins*,[113] the Supreme Court said that a person's confession, obtained in violation of a *Charter* right, "strikes at one of the fundamental tenets of a fair trial, the right against self-incrimination". This is because the confession did not exist prior to the *Charter* violation; it was conscripted evidence from an accused because of the illegal actions of the police. In such instance, the more serious the offence, the more damaging to the system's repute would be an unfair trial, in which case the evidence should be excluded.

In 2009, the Supreme Court replaced the *Collins* test for the admissibility of evidence obtained in breach of a *Charter* right with a new one. In *Grant*[114] the Court recognized that "the concepts of trial fairness and conscription under the first branch of *Collins* introduced new problems of their own".[115] It was held that when faced with an application for exclusion under section 24(2), a court is now required to assess and balance the effect of admitting the evidence on society's confidence in the justice system having regard to: (1) the seriousness of the *Charter*-infringing state conduct, (2) the impact of the breach on the *Charter*-protected interests of the accused, and (3) society's interest in the adjudication of the case on its merits. At the first stage, the nature of the police conduct that infringed the *Charter* and led to the discovery of the evidence must be considered. The more severe or deliberate the state conduct that led to the *Charter* violation, the greater the need for the courts to dissociate themselves from that conduct by excluding evidence linked to that conduct in order to preserve public confidence in and ensure state adherence to the rule of law. The second stage of the inquiry calls for an evaluation of the extent to which the breach actually undermined the interests protected by the infringed right. The Court felt that the more serious the incursion on these interests, the greater the risk that admission of the evidence would bring the administration of justice into disrepute. At the third stage, a court should ask whether the truth-seeking function of the criminal trial process would be better served by admission of the evidence or by its exclusion. At this stage, factors such as the reliability of the evidence and its importance to the Crown's case should be considered.

---

[113] 1987 CarswellBC 94, 1987 CarswellBC 699, [1987] 1 S.C.R. 265, 13 B.C.L.R. (2d) 1, 33 C.C.C. (3d) 1, 56 C.R. (3d) 193, *(sub nom. Collins v. R.)* 38 D.L.R. (4th) 508, [1987] 3 W.W.R. 699, 28 C.R.R. 122, 74 N.R. 276.

[114] 2009 SCC 32, 2009 CarswellOnt 4104, 2009 CarswellOnt 4105, 245 C.C.C. (3d) 1, 66 C.R. (6th) 1.

[115] *Supra* at para. 62.

In *Singh*[116] a majority (5-4) panel of the Supreme Court held that a finding of voluntariness will be determinative of the section 7 *Charter* (right to silence) issue since the question of voluntariness requires the court to scrutinize whether the detainee was denied his or her right to silence. The majority felt that the confessions rule effectively subsumes the constitutional right to silence because the two tests are functionally equivalent. Thus, it was argued, where a statement has survived a thorough inquiry into voluntariness, the accused's *Charter* application alleging that the statement was obtained in violation of the pre-trial right to silence under section 7 cannot succeed. Conversely, if circumstances are such that the accused can show on a balance of probabilities that the statement was obtained in violation of his or her constitutional right to remain silent, the Crown will be unable to prove voluntariness beyond a reasonable doubt. The minority panel, however, was not prepared to accept that the two tests are functionally equivalent. They reasoned that while a confession may be "voluntary" under the common law rule, it may still be obtained by state action that infringes section 7 of the *Charter* where a police interrogator has undermined a detainee's freedom to choose whether to make a statement. It was held that while there is considerable overlap between the *Charter* protection of the right to silence and the common law confessions rule, given their different purposes, they should remain distinct doctrines.

10. THE USE OF TRICKS

The question of police trickery is a distinct inquiry, although related to voluntariness.[117] Its more specific objective is maintaining the integrity of the criminal justice system. Here, the inquiry is not concerned with reliability, but with the authorities' conduct as regards reliability. The test is whether the conduct of the police "shocks the community". If proven, then the confessions will be excluded even though the confession is voluntary in the traditional sense and the accused's right to silence has not been infringed.

An issue that has raised a great deal of judicial discussion has been the practice of placing a police officer, disguised in plainclothes and pretending to be a suspect under arrest, in a cell with an accused for the purpose of

---

[116] 2007 CarswellBC 2588, 2007 CarswellBC 2589, [2007] 3 S.C.R. 405, 225 C.C.C. (3d) 103, 51 C.R. (6th) 199.

[117] *Oickle*, 2000 SCC 38, 2000 CarswellNS 257, 2000 CarswellNS 258, [2000] 2 S.C.R. 3, 187 N.S.R. (2d) 201, 147 C.C.C. (3d) 321, 36 C.R. (5th) 129, 190 D.L.R. (4th) 257, 585 A.P.R. 201, 259 N.R. 227, [2000] S.C.J. No. 38.

actively eliciting incriminating information, or even passively listening to what an accused may say. On the eve of the introduction of the *Charter*, such conduct was not only accepted, but was regarded as reasonably necessary for the pursuit of shrewd and sophisticated criminals.[118]

Almost a decade of the *Charter* witnessed a reversal of that view. In *Hebert*,[119] it was held that the right to silence had to be defined broadly enough to preserve for a detained person the right to choose whether to speak to the authorities or to remain silent. To permit the authorities to trick a suspect into making a confession to them after he or she has exercised the right of conferring with counsel and has declined to make a statement, would permit the authorities to do indirectly what the *Charter* forbids them from doing directly. To do so would effectively deprive a suspect of that choice.

In *Hebert*, statements made by the accused to a plainclothes officer posing as a suspect under arrest were excluded because the accused had said, after he had consulted counsel, that he did not wish to make a statement. The Supreme Court said that the police violated his right to remain silent by using a trick to negate his decision not to speak. However, the Court also stressed that the scope of the right to silence does not go so far as to prohibit the police from obtaining confessions in all cases. The right to silence was subject to the following limits:

1. There is no duty on the police to advise an accused of the right to silence.

2. The police are not prohibited from questioning an accused in the absence of counsel after he has retained counsel. Police persuasion, short of denying the accused the right to choose or of depriving him of an operating mind, does not breach the right to silence.

3. The right to silence applies only after the accused is detained.

4. The right does not affect voluntary statements made to cellmates. The violation of the suspect's rights occurs only when the Crown acts to subvert the suspect's constitutional right to choose not to make a statement to the authorities.

5. A distinction must be made between the use of undercover agents to observe the suspect, and the use of undercover agents to actively elicit

---

[118] *Rothman*, 1981 CarswellOnt 43, 1981 CarswellOnt 93, 59 C.C.C. (2d) 30, 20 C.R. (3d) 97 (S.C.C.).

[119] 1990 CarswellYukon 4, 1990 CarswellYukon 7, [1990] 2 S.C.R. 151, 47 B.C.L.R. (2d) 1, 57 C.C.C. (3d) 1, 77 C.R. (3d) 145, [1990] 5 W.W.R. 1, 49 C.R.R. 114, 110 N.R. 1.

information in violation of the suspect's choice to remain silent. The right to silence is not violated where the undercover agents observe rather than actively elicit.

6. Evidence may, where appropriate, be admitted even where a violation of the accused's right is established. It is only where the court is satisfied that its reception would bring the administration of justice into disrepute that the evidence can be rejected under section 24(2) of the *Charter*. Where the police have acted with due care for the suspect's rights, it is unlikely that the statements they obtain will be held inadmissible.

Cases that have followed *Hebert* have made it clear that not every admission made by an accused to a cellmate will be excluded as violating his right to silence. The right to silence prohibits the police from *actively* eliciting statements from a detainee so as to infringe his right to silence. It does not apply where a police informer has been placed in the accused's cell to obtain incriminating statements from the accused, so long as he acts independently of the police.[120] Nor will the right to silence prevent the admissibility of a confession made to an undercover officer who is placed in the accused's cell, so long as the undercover officer does not actively elicit information from the accused.[121]

The issue for the trial judge to consider is whether the accused has been deprived of the right to "make a choice" whether to speak or not. In *Whittle*,[122] Mr. Justice Sopinka proposed that the test be applied this way:

> Did the action of the police authorities deprive the suspect of making an effective choice by reason of *coercion, trickery* or *misinformation* or the lack of information?[123]

---

[120] *Johnston*, 1991 CarswellOnt 92, 2 O.R. (3d) 771, 64 C.C.C. (3d) 233, 5 C.R. (4th) 185, 47 O.A.C. 66 (C.A.); leave to appeal refused (1991), 67 C.C.C. (3d) vi (S.C.C.); *Gray*, 1991 CarswellOnt 691, 4 O.R. (3d) 33, 66 C.C.C. (3d) 6, 51 O.A.C. 81 (C.A.); leave to appeal refused (1992), 69 C.C.C. (3d) vi, 138 N.R. 411 (note), 56 O.A.C. 79 (note) (S.C.C.).

[121] *Graham*, 1991 CarswellOnt 77, 1 O.R. (3d) 499, 62 C.C.C. (3d) 128, 3 C.R. (4th) 44, 44 O.A.C. 374 (C.A.); leave to appeal refused (1992), 69 C.C.C. (3d) vi (S.C.C.).

[122] 1994 CarswellOnt 1163, 1994 CarswellOnt 91, [1994] 2 S.C.R. 914, 92 C.C.C. (3d) 11, 32 C.R. (4th) 1, 116 D.L.R. (4th) 416, 23 C.R.R. (2d) 6, 170 N.R. 16, 73 O.A.C. 201.

[123] *Ibid.*, at p. 14 [C.R.].

11. EXCLUSION OF EVIDENCE OBTAINED BY AN INVOLUNTARY CONFESSION

At common law, a judge had no discretion to exclude evidence because of the manner in which it was obtained.[124] In 1949 in the *St. Lawrence case*,[125] it was held that where the discovery of some fact confirms the truth of an involuntary confession, the part of the confession that is confirmed by the discovery of the fact is admissible. However, in *S. (K.)*,[126] the Ontario Court of Appeal held that the rule was no longer valid. It was a product of a time when a trial judge had no residual discretion to exclude evidence because of the manner in which it was obtained. All of this has been overtaken by constitutional and judicial development. The Court noted that comments from the Supreme Court of Canada reflect a strong indication that using an involuntary confession is inconsistent with fundamental notions of fairness and the administration of justice. The Court said that, in the light of such developments from the Supreme Court, the rule should be modified to acknowledge that the trial judge has the discretion to exclude the evidence. Moreover, it is only in exceptional circumstances that the confession should not be excluded. Since admitting an involuntary confession runs counter to fundamental aspects of trial fairness, it is difficult to conceive of a basis for exercising the discretion in favour of admission.[127]

---

[124] *Wray* (1970), 1970 CarswellOnt 207F, 1970 CarswellOnt 22, [1971] S.C.R. 272, [1970] 4 C.C.C. 1, 11 D.L.R. (3d) 673, 11 C.R.N.S. 235.

[125] 1949 CarswellOnt 4, [1949] O.R. 215, 93 C.C.C. 376, 7 C.R. 464 (H.C.).

[126] 2000 CarswellOnt 3290, 50 O.R. (3d) 321, 148 C.C.C. (3d) 247, 36 C.R. (5th) 198, 77 C.R.R. (2d) 327, 136 O.A.C. 238, [2000] O.J. No. 3534 (C.A.).

[127] See *Oickle, supra*, note 117, where the Supreme Court held that the underlying consideration when dealing with the admissibility of a confession is the reliability of the evidence.

PART C

Proof at Trial

8
PROOF AT TRIAL

1. GENERALLY

The common law system is known as the adversary or accusatorial system, as opposed to the continental system, which is generally described as the inquisitorial system. Although both systems have many characteristics in common, such as an oral hearing with both the prosecution and the accused separately represented by counsel, and with no compulsion upon the accused to answer questions, there are distinct differences. Under the inquisitorial system, the judge takes an active role in questioning witnesses for the prosecution and in examining the accused and witnesses for the defence. Moreover, prior to trial, a brief or dossier compiled by a *juge d'instruction* or examining magistrate containing the examination of various witnesses is provided to the judge and jury.

The common law system may be described more as a duel between the Crown prosecutor and the defence counsel, with the judge sitting in the middle as an impartial arbiter. There are, however, some limitations on the contestants. It is the duty of counsel for the Crown to bring out all of the facts both for and against the accused. Moreover, it has been said that:

> . . . the business of counsel for the Crown is fairly and impartially to exhibit all the facts to the jury. The Crown has no interest in procuring a convic-

tion. Its only interest is that the right person should be convicted, that the truth should be known, and that justice be done.[1]

On the other hand, it is the duty of counsel for the defence to use all of the legitimate means at hand to obtain an acquittal for his or her client. In fact, the accused need not say anything. The defence need not say or reveal anything until all of the Crown's evidence has been presented to the judge or jury and tested by the defence on every essential element of the offence to the extent that the judge or jury, fully instructed and acting rationally, could convict the accused. Neither the prosecutor nor the judge is entitled to comment to the jury that the accused has remained silent; nor is the judge or jury entitled to draw an adverse inference from the accused's silence. It is only when the Crown has passed the threshold of presenting sufficient evidence on all elements of a charge and the trial judge is satisfied that a jury properly instructed and acting rationally could convict the accused that the defence is required to reveal its position.[2]

The usual steps in the process are these: opening statement by the prosecution; presentation of the prosecution's case; opening statement by the defence; presentation of the evidence for the defence; rebuttal evidence by the prosecution; summation of counsel for the prosecution and for the defence; charge to the jury by the trial judge; verdict of the jury or the judge, where the trial is by judge alone.

2. DISCLOSURE BY THE CROWN

(a) Generally

In a purely adversarial setting, each side would have the right until trial to withhold from the other information pertinent to the success or failure of its case. However, under the common law, it is the duty of the Crown to bring out all facts both for and against the accused "so that the right person should be convicted, that truth be known and that justice be done".[3]

Unfortunately, this was not the case in the early days of common law. In fact, in the early days, there was very little, if any, disclosure. Until the seventeenth century, anyone charged with a felony was kept in close confinement until his trial. The accused was given only a copy of the indict-

---

[1] *Sugarman* (1935), 25 Cr. App. R. 109 at pp. 114-15.
[2] *Chaulk*, 1990 CarswellMan 385, 1990 CarswellMan 239, [1990] 3 S.C.R. 1303, 62 C.C.C. (3d) 193, 2 C.R. (4th) 1.
[3] *Sugarman, supra* note 1.

ment against him when he was asked to plead and only then discovered the evidence against him when it was produced at trial.[4]

It was not until 1848, with the passage of the *Indictable Offences Act*,[5] that a preliminary inquiry was finally held in the presence of the accused and the accused given an opportunity to cross-examine the witnesses against him and to obtain a copy of their depositions. But disclosure, even at the preliminary inquiry stage, was still the exception rather than the norm. The very nature of the adversary system relied upon the element of surprise. Courts were reluctant to allow an accused to use the preliminary inquiry to learn about the case against him. As late as 1970, the Supreme Court of Canada said that the defence could not demand, as of right, the production of statements made by Crown witnesses.[6]

Today, the only statutory disclosure provisions contained in the *Criminal Code* are sections 603 and 605. Section 603 allows an accused, after he or she has been ordered to stand trial, to inspect without charge the indictment, his or her own statement, the evidence and the exhibits, if any, and gives the accused the right to obtain copies of those documents (with the exception of the exhibits) upon payment of a reasonable fee. Section 605 authorizes judge of a superior court or a court of criminal jurisdiction, on summary application on behalf of the accused or the prosecutor, after three days' notice to the accused or prosecutor, to order the release of any exhibit for the purpose of a scientific or other test or examination, subject to such terms as appear to be necessary or desirable to ensure the safeguarding of the exhibit and its preservation for use at the trial. To fill the gap, it has been necessary for the Supreme Court of Canada to impose an obligation upon the Crown to provide the defence with full and frank disclosure of its case against an accused.

(b) Evidence in the Possession of the Crown

It was only a little over two decades ago that the Supreme Court decided to introduce judicial reform and guidance with respect to the question of Crown disclosure. In *Stinchcombe*,[7] the Supreme Court finally rejected the

---

[4] Stephen, *A History of the Criminal Law of England*, Vol. 1 (New York, Franklin reprint, 1964) at pp. 284, 350.

[5] *Sir John Jervis's Act*, c. 42.

[6] *Patterson*, 1970 CarswellAlta 61, [1970] S.C.R. 409, 2 C.C.C. (2d) 227, 9 D.L.R. (3d) 398, 72 W.W.R. 35, 10 C.R.N.S. 55.

[7] (1991), 1991 CarswellAlta 559, 1991 CarswellAlta 192, [1991] 3 S.C.R. 326, 120 A.R. 161, 83 Alta. L.R. (2d) 193, 68 C.C.C. (3d) 1, 8 C.R. (4th) 277, [1992] 1 W.W.R. 97, 18 C.R.R. (2d) 210, 130 N.R. 277, 8 W.A.C. 161.

argument frequently advanced by the Crown that full and frank disclosure of the Crown's evidence could have a serious impact on the success of the case against the accused. The Court pointed out that section 7 of the *Charter*, the right to fundamental justice, gives an accused the right to full disclosure of the Crown's case. It said that the fruits of a police investigation, which are in the possession of the Crown, are not the property of the Crown for its use in securing a conviction. Rather, they are the property of the public to be used to ensure that justice is done. The absolute withholding of information which is relevant to the defence can only be justified on the basis of the existence of a legal privilege which excludes the information from disclosure. This privilege is reviewable, however, on the ground that it is not a reasonable limit on the right to make full answer and defence in a particular case.

The issue in *Stinchcombe* was whether an accused should be allowed to see contradictory statements of Crown witnesses. Under the adversary system, a contradictory statement of a witness is an important tool for the defence to show that a witness's testimony may not be credible. Fairness to an accused, the Court said, demands such disclosure. The Crown has the duty to disclose to the defence all material evidence in its possession, whether favourable to the accused or not, in order to ensure a fair trial and guarantee that an accused can make full answer and defence. This included all statements and notes prepared by the police. If there are no statements or notes, all information in the prosecution's possession relating to any relevant evidence the person could give must be disclosed.

The Supreme Court has also said that the duty to disclose also extends to records relating to findings of serious misconduct by police officers involved in the investigation against the accused. Such records properly fall within the scope of the first party disclosure package due to the Crown from the police where the police misconduct is either related to the investigation or where the finding of misconduct could reasonably have an impact on the case against the accused.[8]

In *Stinchombe*, the Court said that the obligation to disclose is triggered by a request by or on behalf of the accused. The onus is then upon the Crown to justify its refusal to disclose, or to seek a delay because of a claim of privilege. Disclosure by the Crown should be made even before the accused is called upon to elect his or her mode of trial. In those rare cases where an accused is unrepresented by counsel, there is a further duty upon the Crown to advise the accused of the right to disclosure; moreover, the

---

[8] *McNeil*, 2009 SCC 3, 2009 CarswellOnt 116, 2009 CarswellOnt 117, [2009] 1 S.C.R. 66, 238 C.C.C. (3d) 353, 62 C.R. (6th) 1.

trial judge should not take the accused's plea until disclosure has been made. Finally, the obligation to disclose is a continuing one and must be made whenever additional information is received during the course of the investigation or trial.

However, the Supreme Court recognized that the obligation to disclose is not absolute. Rather, it is subject to the Crown's discretion both to the withholding of information and to the timing of disclosure, for example, with respect to the rules of privilege. That discretion is reviewable by the trial judge. Defence counsel can initiate a review and the Crown must justify its refusal to disclose. Since disclosure of all relevant information is the general rule, the Crown is required to bring itself within an exception to the disclosure rule.[9]

The Supreme Court has said there is also an obligation upon the Crown to preserve relevant evidence that is in its possession.[10] For example, in *Bero*,[11] the only issue at trial was whether the accused, who was charged with serious driving offences, was the driver of the car. After the accused was released from the hospital, it was discovered by the defence that his automobile had been turned over to and destroyed by a wrecker. It was held on appeal that although there was no evidence that the Crown had acted with an improper motive, the failure to preserve the vehicle was caused by the failure to look beyond the needs of the prosecution to the wider question of the potential relevance of the vehicle to the defence. The failure to preserve the vehicle revealed an ignorance of, or at least an indifference to, the duty of the Crown and the police to preserve the fruits of their investigation.

(c) Evidence in the Possession of Third Parties

The *Stinchcombe* case only dealt with the question of potential evidence for the defence that was in the possession or under the control of the Crown. What it did not deal with was whether the defence had the right to production of potential evidence not in the possession or under the control of the Crown, but in the possession of third parties. The Supreme Court was faced with this issue four years later in *O'Connor*.[12] In *O'Connor*, the issue was

---

[9] *La*, 1997 CarswellAlta 490, 1997 CarswellAlta 491, [1997] 2 S.C.R. 680, 116 C.C.C. (3d) 97, 8 C.R. (5th) 155.

[10] *Ibid.*

[11] 2000 CarswellOnt 4096, 151 C.C.C. (3d) 545, 39 C.R. (5th) 291 (C.A.).

[12] (1995), 1995 CarswellBC 1098, 1995 CarswellBC 1151, [1995] 4 S.C.R. 411, 103 C.C.C. (3d) 1, 44 C.R. (4th) 1, 130 D.L.R. (4th) 235, [1996] 2 W.W.R. 153, 68 B.C.A.C. 1, 33 C.R.R. (2d) 1, 191 N.R. 1, 112 W.A.C. 1, [1995] S.C.J. No. 98.

whether the Court could order the production of therapeutic records of a complainant in a case involving sexual assaults. The defence wanted to examine the records to see if there was any information in them that might be inconsistent with the evidence that the complainant was expected to give at trial.

This time, the Court drew a distinction between records in the hands of the Crown and records in the hands of a third party. The Court said that where third party records have fallen into the possession of the Crown, any concern relating to their privacy and privilege has disappeared. If the complainant was willing to release this information in order to further the criminal prosecution, then fairness required that the accused be entitled to use it in preparation of his or her defence.

Nevertheless, the Court did accept that the rule should be somewhat different where the records were in the hands of a third party. It said that the onus was on the accused to satisfy the court that the information is *likely* to be relevant. To obtain the records, the accused had to bring a formal written application supported by an affidavit setting out the specific grounds for production, although the court could waive formal notice in the interests of justice. Notice also had to be given to the third party in possession of the documents, as well as to those who had a privacy interest in the records. The accused also had to subpoena the custodian and the records to ensure their attendance in court.

The Court pointed out that the initial application for disclosure had to be made to the judge seized of the trial, and generally before the jury was empanelled. Before ordering production, the trial judge had to be satisfied that there was a reasonable probability that the information was logically probative of an issue at trial, or the competence of a witness to testify. The obligation upon the accused to establish likely relevance was not to be interpreted as an onerous burden, but rather a requirement to prevent speculative, fanciful, disruptive, unmeritorious, obstructive and time-consuming requests for production. If the records were ordered produced, it was the responsibility of the judge to examine them and weigh the salutary and deleterious effects of production in order to determine whether a non-production order would constitute a reasonable limit on the ability of the accused to make full answer and defence. In balancing the competing interest, the judge was required to consider: (1) the extent to which the record was necessary for the accused to make full answer and defence; (2) the probative value of the record; (3) the nature and extent of the reasonable expectation of privacy vested in the record; (4) whether production of the record would be premised upon any discriminatory belief or bias; and (5) the potential prejudice to the complainant's dignity, privacy or security that would be occasioned by production of the record.

The Supreme Court was not unanimous in its view on this issue. In a strong dissent, Madam Justice L'Heureux Dubé argued that it must not be presumed that the mere fact that a victim received treatment or counselling after a sexual assault indicated that the records would contain information that was relevant to the defence. The defence should have the onus of establishing the "likely relevance" of any record before production could be ordered for inspection by the judge. The onus was a significant one and required the defence to show that there was likely to be information in the impugned records which would relate to the complainant's credibility on a particular, material issue at trial. Without establishing "likely relevance" she said, applications before the court could turn into a fishing expedition that would result in the invasion of the privacy of women who have been sexually assaulted and would deter women from reporting the assault for fear of having their past dredged up in court.

The dissenting view of L'Heureux Dubé J. quickly found favour with the government of Canada and legislation was introduced to limit the right of an accused to access to third party records. On May 12, 1997, Parliament proclaimed Bill C-46 to provide statutory rules governing the production of the personal records of all witnesses where an accused is charged with certain specific sexual offences.[13]

Under this legislation, the defence is now required to go through a two-stage procedure to obtain production of third party records from the trial judge. In the first stage, the trial judge must conduct an in-camera hearing and give the complainant or witness the opportunity to make submissions. The judge must then decide, without looking at the records, whether they should be produced to him or her for review. The test which the judge must adopt is whether the record is still "likely relevant to an issue at trial or to the competence of a witness to testify", but it has been supplemented with the further requirement that production "be necessary in the interests of justice." In deciding whether to order production, the judge is required to consider "the salutary and deleterious effects" of that decision on the accused's right to make full answer and defence, and on the right to privacy and equality of the complainant or witness.[14] Section 278.5(5) lists the factors that must be taken into account by the judge in deciding whether to order production. It is only where the records are ordered to be produced that the judge is entitled to review the records and decide whether any or part of the record should be produced.

---

[13] Sections 278.1 to 278.91 of the *Criminal Code*.
[14] Section 278.5.

In effect, what the judge is expected to do in the first stage is to balance the competing interests of the right to make full answer and defence, and the right to privacy without even looking at the records. Although attacks on the new legislation as infringing sections 7 and 11(d) of the *Charter* were successful in the trial courts of some provinces,[15] the Supreme Court has upheld the new legislation. In *Mills*,[16] the Court said that the fact that section 278.2 prevents the automatic disclosure of all relevant and non-privileged information in the possession of the Crown does not deprive the accused of his right to make full answer and defence. The criterion that production be necessary in the interests of justice invests the trial judge with the discretion to consider the full range of rights and interests at issue before ordering production in a manner scrupulously respectful of the requirements of the *Charter*. In other words, section 278.5 now permits the trial judge to exercise a wide discretion in considering a variety of factors in order to preserve the complainant's privacy and equality rights to the maximum extent possible, and also ensures that the accused has access to documents required to make full answer and defence.

(d) Remedies for Failure to Disclose

Generally, the courts have been reluctant to sanction any remedy against the Crown for the failure to provide timely and complete disclosure to the defence, except an order for disclosure, an adjournment, or a mistrial and the imposition of costs. A stay of proceedings has been regarded as a remedy only of "last resort", granted where the adverse effect on the ability of the accused to make full answer and defence cannot be remedied, or where irreparable harm would be caused to the integrity of the justice system if the prosecution was allowed to continue, and even then, only in the clearest of cases.[17]

---

[15] *Mills* (1997), 1997 CarswellAlta 762, 205 A.R. 321, 56 Alta. L.R. (3d) 277, 12 C.R. (5th) 138, [1998] 4 W.W.R. 83, 47 C.R.R. (2d) 104, [1997] A.J. No. 891 (Q.B.); additional reasons 1997 CarswellAlta 921, 12 C.R. (5th) 163 (Q.B.); reversed 1999 CarswellAlta 1055, 1999 CarswellAlta 1056, 139 C.C.C. (3d) 321, 28 C.R. (5th) 207 (S.C.C.) and *Lee*, 1997 CarswellOnt 3636, 35 O.R. (3d) 594 (Gen. Div.).

[16] (1999), 1999 CarswellAlta 1055, 1999 CarswellAlta 1056, [1999] 3 S.C.R. 668, 244 A.R. 201, 75 Alta. L.R. (3d) 1, 139 C.C.C. (3d) 321, 28 C.R. (5th) 207, 180 D.L.R. (4th) 1, [2000] 2 W.W.R. 180, 69 C.R.R. (2d) 1, 248 N.R. 101, 209 W.A.C. 201, [1999] S.C.J. No. 68

[17] *O'Connor*, 1994 CarswellBC 575, 89 C.C.C. (3d) 109, 29 C.R. (4th) 40, 42 B.C.A.C. 105, 20 C.R.R. (2d) 212, 67 W.A.C. 105, [1994] B.C.J. No. 1116 (C.A.); additional reasons 1994 CarswellBC 581, 90 C.C.C. (3d) 257, 30 C.R.

However, the loss or destruction of potential evidence that may be of assistance to the defence has been another matter. Here the Supreme Court has said that the Crown has a duty to explain what has happened to the evidence or risk a stay of proceedings. For example, in *Carosella*,[18] a social worker at a sexual abuse crisis centre, who had interviewed the complainant in a sexual assault case, shredded her notes pursuant to a policy laid down by the centre mandating the shredding of most of the contents of their files in which there was "police involvement". Neither the Crown nor the complainant was aware that this had been done. In fact, both had consented to a disclosure of the contents of the entire file to the trial judge to determine which part of the files should be disclosed to the defence. The trial judge had stayed proceedings on the basis that the destroyed notes were relevant and material, and that they would, more likely than not, assist the accused. However, the Ontario Court of Appeal had set aside the stay because the Court felt that the notes were not a verified account of what the complainant had said, did not constitute a written statement of the complainant, and no realistic appraisal of the probable effect of the lost notes could support the conclusion that the accused's right to make full answer and defence had been compromised.

The Supreme Court, in a majority decision, re-instated the stay of proceedings. Sopinka J., delivering the majority judgment, held that an accused who alleges a breach of his right to make full answer and defence as a result of non-disclosure or non-production is not required to show that the conduct of the defence was prejudiced. If the material that was destroyed meets the threshold test for disclosure or production, the accused's *Charter* right is

---

(4th) 55 (C.A.); affirmed (1995), 1995 CarswellBC 1098, 1995 CarswellBC 1151, [1995] 4 S.C.R. 411, 103 C.C.C. (3d) 1, 44 C.R. (4th) 1, 130 D.L.R. (4th) 235, [1996] 2 W.W.R. 153, 68 B.C.A.C. 1, 33 C.R.R. (2d) 1, 191 N.R. 1, 112 W.A.C. 1, [1995] S.C.J. No. 98; *Stinchcombe*, 1994 CarswellAlta 324, (sub nom. *R. v. Stinchcombe (No. 2))* 149 A.R. 167, 88 C.C.C. (3d) 557, 30 C.R. (4th) 119, 63 W.A.C. 167 (C.A.); affirmed 1995 CarswellAlta 409, 1995 CarswellAlta 27, [1995] 1 S.C.R. 754, 162 A.R. 269, 96 C.C.C. (3d) 318, 38 C.R. (4th) 42, 178 N.R. 157, 83 W.A.C. 269; *Bero*, 2000 CarswellOnt 4096, 151 C.C.C. (3d) 545, 39 C.R. (5th) 291 (C.A.); *Taillefer*, 2003 CarswellQue 2765, 2003 CarswellQue 2766, 179 C.C.C. (3d) 353, 17 C.R. (6th) 57 (S.C.C.).

[18] 1997 CarswellOnt 85, 1997 CarswellOnt 86, [1997] 1 S.C.R. 80, 31 O.R. (3d) 575 (headnote only), 112 C.C.C. (3d) 289, 4 C.R. (5th) 139, 142 D.L.R. (4th) 595, 41 C.R.R. (2d) 189, 207 N.R. 321, 98 O.A.C. 81, [1997] S.C.J. No. 12. See also *MacDonnell*, 1997 CarswellNS 26, 1997 CarswellNS 27, [1997] 1 S.C.R. 305, 158 N.S.R. (2d) 1, 114 C.C.C. (3d) 145, 6 C.R. (5th) 80, 466 A.P.R. 1, 210 N.R. 318, [1997] S.C.J. No. 16.

breached without the requirement of showing additional prejudice. The extent to which the *Charter* violation causes actual prejudice to the accused relates only to the remedy to be fashioned pursuant to section 24(1) of the *Charter*. Sopinka J. held that in the circumstances of the case (a 1¾ hour interview immediately followed by a complaint to the police), a stay of proceedings was the only appropriate remedy. The deliberate destruction of the material in order to deprive the court and the accused of relevant evidence would damage the image of the administration of justice. Confidence in the system would be undermined if the court condoned conduct designed to defeat the processes of the court by an agency that receives money from and whose actions are scrutinized by provincial governments.

Although *Carosella* established that there is no onus upon the defence to establish prejudicial loss where there has been a deliberate destruction of potentially relevant evidence that might be of assistance to the defence, it did not deal with the question of the failure of the authorities to record evidence that might be potentially relevant. The distinction between destroyed evidence and unrecorded interviews remained unclear until a few months later when the Supreme Court released its reasons in *La*.[19] There the accused was charged with the sexual assault of a thirteen-year-old runaway for whom the police were searching. One of the runaway's conversations with a police officer was taped at police headquarters in preparation for a secure treatment application and only notes of her date of birth, address and phone numbers were made. The taped conversation was not for any criminal investigation, as the investigation into the accused's activities had not yet started. The tape was later misplaced. The trial judge had stayed proceedings.

Delivering the main judgment of the Court, Sopinka J. lifted the stay and set out the following principles that should be considered by a judge when dealing with disclosure by the Crown:

> 1. The Crown has the obligation to disclose all relevant information in its possession, inculpatory or exculpatory, whether it intends to rely upon it or not. The right of disclosure is a component of the right to make full answer and defence that is, in turn, a principle of fundamental justice embraced by section 7 of the *Charter*.
>
> 2. The Crown's obligation to disclose all relevant information in its possession gives rise to an obligation to preserve relevant evidence.

---

[19] 1997 CarswellAlta 490, 1997 CarswellAlta 491, [1997] 2 S.C.R. 680, 200 A.R. 81, 51 Alta. L.R. (3d) 181, 116 C.C.C. (3d) 97, 8 C.R. (5th) 155, 148 D.L.R. (4th) 608, [1997] 8 W.W.R. 1, 44 C.R.R. (2d) 262, 213 N.R. 1, 146 W.A.C. 81, [1997] S.C.J. No. 30.

3. When the prosecution has lost evidence that should have been disclosed, the Crown has a duty to explain what has happened to it. In determining whether the Crown's explanation is satisfactory, the Court should analyze the circumstances surrounding the loss of evidence. The main consideration is whether the police or the Crown took reasonable steps to preserve the evidence for disclosure. The relevance that the evidence was perceived to have at the time must be considered. The police cannot be expected to preserve everything on the chance that it will be relevant in the future. Furthermore, even the loss of relevant evidence will not result in a breach of the duty to disclose if the conduct of the police is reasonable.

4. The degree of care that is expected of the police for the preservation of the evidence will increase with the relevancy of the evidence.

5. If the explanation satisfies the trial judge that the evidence has not been destroyed or lost owing to unacceptable negligence, then the duty to disclose has not been breached. Nevertheless, the loss of a document may be so prejudicial that it impairs the right of an accused to make full answer and defence and to receive a fair trial. To establish a breach of section 7 of the *Charter* on the ground of lost evidence, the accused must establish actual prejudice to his or her right to make full answer and defence.

6. If the explanation for the lost evidence does not satisfy the trial judge, then section 7 of the *Charter* has been breached. Such failure may also suggest that an abuse of process has occurred. Conduct amounting to abuse of process will include the deliberate destruction of material by the police or other officers of the Crown for the purpose of defeating the Crown's obligation to disclose and, even absent proof of improper motive, an unacceptable degree of negligent conduct.

7. An accused need not establish abuse of process for the Crown to have failed to meet its section 7 *Charter* obligation to disclose.

8. The appropriateness of a stay of proceedings depends upon the effect of the conduct amounting to an abuse of process or other prejudice on the fairness of the trial and will be best assessed in the context of the trial as it unfolds. The trial judge has a discretion whether to rule on the application for a stay immediately or after hearing some or all of the evidence. It will usually be preferable for the judge to reserve on the application unless it is clear that no other course of action will cure the prejudice that is occasioned by the conduct giving rise to the abuse. This will enable the judge to assess the degree of prejudice and whether measures to minimize that prejudice have borne fruit.

9. Even if the trial judge rules on the motion at an early stage of the trial and the motion is unsuccessful, it may be renewed if there is a material change of circumstances.

3. THE CASE FOR THE CROWN

(a) The Opening Statement

In a jury trial, but not necessarily in a trial by judge alone, the prosecution will begin with an opening speech to the jury. The purpose of the speech is to lay before the jury a brief summary of the facts upon which the prosecution relies to establish its case and of the evidence that it expects each prosecution witness will give. The Crown must always be fair in the opening address, as well as in the prosecution in general. There is a duty to be impartial and to guard against injecting comments likely to excite or inflame the jury against the accused. If evidence to be introduced will require a ruling by the trial judge as to its admissibility, such as an admission or a confession, the Crown will make no mention of it in the opening address. If the Crown does refer to evidence that will require a ruling by the judge and the judge rules the evidence to be inadmissible, the result will usually be a mistrial and a new jury will have to be impanelled.

(b) The Evidence Generally

When the address of the Crown prosecutor is completed, the trial judge will call upon the prosecutor to present the case for the Crown. The prosecution will begin by calling witnesses who will be examined in-chief. In an examination-in-chief, the prosecution must be careful not to lead the witness on matters crucial to its case. A leading question is one that suggests the answer to the witness. For example, it is not permissible to ask the witness, "Did you see the accused shoot his wife", because it assumes the accused shot his wife. A leading question is one that takes for granted evidence that a witness has not yet given. The question, "When did you stop beating your wife?" is leading because it assumes that the witness has already said that he beat his wife in the past and has stopped doing so. On the other hand, there is no prohibition against the Crown leading a witness on matters that are not contentious or crucial to the defence. It is the duty and responsibility of the trial judge to intervene and prevent Crown counsel from putting leading questions to the witness.[20]

---

[20] *Rose*, 2001 CarswellOnt 955, 53 O.R. (3d) 417, 153 C.C.C. (3d) 225, 42 C.R. (5th) 183 (C.A.).

The Supreme Court has said that the Crown is not prohibited from leading evidence of the criminal record of its witnesses called in-chief who have been associated with the accused. Although it has been argued that doing so has the indirect effect of permitting the Crown to lead evidence of the accused's bad character by his association with criminals, which it is not entitled to do directly, the Court has said that prior convictions can bear to some extent upon the credibility of a witness and a jury is entitled to know of them. Nevertheless, the trial judge has the discretion to exclude such evidence if the Crown is leading it for an oblique motive.[21]

On the other hand, the Crown is not permitted to adduce evidence of the accused's bad character either by evidence of reputation or specific acts unless the accused has put character in issue or the evidence is otherwise relevant to an issue.[22] While such evidence may be relevant, it is excluded on the grounds that its prejudicial effect is apt to outweigh its probative value. In other words, the danger exists that a jury may convict on the basis of the accused's reputation rather than on the basis of the evidence.[23]

Although the Crown is bound by a strict duty to ensure that the integrity of the criminal justice system is preserved, it must operate within the context of an adversarial procedure. So long as the Crown has given full disclosure of its case within the guidelines set down by the Supreme Court in *Stinchcombe*,[24] the responsibility for choosing what witnesses are necessary to establish its case rests upon the Crown. Neither the defence nor the trial judge has any right to dictate to the Crown what evidence it should call.[25] This fundamental principle was reaffirmed by the Supreme Court in *Cook*.[26] In *Cook*, the accused was convicted of assault causing bodily harm on a male victim arising out of an incident in a woman's apartment. The woman had testified, but not the male victim. On appeal, the New Bruns-

---

[21] *Corbett*, 1988 CarswellBC 756, 1988 CarswellBC 252, [1988] 1 S.C.R. 670, 41 C.C.C. (3d) 385, 64 C.R. (3d) 1. Followed in *Gibson*, 2001 CarswellBC 885, 153 C.C.C. (3d) 465, 41 C.R. (5th) 213 (C.A.).

[22] See Chapter 5.

[23] *Arcangioli*, 1994 CarswellOnt 1151, 1994 CarswellOnt 51, [1994] 1 S.C.R. 129, 87 C.C.C. (3d) 289, 27 C.R. (4th) 1 at paras. 26-27.

[24] (1991), 1991 CarswellAlta 559, 1991 CarswellAlta 192, [1991] 3 S.C.R. 326, 120 A.R. 161, 83 Alta. L.R. (2d) 193, 68 C.C.C. (3d) 1, 8 C.R. (4th) 277, [1992] 1 W.W.R. 97, 18 C.R.R. (2d) 210, 130 N.R. 277, 8 W.A.C. 161.

[25] *V. (J.)*, 1994 CarswellQue 1356, 1994 CarswellQue 2494, 91 C.C.C. (3d) 284 (C.A.).

[26] 1997 CarswellNB 126, 1997 CarswellNB 125, [1997] 1 S.C.R. 1113, 188 N.B.R. (2d) 161, 114 C.C.C. (3d) 481, 7 C.R. (5th) 51, 146 D.L.R. (4th) 437, 480 A.P.R. 161, 210 N.R. 197, [1997] S.C.J. No. 22.

wick Court of Appeal set aside the conviction on the basis that the accused had the right to be faced by his accuser and to cross-examine him. Although recognizing that the Crown has the discretion to call, or not call, whatever witnesses it considers necessary for the presentation of its case, the Court of Appeal said that Crown was not entitled to hold back evidence that could assist the accused. There was a duty upon the trial judge to inquire why a complainant was not being called, and to determine whether or not the witness should be called to avoid a miscarriage of justice.

The Supreme Court, however, disagreed. The Court noted that, historically, fairness has been the main ground for opposing the Crown's discretionary authority to choose which witnesses to call. It pointed out that since the Crown is now required to disclose all relevant information it possesses, the defence is made aware of potentially exculpatory evidence discovered by the Crown and of material inconsistencies in its evidence; it has the ability to call those witnesses. The Court also rejected the argument that an accused who is not given a free opportunity to cross-examine every potential witness, whether or not the Crown wishes to call them, is necessarily prejudiced in his or her defence. Nor did the Court accept that a failure on the Crown's part to call a witness could result in prejudice to the accused in losing the right to address the jury last. Rather, the failure to call a witness was only a factor for the trial judge to consider in deciding whether or not he or she should call that witness. It was a matter to be left to each judge's discretion, to be exercised only in rare cases so as to avoid overly interfering with the adversarial nature of the proceedings. Unless improper motives could be imputed to the prosecution, such as, for example, the desire to hide exculpatory evidence, Crown counsel would be considered to have properly executed his or her function in the criminal trial.

(c) A Confession or Admission by the Accused

If Crown counsel intends to introduce a statement or admission made by the accused, he or she will indicate to the judge that a *voir dire* is required to determine the voluntariness of the statement or admission.[27] The defence may, however, be prepared to admit that the statement is voluntary, in which case a *voir dire* will not be necessary.[28] If the trial judge rules that the statement was made voluntarily by the accused, or if the defence admits

---

[27] *Piche* (1970), 1970 CarswellMan 62, 1970 CarswellMan 81, [1971] S.C.R. 23, [1970] 4 C.C.C. 27, 11 D.L.R. (3d) 700, 74 W.W.R. 674, 12 C.R.N.S. 222.

[28] *Park*, 1981 CarswellOnt 100, 1981 CarswellOnt 52, [1981] 2 S.C.R. 64, 59 C.C.C. (2d) 385, 21 C.R. (3d) 182 (Eng.), 26 C.R. (3d) 164 (Fr.), 122 D.L.R. (3d) 1, 37 N.R. 501.

that it was made voluntarily, then the statement is usually introduced through the officer or person who took the statement, and will be made an exhibit, if it is in writing or is by video or audio. A statement that has been ruled to be involuntary may not be introduced by the Crown and is inadmissible for all purposes. For example, it cannot be used by the Crown or by a co-accused to cross-examine an accused who enters the witness stand and gives evidence inconsistent with what he or she said in their statement.

The Crown is not barred from introducing a statement ruled inadmissible in a prior proceeding. The trial judge is required to consider the admissibility issue afresh based on the evidence adduced on the *voir dire*. The judge presiding at the subsequent hearing does not owe deference to factual or credibility findings made at an earlier hearing.[29] The Supreme Court has said that the doctrine of issue estoppel does not apply to statement *voir dires*.[30]

The Crown may not wish to introduce an accused's statement because it is exculpatory, but may still wish to be able to use it to cross-examine the accused if he or she gives evidence contrary to the contents of the statement. The courts, however, have said that it will not allow the Crown to lie in wait and permit the accused to trap him or herself.[31] Some authorities have suggested that if the statement is relevant to a fact in issue, even if it does not directly incriminate the accused, then the statement should be advanced as part of the Crown's case in chief, unless it is marginally, minimally or doubtfully relevant.[32] Other authorities have said that although the Crown need not introduce the statement in chief, it must at least attempt to prove its voluntariness during the presentation of the prosecution case in chief.[33] If the statement is proved to be voluntary, this will at least alert the accused to the fact that it may be used by the Crown to cross-examine him if he gives evidence which conflicts with the contents of the statement.

Although the Crown is not entitled to cross-examine an accused on a statement that the trial judge has found not be voluntary, that ruling will not

[29] *Banwait*, 2010 ONCA 869, 2010 CarswellOnt 9673, 265 C.C.C. (3d) 201, 82 C.R. (6th) 87; leave to appeal refused 2011 CarswellOnt 6017, 2011 CarswellOnt 6018 (S.C.C.); reversed 2011 CarswellOnt 11786, 2011 CarswellOnt 11787, 276 C.C.C. (3d) 385, 88 C.R. (6th) 116 (S.C.C.).

[30] *Duhamel*, 1984 CarswellAlta 174, 1984 CarswellAlta 418, [1984] 2 S.C.R. 555, 15 C.C.C. (3d) 491, 43 C.R. (3d) 1.

[31] *Drake* (1970), 1970 CarswellSask 37, 1 C.C.C. (2d) 396, [1971] 1 W.W.R. 454, 12 C.R.N.S. 220 (Q.B.).

[32] *Bruno*, 1975 CarswellOnt 1076, 27 C.C.C. (2d) 318 (C.A.).

[33] *Lizotte*, 1980 CarswellQue 25, 61 C.C.C. (2d) 423, 18 C.R. (3d) 364 (C.A.).

necessarily apply where the statement has been declared inadmissible because of a breach of the accused's *Charter* rights. For example, in *Calder*,[34] the trial judge had excluded the statement of an accused which the Crown sought to introduce in chief because his right to counsel had been violated. When the accused gave evidence in his defence, the Crown applied to the trial judge to be allowed to use the statement to impeach his credibility. It was argued by the Crown that when an accused gives evidence, he brings his credibility into issue and cannot argue that the use of such statements for credibility violates his right against self-incrimination. Although the trial judge rejected that argument, it found favour with two of the three judges of the Ontario Court of Appeal who, however, dismissed the appeal for other reasons. On a further appeal by the Crown, the Supreme Court, in a majority decision, held that the trial judge was correct in refusing to permit cross-examination on the excluded statement.

Sopinka J., speaking for the majority, said that since the exclusion order made by the trial judge under section 24(1) of the *Charter* was made under the authority of a constitutional provision, the condition under which the trial judge may reconsider his decision must be at least as stringent as that in respect of an order made under the authority of a statute. He rejected the notion that a distinction should be made between the prohibited use for all purposes of a statement ruled involuntary and one excluded for a *Charter* violation. He was of the view that although the rule against the admission of an involuntary statement is based primarily on reliability concerns, the law has now developed to the extent that the voluntariness rule is supported in part on fairness in the criminal process.[35]

> The effect of destroying the credibility of an accused who takes the stand in his or her defence using evidence obtained from the mouth of the accused in breach of his or her *Charter* rights will usually have the same effect as the use of the same evidence when adduced by the Crown in its case in chief for the purpose of incrimination. The fact that a jury carefully instructed can apply the distinction does not mean that the use for the purpose of impeach-

---

[34] 1994 CarswellOnt 94, 19 O.R. (3d) 643, 92 C.C.C. (3d) 97, 32 C.R. (4th) 197, 23 C.R.R. (2d) 94, 74 O.A.C. 1 (C.A.); leave to appeal refused (1995), 94 C.C.C. (3d) vii (note), 37 C.R. (4th) 400 (note) (S.C.C.); affirmed 1996 CarswellOnt 1405, 1996 CarswellOnt 1405F, [1996] 1 S.C.R. 660, 27 O.R. (3d) 258 (headnote only), 105 C.C.C. (3d) 1, 46 C.R. (4th) 133, 132 D.L.R. (4th) 577, 34 C.R.R. (2d) 189, 194 N.R. 52, 90 O.A.C. 18.

[35] Referring to *Whittle*, 1994 CarswellOnt 1163, 1994 CarswellOnt 91, [1994] 2 S.C.R. 914, 92 C.C.C. (3d) 11, 32 C.R. (4th) 1, 116 D.L.R. (4th) 416, 23 C.R.R. (2d) 6, 170 N.R. 16, 73 O.A.C. 201 at para. 27.

ment will, in the eyes of the jury, have a less detrimental effect on the case for the accused.[36]

Nevertheless, he did not rule out the use of such evidence entirely and accepted that it could be used in "very limited circumstances". But before it could be used, the Crown was required to seek a ruling from the trial judge during its case or before cross-examining the accused. In such instance, a *voir dire* would be necessary in which the trial judge would have to consider the admissibility of the statement for the limited purpose for which the Crown intended to use the statement.

McLachlin J., disagreed that the use of a statement excluded for the breach of a *Charter* right should occur only "in very limited circumstances". As far as she was concerned, this was not a proper test because the trial judge, before excluding evidence obtained in breach of the *Charter*, is required under section 24(2) to consider "all the circumstances", not "limited circumstances". The addition of a requirement of "very limited circumstances" would contradict the plain words of the statute. She summed up her dissenting opinion this way:

> It may be seen as unfair to tender against an accused as substantive evidence a statement which the state obtained from him in violation of his *Charter* rights. However, where the accused chooses to take the stand and place his credibility in issue, vouching to the jury that what he is telling them is the whole truth and nothing but the truth, it is more difficult to say that it is unfair to permit the Crown to cross-examine him on his prior inconsistent statement and to put to him the vital question of which version is true. These are important considerations which must be weighed against any unfairness arising from the way the statement was taken, if the judge is to properly determine whether admission of the statement would bring the administration of justice into disrepute.[37]

McLachlin J. felt that it is important to permit the jury to judge fairly the truthfulness of the witness. It was equally important not to permit witnesses to take the stand and fabricate lies, free from fear that they may be cross-examined on earlier contradictory statements. Thus, she argued, the trial judge must consider "all the circumstances" as required by section 24(2), not simply the "limited circumstances" suggested by the majority members of the Court.

---

[36] *Supra* note 34, at p. 15 [C.C.C. (3d)].

[37] *Supra* note 34 at p. 27 [C.C.C. (3d)]

(d) Introduction of Prior Testimony

Section 715(1) of the *Criminal Code* permits evidence given by a witness at the accused's previous trial on the same charge, or evidence of the witness taken in the investigation of the accused or at the preliminary hearing into the charge, to be read as evidence at trial if the witness refuses to be sworn or give evidence, or is dead, insane, too ill to travel or testify, or is absent from Canada. However, section 715(1) also gives the trial judge discretion to refuse to allow the evidence to be read if the accused satisfies the judge that he or she did not have "full opportunity" to cross-examine the witness when the evidence was given or taken.

The "full opportunity" to cross-examine requirement in section 715(1) has been held to be limited to those cases where the witness refuses to answer questions in cross-examination, dies or disappears in the midst of cross-examination, or where the presiding judge curtails cross-examination by imposing improper limitations or restrictions. It has been held not to apply where failure to cross-examine the witness stems from the accused's ignorance of potentially useful information, no matter the cause or reason. Those situations have been said to be best dealt with under trial fairness, where the reason for the missing information can properly be taken into account as a factor.[38]

For some time, it was generally held that once the Crown complied with section 715, the trial judge was required to admit the transcript of the previous testimony. The judge had no discretion to exclude it. However, in *Potvin*,[39] the Supreme Court decided that a trial judge has the discretion to refuse to admit such evidence where it is obtained in a manner that is unfair to the accused. For example, the fact that a witness is absent from Canada will not necessarily result in the admission of the witness's testimony if the Crown could obtain the witness's attendance by some minimal degree of effort. A judge might also refuse to permit the Crown to introduce transcript evidence if the Crown was aware at the time the witness previously testified that he or she would not be available to testify at trial and failed to inform the defence so that they could use their best efforts in cross-examination.[40] Similarly, the failure of the Crown to disclose information which could

---

[38] *Michaud*, 2000 CarswellNB 69, 144 C.C.C. (3d) 62 (C.A.); *Lewis*, 2009 ONCA 874, 2009 CarswellOnt 7685, 249 C.C.C. (3d) 265. But see *Barembruch*, 1997 CarswellBC 1837, 119 C.C.C. (3d) 185 (C.A.).

[39] *Potvin*, 1989 CarswellQue 16, 1989 CarswellQue 104, [1989] 1 S.C.R. 525, 47 C.C.C. (3d) 289, 68 C.R. (3d) 193, 42 C.R.R. 44, 93 N.R. 42, 21 Q.A.C. 258.

[40] *Kaddoura* (1987), 1987 CarswellAlta 251, 82 A.R. 347, 56 Alta. L.R. (2d) 126, 41 C.C.C. (3d) 371, 60 C.R. (3d) 393, [1988] 1 W.W.R. 693 (C.A.); leave to

have been used by the defence in cross-examination to attack the credibility of the complainant at the preliminary inquiry has been held to be a reason to deny the Crown the right to introduce transcript evidence, as a denial of the accused's right to full answer and defence.[41]

The Ontario Court of Appeal has said that to satisfy the necessity requirement, it is not sufficient for the Crown to simply show that a witness is not compellable because he or she is out of the jurisdiction. Efforts should be made to pursue other options such as teleconferencing or taking commission evidence before one reaches the conclusion that admitting evidence by way of a hearsay statement is necessary. Since evidence under section 715(1)(d) is hearsay, the trial judge is required to enter into a necessity/reliability analysis before admitting such evidence. Necessity cannot be equated with the unavailability of a witness. Rather, it must be shown that hearsay is the only available means of putting the evidence before the court. Sections 714.2 and 714.4 of the *Criminal Code* added in 1999 specifically recognize the reception of evidence given by a witness outside Canada by means of technology that permits the witness to testify in the virtual presence of the parties.[42]

[56] It seems to me that when s. 715(1)(d) is read together with ss. 714.2 and 714.4, it is incumbent on a trial judge to include, as a consideration before making the order, the possibility of taking the evidence in a live manner via audio or video technology.

An unusual example of where the Crown was refused the right to lead transcript evidence under section 715 was *Hawkins*.[43] At issue was whether the evidence of a woman who had testified against the accused at his preliminary hearing and then subsequently married him, could be read in under section 715. The Supreme Court said that it could not. Spousal incompe-

---

appeal refused (1988), 87 A.R. 160n, 60 Alta. L.R. (2d) lv, 64 C.R. (3d) xxx (S.C.C.).

[41] *Barembruch*, 1997 CarswellBC 1837, 119 C.C.C. (3d) 185, 96 B.C.A.C. 215, 155 W.A.C. 215, [1997] B.C.J. No. 2029 (C.A.).

[42] *Li*, 2012 ONCA 291, 2012 CarswellOnt 5530, 284 C.C.C. (3d) 207. See also See *Orpin*, 2002 CarswellOnt 1327, 165 C.C.C. (3d) 56 (C.A.); *O'Connor*, 2002 CarswellOnt 3955, 62 O.R. (3d) 263, 170 C.C.C. (3d) 365, 7 C.R. (6th) 205 (C.A.) and *Finta*, 1992 CarswellOnt 96, 73 C.C.C. (3d) 65, 14 C.R. (4th) 1 (C.A.); affirmed 1994 CarswellOnt 61, 1994 CarswellOnt 1154, 88 C.C.C. (3d) 417, 28 C.R. (4th) 265 (S.C.C.); reconsideration / rehearing refused (June 23, 1994), Doc. 23023, 23097 (S.C.C.). As Feldman J.A. noted in *Li*.

[43] 1996 CarswellOnt 4063, 1996 CarswellOnt 4062, [1996] 3 S.C.R. 1043, 30 O.R. (3d) 641 (headnote only), 111 C.C.C. (3d) 129, 2 C.R. (5th) 245, 141 D.L.R. (4th) 193, 204 N.R. 241, 96 O.A.C. 81, [1996] S.C.J. No. 117.

tency does not represent a refusal to give evidence as required by the section. The common law rule of spousal incompetency disqualifies a spouse from giving evidence regardless of the spouse's choice.

(e) Videotape Testimony of a Victim or Witness under 18 or Disabled

The common law has recognized, at least since the 18th century, that an accused has the right to face an accuser and subject the testimony of that accuser to the test of cross-examination. That right has been constitutionally recognized by section 11(d) of the *Charter* which guarantees an accused the right "to be presumed innocent until proven guilty according to law in a fair and public hearing by an independent and impartial tribunal". Section 7 of the *Charter* also recognizes "the right to life, liberty and security of the person and the right not to be deprived thereof except in accordance with the principles of fundamental justice".

The Supreme Court, however, has accepted that section 715.1 of the *Criminal Code* is a legitimate exception to sections 11(d) and 7.[44] Section 715.1 allows for the reception of videotaped evidence of a victim or other witness under the age of 18 years at the time the offence was alleged to have been committed. Section 715.2 also permits the reception of video-taped evidence of a victim or other witness who is able to communicate evidence but may have difficulty doing so by reason of mental or physical disability. There are three conditions that must be satisfied before the video-tape will be admitted. The first is that the videotaped interview must have been made within a reasonable time after the alleged offence. Here, what constitutes a reasonable time will depend on all of the circumstances of the case. For example, in *Scott*,[45] the videotaped interview took place about four and a half months after the assault. In admitting the videotaped interview, the trial judge took into account the fact that the child in the particular circumstances of the case was reluctant to disclose the assault. Similarly, in *G.(S.)*,[46] a three year delay of a 13-year-old-complainant's videotaped statement was admitted because of the complainant's fear of the accused and her mother's failure to take action once the complainant told her of the incident.

---

[44] *L. (D.O.)*, 1993 CarswellMan 348, 1993 CarswellMan 24, [1993] 4 S.C.R. 419, 85 C.C.C. (3d) 289, 25 C.R. (4th) 285, 18 C.R.R. (2d) 257, 88 Man. R. (2d) 241, 161 N.R. 1, 51 W.A.C. 241; reversing 1991 CarswellMan 10, 65 C.C.C. (3d) 465, 6 C.R. (4th) 277, 73 Man. R. (2d) 238, 3 W.A.C. 238 (C.A.).

[45] 1993 CarswellOnt 142, 87 C.C.C. (3d) 327, 27 C.R. (4th) 55, 67 O.A.C. 213 (C.A.).

[46] 2007 CarswellOnt 3570, 221 C.C.C. (3d) 439 (S.C.J.).

Where the accused is alleged to have committed sexual offences over a period of time, it has been held that the operative date must be the last incident of abuse, not when the first abuse occurred.[47]

The second condition is that the videotaped interview must describe "the acts complained of".[48] The *Scott* case also recognized that the description of the acts may include more than the bare visible acts constituting the assault. It was held that if the section is to serve its purpose, the victim or witness must be allowed to give her version of the events underlying the charge. This can include everything that happened from the time she first met her assailant until he left her, including a description of his physical features, or his name, if known to her, and any statements made by him during the assault.[49]

The final condition that must be satisfied is that the videotaped interview must be adopted by the victim or the witness in his or her testimony, although what constitutes adoption for the purposes of section 715.1 has been the subject of some judicial dispute.[50]

In *F.(C.)*,[51] the Supreme Court said that section 715.1 is a statutory exception to the hearsay rule and "permits an out-of-court statement to be admitted for the truth of its contents provided that certain conditions are met".[52] Cory J., for the Court, recognized that a witness who could not remember the events could not be cross-examined effectively. Nevertheless, the fact that the statement had to be made within a reasonable time, that the trier can watch the entire interview and observe and assess the personality and intelligence of the child, and the requirement that the child attest that he or she was attempting to be truthful when the videotaped interview was

---

[47] *Archer*, 2005 CarswellOnt 4964, 202 C.C.C. (3d) 60, 34 C.R. (6th) 271 (C.A.).

[48] It does not include additional assaults not charged in the indictment which may be introduced as similar fact evidence: *A. (J.F.)*, 1993 CarswellOnt 1174, 82 C.C.C. (3d) 295 (C.A.).

[49] *Meddoui* (1990), 1990 CarswellAlta 187, 111 A.R. 295, 77 Alta. L.R. (2d) 97, 61 C.C.C. (3d) 345, 2 C.R. (4th) 316, [1991] 2 W.W.R. 289, 5 C.R.R. (2d) 294 (C.A.); leave to appeal refused (1991), [1991] 3 S.C.R. ix, 82 Alta. L.R. (2d) lxv (note), 69 C.C.C. (3d) vi, [1992] 1 W.W.R. lxv (note), 6 C.R.R. (2d) 192 (note), 137 N.R. 389 (note).

[50] *Meddoui, ibid.*, and *T. (W.P.)*, 1993 CarswellOnt 1056, 14 O.R. (3d) 225, 83 C.C.C. (3d) 5, 16 C.R.R. (2d) 49, 63 O.A.C. 321 (C.A.). See Chapter 3, 7. Statutory Exceptions (b) Videotaped Evidence of a Complainant.

[51] 1997 CarswellOnt 4448, 1997 CarswellOnt 4449, (sub nom. *R. v. F. (C.C.)*) [1997] 3 S.C.R. 1183, 120 C.C.C. (3d) 225, 11 C.R. (5th) 209, 154 D.L.R. (4th) 13, 220 N.R. 362, 104 O.A.C. 321, [1997] S.C.J. No. 89.

[52] *Ibid.*, at p. 216 [C.R.].

made, provided, as far as he was concerned, the requisite reliability of the statement. He also rejected the argument that the videotaped evidence adds nothing to the testimony when the complainant has an independent present memory of the events. It was his view that both the adopted videotaped statement together with the viva voce evidence given at trial are to comprise the whole of the evidence-in-chief of the complainant. As he noted:

> The admission of the videotaped statements made shortly after the events in issue may be of great assistance in augmenting a child's testimony at trial by the account of events given in the statement when the incidents were fresh in the child's mind.[53]

Cory J. felt that the primary goal of section 715.1 is to create a record of what is probably the best recollection of the event. A subsidiary aim of the section is to prevent, or reduce materially, the likelihood of inflicting further injury upon a child as a result of participating in court proceedings by reducing the number of interviews that the child must undergo and by conducting them in less overwhelming surroundings. He also stressed that videotaping may increase the accuracy of the testimony since the child may feel more comfortable and be more forthcoming.

One of the concerns often expressed by the defence, which was not adequately addressed in *F.(C.)*, is that a child may be subjected to a pre-video interview involving suggestive questioning and persistent pressure, not only by the police, but also by social workers whose primary concern will be the treatment of the child, not the prosecution of the abuser. Cory J. did say that it was preferable, where reasonably possible, that the police not conduct a pre-video interview. However, if the police felt that one was necessary, they should ask simple open-ended questions, although it may be necessary in some instances to ask the child leading questions. Nevertheless, any pre-video interviewing by the police would not affect the admissibility of the videotaped statement, only its weight. He was not prepared to grant to the trial judge the right to exclude a videotaped statement altogether where the judge was convinced that the pre-video interview questioning was so tainted by the method of questioning the child that it would be dangerous to admit it.

(f) No Case-Splitting by the Crown

The Crown is required to call all of its evidence to prove its case before the defence is called upon. This is known as the rule against case-splitting. It is based upon the principle that an accused should not be taken by surprise and need not incriminate him or herself until the defence has heard

---

[53] *Ibid.*, at pp. 222-23 [C.R.].

and thoroughly explored the entire case that the Crown intends to present against the accused. It has been said to provide "a safeguard against the importance of a piece of evidence, by reason of its late introduction, being unduly emphasized or magnified in relation to the other evidence".[54]

Although the rule requires the Crown to prove each and every element of the charge, it does not require the Crown to anticipate every defence that may be raised. For example, the Crown is not required to lead evidence-in-chief that could rebut an alibi of the accused, even if it has received notice from the defence prior to trial that the defence intends to introduce alibi evidence and has been given particulars of that alibi.[55] Nor is the Crown required to lead evidence that an accused is not suffering from a mental disorder that would exempt the accused from criminal responsibility. Section 16(2) of the *Criminal Code* presumes that a person is not suffering from a mental disorder so as to be exempt from criminal responsibility "until the contrary is proved on the balance of probabilities".[56]

(g) Admissions by the Defence

The defence is entitled to admit a fact in issue thereby avoiding the necessity of the Crown proving the fact. Section 655 of the *Criminal Code* provides that:

> Where an accused is on trial for an indictable offence, he or his counsel may admit any fact alleged against him for the purpose of dispensing with proof thereof.

For example, counsel for the defence may admit that a statement given by the accused was voluntary, dispensing with the necessity of holding a *voir dire*.[57]

However, the Crown is not required to accept an admission by the defence where to do so might preclude the Crown from leading evidence on a

---

[54] *Per* Martin J.A. in *Campbell*, 1977 CarswellOnt 6, 17 O.R. (2d) 673 at 699, 38 C.C.C. (2d) 6 at 32, 1 C.R. (3d) S-49 (C.A.) at p. 334 [C.R.].

[55] *Rafferty*, 1983 CarswellAlta 69, 43 A.R. 323, 25 Alta. L.R. (2d) 334, 6 C.C.C. (3d) 72, [1983] 4 W.W.R. 511 (C.A.); *Andrews*, 1979 CarswellBC 546, 8 C.R. (3d) 1 (C.A.); leave to appeal refused (1979), 28 N.R. 537n (S.C.C.).

[56] *Chaulk* (1990), 1990 CarswellMan 385, 1990 CarswellMan 239, [1990] 3 S.C.R. 1303, 62 C.C.C. (3d) 193, 2 C.R. (4th) 1, [1991] 2 W.W.R. 385, 1 C.R.R. (2d) 1, 69 Man. R. (2d) 161, 119 N.R. 161, [1990] S.C.J. No. 139.

[57] *Park*, 1981 CarswellOnt 100, 1981 CarswellOnt 52, [1981] 2 S.C.R. 64, 59 C.C.C. (2d) 385, 21 C.R. (3d) 182 (Eng.), 26 C.R. (3d) 164 (Fr.), 122 D.L.R. (3d) 1, 37 N.R. 501.

vital issue. For example, in *Castellani*,[58] the accused was charged with the capital murder of his wife. She had died of arsenic poisoning after ingesting quantities of arsenic over several months prior to her death. At trial, counsel for the defence wanted to admit that the accused had been having an extra-marital affair with another woman to prevent the Crown from leading evidence-in-chief that the accused and the other woman were planning to marry immediately after his wife was dead, and that these plans were made while she was critically ill. In other words, the admission was to prevent the Crown from showing a motive by the accused to commit the murder. It was held by the Supreme Court that the trial judge was correct in refusing to permit the admission. It was not open for an accused to frame the Crown's allegations so as to conform to his own purpose and then insist on admitting them.

4. CROSS-EXAMINATION BY THE DEFENCE

(a) The Nature of the Cross-examination

When the prosecution has completed its examination-in-chief of a witness, the defence may cross-examine that witness. The purpose of cross-examination is to show that the witness is mistaken or lying, or it may be directed towards bringing out facts favourable to the defence that were not brought out in chief by the prosecution. Here questions that suggest the answer are not only permitted, they will often be put to the witness by the cross-examiner.

The general rule is that questions on cross-examination must relate either to a fact in issue or to the impeachment of the witness's credibility. Impeachment of the witness's credibility allows the cross-examiner to ask the witness questions about misconduct on unrelated matters which may not have resulted in a conviction.[59] The purpose is to suggest that the witness should not be believed because of such bad character. The witness may also be cross-examined regarding an outstanding charge against him for the purpose of showing a possible motivation to seek favour with the Crown.[60]

---

[58] (1969), 1969 CarswellBC 187, 1969 CarswellBC 259, [1970] S.C.R. 310, [1970] 4 C.C.C. 287, 11 D.L.R. (3d) 92, 71 W.W.R. 147, 9 C.R.N.S. 111.

[59] *Davison*, 1974 CarswellOnt 559, 6 O.R. (2d) 103, 20 C.C.C. (2d) 424 (C.A.); leave to appeal refused [1974] S.C.R. viii, 6 O.R. (2d) 103n, 20 C.C.C. (2d) 424n.

[60] *Titus*, 1983 CarswellOnt 806, 1983 CarswellOnt 64, [1983] 1 S.C.R. 259, (sub nom. *Titus v. R.*) 2 C.C.C. (3d) 321, 33 C.R. (3d) 17, 144 D.L.R. (3d) 577, 46 N.R. 477; *Gonzague*, 1983 CarswellOnt 81, 4 C.C.C. (3d) 505, 34 C.R. (3d) 169 (C.A.).

Impeachment of the witness's credibility also allows the cross-examiner to ask the witness questions not related to a fact in issue to show that the witness may have a motive to lie, may be biased against the accused or may be a person not worthy of belief. If the question is not relevant to a fact in issue or to the witness's credibility, the trial judge has the duty to disallow it even if the opposing counsel does not object.[61]

Although the defence is entitled to cross-examine a witness about testimony that was introduced by other witnesses, what is not permitted is to ask the witness to comment upon the credibility of another witness. That calls for speculation on the part of the witness as to the motives of those witnesses and an opinion as to whether they are lying, which is irrelevant to the inquiry. It is the responsibility of the trier of fact, not the witness, to assess the credibility of the witnesses.[62]

The trial judge also has the duty to prevent the cross-examiner from putting a question to the witness which is vexatious or has the effect of misleading or leaving a false impression with the court.[63] In *Rowbotham*, Judge Borins (as he then was) described that duty this way:

> The trial judge may disallow any question put in cross-examination which may appear to him vexatious and not relevant to any matter proper to be inquired into, e.g., questions as to alleged improprieties of remote date or of such a nature as not seriously to affect present credibility. Thus, the trial judge may ask himself or herself in any particular situation whether the danger of unfair prejudice against the witness and the party calling him from character impeachment outweighs the probable value of the light shed on credibility. The court has a responsibility to ensure that witnesses are dealt with fairly and to prevent victimization. It is not the witness who is on trial.

---

[61] *Rowbotham (No. 5)*, 1977 CarswellOnt 8, 2 C.R. (3d) 293 (G.S.P.); *Bourassa*, 1991 CarswellQue 130, 1991 CarswellQue 1991, 67 C.C.C. (3d) 143, 38 Q.A.C. 10 (C.A.).

[62] *Markadonis*, 1935 CarswellNS 50, [1935] S.C.R. 657, 64 C.C.C. 41, [1935] 3 D.L.R. 424; *Brown*, 1982 CarswellAlta 470, 41 A.R. 69, 1 C.C.C. (3d) 107 (C.A.); affirmed (1985), 1985 CarswellAlta 184, 1985 CarswellAlta 614, (sub nom. *Brown and Murphy v. The Queen*) [1985] 2 S.C.R. 273, 40 Alta. L.R. (2d) 193, 21 C.C.C. (3d) 477, 21 D.L.R. (4th) 761, [1986] 1 W.W.R. 97, 62 N.R. 241; *Yakeleya*, 1985 CarswellOnt 105, 20 C.C.C. (3d) 193, 46 C.R. (3d) 282, 14 C.R.R. 381, 9 O.A.C. 284 (C.A.).

[63] *Anderson*, 1938 CarswellMan 23, 70 C.C.C. 275, [1938] 3 D.L.R. 317, [1938] 2 W.W.R. 49, 46 Man. R. 97 (C.A.); *Bourassa*, 1991 CarswellQue 130, 1991 CarswellQue 1991, 67 C.C.C. (3d) 143, 38 Q.A.C. 10 (C.A.); *Hehr*, 1982 CarswellAlta 254, 24 Alta. L.R. (2d) 59, 18 M.V.R. 244 (Q.B.).

Counsel who proceeds on that premise frequently fails to assess the situation carefully.[64]

If the defence intends to introduce evidence contradicting the testimony of a witness on a significant fact in issue, it is generally recognized that counsel for the defence has the obligation during cross-examination to put the substance of that evidence to the witness so that the witness can have the opportunity of explaining the contradiction.[65] If the witness is not cross-examined by the defence on matters that are of significance to the facts in issue, and the defence then leads evidence which contradicts that witness on those issues, the trier of fact may take the failure to cross-examine into consideration in assessing the credibility of that witness and the contradictory evidence offered by the other side.[66]

This rule, known as the rule in *Browne v. Dunn*, is based on fairness to prevent a witness from being ambushed; it does not mean that the defence is required to slog through a prosecution witness's evidence in chief putting the witness on notice of every detail that the defence does not accept.[67] The failure to challenge a witness's version of events on significant matters that are later contradicted in evidence by the defence is not controlled by a hard and fast rule; it will depend on the circumstances of the case. In some circumstances, the position of the defence on a significant matter will be clear even without cross-examination; or when considered in the overall context of the case, the fact in issue may turn out to be not significant at all. On the other hand, where the central feature of a complainant's evidence is left untouched, or even implicitly accepted in cross-examination, then the absence of cross-examination may have a negative impact on the accused's credibility.[68]

There is no requirement that a cross-examiner only put suggestions to a witness that he or she can prove. That issue was clearly settled in *Bencardino*[69] and confirmed by the Supreme Court in *Lyttle*[70] In *Bencardino*, a

---

[64] *Supra*, *Rowbotham (No. 5)*, note 61, at p. 299 [C.R.].

[65] *Browne v. Dunn* (1893), 6 R. 67 (U.K. H.L.).

[66] *Paris*, 2000 CarswellOnt 4771, 150 C.C.C. (3d) 162, 138 O.A.C. 287 (C.A.); leave to appeal refused 2001 CarswellOnt 2137, 2001 CarswellOnt 2138, 154 C.C.C. (3d) iv (note) (S.C.C.).

[67] *Verney*, 1993 CarswellOnt 1157, 87 C.C.C. (3d) 363, 67 O.A.C. 279 (C.A.).

[68] *Carter*, 2005 CarswellBC 1766, 199 C.C.C. (3d) 74, 32 C.R. (6th) 1 (C.A.).

[69] 1973 CarswellOnt 51, 2 O.R. (2d) 351, 15 C.C.C. (2d) 342, 24 C.R.N.S. 173 (C.A.).

[70] 2004 CarswellOnt 510, 2004 CarswellOnt 511, 180 C.C.C. (3d) 476, 17 C.R. (6th) 1 (S.C.C.).

Crown witness had given evidence incriminating the accused, and had then testified for the defence changing his evidence. The Crown then called a barrister who had acted for the witness on his own trial seeking to prove what the barrister had told the Crown. The trial judge had refused to allow the Crown to elicit such evidence. Jessup J.A., delivering the judgment of the Ontario Court of Appeal, said that he deprecated the tactics of the Crown counsel in implying "without evidence to support such an implication", a lack of integrity on the part of defence counsel. However, he was unable to say any illegality was involved. He went on to adopt the words of Lord Radcliffe in *Fox v. General Medical Council*,[71] where he said:

> An advocate is entitled to use his discretion as to whether to put questions in the course of cross-examination which are based on material which he is not in a position to prove directly. The penalty is that, if he gets a denial or some answer that does not suit him, the answer stands against him for what it is worth.[72]

In *Lyttle*[73] (the Supreme Court stressed that the right of an accused to cross-examine prosecution witnesses without significant and unwarranted constraint is an essential component of the right to make a full answer and defence. The right of cross-examination, which is protected by sections 7 and 11(d) of the *Canadian Charter of Rights and Freedoms*, must be jealously protected and broadly construed. A question can be put to a witness in cross-examination regarding matters that need not be proved independently, *provided that counsel has a good faith basis for putting the question*. It is not uncommon for counsel to believe what is in fact true without being able to prove it otherwise than by cross-examination. "A good faith basis" is a function of the information available to the cross-examiner, his or her belief in its likely accuracy, and the purpose for which it is used. The information may fall short of admissible evidence and may be incomplete or uncertain, provided the cross-examiner does not put suggestions to the witness recklessly or that he or she knows to be false. The cross-examiner may pursue any hypothesis that is honestly advanced on the strength of reasonable inference, experience or intuition; there is no requirement of an evidentiary foundation for every factual suggestion put to a witness in cross-examination. Where a question implies the existence of a disputed fact that is manifestly tenuous or suspect, a trial judge may seek assurance that a good faith basis exists for the question. If the judge is satisfied in this regard and the

---

[71] [1960] 3 All E.R. 225, [1960] 1 W.L.R. 1017 (P.C.).

[72] *Ibid.*, at p. 1023 [W.L.R.].

[73] *Supra*, note 70.

question is not otherwise prohibited, counsel should be permitted to put the question to the witness.

(b) Questions as to Credibility — Rule Against Collateral Evidence

As noted previously, impeachment of the witness's credibility allows the cross-examiner to ask the witness questions not related to a fact in issue to show that the witness may have a motive to lie, may be biased against the accused or may be a person not worthy of belief. Questions in cross-examination that are directed solely to the credibility of a witness and not to a fact in issue are said to be collateral. The rule is that except for questions in cross-examination pertaining to the witness's previous criminal record and other recognized exceptions, neither the defence nor the Crown is allowed to call evidence to refute the answer given by the witness. (See Chapter 1, The Rule Against Collateral Facts). The reason why evidence to refute the witness is not permitted, even though it may show that the witness is not a believable person, is because it is too remote and may distract the jury from the main issue in the case. There is a concern that it would only encourage a series of mini-trials on the credibility of each witness and unduly prolong the length of the trial.

One statutory exception to the rule — section 12 of the *Canada Evidence Act* — relates to previous convictions and will be dealt with in the next section. Another exception to the collateral facts rule is evidence that demonstrates bias or partiality by a witness.[74] For example, in *M. (P.)*,[75] where the accused was charged with sexual assault and gross indecency involving a 12-year-old, reply evidence was permitted to show bias on the part of the complainant's mother who had lived with the accused for about six years. Medical evidence to demonstrate that a witness suffers from a mental disease or abnormality of the mind which may affect the reliability of his evidence is another exception to the collateral facts rule.[76] Here evidence may be led, not only as to the foundation of and the reason for the diagnosis, but also the extent to which the credibility of the witness is affected. Finally, it

---

[74] *McDonald* (1959), 1959 CarswellOnt 38, [1960] S.C.R. 186, 126 C.C.C. 1, 32 C.R. 101; *Babinski*, 1999 CarswellOnt 1360, 44 O.R. (3d) 695, 135 C.C.C. (3d) 1, 122 O.A.C. 1, [1999] O.J. No. 1407 (C.A.).

[75] 1990 CarswellOnt 696, 1 O.R. (3d) 341, 42 O.A.C. 153 (C.A.).

[76] *Hawke*, 1975 CarswellOnt 4, 7 O.R. (2d) 145, 22 C.C.C. (2d) 19, 29 C.R.N.S. 1 (C.A.); *French*, 1977 CarswellOnt 1011, 37 C.C.C. (2d) 201 (C.A.); affirmed (1979), 1979 CarswellOnt 709F, 1979 CarswellOnt 709, [1980] 1 S.C.R. 158, 47 C.C.C. (2d) 411, 98 D.L.R. (3d) 385, 28 N.R. 100.

has been recognized that evidence may be called to show that the witness cannot be believed on oath. Here the evidence is restricted. The witness may only be asked whether he or she knows the witness's reputation for veracity and whether, from such knowledge, he or she would believe the witness on oath.[77] Although a strict application of the rule could in some instances cause a miscarriage of justice, the courts have been reluctant to relax its strict enforcement. For example, in instances of alleged sexual abuse where there are no witnesses other than the victim and the accused, and the defence is that the assault never happened, evidence that the victim has made other false allegations would undoubtedly be relevant not only to her general credibility but also to the issue of whether or not a sexual assault occurred. However, the courts have refused to permit the defence to call evidence of other false accusations because "it would introduce a collateral issue of credibility which would be as difficult to resolve as those contained in the complaints of which the trial judge was seized".[78] For example, in *Riley*,[79] the accused, who was charged with sexual assault, alleged that the accusation was false and that the complainant had made a false accusation against one R, who had been acquitted of a similar accusation against him. However, the trial judge had curtailed the defence's cross-examination of the complainant on the alleged false accusation and refused to allow R to be called to testify as to the falsity of the accusation against him. The Ontario Court of Appeal held that the trial judge's ruling was correct. It noted that even if they had a proper record of R's trial, a not guilty verdict, standing by itself, could not establish that the prosecution was based on fabricated evidence by the complainant.

Even a trial judge's finding in another trial that a police officer was a compulsive liar has been considered by the Ontario Court of Appeal to be nothing more than an opinion by the judge on unrelated testimony given by the officer in the context of another case.[80] In *Ghorvei*,[81] the accused had

---

[77] *Toohey v. Metropolitan Police Commissioner*, [1965] A.C. 595, [1965] 1 All E.R. 506, 49 Cr. App. R. 148 (U.K. H.L.); *Gonzague, supra*, note 60. But see a criticism of the exception in *Clarke*, 1998 CarswellOnt 3447, 129 C.C.C. (3d) 1, 18 C.R. (5th) 219, 112 O.A.C. 233, [1998] O.J. No. 3521 (C.A.).

[78] *Riley*, 1992 CarswellOnt 707, 11 O.R. (3d) 151 (C.A.) at p. 154 [O.R.], ; leave to appeal refused [1993] 2 S.C.R. x, 13 O.R. (3d) xvi, 154 N.R. 400 (note), 64 O.A.C. 400 (note); *Harper*, 1997 CarswellPEI 37, 149 Nfld. & P.E.I.R. 295, 467 A.P.R. 295, [1997] P.E.I.J. No. 41 (C.A.).

[79] *Ibid.*

[80] *Ghorvei*, 1999 CarswellOnt 2763, 46 O.R. (3d) 63, 138 C.C.C. (3d) 340, 29 C.R. (5th) 102, 124 O.A.C. 301 (C.A.).

[81] *Ibid.*

been convicted of trafficking and breach of recognizance. On appeal, he sought to introduce fresh evidence of that finding by a trial judge against the police officer in the form of a transcript of a previous trial of another accused. It was held that if there had been a conviction of the police officer for perjury or for giving contradictory evidence under oath with respect to the facts of the other trial, that conviction could have been used on cross-examination of the officer. However, since the finding of the trial judge was nothing more than a rejection of the officer's evidence, it was a collateral issue and not admissible.

The no-collateral evidence will not necessarily apply where the Crown calls a witness to whom a complaint of sexual assault was made and to whom the complainant also recanted previous allegations of sexual assaults by other persons. For example in *Green*,[82] the complainant had on two prior occasions alleged that she had been sexually assaulted by other persons only to later recant those allegations. The trial judge had refused to admit evidence of the recantations holding it was collateral to the issue of whether the accused had sexually assaulted the complainant. It was held that the trial judge had erred. The questions were proper questions to put to the complainant on cross-examination. Moreover, evidence of her recantations to the very witness to whom she had complained of sexual assault by the accused was relevant in assessing the complainant's general credibility and the reliability of her statement to the witness that she had just been sexually assaulted by the accused.

English courts, however, have shown signs of a more liberal approach to allowing such rebuttal evidence by the defence. For example, in an English case, *Chandu Nagrecha*,[83] the accused, an owner of a restaurant, was charged with indecently assaulting the complainant, one of his employees. The only witnesses were the complainant and the accused. The defence was not that the complainant consented but that the alleged assault had never happened. At trial, counsel for the accused cross-examined the complainant about allegations of sexual impropriety that she had made against other men but she denied them. The trial judge had refused to allow the defence to call evidence as to the making of those complaints. The Court of Appeal held that the judge had erred. The Court said that the evidence went not merely to credit, but to the heart of the case. In other words, the fact that the complainant had made a false complaint against other men went to the issue of

---

[82] 2013 ONCA 74.

[83] [1997] 2 Cr. App. R. 401; see also *R. v. Busby* (1981), 75 Cr. App. R. 79 (Eng. C.A.); *Funderburk* (1990), Cr. App. R. 466; *Marsh* (1985), 83 Cr. App. R. 165.

whether she had made a false complaint against the accused and was relevant to her credibility.

The practice of putting questions that are directed only to credibility and are collateral to the issues in the case can often be abused. A good example was the common practice of defence counsel, in a sexual assault prosecution before the enactment of section 276 of the *Criminal Code*, of asking the complainant whether she ever had sexual intercourse with a person other than the accused. The fact that the complainant had sexual intercourse with another male person who was not her husband was not then, nor is it now, relevant to the issue of whether she consented to intercourse with the accused. Nevertheless, the courts permitted the question under the guise that it tested her credibility, although it was more likely allowed because of the stereotypical belief that a woman who had sexual relations with someone other than her husband was more likely to have consented to having sexual relations with the accused and was, therefore, not worthy of belief. If the complainant denied the allegation, the defence was not allowed to call evidence to refute it. It was collateral to the issue of whether she consented to sexual intercourse with the accused and the defence was bound by her answer. However, damage to the complainant's credibility was often caused by the mere asking of the question. If she answered truthfully and admitted that she had, there was the concern that she would be judged on her morality rather than her credibility. Section 276 has now put an end to this practice unless the defence can establish that the question is relevant to a fact in issue.

Section 276 prohibits, with respect to certain listed offences, any evidence that a complainant has engaged in sexual activity, whether with the accused or with any other person, to support an inference that, by reason of the sexual nature of that activity, the complainant (a) is more likely to have consented to the sexual activity that forms the subject matter of the charge; or (b) is less worthy of belief. In *Osolin*,[84] Cory J. expressed his view of the goal of section 276.

> Generally, a complainant may be cross-examined for the purpose of eliciting evidence relating to consent and pertaining to credibility when the probative value of that evidence is not substantially outweighed by the danger of unfair prejudice which might flow from it. Cross-examination for the purposes of showing consent or impugning credibility which relies upon "rape myths" will always be more prejudicial than probative. Such evidence can fulfil no legitimate purpose and would therefore be inadmissible to go to consent or credibility. Cross-examination which has as its aim to elicit

---

[84] 1993 CarswellBC 512, 1993 CarswellBC 1274, [1993] 4 S.C.R. 595, 86 C.C.C. (3d) 481, 26 C.R. (4th) 1.

such evidence should not be permitted. It will be up to the trial judge to take into consideration all of the evidence presented at the voir dire and to then determine if there is a legitimate purpose for the proposed cross-examination.

In each case the trial judge must carefully balance the fundamentally important right of the accused to a fair trial against the need for reasonable protection of a complainant, particularly where the purpose of the cross-examination may be directed to "rape myths". In order to assure the fairness of the trial, where contentious issues arise as to the cross-examination of the complainant a voir dire should be held. In the voir dire it will be necessary to show either by way of submissions of counsel, affidavit or viva voce evidence that the proposed cross-examination is appropriate. If at the conclusion of the voir dire the cross-examination is permitted then the jury must be advised as to the proper use that can be made of the evidence derived from the cross-examination. As a general rule the trial of an accused on a charge of sexual assault need not and should not become an occasion for putting the complainant's lifestyle and reputation on trial. The exception to this rule will arise in those relatively rare cases where the complainant may be fraudulent, cruelly mischievous or maliciously mendacious.

(c) Previous Criminal Record of the Witness

Section 12 of the *Canada Evidence Act* is a statutory exception to the rule against admitting collateral evidence that allows a cross-examiner to ask a witness whether he or she has been convicted of "any offence". If the witness denies the fact or refuses to answer, the opposite party is allowed to prove the conviction, even though such evidence is strictly collateral to the facts in issue. The rationale underlying section 12 is that the question goes to the credibility of the witness. In other words, the fact that a witness has a criminal record goes to the issue of whether the witness is worthy of belief.[85] Presumably, it is based on the assumption that a person who has a criminal record is less likely to tell the truth than a person who does not. At the same time, the judge is required to instruct the jury that they are only entitled to consider the record of the witness for the purpose of assessing the witness's credibility with respect to the issue before the court. It is assumed that the jury will honour the judge's instructions.

Section 12(1) authorizes the cross-examiner to ask the witness whether he or she "has been convicted of any offence". The plain language of the section would seem to restrict the cross-examiner to questioning the witness about the particulars of the offence and not the underlying facts resulting in the conviction. The Ontario Court of Appeal, however, has said that since

---

[85] *Pleich*, 1980 CarswellOnt 44, 55 C.C.C. (2d) 13, 16 C.R. (3d) 194 (C.A.).

section 12 is permissive in its terms, cross-examination must be limited within the bounds of relevance and propriety.[86] The Court reasoned that since cross-examination on the underlying facts of the conviction may be relevant "to discreditable conduct and associations, unrelated to the subject-matter of the testimony, as a ground for disbelieving" the witness's testimony, the trial judge could allow such cross-examination.

A good example of where cross-examination on the underlying facts went to the issue of the credibility of the main witness for the Crown was *Burgar*[87] There, the accused was convicted of arson based primarily on the evidence of the complainant, his former common-law wife. Although the trial judge permitted defence counsel to cross-examine the complainant on her criminal record, counsel was prohibited from cross-examining the complainant about the facts underlying her conviction. The argument that the questions were intended to attack the complainant's credibility and to show that it was she who had committed the arson was rejected. On appeal, it was held that the trial judge had erred in refusing permission to cross-examine on the substance of the convictions. Cross-examination on a witness's previous convictions was proper and could go beyond the bare fact of the conviction and investigate the facts of the witness's previous bad conduct.

The expression "conviction" used in section 12 has been interpreted to include the sentence imposed by the court so that the cross-examiner may question the witness about the penalty imposed.[88] The words "any offence" in section 12 have also been interpreted to mean any offence under a federal statute even though it does not truly relate to the criminal law power of the federal government.[89] Those words have also been interpreted to include convictions for offences committed outside of Canada so long as the process of adjudication of guilt is of a character that would constitute a conviction under Canadian law.[90]

On the other hand, it is considered improper to cross-examine a witness with respect to a conviction for which he or she has been granted a pardon.

---

[86] *Miller*, 1998 CarswellOnt 4983, 131 C.C.C. (3d) 141, 21 C.R. (5th) 178, 116 O.A.C. 331, [1998] O.J. No. 5356 (C.A.); *Gassyt*, 1998 CarswellOnt 3241, 127 C.C.C. (3d) 546, 114 O.A.C. 147 (C.A.); leave to appeal refused (1999), 136 C.C.C. (3d) vi, 244 N.R. 400 (note), 126 O.A.C. 200 (note) (S.C.C.).

[87] 2010 CarswellAlta 2124, 263 C.C.C. (3d) 521 (C.A.).

[88] *Boyce*, 1974 CarswellOnt 46, 7 O.R. (2d) 561, 23 C.C.C. (2d) 16, 28 C.R.N.S. 336 (C.A.).

[89] *Watkins*, 1992 CarswellOnt 1062, 70 C.C.C. (3d) 341, 54 O.A.C. 200 (C.A.).

[90] *Stratton*, 1978 CarswellOnt 29, 21 O.R. (2d) 258, 42 C.C.C. (2d) 449, 3 C.R. (3d) 289, 90 D.L.R. (3d) 420 (C.A.).

Section 748(3) of the *Criminal Code* provides that a person granted a free pardon is deemed never to have committed the offence in respect of which the pardon is granted. Although section 5 of the *Criminal Records Act*, which formerly provided that a pardon is evidence of the fact that the conviction in respect of which the pardon is granted should no longer reflect adversely on the convicted person's character, was repealed,[91] section 9 of the Act provides that nothing in the amended provisions limits or affects the *Criminal Code* relating to pardons.[92] It has also been held that section 12 does not permit cross-examination of a witness on an offence of which he or she was found guilty and granted a discharge, or a conditional discharge and the conditions were subsequently fulfilled. Section 730(3) provides that an offender who has been discharged of an offence, "shall be deemed not to have been convicted of the offence". Therefore, an adjudication of guilt followed by the granting of a discharge is not a conviction within s. 12(1) of the *Canada Evidence Act*.[93]

(d) Protection from Self-Incrimination

Section 7 of the *Charter* guarantees everyone the right to life, liberty and security of the person and the right not to be deprived thereof except in accordance with the principles of fundamental justice. This right has been interpreted by the Supreme Court of Canada to encompass the right to remain silent and is broader than the common law confession rule and the rule against self-incrimination.[94] Nevertheless, a witness who is facing the same or similar charges as the accused does not have an absolute right to silence protected by section 7 if that witness is subpoenaed to testify at the accused's separate trial. In *S. (R.J.)*,[95] the Supreme Court said that although a statutory compulsion to testify engages a witness's liberty interest under section 7, that interest can only be affected in accordance with the principles of fundamental justice. The Court reasoned that since sections 11(c)

---

[91] 2012, c. 1, s. 119.

[92] *Paterson*, 1998 CarswellBC 122, 122 C.C.C. (3d) 254, 102 B.C.A.C. 200, 166 W.A.C. 200 (C.A.); leave to appeal refused (1999), 134 C.C.C. (3d) iv, 132 B.C.A.C. 139 (note), 242 N.R. 199 (note), 215 W.A.C. 139 (note) (S.C.C.).

[93] *Danson*, 1982 CarswellOnt 1345, 35 O.R. (2d) 777, 66 C.C.C. (2d) 369 (C.A.).

[94] *Hebert*, 1990 CarswellYukon 4, 1990 CarswellYukon 7, [1990] 2 S.C.R. 151, 47 B.C.L.R. (2d) 1, 57 C.C.C. (3d) 1, 77 C.R. (3d) 145, [1990] 5 W.W.R. 1, 49 C.R.R. 114, 110 N.R. 1.

[95] 1995 CarswellOnt 2, 1995 CarswellOnt 516, [1995] 1 S.C.R. 451, 21 O.R. (3d) 797 (note), 96 C.C.C. (3d) 1, 36 C.R. (4th) 1, 121 D.L.R. (4th) 589, 26 C.R.R. (2d) 1, 177 N.R. 81, 78 O.A.C. 161.

and 13 of the *Charter* prevent the witness's testimony and a limited class of evidence derived from that witness's testimony being used against him or her in other proceedings, save for proceedings in respect of perjury or for the giving of contradictory evidence, fundamental justice is satisfied.

The Court, however, did stress that the *Charter* protections contained in sections 11(c) and 13 do not authorize the Crown or the defence to engage in all types of inquisition. It noted that although the principle against self-incrimination generally finds recognition not only in section 13 but also under section 24(2) of the *Charter*, derivative evidence which could not have been obtained, or the significance of which could not have been appreciated, but for the testimony of the witness, should generally be excluded under section 7 in the interests of trial fairness. The Court reasoned that, although such evidence is not created by the accused and thus not self-incriminatory by definition, it is self-incriminatory nonetheless because the evidence could not have otherwise become part of the Crown's case. In such instance, the witness must be protected against assisting the Crown in creating a case to meet.

The Court did not feel that there should be an automatic rule of exclusion for derivative evidence. It said that exclusion should be governed by the trial judge's discretion. The exercise of that discretion should depend upon the probative effect of the evidence balanced against the prejudice caused to the accused by its admission. Moreover, the burden is on the accused to demonstrate that the proposed evidence is derivative evidence deserving of protection from being used against the accused.

5. THE REQUIREMENT FOR CORROBORATION

Although it is often said that the common law system is distinguishable from the civil law system because the court is entitled to reach a decision on the unsupported evidence of one witness, it was not always the rule. In its infancy, the jury system required that a certain number of persons swear upon oath that an accused was guilty or not guilty, although it might be said that the witnesses were really giving evidence as to the accused's character rather than probative evidence on the question of his or her guilt or innocence. Later, as the jury system became more like what it is today, certain rules developed. One was the requirement that no prosecution for treason could succeed upon the evidence of one witness; another was that a prosecution for perjury required clear corroborating testimony. A rule of practice also developed requiring the corroboration of the testimony of accomplices, complainants in sexual cases and children.

The historical rationale requiring corroboration of an accomplice was stated as early as 1775 by Lord Mansfield in *Rudd*:[96]

> And though, under this practice, they are clearly competent witnesses, their single testimony alone is seldom of sufficient weight with a jury to convict the offenders; it being so strong a temptation to a man to commit perjury, if by accusing another he can escape himself.

Support for the corroboration of women complainants in sexual cases was based on the belief that:

> ... these cases are particularly subject to the danger of deliberately false charges, resulting from sexual neurosis, fantasy, jealousy, spite or simply a girl's refusal to admit that she consented to an act of which she is now ashamed.[97]

For the corroboration of children, it was argued that:

> Children are suggestible and sometimes given to living in a world of make-believe. They are egocentric, and only slowly learn the duty of speaking the truth ... a child's power of observation and memory tends to be even less reliable than that of an adult.[98]

The requirement for corroboration of the testimony of women, children and accomplices was eventually swept away by legislation and case law. The rigid rule that had been in place for over two centuries was replaced with judicial discretion. In *Vetrovec*,[99] the Supreme Court questioned the rationale for retention of the rule requiring corroboration of the testimony of an accomplice. Dickson J. (as he then was), delivering the judgment of the Court, had grave doubts about the utility of its continuance. He wrote:

> None of these arguments can justify a fixed and invariable rule regarding all accomplices. All that can be established is that the testimony of some accomplices may be untrustworthy. But this can be said of many other categories of witnesses. There is nothing inherent in the evidence of an accomplice which automatically renders him untrustworthy. To construct a universal rule singling out accomplices, then, is to fasten upon this branch of the law a blind and empty formalism. Rather than attempting to pigeon-hole a witness into a category and then recite a ritualistic incantation, the trial judge might better direct himself to the facts of the case and thoroughly examine all the factors which might impair the worth of a particular witness. If, in

---

[96] (1775), 1 Cowp. 331, 98 E.R. 1114 (K.B.) at p. 336 [Cowp.].

[97] Glanville Williams, *Proof of Guilt*, 3rd ed. at p. 159.

[98] *Ibid.*, at pp. 178-79.

[99] (1982), 1982 CarswellBC 663, 1982 CarswellBC 682, [1982] 1 S.C.R. 811, (sub nom. *R. v. Gaja)* 67 C.C.C. (2d) 1, 27 C.R. (3d) 304, 136 D.L.R. (3d) 89, [1983] 1 W.W.R. 193, 41 N.R. 606.

his judgment, the credit of the witness is such that the jury should be cautioned, then he may instruct accordingly. If on the other hand, he believes the witness to be trustworthy, then, regardless of whether the witness is technically an "accomplice" no warning is necessary.[100]

Instead of a technical set instruction, what was appropriate from the trial judge was:

> . . . in some circumstances [is] a clear and sharp warning to attract the attention of the juror to the risks of adopting, without more, the evidence of the witness.[101]

Dickson J., however, recognized that there were cases where a jury might require some instruction.

> It does not, however, always follow that the presiding judge may always simply turn the jury loose upon the evidence without any assisting analysis as to whether or not a prudent finder of fact can find confirmation, somewhere in the mass of evidence, of the evidence of a witness . . . However, there is in some circumstances, particularly in lengthy trials, the need for helpful direction on the question of sifting the evidence where guilt or innocence might, and probably will, turn on the acceptance or rejection, belief or disbelief, of the evidence of one or more witnesses.[102]

Although the *Vetrovec* case seemed to suggest that the need for a warning was entirely a matter for the discretion of the trial judge who was in the best position to assess the credibility of the witness, subsequent decisions of the Supreme Court and provincial appellate courts have said that the trial judge's discretion is not untrammeled.[103] Two considerations are paramount in determining whether a warning must be given: the credibility of the witness; and the importance of the witness's evidence to the Crown's case. If a witness's evidence is highly important, a jury warning may be mandatory.

An example of where one would expect a mandatory warning is in the case of a jailhouse informant. As a matter of common sense, a jailhouse informant who is prepared to bargain his credibility for a lighter sentence should always be subject to an inference of untrustworthiness. However, it

---

[100] *Ibid.*, at p. 11 [C.C.C.].

[101] *Ibid.*, at p. 17.

[102] *Ibid.*, at pp. 17-18.

[103] *Brooks*, 2000 SCC 11, 2000 CarswellOnt 292, 2000 CarswellOnt 293, [2000] 1 S.C.R. 237, 46 O.R. (3d) 640 (headnote only), 141 C.C.C. (3d) 321, 30 C.R. (5th) 201, 182 D.L.R. (4th) 513, 250 N.R. 103, 129 O.A.C. 205, [2000] S.C.J. No. 12; *Bromley*, 2001 NFCA 5, 2001 CarswellNfld 19, 197 Nfld. & P.E.I.R. 316, 151 C.C.C. (3d) 480, 591 A.P.R. 316.

has been said that if the trial judge believes the witness can be trusted, then regardless of whether the witness is an accomplice or a jailhouse informant, a warning is not necessary.[104]

Where a trial judge decides that a *Vetrovec* warning is required to be given to the jury, there are four main elements of the caution. The first is that the attention of the jury must be drawn to the testimonial evidence requiring special scrutiny. The second is that the jury should be told why this evidence is subject to special scrutiny. The third is they should be cautioned that it is dangerous to convict on unconfirmed evidence of this sort, although they are entitled to do so if satisfied that the evidence is true. Finally, in determining the veracity of the suspect evidence, they should look for evidence from another source tending to show that the untrustworthy witness is telling the truth as to the guilt of the accused. Their attention should then be drawn to evidence capable of confirming or supporting material parts of the witness's evidence. Evidence that is tainted by connection to the witness cannot serve to confirm his or her testimony. To be confirmatory, evidence should give comfort that the witness can be trusted.[105]

In the absence of evidence of collusion or collaboration, the evidence of one unsavoury witness can confirm the testimony of another.[106] Confirmatory evidence must be independent of the tainted witness, but need not implicate the accused.[107]

Legislation has swept away the requirement for corroboration of the evidence of children and of complainants in sexual cases. In 1980, section 274 was added to the *Criminal Code* providing that:

> If an accused is charged with an offence under section 151, 152, 153, 153.1, 155, 159, 160, 170, 171, 172, 173, 212, 271, 272 or 273, no corroboration is required for a conviction and the judge shall not instruct the jury that it is unsafe to find the accused guilty in the absence of corroboration.

In 1993, section 659 of the *Code* was amended to provide that:

> Any requirement whereby it is mandatory for a court to give the jury a warning about convicting an accused on the evidence of a child is abrogated.

---

[104] *Ibid.*

[105] *Khela*, 2009 SCC 4, 2009 CarswellBC 69, 2009 CarswellBC 70, [2009] 1 S.C.R. 104, 238 C.C.C. (3d) 489, 62 C.R. (6th) 197.

[106] *Roks*, 2011 CarswellOnt 6853, 274 C.C.C. (3d) 1, 87 C.R. (6th) 144 (C.A.) at para. 67; additional reasons 2011 CarswellOnt 10380, 284 C.C.C. (3d) 510 (C.A.).

[107] *Khela*, *supra* note 104 at paras. 39–41.

Although there is no longer an obligation upon the trial judge to warn the jury about the need for corroboration, the Supreme Court has recognized that a cautionary warning may be necessary in some circumstances. In *W. (R.)*,[108] Madam Justice McLachlin, in dealing with the evidence of children, noted:

> The repeal of provisions creating a legal requirement that children's evidence be corroborated does not prevent the judge or jury from treating a child's evidence with caution where such caution is merited in the circumstances of the case. But it does revoke the assumption formerly applied to all children, often unjustly, that children's evidence is always less reliable than the evidence of adults. So if a court proceeds to discount a child's evidence automatically, without regard to the circumstances of the particular case, it will have fallen into an error.[109]

Later she said:

> It is neither desirable nor possible to state hard and fast rules as to when a witness's evidence should be assessed by reference to "adult" or "child" standards — to do so would create anew stereotypes potentially as rigid and unjust as those which the recent developments in the law's approach to children's evidence have been designed to dispel. Every person giving testimony in court, of whatever age, is an individual, whose credibility and evidence must be assessed by reference to criteria appropriate to her mental development, understanding and ability to communicate. But I would add this. In general, where an adult is testifying as to events which occurred when she was a child, her credibility should be assessed according to criteria applicable to her as an adult witness. Yet with regard to her evidence pertaining to events which occurred in childhood, the presence of inconsistencies, particularly as to peripheral matters such as time and location, should be considered in the context of the age of the witness at the time of the events to which she is testifying.[110]

The only surviving requirement for corroboration lies in prosecutions for high treason or treason,[111] perjury[112] and procuring a feigned marriage.[113] There can be no conviction for any of these offences on the evidence of one

---

[108] 1992 CarswellOnt 991, 1992 CarswellOnt 90, (sub nom. *R. c. W.)* [1992] 2 S.C.R. 122, 74 C.C.C. (3d) 134, 13 C.R. (4th) 257, 137 N.R. 214, 54 O.A.C. 164, [1992] S.C.J. No. 56; reconsideration / rehearing refused (November 18, 1992), Doc. 21820 (S.C.C.).

[109] *Ibid.*, at p. 266 [C.R.].

[110] *Ibid.*, at pp. 267-68.

[111] *Criminal Code*, s. 47(3).

[112] *Ibid.*, s. 133.

[113] *Ibid.*, s. 292(2).

witness unless that evidence is "corroborated in a material particular by evidence that implicates the accused." Corroborative evidence is thus independent confirmatory evidence of a witness that shows or tends to show not only that a crime was committed, but also that the accused committed it. The law is that the trial judge is required to specify for the jury what items of evidence are capable of being corroborative, leaving to them the ultimate question of deciding whether such items are, in fact, corroborative. If the items viewed cumulatively, (but not alone), are capable of constituting corroboration, the trial judge must specify those items which may be considered part of the cumulative package.[114]

At common law, corroborative evidence had to be independent testimony which affected the accused by connecting or tending to connect him with the crime. The evidence could be either direct or circumstantial in nature.[115] The common law also required that the evidence emanate independently from the witness.[116]

The common law rule has been modified in the last quarter century. Corroborative evidence need no longer emanate independently of the suspect witness.[117] The evidence need only satisfy the trier of fact that the witness is telling the truth about a salient matter in the time frame in question; it need not point specifically to the guilt of the accused.[118] Evidence given by an accomplice that is contradicted or explained by an accused may still constitute corroborative evidence; it is for the jury to decide whether the evidence, in fact, is corroborative.[119] Finally, although a piece of evidence viewed in isolation may not constitute corroboration, a number of pieces viewed collectively may constitute corroboration.

---

[114] *McNamara (No. 1)*, 1981 CarswellOnt 1243, 56 C.C.C. (2d) 193 (C.A.); leave to appeal refused [1981] 1 S.C.R. xi; affirmed 1985 CarswellOnt 939, 1985 CarswellOnt 96, (sub nom. *R. v. Canadian Dredge & Dock Co.)* [1985] 1 S.C.R. 662, 19 C.C.C. (3d) 1, 45 C.R. (3d) 289, 19 D.L.R. (4th) 314, 59 N.R. 241, 9 O.A.C. 321.

[115] *Baskerville* (1916), [1916-17] All E.R. Rep. 38, 25 Cox C.C. 524, 12 Cr. App. R. 81, 80 J.P. 446, [1916] 2 K.B. 658 (C.A.).

[116] *Thomas*, 1952 CarswellOnt 16, [1952] 2 S.C.R. 344, 103 C.C.C. 193, 15 C.R. 1, [1952] 4 D.L.R. 306.

[117] *Murphy* (1976), 1976 CarswellBC 205, 1976 CarswellBC 320, [1977] 2 S.C.R. 603, 29 C.C.C. (2d) 417, 70 D.L.R. (3d) 42, [1976] 5 W.W.R. 65, 35 C.R.N.S. 44, 9 N.R. 329.

[118] *McCaw*, 1998 CarswellOnt 724, [1998] O.J. No. 730 (C.A.); leave to appeal refused (1998), 234 N.R. 197 (note), 118 O.A.C. 198 (note), [1998] S.C.C.A. No. 173.

[119] *McNamara (No.1)*, *supra*, note 114.

6. RE-EXAMINATION OF A CROWN WITNESS

When the defence has completed the cross-examination of the Crown witness, Crown counsel will be permitted to re-examine the witness. The purpose of re-examination is to deal only with new evidence or clarify matters raised by the defence during cross-examination, and only to reply to those new facts. The Crown is not entitled to rehash or ask the witness to repeat evidence already given by him or her in-chief. If there has been no cross-examination, there is no right to re-examine. Moreover, in re-examination the rule against leading questions applies.[120]

The rule against case-splitting prevent is designed to prevent the Crown from intentionally putting their case in piecemeal and raising new matters in re-examination. However, the trial judge has the right to permit Crown counsel to adduce a matter that he or she innocently forgot to raise in-chief.[121] Counsel for the defence will be entitled to cross-examine on that particular matter.

7. REOPENING THE CASE FOR THE CROWN

Occasionally, a prosecutor may discover that he or she has closed the case too soon and has omitted evidence crucial to the case for the Crown. The prosecutor will then apply to the trial judge to be permitted to re-open the Crown's case. Whether or not the prosecutor will be permitted to do so is a discretionary matter for the trial judge.

Historically, there were three stages in the trial where it was recognized that the trial judge had the discretion to allow the Crown to reopen its case. The first was before the Crown closed its case. Here, the trial judge had a wide latitude in allowing the Crown to recall a witness to prove an omitted element of the case or correct earlier testimony. The second stage was after the Crown had closed its case. Here the trial judge had the discretion to allow the Crown to reopen its case to correct some oversight or prove a matter that it had failed to do so inadvertently, provided that there was no prejudice to the accused. However, once the defence had begun to present its case, the trial judge's discretion was narrowly restricted. The Crown was only allowed to reopen its case to prove a matter, *ex improviso*, which no human ingenuity could have foreseen.[122]

---

[120] *Moore*, 1984 CarswellOnt 1178, 15 C.C.C. (3d) 541 (C.A.); leave to appeal refused (1985), 15 C.C.C. (3d) 541 (note) (S.C.C.).

[121] *Kozodoy*, 1957 CarswellOnt 132, 117 C.C.C. 315 (C.A.).

[122] *Cachia*, 1974 CarswellOnt 15, 17 C.C.C. (2d) 173, 26 C.R.N.S. 302 (H.C.).

Allowing the prosecution to re-open its case after the defence was called upon to meet it was regarded as an indirect breach of the fundamental rule that an accused was not required to respond to the allegation until the Crown established that there was a "case to meet". Once there was a case to meet, then the accused could no longer remain passive and was required to answer the case against him or risk conviction.

However, in 1978, the Supreme Court of Canada seemed to sweep away these principles in *Robillard*.[123] There the Court indicated that there was absolutely no restriction on the trial judge's discretion. It said that the *ex improviso* rule did not apply to Canada and the trial judge had a wide discretion to allow the Crown to reopen its case, even where the defence had been put to its election whether it intended to call evidence and had elected not to do so.

In 1994, in *P. (M.B.)*,[124] the Supreme Court reconsidered its decision in *Robillard*. The Court said that although Canadian jurisprudence has not applied the strict *ex improviso* rule as it has been applied at common law, the circumstances in which the Crown may be allowed to reopen its case after the defence has begun its case should be narrow and the *Robillard* case should be construed as applying only to situations where the Crown is seeking to reopen in order to correct a matter of form. The Court gave three examples where a judge could exercise his discretion:

1. Where the conduct of the defence, either directly or indirectly, has contributed to the Crown's failure to adduce certain evidence before closing its case.[125]

2. Where the Crown's omission or mistake was over a non-controversial issue to do with purely formal procedural or technical matters, having nothing to do with the substance or merits of a case.[126]

---

[123] 1978 CarswellQue 132, 1978 CarswellQue 132F, [1978] 2 S.C.R. 728, 41 C.C.C. (2d) 1, 5 C.R. (3d) 186, 85 D.L.R. (3d) 449, 21 N.R. 557.

[124] 1994 CarswellOnt 1153, 1994 CarswellOnt 65, [1994] 1 S.C.R. 555, 17 O.R. (3d) 782 (note), 89 C.C.C. (3d) 289, 29 C.R. (4th) 209, 113 D.L.R. (4th) 461, 21 C.R.R. (2d) 1, 165 N.R. 321, 70 O.A.C. 161.

[125] *Champagne* (1969), 1969 CarswellBC 268, [1970] 2 C.C.C. 273 (C.A.); *Crawford*, 1984 CarswellOnt 84, 43 C.R. (3d) 80, 33 M.V.R. 45 (Co. Ct.).

[126] *Kissick (No. 1)*, 1952 CarswellMan 1, (sub nom. *Kissick v. R.)* [1952] 1 S.C.R. 343, 102 C.C.C. 129, 14 C.R. 1; *Huluszkiw* (1962), 1962 CarswellOnt 12, [1963] 1 O.R. 157, 133 C.C.C. 244, 37 C.R. 386, 37 D.L.R. (2d) 309 (C.A.); *Assu*, 1981 CarswellBC 724, 64 C.C.C. (2d) 94 (C.A.).

3. Where the interests of the accused warrant reopening the Crown's case.[127]

It is often forgotten that there is a clear difference between an application by the Crown to reopen its case in order to call additional evidence and reply evidence called by the Crown after the defence has completed its case. When the Crown applies to reopen its case and lead additional evidence before the defence is called upon to present its case, it accepts that the additional evidence is relevant to a factual issue which was material during its case, and that should have and would have been led during its case. It also offers an explanation for failing to do so, which it contends justifies departing from the normal trial format. If the evidence is an attempt to fill a gap in the Crown's case revealed by the defence after the defence has presented it case, or if it effectively changes the case which the defence undertook to answer when it elected to call evidence, then the application will usually be refused, except in the rarest of cases.[128]

The right to adduce reply evidence, on the other hand, arises where the defence has led evidence which the Crown could not reasonably have anticipated. In other words, the reply evidence will take on its significance from evidence that the defence tendered during its case, not something that the Crown should have led in chief.

8. MOTION FOR DIRECTED VERDICT OR NO-CASE TO ANSWER

If the Crown has presented a *prima facie* case, the trial judge will then call upon the defence to present its case. However, the defence may ask the trial judge to direct the jury to return a verdict of acquittal on the basis that there is no prima facie case to answer. Where a judge presides without a jury, the defence will ask the judge to enter a verdict of not guilty.

The test that the trial judge must apply in determining if the Crown has established a prima facie case is whether there is any evidence upon which a reasonable jury properly instructed could convict the accused. The judge must remember that at this stage of the proceedings, the question of proof beyond a reasonable doubt does not arise. The judge is not entitled to take the case away from the jury and direct them to render a verdict of acquittal because he or she concludes that the evidence is manifestly unreliable. In

---

[127] *Nelson*, 1993 CarswellOnt 2534, [1993] O.J. No 1899 (Gen. Div.).
[128] *M. (F.S.)*, 1996 CarswellOnt 3364, 111 C.C.C. (3d) 90, 93 O.A.C. 201 (C.A.).

other words, the judge is not entitled to weigh the quality or reliability of the evidence even when sitting without a jury.

Although the test appears relatively straightforward, its application to the facts of any case often creates difficulty for the trial judge. Exactly what does "any evidence" mean? In *Charemski*,[129] where the accused was charged with the murder of his estranged wife, the trial judge had directed a verdict of acquittal on the basis that the Crown had failed to adduce evidence of causation. The forensic evidence had failed to establish definitely whether the deceased had died from natural causes, or as a result of an accident, suicide or homicide. The Supreme Court was of the view that the trial judge had erred in directing a verdict of acquittal. In a majority judgment, the Court was satisfied that the condition and position of the body as found could have led to the inference that the deceased was the victim of foul play. In a dissenting judgment, McLachlin J. said that to pass the hurdle of a directed verdict of acquittal, the Crown must adduce sufficient evidence on the issues of identity, causation and the requisite mental state to sustain a verdict beyond a reasonable doubt, and the Crown had failed to do so.

This means that the trial judge must, of necessity, enter into a weighing process. The judge's determination of whether there is *any evidence* to go to the jury requires him or her to weigh the evidence presented by the Crown to determine whether "a reasonable jury properly instructed could convict the accused". Since no reasonable jury could convict unless there was some evidence of substance, the judge must determine whether it is sufficient to meet this threshold test. However, in assessing the sufficiency of the evidence, the trial judge must never assess its quality or reliability. In other words, what the judge must never do is to enter the province of the jury and decide whether the testimony of the witnesses is manifestly unreliable or, where the evidence is entirely circumstantial, whether that evidence is consistent with any conclusion other than the guilt of the accused. In a jury trial, the question of the weight of the evidence on the issue of proof beyond a reasonable doubt belongs to the jury not the judge, and the judge must be careful not to usurp their function. Although one might wonder why the same rule applies in trials by judge alone where the judge is also the trier of the facts, the rule is still strictly enforced.

[129] 1998 CarswellOnt 1199, 1998 CarswellOnt 1200, [1998] 1 S.C.R. 679, 123 C.C.C. (3d) 225, 15 C.R. (5th) 1, 157 D.L.R. (4th) 603, 224 N.R. 120, 108 O.A.C. 126, [1998] S.C.J. No. 23.

In *Monteleone*,[130] Mr. Justice McIntyre described the rule this way:

> Where there is before the court any admissible evidence, whether direct or circumstantial, which, if believed by a properly-charged jury acting reasonably, would justify a conviction, the trial judge is not justified in directing a verdict of acquittal. It is not the function of the trial judge to weigh the evidence, to test its quality or reliability once a determination of its admissibility has been made. It is not for the trial judge to draw inferences of fact from the evidence before him. These functions are for the trier of fact, the jury.

Although some legal scholars have argued that a trial judge should go so far as to determine whether the evidence is sufficient to prove guilt beyond a reasonable doubt before it goes to the jury, that view fails to recognize and understand the different roles played by the judge and the jury in a criminal trial. They argue that such a threshold test ensures that section 7 of the *Charter of Rights and Freedoms*, which guarantees an accused fundamental justice and section 11(d), which presumes an accused innocent until proven guilty, can be satisfied and given their full meaning.[131]

It must be remembered, however, that the accused has chosen a jury, not a judge, to determine whether the Crown has established his or her guilt beyond a reasonable doubt and it is assumed that the jury will obey the judge's instructions on this issue. To ask a judge to decide whether the Crown has established the guilt of the accused beyond a reasonable doubt before allowing the case to go to the jury carries the danger that if the case is allowed to go to the jury, they might feel compelled to agree with the judge's decision on that issue and find the accused guilty even if they have a reasonable doubt. Moreover, a finding of not guilty by a jury, in the face of a legal ruling by the judge that the evidence has established the accused's guilt beyond a reasonable doubt, might cause the public generally to feel that the administration of justice has been brought into disrepute.

If the judge agrees that there is no case to answer, he or she will direct the jury that, as a matter of law, they must acquit the accused. Even though the decision is a legal one, the common law rule was that once an accused had elected trial by jury and had been placed in the jury's charge at the beginning of the trial, only the jury, not the judge, had jurisdiction to formally pronounce the verdict of not guilty and deliver the accused from their

---

[130] 1987 CarswellOnt 970, 1987 CarswellOnt 106, [1987] 2 S.C.R. 154, 35 C.C.C. (3d) 193, 59 C.R. (3d) 97, 41 D.L.R. (4th) 746, 78 N.R. 377, 23 O.A.C. 241 at p. 103 [C.R.].

[131] See David Tanovich, "Annotation", 27 C.R. (4th) 174.

charge.[132] This often placed the judge in an embarrassing position if the jury was reluctant to follow the judge's instructions. In 1994 in *Rowbotham*,[133] the Supreme Court decided to modify the rule and allow the judge to tell the jury that he or she was withdrawing the case from them and entering a verdict of acquittal. In trials by judge alone, the judge will simply render a verdict of not guilty and dismiss the charge.

9. THE CASE FOR THE DEFENCE

(a) Making an Opening Address

If there is some evidence upon which a jury properly instructed could convict the accused, the judge will call upon the defence to present its case. The defence may or may not call evidence. If the defence elects to call evidence, section 651(2) of the *Criminal Code* authorizes counsel for the accused, or the accused where he or she is not represented by counsel, to make an opening address to the jury. The defence has no right to make an opening address unless the defence intends to call evidence. The purpose of the opening address is to outline to the jury essentially what the defence is all about and what the defence witnesses, including the accused if it is intended to call the accused to give evidence, are expected to say. If the defence does not intend to call witnesses, then the Crown will be directed by the trial judge to sum up its case to the jury and the defence is entitled to address the jury last.[134]

If two or more accused are tried jointly, the judge must, at the conclusion of the Crown's case, call upon the accused first named in the indictment to indicate whether he or she intends to call evidence. If first named accused elects to call evidence, then that accused must open to the jury first and call all of the witnesses that are intended to be called before the next named accused is called upon. The trial judge must then proceed in the same manner with respect to each accused in the order that the accused appears on the indictment.

If an accused, or any of the accused jointly tried, calls any witnesses, the proceedings are reversed. The right to address the jury last for all accused will be lost if any accused jointly tried chooses to call any evidence. The witnesses will be examined in chief by counsel for the defence (or the ac-

---

[132] See Lord Devlin, Trial by Jury, The Hamlyn Lecture (8th) Series, 1966, Steven and Sons Ltd., at p. 78.

[133] 1994 CarswellOnt 76, 1994 CarswellOnt 2265, (sub nom. *R. v. Roblin)* [1994] 2 S.C.R. 463, 90 C.C.C. (3d) 449, 30 C.R. (4th) 141, 22 C.R.R. (2d) 193 at 195, 168 N.R. 220, 72 O.A.C. 98.

[134] *Criminal Code*, s. 651.

cused if unrepresented), cross-examined by counsel for the Crown and re-examined by counsel for the accused. Co-accused (or their counsel) have the right to cross-examine the accused and the accused's witnesses but any cross-examination by co-accused must be conducted before the Crown is called upon to conduct its own cross-examination of the witness. Cross-examination by co-accused must be conducted in the order of appearance on the indictment, unless the defence agrees otherwise or the judge so directs.

Although there have been cases where the trial judge has permitted the defence to make an opening statement immediately after the Crown's opening statement,[135] it is submitted that this practice is improper for a number of reasons. First of all, it directly contravenes section 651(2) of the Code which states that counsel for the accused or the accused, at the end of the Crown's case, is entitled to open for the defence, then call evidence and then to sum up the case for the accused. Secondly, and most importantly, permitting the accused to address the jury after the Crown assumes that the accused will call evidence. But what if the defence decides at the end of the Crown's case not to call evidence? Does the trial judge declare a mistrial? Finally, section 651(2) authorizes the defence to make an opening statement at the end of the Crown's case. Does that mean that the defence is entitled to a second opening if it calls evidence?

(b) The Right to Adduce Evidence

The common law of England did not permit an accused to give evidence in his own defence and it was not until 1640 that an accused charged with a felony could call witnesses on his behalf. Even then, witnesses were not allowed to give their evidence under oath in the belief that if they contradicted the witness for the Crown, they would probably be lying. Although an accused was not allowed to testify in his own defence, he was allowed to make a statement from the prisoner's dock after the Crown had presented all of its evidence. The statement, however, could not be under oath and therefore did not possess the sanctity of sworn testimony that was considered essential to the dignity of a criminal trial. His lawyer, if he could afford one, was not allowed to ask him questions that might be germane to the issues in the case or even direct him to those matters pertinent to the defence. Finally, in 1898 the British Parliament decided to heed the cries of law reformers and abolished the rule disqualifying an accused from testify-

---

[135] *Morgan*, 1997 CarswellOnt 5620, 125 C.C.C. (3d) 478 (Gen. Div.); *Bekar*, 2003 CarswellBC 1333, 175 C.C.C. (3d) 97 (C.A.). But see *D. (A.)*, 2003 CarswellOnt 4149, 180 C.C.C. (3d) 319 (S.C.J.).

ing in his own behalf. Canada had taken the lead five years earlier and abolished the rule in 1893 for all offences, including treason. Section 4(1) of the *Canada Evidence Act* provides,

> 4. (1) Every person charged with an offence, and, except as otherwise provided in this section, the wife or husband, as the case may be, of the person so charged, is a competent witness for the defence, whether the person so charged is charged solely or jointly with any other person.

Today, an accused has the right to call any witness for the defence including a witness previously called by the prosecution. Neither the Crown nor the defence has a proprietary interest in a witness who has been called. Nor is the defence under any obligation to call any witness, although the prosecution may comment on the failure to call a particular witness. The judge may not do so.[136] Although it is not improper for a co-accused to comment upon the failure of the accused to testify[137]., the judge and the prosecutor are prohibited from commenting upon the failure of the accused or his or her spouse to testify.[138]

A judge has the power to exclude relevant evidence tendered by the Crown on the basis simply that its prejudicial effect outweighs its probative value. However, the power to exclude relevant defence evidence is narrower and constrained by the fundamental tenet that an innocent person should not be convicted. That tenet now has constitutional protection in section 7 of the *Charter*.[139] The reason was explained by McLachlin J. in *Seaboyer*,[140]

> Canadian courts, like courts in most common law jurisdictions, have been extremely cautious in restricting the power of the accused to call evidence in his or her defence, a reluctance founded in the fundamental tenet of our judicial system that an innocent person must not be convicted. It follows from this that the prejudice must substantially outweigh the value of the evidence before a judge can exclude evidence relevant to a defence allowed by law.

> These principles and procedures are familiar to all who practise in our criminal courts. They are common sense rules based on basic notions of fairness,

---

[136] *Zehr*, 1980 CarswellOnt 1269, 54 C.C.C. (2d) 65 (C.A.).

[137] *Prokofiew*, 2012 SCC 49, 2012 CarswellOnt 12411, 2012 CarswellOnt 12412, 290 C.C.C. (3d) 280, 96 C.R. (6th) 57

[138] Section 4(6) of the *Canada Evidence Act*.

[139] *Seaboyer*, 1991 CarswellOnt 109, 1991 CarswellOnt 1022, [1991] 2 S.C.R. 577, 66 C.C.C. (3d) 321, 7 C.R. (4th) 117 at pp. 611-12 [S.C.R.] and *Clarke*, 1998 CarswellOnt 3447, 129 C.C.C. (3d) 1, 18 C.R. (5th) 219 (C.A.) at para. 33.

[140] *Ibid.*

and as such properly lie at the heart of our trial process. In short, they form part of the principles of fundamental justice enshrined in s. 7 of the Charter. They may be circumscribed in some cases by other rules of evidence, but as will be discussed in more detail below, the circumstances where truly relevant and reliable evidence is excluded are few, particularly where the evidence goes to the defence. In most cases, the exclusion of relevant evidence can be justified on the ground that the potential prejudice to the trial process of admitting the evidence clearly outweighs its value.

Thus, it is open for an accused to blame a third party or to call a witness to confess their guilt for a crime that the accused is charged with committing. Martin J.A. explained the rational and test for the admission of alternate or third party suspect evidence in *McMillan*,[141]

> It follows that evidence of the disposition of a third person to commit the crime in question, like other circumstantial evidence, is admissible, if relevant, to prove that the crime was committed by the third person.

> Where the character is that of a third person, not a party to the cause, the reasons of policy (noted ante, subsection 64) for exclusion seem to disappear or become inconsiderable; hence, if there is any relevancy in the fact of character, i.e. if some act is involved upon the probability of which a moral trait can throw light, the character may well be received. (Wigmore at p. 488.)

> Obviously, unless the third person is connected with the crime under consideration by other circumstances, evidence of such person's disposition to commit the offence is inadmissible on the ground of lack of probative value. For example, if A is charged with murdering X, in the absence of some nexus with the alleged offence, evidence that B has a propensity or disposition for violence, by itself, is inadmissible to prove B is the murderer because standing alone it has no probative value with respect to the probability of B having committed the offence. If, however, it is proved that A, B and X all lived in the same house when X was killed, and that B had a motive to kill X, then evidence that B had a propensity for violence may have probative value on the issue whether B, and not A, killed X, and is accordingly admissible.

This means that before a third party or alternate suspect evidence can be admitted, the accused bears the burden of showing that the proposed evidence has "some nexus with the alleged offence". Without the nexus, the evidence would lack probative value.[142] However, where an accused pro-

---

[141] 1975 CarswellOnt 7, 7 O.R. (2d) 750, 23 C.C.C. (2d) 160 (C.A.) at p. 758 [O.R.], affirmed 1977 CarswellOnt 474, 1977 CarswellOnt 474F, 33 C.C.C. (2d) 360 (S.C.C.). See also *Grandinetti*, 2005 SCC 5, 2005 CarswellAlta 81, 2005 CarswellAlta 82, 191 C.C.C. (3d) 449, 25 C.R. (6th) 1 at paras. 46–48.
[142] *Murphy*, 2012 ONCA 573, 2012 CarswellOnt 10836.

poses to call direct evidence from another person taking responsibility for the crimes charged, the evidence itself constitutes a sufficient nexus or connection. Nothing more need be shown and no formal application is necessary. The defence has always been permitted to call or adduce evidence that some other person committed the crime with which the accused has been charged.

(c) Alibi Evidence

Under Canadian law, everyone accused of a crime has the right to remain silent. A jury is not entitled to draw any inference against an accused who chooses to exercise that right. That right, however, is not an absolute one. One exception arises where the defence is alibi. In such instance, the failure to disclose a defence of alibi in a timely manner may be considered by the trier in assessing the credibility of that defence.[143] The purpose of this exception is to guard against surprise alibis fabricated in the witness box which the prosecution is almost powerless to challenge.[144]

At one time, the rule required the defence to disclose an alibi immediately upon arrest.[145] However, this put the accused in an untenable position because it conflicted with the accused's right to remain silent. In *Cleghorn*,[146] the Supreme Court decided to modify the rule to define timely disclosure to mean "when it allows the prosecution and police to investigate the alibi evidence before trial". The Court said that the criteria of timeliness and adequacy should be evaluated on the basis of whether a meaningful investigation could have been undertaken as a result of disclosure. The new rule is that the failure to disclose an alibi at a sufficiently early time to permit the alibi to be investigated by the police is a factor that may be considered by the trier in determining the weight to be given to it. The Court also said that timely disclosure of the alibi no longer has to be made by the accused. The right to silence at the investigative stage permits disclosure of the alibi by a third party who is a witness to the alibi. The Court in *Cleghorn* also indi-

---

[143] *Chambers*, 1990 CarswellBC 217, 1990 CarswellBC 761, [1990] 2 S.C.R. 1293, 49 B.C.L.R. (2d) 299, 59 C.C.C. (3d) 321, 80 C.R. (3d) 235, [1990] 6 W.W.R. 554, (sub nom. *R. v. Chambers (No. 2)*) 119 N.R. 321, *per* Cory J at p. 343 [C.C.C.]. See also *Russell*, 1936 CarswellBC 118, 67 C.C.C. 28, [1936] 4 D.L.R. 744 (S.C.C.).

[144] *Cleghorn*, 1995 CarswellOnt 126, 1995 CarswellOnt 802, [1995] 3 S.C.R. 175, 100 C.C.C. (3d) 393, 41 C.R. (4th) 282, 32 C.R.R. (2d) 41, 186 N.R. 49, 85 O.A.C. 129.

[145] *Russell*, *supra*, note 143.

[146] *Supra*, note 144.

cated that disclosure should be given with sufficient particularity to enable the authorities to conduct a meaningful investigation. Three pieces of information are necessary: a statement that the accused was not present at the location of the crime; the whereabouts of the accused at that time; and, the names of any witness to the alibi.

Of course, whether an accused is required to make timely disclosure will depend upon whether the Crown requires disclosure in order to be in a position to effectively investigate and respond to the defence actually advanced by the accused. For example, in *Wright*[147], the accused was charged with the robbery of H and other related offences. The theory of the Crown was that the accused and another person went to H's apartment to buy marijuana, and while there, attacked and robbed him. At trial, the defence called R who said that on the day of the robbery, she was approached by three young men who wanted to purchase marijuana. She said that she took two of the young men to see A, who was a user of marijuana. The accused did not go with them and stayed with her. It was held that the trial judge erred in characterizing the evidence of R as alibi evidence and charging the jury that they could draw an adverse inference from the fact that her evidence was only disclosed shortly before trial. The police had become aware of R's involvement in the offence shortly after it had occurred and had the opportunity to question her if they wanted.

To constitute an alibi, the explanation advanced by the defence must be determinative of the final issue of guilt or innocence of the accused. In other words, it must be essential to the Crown's case against the accused. For example, in *Hill*,[148] the accused was convicted of perjury, insurance fraud and arson in connection with the burning of his boat to collect insurance money. The case for the Crown depended on the evidence of a disgruntled former employee who said that he had a meeting with the accused on a certain date at which time the accused solicited him to set fire to the boat and did so at his request. The accused testified that he could not have met with his employee on the date alleged because he was elsewhere. The trial judge charged the jury that the accused had raised an alibi defence, and that they could, in considering the weight to be given to the alibi, take into account the fact that it was not disclosed to the police. It was held that the trial judge mischaracterized his defence as an alibi one. At best, the accused's explanation of his whereabouts might demonstrate that the conversations could not have taken place when they were alleged to have taken

---

[147] 2009 ONCA 623, 2009 CarswellOnt 4967, 247 C.C.C. (3d) 1.

[148] 1995 CarswellOnt 127, 25 O.R. (3d) 97, 102 C.C.C. (3d) 469, 41 C.R. (4th) 299, 83 O.A.C. 99 (C.A.).

place, not that they never took place. Thus the date when the accused claimed to have been elsewhere was not essential to the Crown's case against him.

Although the rationale underlying *Hill* is sound, its application to the facts in that case is difficult to understand. The facts set out in the reported judgment indicate that the case for the Crown was that the meeting between the accused and the former employee took place at a certain time and place during which the accused solicited the employee to burn his boat. The accused's defence was that he could not have met with his employee on the date alleged because he was elsewhere. Thus, the suggestion by the Court that the date when the accused claimed to have been elsewhere was not essential to the Crown's case against him and therefore not strictly alibi evidence, flies in the face of the theory of the Crown.

Where the defence has given notice to the Crown prior to trial that it intends to adduce alibi and has given details of that alibi, the Crown is not required to lead evidence-in-chief which could rebut that alibi. The Crown is entitled to wait until the accused has testified and then lead that evidence in rebuttal. The rule is that the Crown is only required to lead evidence where it is relevant to the case it is presenting; there is no obligation upon the Crown to foresee that certain evidence might later become relevant.[149]

The trial judge is required to instruct the jury that the mere fact that they disbelieve the alibi does not necessarily mean that it is concocted. It is only where they conclude that the alibi was deliberately fabricated by the accused that they are entitled to draw the inference that he did so by consciousness of guilt.[150] Although the logic of the distinction may be difficult for a juror to understand, the rationale underlying the rule is that it is a necessary safeguard to prevent the jury from short-circuiting the Crown's obligation to prove guilt beyond a reasonable doubt by moving directly from disbelief to a finding of guilt.

---

[149] *Rafferty*, 1983 CarswellAlta 69, 43 A.R. 323, 25 Alta. L.R. (2d) 334, 6 C.C.C. (3d) 72, [1983] 4 W.W.R. 511 (C.A.); *Andrews*, 1979 CarswellBC 546, 8 C.R. (3d) 1 (C.A.); leave to appeal refused (1979), 28 N.R. 537n (S.C.C.).

[150] *Hibbert*, 2002 CarswellBC 847, 2002 CarswellBC 848, 163 C.C.C. (3d) 129, 50 C.R. (5th) 209 (S.C.C.); *Maracle*, 2006 CarswellOnt 807, 206 C.C.C. (3d) 36 (C.A.); *Carey*, 1996 CarswellQue 1070, 113 C.C.C. (3d) 74 (C.A.); *Tessier*, 1997 CarswellBC 451, 113 C.C.C. (3d) 538, 87 B.C.A.C. 269, 143 W.A.C. 269, [1997] B.C.J. No. 515 (C.A.).

10. CROSS-EXAMINATION OF DEFENCE WITNESSES

(a) Generally

Although witnesses for the defence are open to the same kind of attack as witnesses for the prosecution, an accused who testifies occupies a special position when he is being cross-examined by Crown counsel. In *Davison*,[151] Mr. Justice Martin succinctly summed up that position:

> An accused who gives evidence has a dual character. As an accused he is protected by an underlying policy rule against the introduction of evidence by the prosecution tending to show that he is a person of bad character, subject of course, to the recognized exceptions to that rule. As a witness, however, his credibility is subject to attack. If the position of an accused who gives evidence is assimilated in every respect to that of an ordinary witness he is not protected against cross-examination with respect to discreditable conduct and associations.
>
> If the accused could in every case be cross-examined with a view to showing that he is a professional criminal under the guise of an attack upon his credibility as a witness it would be virtually impossible for him to receive a fair trial on the specific charge upon which he is being tried. It is not realistic to assume that, ordinarily, the jury will be able to limit the effect of such a cross-examination to the issue of credibility in arriving at a verdict.
>
> In my view the policy rule which protects an accused against attack upon his character lest it divert the jury from the issue which they are called upon to decide, namely, the guilt or innocence of the accused on the specific charge before the Court, is not wholly subordinated to the rule which permits an accused who elects to give evidence to be cross-examined on the issue of his credibility. In this area of the law, as in so many areas, a balance has been struck between competing interests, which endeavours so far as possible to recognize the purpose of both rules and does not give effect to one to the total exclusion of the other.
>
> Consequently, limitations are imposed with respect to the cross-examination of an accused which do not apply in the case of an ordinary witness ...
>
> I conclude that, save for the cross-examination as to previous convictions permitted by s.12 of the Canada *Evidence Act*, an accused may not be cross-examined with respect to misconduct or discreditable associations unrelated to the charge on which he is being tried for the purpose of leading to the conclusion that by reason of his bad character he is a person whose evidence ought not be believed. Cross-examination, however, which is directly

---

[151] 1974 CarswellOnt 559, 6 O.R. (2d) 103, 20 C.C.C. (2d) 424 (C.A.); leave to appeal refused [1974] S.C.R. viii, 6 O.R. (2d) 103n, 20 C.C.C. (2d) 424n, approved in *Stewart*, 1991 CarswellOnt 1317, 62 C.C.C. (3d) 289, 43 O.A.C. 109 (C.A.).

relevant to prove the falsity of the accused's evidence does not fall within the ban notwithstanding that it may incidentally reflect upon the accused's character by disclosing discreditable conduct on his part.

(b) Prohibited Questions by the Crown

There are other questions that may be asked by the Crown that are considered to be improper. For example, asking the accused to express an opinion whether another witness for the prosecution is telling the truth or is lying is improper because the opinion of one witness about the veracity of another witness is a matter solely for the trier to consider, not the accused or any other defence witness.[152] Questions that could leave the jury with the mistaken impression that there is an onus upon the accused to disprove the allegations against him are considered improper. For example, it is considered improper for the Crown to ask the accused why a complainant would make up the allegations; such questions place an obligation upon the accused to provide some motive for the complainant to lie.[153] Similarly, it is improper to ask an accused why the investigating officer would have a motive to make a false accusation against him.[154] Again, it is improper to ask an accused why other witnesses have not been called to testify on his behalf.[155] Such questions could leave the jury with the impression that there was an onus upon the accused to prove his innocence.

It is improper for the Crown to ask the accused, as well as an ordinary witness, questions that are designed to demean or denigrate the accused, or are laced with sarcasm or contempt.[156] Questions put by Crown counsel which inject his or her personal views or are editorial comment are improper because the Crown's opinion as to the guilt of the accused is irrelevant.[157]

Questions that suggest or imply that the accused has exercised his or her constitutional rights are prohibited; the Crown is not entitled to turn the

---

[152] *Markadonis*, 1935 CarswellNS 50, [1935] S.C.R. 657, 64 C.C.C. 41, [1935] 3 D.L.R. 424; *Vandenberghe*, 1995 CarswellOnt 1806, 96 C.C.C. (3d) 371, [1995] O.J. No. 243 (C.A.); *Rose*, 2001 CarswellOnt 955, 53 O.R. (3d) 417, 153 C.C.C. (3d) 225, 42 C.R. (5th) 183, 143 O.A.C. 163 (C.A.).

[153] *F. (A.)*, 1996 CarswellOnt 3157, 30 O.R. (3d) 470, 1 C.R. (5th) 382, 93 O.A.C. 102 (C.A.). But see *P. (H.P.)*, 1996 CarswellMan 586, 112 C.C.C. (3d) 140, 113 Man. R. (2d) 271, 131 W.A.C. 271 (C.A.).

[154] *F. (A.)*, 1996 CarswellOnt 3157, 1 C.R. (5th) 382 (C.A.).

[155] *Bouhsass*, 2002 CarswellOnt 3613, 169 C.C.C. (3d) 444 (C.A.).

[156] *V. (E.)*, 1994 CarswellOnt 73, 90 C.C.C. (3d) 484, 30 C.R. (4th) 78 (C.A.).

[157] *Gormley*, 1999 CarswellPEI 83, 140 C.C.C. (3d) 110 (C.A.).

exercise of a constitutionally protected *Charter* right into a trap. For example, where the accused chooses to exercise the right to remain silent, it is improper for the Crown to suggest that if the accused's testimony were true, he or she would have given the police the same explanation being given in the witness stand.[158] Similarly, it is improper for the Crown to ask an accused questions directed to his failure to provide the police with information or an explanation for what had occurred; such questions breach an accused's right to silence and presumption of innocence.[159]

Questions about trial tactics may be prejudicial and unfair. For example, it is improper for Crown counsel to ask the accused about the trial tactics used by his defence counsel, such as asking the accused why his lawyer did not cross-examine Crown witnesses upon evidence that the defence was intending to contradict with its own witnesses, or suggest that the accused is responsible for the tactical decisions of his trial counsel, or questions about his plea.[160] Similarly, questions that insinuate that the accused has tried, in vain, to keep evidence of his or her statement to the police from the jury by requiring the Crown to prove the voluntariness of the statement on a *voir dire* are highly improper.[161] Again, it is improper for the Crown to ask the accused why another expert opinion was not sought concerning a DNA sample and to invite the jury to infer that an innocent person would have done so.[162]

Questions as to what the accused, charged with murder by stabbing the victim, had been advised by his counsel with regard to self-defence and when he had received such advice have been regarded as improper infringing upon the solicitor-client relationship.[163] Similarly, an inquiry of the accused whether he or she will consent to provide a sample of his blood for the purposes of forensic analysis in order to determine whether or not the blood found at the scene of the alleged crime may belong to the accused is

---

[158] *Chambers*, 1990 CarswellBC 217, 1990 CarswellBC 761, 59 C.C.C. (3d) 321, 80 C.R. (3d) 235 (S.C.C.) at pp. 340–43 [C.C.C.]; *Creighton*, 1995 CarswellOnt 12, 1995 CarswellOnt 523, (sub nom. *R. v. Crawford*) 96 C.C.C. (3d) 481, 37 C.R. (4th) 197 (S.C.C.) at pp. 500–02 [C.C.C.].

[159] *Wojcik*, 2002 CarswellMan 272, 166 C.C.C. (3d) 418, 3 C.R. (6th) 92 (C.A.).

[160] *Henderson* (1999), 134 C.C.C. (3d) 131 (Ont. C.A.).

[161] *C. (G.)*, 1996 CarswellNfld 222, 110 C.C.C. (3d) 233 (C.A.).

[162] *Usereau*, 2010 CarswellQue 4219, (sub nom. *R. v. Usereau)*) 256 C.C.C. (3d) 499 (C.A.); leave to appeal refused 2010 CarswellQue 13352, 2010 CarswellQue 13353 (S.C.C.).

[163] *Nealy*, 1986 CarswellOnt 136, 30 C.C.C. (3d) 460, 54 C.R. (3d) 158 (C.A.).

improper.[164] It is also improper to threaten the accused or any witness for the defence with perjury, the mere threat which will prejudice the fair trial of the accused.[165]

Generally, it is improper for Crown counsel to suggest to the accused that his evidence should be discounted because he had received full disclosure before trial and had only been subjected to cross-examination on one occasion. Although questions concerning disclosure are "always potentially dangerous", they are not always considered improper. For example, where an accused has suggested that records in the Crown disclosure confirm aspects of his testimony, it has not been considered improper for the Crown to cross-examine on the fact that the accused received and reviewed disclosure prior to trial so that his or her testimony can be viewed in that light.[166] Similarly, it has not been considered improper for the Crown to refer to an accused's receipt of disclosure in order to undermine a defence of alibi — particularly an alibi with no particulars — in order to suggest that the accused has tailored his evidence to fit the disclosure.[167]

As noted above, other witnesses for the defence do not have the same protection. They are subject to the same attack as any other witness and may be cross-examined with respect to misconduct on unrelated matters which have not resulted in a conviction[168] with a view to showing that the witness ought not to be believed because of such bad character.[169] Impeachment of the witness's credibility also allows the cross-examiner to ask the witness questions not related to a fact in issue to show that the witness

---

[164] *Charlebois*, 1999 CarswellQue 77, 1999 CarswellQue 4728, (sub nom. *R. v. Charlebois*) 135 C.C.C. (3d) 414 (C.A.) at pp. 427-428 [C.C.C.]; affirmed 2000 CarswellQue 2306, 2000 CarswellQue 2307, (sub nom. *R. v. Charlebois*) 148 C.C.C. (3d) 449, 37 C.R. (5th) 253 (S.C.C.).

[165] *Provencher*, 1955 CarswellQue 16, 114 C.C.C. 100, 22 C.R. 407 (S.C.C.) at p. 106 [C.C.C.].

[166] *White*, 1999 CarswellOnt 298, 132 C.C.C. (3d) 373, 22 C.R. (5th) 56 (C.A.); *Thain*, 2009 CarswellOnt 1310, 243 C.C.C. (3d) 230 (C.A.).

[167] *Khan*, 1998 CarswellBC 1344, 126 C.C.C. (3d) 523 (C.A.); additional reasons 2001 CarswellBC 24 (C.A.); leave to appeal refused 2001 CarswellBC 1487, 2001 CarswellBC 1488 (S.C.C.); *Marshall*, 2005 CarswellOnt 4716, 200 C.C.C. (3d) 179 (C.A.); leave to appeal refused 2006 CarswellOnt 5556, 2006 CarswellOnt 5557 (S.C.C.).

[168] *Davison*, *supra*, note 151.

[169] *Titus*, 1983 CarswellOnt 806, 1983 CarswellOnt 64, [1983] 1 S.C.R. 259, (sub nom. *Titus v. R.*) 2 C.C.C. (3d) 321, 33 C.R. (3d) 17, 144 D.L.R. (3d) 577, 46 N.R. 477; *Gonzague*, 1983 CarswellOnt 81, 4 C.C.C. (3d) 505, 34 C.R. (3d) 169 (C.A.).

may have a motive to lie, may be biased in favour of the accused or may be a person not worthy of belief.

(c) Questions as to Credibility — Rule Against Collateral Evidence

As noted earlier, the general rule is that questions in cross-examination must relate either to a fact in issue or to the impeachment of the witness's credibility. Generally, the Crown is entitled to call evidence in reply to refute an answer given by the accused or a defence witness to a fact in issue. However, the rule is different where the question is asked to test the credibility of the witness and does not relate to a fact in issue. Here, the prosecution is not allowed to call evidence to refute the answer given by the witness or the accused; the prosecution is bound by the answer. An exception to that rule is where the questions pertain to the previous criminal record of the accused or the witness for the defence. In such instance, section 12 of the *Canada Evidence Act* permits the cross-examiner to prove the record if the accused or a defence witness refuses to admit it.

One might question the wisdom of a rule that allows one side to ask a question to test credibility but does not allow evidence in reply to prove that the witness is being untruthful on that issue. The reason for the rule is to ensure that the trier concentrates on the issue in dispute and avoids a multiplicity of proceedings. If the cross-examiner were allowed to call impeachment evidence on every question that was put to a witness, it would mean that trials would be sidetracked and unduly prolonged by a series of mini-trials to refute a witness's testimony.

(d) Criminal Record of the Accused

Section 12 of the *Canada Evidence Act* provides that a witness (which includes the accused) "may be questioned as to whether he has been convicted of any offence" and, if he or she denies the fact or refuses to answer, the opposite party may prove the conviction. When it comes to the accused, as opposed to an ordinary witness, the word "conviction" has been strictly construed. Section 12 does not permit the Crown to go beyond prior convictions and to cross-examine an accused as to discreditable conduct or association with disreputable individuals in order to attack an accused's credibility.[170] Nor does it permit cross-examination where the accused was found guilty and granted an absolute discharge, or a conditional discharge and the

---

[170] *Davison, supra,* note 151.

conditions were subsequently fulfilled.[171] Section 730(3) provides that an offender who has been discharged of an offence, "shall be deemed not to have been convicted of the offence". Therefore, an adjudication of guilt followed by the granting of a discharge is not a conviction within s. 12(1) of the *Canada Evidence Act*. Similarly, it is considered improper to cross-examine a witness with respect to a conviction for which he or she has been granted a pardon. Section 749(3) of the *Criminal Code* provides that a person who is granted a free pardon is deemed never to have committed the offence in respect of which the pardon is granted.[172]

The risk of such questions in the case of the accused, unlike a witness, is that the jury may conclude that because the accused has been convicted of an offence on a previous occasion, he or she is probably guilty of the offence that they are trying. This imposes upon the trial judge the responsibility of instructing the jury that they must not draw this inference against the accused. The jury must be specifically told that they may not use the accused's prior criminal record to show that the accused was likely to have committed the offence charged.[173] The judge must also instruct the jury that they are only entitled to consider the criminal record of the accused for the purpose of assessing his credibility with respect to the issues before the court. The jury system assumes that the jury will honour those instructions.[174]

For some time, the law was uncertain as to whether the trial judge had any discretion to disallow questions about prior convictions where it was prejudicial to an accused, such as where the conviction was an old one, or where it bore no relationship to the issue of credibility (unlike convictions for dishonesty such as forgery, cheating and the like).[175] Some trial judges felt that the word "may" in section 12 gave the judge the discretion to disal-

---

[171] Section 730(3); *Sark*, 2004 CarswellNB 2, 2004 CarswellNB 3, 182 C.C.C. (3d) 530 (C.A.).

[172] *Paterson*, 1998 CarswellBC 122, 122 C.C.C. (3d) 254, 102 B.C.A.C. 200, 166 W.A.C. 200 (C.A.); leave to appeal refused (1999), 134 C.C.C. (3d) iv, 132 B.C.A.C. 139 (note), 242 N.R. 199 (note), 215 W.A.C. 139 (note) (S.C.C.).

[173] *Todish*, 1985 CarswellOnt 1394, 18 C.C.C. (3d) 159, 7 O.A.C. 336 (C.A.); *P. (M.)*, 2001 CarswellOnt 66, 52 O.R. (3d) 631, 151 C.C.C. (3d) 193, 139 O.A.C. 129 (C.A.).

[174] *Corbett*, 1988 CarswellBC 756, 1988 CarswellBC 252, [1988] 1 S.C.R. 670, 28 B.C.L.R. (2d) 145, 41 C.C.C. (3d) 385, 64 C.R. (3d) 1, [1988] 4 W.W.R. 481, 34 C.R.R. 54, 85 N.R. 81.

[175] *Morris* (1978), 1978 CarswellQue 38, 1978 CarswellQue 150, [1979] 1 S.C.R. 405, 43 C.C.C. (2d) 129, 6 C.R. (3d) 36, 91 D.L.R. (3d) 161, 23 N.R. 109 at p. 153 [C.C.C.].

low the question in a proper case.[176] In *Stratton*,[177] the Ontario Court of Appeal appeared to put the issue to rest when it concluded that there was no judicial discretion to exclude evidence rendered admissible by the section.

Eight years later, the Supreme Court of Canada examined the entire issue in *Corbett*.[178] There, the constitutionality of section 12 of the *Canada Evidence Act* was challenged on the basis that it infringed an accused's presumption of innocence guaranteed by section 11(d) of the *Charter*. In a majority decision, that argument was rejected. The Court said that the fact that the accused has a criminal record does not mean that he or she should not be believed. It is only a factor that may be taken into account by the trier in assessing an accused's credibility. However, the Court recognized that a trial judge does have a discretion to exclude evidence of previous convictions of an accused in those cases where a mechanical application of section 12 of the *Canada Evidence Act* would undermine the right of an accused to a fair trial as guaranteed by the *Charter*.

Chief Justice Dickson, who delivered the main majority judgment, recognized that there was always a risk that a jury, if told that the accused had a criminal record, might make more of that fact than it should. On the other hand, he also recognized that there was the risk that concealing the prior record of an accused who testified would deprive the jury of information relevant to his credibility, and create a serious risk that they would be presented with a misleading picture. Although accepting that the trial judge has a discretion to exclude prejudicial evidence in an appropriate case, he felt that often the best way to balance and alleviate these risks was to give the jury all of the information and at the same time require the trial judge to give them clear directions as to the limited use that they were to make of such information. Nevertheless, he accepted that the catalogue of factors listed by La Forest J. in his dissenting judgment were useful in determining how a trial judge's discretion should be exercised.

La Forest J. recognized that evidence of an accused's prior convictions harbours the potential to prejudice profoundly the fairness of his trial. It was his view that section 12 gives the trial judge the discretion to exclude prejudicial evidence of previous convictions in an appropriate case. Although it was impossible to provide an exhaustive catalogue of factors in assessing

---

[176] *Powell*, 1977 CarswellOnt 1171, 37 C.C.C. (2d) 117 (Gen. Div.); *Skehan*, 1978 CarswellOnt 1337, 39 C.C.C. (2d) 196 (H.C.).

[177] 1978 CarswellOnt 29, 21 O.R. (2d) 258, 42 C.C.C. (2d) 449, 3 C.R. (3d) 289, 90 D.L.R. (3d) 420 (C.A.).

[178] 1988 CarswellBC 756, 1988 CarswellBC 252, [1988] 1 S.C.R. 670, 28 B.C.L.R. (2d) 145, 41 C.C.C. (3d) 385, 64 C.R. (3d) 1, [1988] 4 W.W.R. 481, 34 C.R.R. 54, 85 N.R. 81.

the probative value or potential prejudice of such evidence, he considered that a began, however, by stating that he regarded the nature of the prior conviction as the most important conviction which involved acts of deceit, fraud, cheating or stealing was more probative of a person's honesty and integrity than an act of violence that had little or no direct bearing on a person's veracity. Another factor creating potential prejudice was the similarity of the prior conviction to the charge before the court.[179] He felt that a trial judge should be wary of admitting such evidence unless it met the stringent test for admitting similar fact evidence. The remoteness or nearness of the previous conviction was also a factor to be considered. He was of the view that a conviction, even one involving an act of dishonesty, which occurred long before, should be generally excluded on the ground of remoteness.

One issue that gave Mr. Justice La Forest concern is the fairness to the Crown of prohibiting the cross-examination of an accused on prior convictions where the defence has made a deliberate attack upon the credibility of a Crown witness, particularly where the case boils down to a credibility contest between the accused and that witness. He was prepared to recognize that, in such instance, the jury was entitled to have before it the record of the accused attacking the character of the Crown witness in order to determine whether the accused was any more worthy of belief than the person attacked. Nevertheless, this was not a factor that should override the concern for a fair trial.

Cases decided since *Corbett* have generally held that the test in determining whether the criminal record of an accused should be excluded is a balancing of interest, that is, a balancing of probative value against prejudicial effect. The right to a fair trial is the context in which the balancing exercise must be considered. The outcome of the balancing of probative value and prejudicial effect is the preservation of a fair trial.[180] For example, in *Saroya*,[181] the accused was charged with aggravated assault and assault causing bodily harm. It was held that the trial judge was correct in not excluding a previous conviction for attempted murder. To deprive the jury of the accused's criminal record would leave the jury with incomplete and

---

[179] *P. (G.F.)*, 1994 CarswellOnt 67, 18 O.R. (3d) 1, 89 C.C.C. (3d) 176, 29 C.R. (4th) 315, 70 O.A.C. 350 (C.A.); *Trudel*, 1994 CarswellQue 167, 1994 CarswellQue 2492, [1994] R.J.Q. 678, 90 C.C.C. (3d) 318, 60 Q.A.C. 138, [1994] A.Q. No. 114 (C.A.).

[180] *Saroya*, 1994 CarswellOnt 122, 36 C.R. (4th) 253, 76 O.A.C. 25, [1994] O.J. No. 2920 (C.A.); *Wilson*, 2006 CarswellOnt 3749, 210 C.C.C. (3d) 23, 39 C.R. (6th) 345 (C.A.).

[181] *Ibid.*

therefore incorrect information about the accused's credibility as a witness and hinder their ability to correctly appreciate the facts. On the other hand, in *Brooks*,[182] the accused was charged with and convicted of murder in the death of a child. The trial judge had permitted the Crown to examine the accused on his entire criminal record including offences of theft under, fraud, breach of probation, failure to comply with a recognizance and assault. The only persons who could have had access to the child on the night of the murder were the accused and the child's mother. Although an appeal was dismissed, it was held that acts of violence such as assault have less bearing on a person's credibility than do acts of dishonesty, such as fraud and theft, and trial judges should be wary of admitting acts of violence to avoid the possibility that the jury might convict the accused on the basis of his disposition to commit such acts.

Whether the Crown will raise the accused's criminal record during cross-examination is usually a crucial factor in the decision of the defence whether to call the accused. In Ontario, it was the common practice for such applications to be raised by the defence before the accused testified and for the trial judge to hear and give a conditional ruling. Thus, for example, if an accused (with convictions for violence) entered the witness box and gave evidence suggesting that he was a peace-loving person and would not commit the offence before the court, the trial judge would permit the Crown to bring out the convictions for violence. The trial judge would frequently inquire as to the nature of the defence and indicate that the ruling might be withdrawn if the defence changed.

Not all courts, however, agreed with this practice. In *Hoffman*,[183] the Alberta Court of Appeal said that the trial judge should not accede to a request by the defence for a ruling whether the Crown would ask him questions about his criminal record before the accused was called. The Court reasoned that since the trial judge's discretion to exclude such evidence was only permitted where the accused's criminal record was of minimal probative value and of such prejudicial effect that a suitable warning to the jury would not suffice against possible misuse, the exercise of his discretion would depend very much on the nature of the evidence of the accused.

---

[182] 1998 CarswellOnt 3866, 41 O.R. (3d) 661, 129 C.C.C. (3d) 227, 20 C.R. (5th) 116, 113 O.A.C. 201, [1998] O.J. No. 3913 (C.A.); reversed 2000 SCC 11, 2000 CarswellOnt 292, 2000 CarswellOnt 293, [2000] 1 S.C.R. 237, 46 O.R. (3d) 640 (headnote only), 141 C.C.C. (3d) 321, 30 C.R. (5th) 201, 182 D.L.R. (4th) 513, 250 N.R. 103, 129 O.A.C. 205, [2000] S.C.J. No. 12.

[183] 1994 CarswellAlta 325, 155 A.R. 275, 32 C.R. (4th) 396, 73 W.A.C. 275 (C.A.).

The issue was eventually resolved by the Supreme Court in *Underwood*.[184] There the Court said that the proper time for the defence to bring a *Corbett application* is after the close of the case for the Crown. At that time, the trial judge should decide, before calling upon the defence, whether the accused's criminal record should be revealed. The trial judge could also, if he or she believed it to be necessary, hold a *voir dire* and inquire what evidence the defence intended to call so that a fully informed ruling could be made on the application. The Court said that the *voir dire* is not a "defence disclosure" and does not create independent rights in the Crown. It should not be treated as an excuse for the Crown to deeply probe the case for the defence. It was pointed out that although the defence always retains the right to lead evidence that was not disclosed at the *voir dire*, the trial judge is entitled to change his or her ruling if the judge believes that the undisclosed evidence would have had a material impact on the Corbett application.

The ruling in *Underwood* is based on the principle that, before the accused decides to call evidence, he or she is entitled to know the case that must be met. The extent to which the accused's criminal record will be admissible will encompass part of the Crown's case. It is justified as part of the broader principle against self-incrimination which has its roots in the presumption of innocence and the power imbalance between the state and the individual. Once the trial judge rules that the prior convictions have probative value in relation to the accused's credibility, it is up to defence counsel to decide how the evidence is to be treated and whether to bring out the particulars of the record.[185]

(e) Cross-examination of a Co-Accused

The right of an accused to full answer and defence gives him the right to cross-examine a co-accused who has testified and given damaging evidence

---

[184] (1997), 1997 CarswellAlta 1080, 1997 CarswellAlta 1081, [1998] 1 S.C.R. 77, 209 A.R. 276, 67 Alta. L.R. (3d) 81, 121 C.C.C. (3d) 117, 12 C.R. (5th) 241, 155 D.L.R. (4th) 13, [1999] 4 W.W.R. 326, 48 C.R.R. (2d) 205, 221 N.R. 161, 160 W.A.C. 276; See also *MacDonald*, 2000 CarswellOnt 2416, 146 C.C.C. (3d) 525, 35 C.R. (5th) 130 (C.A.).

[185] *Boyce*, 1974 CarswellOnt 46, 23 C.C.C. (2d) 16 (C.A.); *Poitras*, 2002 CarswellOnt 26, 1 C.R. (6th) 366 (C.A.)

against him.[186] In such instance, the protection given by *Davison*[187] does not apply to the co-accused. This means that it is open for an accused to cross-examine a co-accused about his character to show that the co-accused is a disreputable person not worthy of belief.[188] The policy of the law is that the right of a co-accused to full answer and defence does not allow him to hide under that umbrella of protection thereby impairing the right of an accused to full answer and defence by asking questions pertinent to his defence. It is generally assumed that a co-accused, who claims that he will be prevented from having a fair trial if the accused is allowed to cross-examine him, will apply to the court to have his trial severed from that of the accused.

Moreover, a co-accused, who exercised his right to remain silent when he was questioned by the police and who testifies at trial against an accused, cannot use the fact that he exercised that right to deprive the accused of the right to challenge his testimony by a full attack on his credibility. In other words, he cannot immunize himself from an attack by the accused to the effect that he said nothing when questioned by the police.[189] However, although an accused can cross-examine his co-accused on the fact that he remained silent when questioned by the police for the purpose of dispelling any evidence given by the co-accused implicating him, he cannot go further. An accused is not permitted to ask the trier of fact to consider the evidence of the co-accused's silence as positive evidence of his guilt on which the Crown may rely to convict him.

Ironically, the right to attack a co-accused who has exercised the right to remain silent places that co-accused in an anomalous situation. As was noted by McLachlin J. in *Creighton*,[190] it obliges the co-accused to make a prior consistent statement in order to avoid cross-examination on his silence. However, it renders him unable to tender that evidence in support of his own credibility because the law of evidence precludes the admission of

---

[186] *Creighton*, 1995 CarswellOnt 12, 1995 CarswellOnt 523, (sub nom. *R. v. Crawford*) [1995] 1 S.C.R. 858, 22 O.R. (3d) 288 (note), 96 C.C.C. (3d) 481, 37 C.R. (4th) 197, 27 C.R.R. (2d) 1, 179 N.R. 161, 81 O.A.C. 359.

[187] 1974 CarswellOnt 559, 6 O.R. (2d) 103, 20 C.C.C. (2d) 424 (C.A.); leave to appeal refused [1974] S.C.R. viii, 6 O.R. (2d) 103n, 20 C.C.C. (2d) 424n.

[188] *Jackson*, 1991 CarswellOnt 119, 68 C.C.C. (3d) 385, 9 C.R. (4th) 57, 51 O.A.C. 92 (C.A.); affirmed 1993 CarswellOnt 997, 1993 CarswellOnt 136, [1993] 4 S.C.R. 573, 86 C.C.C. (3d) 385, 26 C.R. (4th) 178, 109 D.L.R. (4th) 318, 162 N.R. 113, 68 O.A.C. 161.

[189] *Creighton, supra,* note 186.

[190] *Ibid.*

a prior consistent statement to bolster his credibility. She would have precluded the accused from attacking the co-accused's exercise of the right to silence. As far as she was concerned, pre-trial silence was either a right or it was not a right. If it was a right, the trier of fact should not be permitted to draw an adverse inference from its exercise. If adverse inferences were permitted, the right to silence would be effectively lost; no accused jointly charged who wishes to preserve the possibility of putting forth his story at trial could afford to exercise it. If the right to silence means anything, she argued, it means that a suspect has a right to refuse to talk to the police and not be penalized for it. Moreover, once an accused has been informed by the police of his right not to speak, the exercise of this right should not logically found an inference as to his credibility if he later testifies.

11. REBUTTAL EVIDENCE FOR THE PROSECUTION

The general rule as to the order of proof is that the prosecution must introduce all the evidence in its possession that it relies upon to establish its case before it closes. The rule ensures that the defence knows exactly what case it has to meet in response to the case for the Crown.[191] It is intended to prevent an accused from being taken by surprise, and to enable him to investigate by cross-examination the reliability of such evidence before he is called upon to introduce his defence. It is also intended to prevent the undue emphasis or magnification of evidence in relation to other evidence by reason of its late introduction.[192]

The Crown, however, is not expected to anticipate what the defence may be and to lead evidence to refute that defence in advance. For example, the Crown is not required to lead evidence in chief to rebut the defence of alibi, even where the defence has given notice that it intends to raise that issue when called upon to present its case. The Crown is entitled to wait until the defence has called its alibi evidence and lead its evidence by way of rebuttal.[193] Similarly, where the onus is upon the accused to raise a defence under section 16 of the *Criminal Code*, that the accused is not responsible

---

[191] *Krause* (1986), 1986 CarswellBC 330, 1986 CarswellBC 761, [1986] 2 S.C.R. 466, 7 B.C.L.R. (2d) 273, 29 C.C.C. (3d) 385, 14 C.P.C. (2d) 156, 54 C.R. (3d) 294, 33 D.L.R. (4th) 267, [1987] 1 W.W.R. 97, 71 N.R. 6.

[192] *Campbell*, 1977 CarswellOnt 5, 17 O.R. (2d) 673, 38 C.C.C. (2d) 6, 1 C.R. (3d) 309 (C.A.); varied 1977 CarswellOnt 6, 17 O.R. (2d) 673 at 699, 38 C.C.C. (2d) 6 at 32, 1 C.R. (3d) S-49 (C.A.).

[193] *Andrews*, 1979 CarswellBC 546, 8 C.R. (3d) 1 (C.A.); leave to appeal refused (1979), 28 N.R. 537n (S.C.C.); *Rafferty*, 1983 CarswellAlta 69, 43 A.R. 323, 25 Alta. L.R. (2d) 334, 6 C.C.C. (3d) 72, [1983] 4 W.W.R. 511 (C.A.).

because he or she was suffering from a mental disorder, the Crown is not required to lead evidence that the accused was not suffering from a mental disorder as part of its case in chief.[194]

Generally speaking, rebuttal evidence is restricted to evidence to meet new facts presented by the defence. But the accused's mere denial of the prosecution's case during the course of his or her testimony does not constitute new facts permitting the prosecution to repeat its case or to introduce additional evidence to support it. However, the trial judge does have the discretion to admit, in reply, evidence relevant to the Crown's case as a result of defence evidence that the prosecution could not reasonably be expected to anticipate.

For example, evidence that is of marginal importance during the Crown's case may take on added significance as a result of the defence evidence. If that evidence was not a live issue at the end of the Crown's case, then the Crown may be permitted to call evidence in reply to that issue, provided the admission of the evidence would not work an unfairness to the accused.[195] Rebuttal evidence will also be admitted where it is related to an essential issue which may be determinative of the case and which the Crown could not have foreseen would be necessary to prove its case.[196]

An example is *Aalders*.[197] There, the accused, who was charged with first degree murder and robbery in the course of a break-in at the victim's residence and theft of the victim's belongings, had testified that the money found in his possession when he was arrested came in part from his welfare allowance. By way of reply, the trial judge had allowed the Crown to call two welfare workers to testify that the accused had never received social assistance. It was held that the trial judge had not erred in doing so, even though the accused had admitted the robbery. Evidence as to the details of the robbery formed an integral part of the Crown's case, and it was important that any confusion with regard to the accused's statement and testimony on this essential issue be clarified. The Court said that evidence from the welfare officials that the accused had never received welfare payments was relevant and important because it would establish that the robbery was,

[194] *Chaulk* (1990), 1990 CarswellMan 385, 1990 CarswellMan 239, [1990] 3 S.C.R. 1303, 62 C.C.C. (3d) 193, 2 C.R. (4th) 1, [1991] 2 W.W.R. 385, 1 C.R.R. (2d) 1, 69 Man. R. (2d) 161, 119 N.R. 161, [1990] S.C.J. No. 139.

[195] *P. (G.)*, 1996 CarswellOnt 4538, 31 O.R. (3d) 504, 112 C.C.C. (3d) 263, 4 C.R. (5th) 36, 95 O.A.C. 200 (C.A.).

[196] *Aalders*, 1993 CarswellQue 13, 1993 CarswellQue 2043, (sub nom. *R. v. Aalders*) [1993] 2 S.C.R. 482, 82 C.C.C. (3d) 215, 21 C.R. (4th) 141, 103 D.L.R. (4th) 700, 154 N.R. 161, 55 Q.A.C. 161.

[197] *Ibid.*

in all probability, the source of all the money in his possession at the time of his arrest.

Another example of where rebuttal evidence was held to be properly introduced is *Sparrow*,[198] a murder case. There, the accused's car was found containing shell cartridges from the same type of gun used to kill the deceased. Blood stains from the same grouping as the deceased were also found on the trunk of the car. The accused, during the course of his cross-examination, "guessed" that the bloodstains were as a result of a fistfight between the deceased and a friend several days before the killing. The Crown was allowed to call in reply a professor of criminalistics to testify as to the age of the bloodstains because that issue was not a live one until the accused testified.

Atikian,[199] on the other hand, is a straightforward example of the Crown improperly splitting its case and calling, by way of rebuttal, evidence that should have been lead in chief. In *Atikian*, the parents of a 17-month-old infant who had died from malnutrition and bronchial pneumonia were charged with failing, without lawful excuse, to provide the infant with the necessaries of life thereby causing her death. Their defence was that they were simply following the advice of an herbalist and honestly believed that this advice would restore their child to good health. After the defence completed its case, the Crown was allowed by the trial judge to call, by way of rebuttal, the accused's 16-year-old daughter who had given to the police a prior statement in which she told them that her father did not believe in herbalists and that he was constantly urging her mother to take the baby to a doctor or to a hospital. It was held by the Ontario Court of Appeal that the trial judge erred in allowing the Crown to split its case this way. The reply evidence went to the very heart of the case. It was unfair to allow the Crown to lead that evidence in reply when neither parent had been confronted with their daughter's statement during cross-examination, nor given the opportunity to refute it.

However, the rule is not always easy to apply. Appellate courts often disagree as to what constitutes evidence properly the subject of rebuttal, and evidence of facts relevant to prove guilt that should have been called by the Crown during its case in chief. For example, in *Biddle*,[200] the accused was

---

[198] 1979 CarswellOnt 55, 51 C.C.C. (2d) 443, 12 C.R. (3d) 158 (C.A.).

[199] 1990 CarswellOnt 70, 1 O.R. (3d) 263, 62 C.C.C. (3d) 357, 3 C.R. (4th) 77, 42 O.A.C. 214 (C.A.).

[200] 1995 CarswellOnt 7, 1995 CarswellOnt 521, [1995] 1 S.C.R. 761, 22 O.R. (3d) 128 (note), 96 C.C.C. (3d) 321, 36 C.R. (4th) 321, 123 D.L.R. (4th) 22, 178 N.R. 208, 79 O.A.C. 128.

charged with two counts of assault causing bodily harm and two counts of choking, arising out of two separate attacks on women. The victim of the second incident testified that she was attacked in her apartment building between 10:00 p.m. and 10:30 p.m. The accused testified that he was at a show from around 7:30 p.m. to 9:15 p.m. He claimed that after he left the show, he walked his dog and went to visit a friend who was not at home. He then drove to two bars and left his car at a parking garage around 11:25 p.m. and was arrested upon returning to it. The Crown was allowed by the trial judge to call, by way of rebuttal, the evidence of a woman who claimed to have been followed by the accused in his car around 8:30 p.m. while she was driving to the garage of her apartment building. Although that evidence did not directly relate to the time of the attack on the victim, its admission cast doubt on the credibility of the accused with respect to where he was at the time of the attack.

The Ontario Court of Appeal was of the view that the trial judge had not erred in permitting the Crown to call reply evidence. The Supreme Court of Canada, however, disagreed and ordered a new trial. The Court said that since the accused had given an explanation to the police as to his whereabouts that evening, the Crown therefore knew that the defence intended to challenge the identification evidence of the victim and should have called in chief the evidence of the woman who saw him at 8:30 p.m.. Presumably, if the accused had not given an explanation of his whereabouts to the police and offered that explanation for the first time at trial, the evidence of the woman would have been admissible in reply because it could not have been anticipated by the Crown.

Another example of appellate disagreement as to the appropriateness of reply evidence is *Melnichuk*.[201] There the accused borrowed money from the complainant, representing that the loan would be secured by a valid mortgage on his cottage property. The accused gave the complainant a document that he said was a mortgage on the cottage property and represented that he would see that it was registered. However, the document was a forgery and was never registered. The accused then obtained a mortgage from a third party and registered it on his property as a first mortgage. The accused defaulted on the complainant's mortgage. As part of its case in chief, the Crown called a lawyer who testified that the first purported mortgage was a forgery and had not been prepared by his office. In his testimony, the

---

[201] 1995 CarswellOnt 911, 104 C.C.C. (3d) 160, 87 O.A.C. 336 (C.A.); leave to appeal refused (1996), 105 C.C.C. (3d) vi, 204 N.R. 74 (note), 94 O.A.C. 80 (note) (S.C.C.); reversed 1997 CarswellOnt 798, 1997 CarswellOnt 799, [1997] 1 S.C.R. 602, 114 C.C.C. (3d) 503, 146 D.L.R. (4th) 686, 209 N.R. 321, 99 O.A.C. 218.

accused said that he believed the complainant's mortgage had been registered and that he was led to believe that the third party mortgage was a second mortgage on his property. This belief, he said, was based on a letter that he received from the lawyer and he then produced the letter. However, the letter had not been shown to the lawyer during his cross-examination by defence counsel. The trial judge had allowed the Crown in reply to call the lawyer to say that he would not have placed a second mortgage on the property and was certain that the accused had advised him that the third party's mortgage was to be a first mortgage. The majority of the Court held that the introduction of the letter for the first time by the accused could not have been reasonably anticipated by the Crown. In dissent, Doherty J.A. held that the issue of whether the third party mortgage was a first mortgage or a second mortgage was part of its case and that such evidence should have been led in chief. A further appeal by the accused was allowed by the Supreme Court[202] who held, relying on the reasons given by Doherty J.A., that the trial judge had erroneously permitted the Crown to call reply evidence.

As was pointed out previously, rebuttal evidence is only allowed where the evidence relates to a fact in issue. The Crown is not allowed to call rebuttal evidence to contradict a collateral matter. Again, the purpose of the rule is to ensure that the trier of fact concentrates on the issue in dispute and is not sidetracked by a collateral matter. Thus, if an accused goes into the witness box and gives evidence about a matter that is not relevant to a fact in issue, he cannot be contradicted by evidence in reply. The Crown is bound by his answer.

Unfortunately, the rule allows an accused to go into the witness stand and make all kinds of unfounded allegations against the witnesses for the Crown that cannot be refuted by evidence in reply. It does not mean that the trier has to accept the evidence given by the accused. It only means that the Crown cannot call evidence to directly contradict the accused on that issue.

An example of where this occurred is *Krause*.[203] In *Krause*, a murder case, it was alleged that the killing arose out of a drug deal between the accused and the deceased. At trial, the accused testified that it was a regular thing during the investigation for the police to take him down to the police station and for them to threaten to harass other drug dealers and say that they had been given the dealer's names by the accused. He also testified that the police had shown him a gory photograph of the deceased on the

---

202 1997 CarswellOnt 798, 1997 CarswellOnt 799, [1997] 1 S.C.R. 602, 114 C.C.C. (3d) 503, 146 D.L.R. (4th) 686, 209 N.R. 321, 99 O.A.C. 218.
203 1986 CarswellBC 330, 1986 CarswellBC 761, [1986] 2 S.C.R. 466, 7 B.C.L.R. (2d) 273, 29 C.C.C. (3d) 385, 14 C.P.C. (2d) 156, 54 C.R. (3d) 294, 33 D.L.R. (4th) 267, [1987] 1 W.W.R. 97, 71 N.R. 61.

first interview. The trial judge had permitted the Crown to call evidence to rebut the allegations. The Supreme Court said that he had erred in doing so. Evidence as to police integrity and their conduct in relation to the accused during the investigation was collateral to the main and only issue in the case, that is, whether the accused had killed the deceased, and should not have been admitted by the trial judge.

12. SURREBUTTAL BY THE DEFENCE

As a general rule, the Crown is allowed the last opportunity to call evidence by way of rebuttal to new facts raised by the defence that the Crown could not have reasonably anticipated. However, some authorities have extended a right of rebuttal, or what might be more properly called surrebuttal, to the defence. A closer look at those authorities reveals that they have not created new law. They have merely given the defence the right to rebut facts raised by the Crown for the first time in response to a defence that must be raised by an accused, such as a mental disorder that renders him incapable of appreciating the nature and quality of his act or omission or of knowing that it was wrong.

As Chief Justice Lamer noted in *Chaulk*[204] where the defence was insanity (now not guilty by reason of mental disorder):

> First, the Crown cannot be expected to adduce evidence as part of its case-in-chief to meet a defence that the accused might possibly raise; this principle is not altered by the fact that the accused may warn the Crown that it intends to raise a particular defence. Secondly, a requirement that the Crown adduce evidence in chief to establish the sanity of the accused would defeat the presumption contained in s. 16(4).[205]

For example, in *Ewart*,[206] the accused, who was charged with first degree murder, raised the defence of insanity and called a psychologist who testified that the accused was suffering from a particular disease of the mind. In reply, the Crown called three psychiatrists who said that the accused did not have that particular disease of the mind, but had a psychopathic personality. Following that testimony, the accused attempted to re-call its expert to reply to that evidence, but was refused by the trial judge. It was held by the British Columbia Court of Appeal that since the Crown's evidence was not a

---

[204] (1990), 1990 CarswellMan 385, 1990 CarswellMan 239, [1990] 3 S.C.R. 1303, 62 C.C.C. (3d) 193, 2 C.R. (4th) 1, [1991] 2 W.W.R. 385, 1 C.R.R. (2d) 1, 69 Man. R. (2d) 161, 119 N.R. 161, [1990] S.C.J. No. 139.

[205] *Ibid.*, at p. 52 [C.R.].

[206] 1989 CarswellBC 598, 52 C.C.C. (3d) 280 (C.A.).

denial of the thesis advanced by the defence, but an alternative explanation of the accused's conduct, the rules regarding the permissible scope of surrebuttal must be applied liberally in order to allow the accused to make full answer and defence.

Similarly, in *Rhodes*,[207] the accused was charged with first degree murder based on an allegation of a killing during the commission of a rape. The defence called expert evidence to show that the accused did not suffer from a predisposition to engage in sexual assaults. By way of rebuttal, the Crown was then allowed to call a witness who said that she had been raped by the accused two months before the killing. However, the defence was denied the right to call evidence to rebut the witness's allegations. It was held that since such reply evidence went to show the pre-disposition that the defence psychiatrist had rejected, the trial judge erred in refusing the accused the right to call witnesses in surrebuttal as to the rape allegations.

One final matter should be noted in respect of surrebuttal evidence. Surrebuttal will not, as a general proposition, cure the improper admission by a trial judge of rebuttal evidence by the Crown that should have been introduced in chief.[208] In other words, where the Crown has been allowed to lead evidence in rebuttal that should have been led in chief, the Crown cannot argue that the defence has not been prejudiced by the admission of such evidence because it has been allowed to call surrebuttal evidence in reply to that evidence.

13. ADDRESSES OF COUNSEL AND THE CHARGE TO THE JURY

When all of the evidence is completed, counsel (or the accused where unrepresented by counsel) are entitled to address the jury or, in the case of trial by judge alone, the judge. Section 651(1) of the *Criminal Code* requires the accused, or the accused's counsel where the accused is represented by counsel, to address the jury first if the defence has called any evidence. The same rule usually applies where the accused has elected trial by judge alone, although the trial judge may order otherwise. If the defence has called no evidence, then section 651(3) of the *Code* gives the defence the right to address the jury last. The same practice is generally followed where the trial is by judge alone, subject to the discretion of the trial judge.

---

[207] 1981 CarswellBC 445, 59 C.C.C. (2d) 426, 21 C.R. (3d) 245 (C.A.).
[208] *Biddle, supra*, note 200.

It is generally recognized that both counsel are entitled to a fair degree of latitude in their closing addresses to the jury. As the Ontario Court of Appeal said in *Daly*[209]

> A closing address is an exercise in advocacy. It is a culmination of a hard fought adversarial proceeding. Crown counsel, like any other advocate, is entitled to advance his or her position forcefully and effectively. Juries expect that both counsel will present their positions in that manner and no doubt expect and accept a degree of rhetorical passion in that presentation.

However, there are well-settled limits on the Crown's address. Crown counsel is only entitled to put before the jury matters which are supported by the evidence presented at trial, not from his or her personal experiences or observations.[210] The Crown must abstain from inflammatory rhetoric, demeaning commentary and sarcasm. Crown counsel must not misstate the facts or the law or invite the jury to engage in speculation. Moreover, it is improper for Crown counsel to express a personal opinion about the veracity of any witnesses, particularly the accused, or to express an opinion about the guilt of the accused.[211]

There are two reasons for this rule. The first is that it is irrelevant; the veracity of the witnesses or the guilt of the accused is a matter for the jury or judge where the trial is by judge alone. For that reason, similar submissions by the defence are not permitted. The second is that such comments made by a representative of the Crown may unfairly influence the jury.

In the charge to the jury, the judge is required to review the evidence presented at trial and instruct the jury on the law which they are to apply to that evidence. Although the judge is entitled to express an opinion about the importance of any evidence presented or the credibility of any witness, it must be made clear to the jury that they are not bound to accept that opinion. The judge must remember the enormous influence that he or she has with the jury and must try to maintain a balance of fairness. On the other hand, the judge does have the duty to stress to the jury that while they are the sole judges of the facts and the weight to be given to the evidence presented, they must accept the law that he or she has given them.

---

[209] 1992 CarswellOnt 774, 57 O.A.C. 70 (C.A.) at p. 76 [O.A.C.]; see also See also *Mallory*, 2007 ONCA 46, 2007 CarswellOnt 348, 217 C.C.C. (3d) 266 at para. 339 and *Boudreau*, 2012 ONCA 830, 2012 CarswellOnt 14986.

[210] *Pisani* (1970), 1970 CarswellOnt 210, 1970 CarswellOnt 210F, [1971] S.C.R. 738, 1 C.C.C. (2d) 477, 15 D.L.R. (3d) 1.

[211] *Boucher* (1954), 1954 CarswellQue 14, *(sub nom. Boucher v. R.)* [1955] S.C.R. 16, 110 C.C.C. 263, 20 C.R. 1.

The trial judge must explain to the jury that the burden of proof throughout is on the Crown and that they must, as a matter of law, acquit the accused if they have a reasonable doubt as to his or her guilt. In assessing whether the Crown has met that burden of proof, the jury must be told that they must consider the evidence as a whole.[212] It is improper for the judge to tell the jury that they must be satisfied beyond a reasonable doubt with respect to each piece of evidence upon which the Crown relies to prove the accused's guilt. That rule also applies with respect to any statement or admission made by the accused.[213] The trial judge must also outline to the jury what verdicts they are entitled to return on each count with respect to possible included offences. It is improper, however, for the judge to ask the jury to particularize their verdict, as is common in England. In England, the jury is frequently asked to explain the basis of their verdict in manslaughter prosecutions so that the judge will know upon what factual basis to sentence the accused.[214] The Canadian rule is that since the jury is entitled to arrive at a unanimous verdict for different reasons and on separate evidential bases, they have right to return a general verdict and need not explain it.[215]

Upon completion of the charge to the jury, they will be asked to retire to consider their verdict. In the case of a judge alone, the judge may deliver his or her verdict at the conclusion of argument by counsel, or the judge may reserve and deliver judgment at a future time.

14. RE-OPENING THE CASE FOR THE DEFENCE

The defence is entitled to apply to the judge to re-open the case in order to permit the defence to introduce further evidence on behalf of an accused at any time before the jury (or the judge, in a case of trial by judge alone) has rendered its verdict. Although such an application may also be made after a conviction has been entered in a case of trial by judge alone, no such application may be made after the jury has rendered its verdict. The reason

---

[212] *Morin*, 1988 CarswellOnt 82, 1988 CarswellOnt 967, [1988] 2 S.C.R. 345, 44 C.C.C. (3d) 193, 66 C.R. (3d) 1, 88 N.R. 161, 30 O.A.C. 81.

[213] *MacKenzie*, 1993 CarswellNS 12, 1993 CarswellNS 270, [1993] 1 S.C.R. 212, 118 N.S.R. (2d) 290, 78 C.C.C. (3d) 193, 18 C.R. (4th) 133, 327 A.P.R. 290, 146 N.R. 321.

[214] *Solomon* (1984), 6 Cr. App. R. 120, [1984] Crim. L.R. 433 (Eng. C.A.).

[215] *Tuckey*, 1985 CarswellOnt 100, 20 C.C.C. (3d) 502, 46 C.R. (3d) 97, 9 O.A.C. 218 (C.A.).

in the latter case is that once a jury has rendered its verdict, the trial judge becomes *functus*.

If the application is made before conviction, the judge must first be satisfied that the proposed evidence is relevant to a material issue in the case.[216] Once it is determined that the witness has relevant evidence, the judge must consider the potential prejudice to the other party should the defence be permitted to re-open the evidence. Finally, the judge must consider the effect of re-opening the evidence on the orderly and expeditious conduct of the trial. If the application to re-open the evidence is based on nothing more than a desire to reverse an earlier tactical decision, then the judge is entitled to refuse the application as being detrimental to the orderly conduct of the trial proceedings.

Where the trial is by judge alone and the trial judge has convicted the accused, a more rigorous test is required to protect the integrity of the process, including the enhanced interest in finality. Here the judge is usually required to apply the criteria for admissibility of fresh evidence on appeal.[217] Under that test, evidence will generally not be admitted if, by due diligence, it could have been adduced at trial subject to the recognition that this general principle will not be applied as strictly in a criminal case as in a civil case. The evidence should also be relevant in the sense that it bears upon a decisive or potentially decisive issue in the trial. It should also be credible in the sense that it is reasonably capable of belief. Finally, the evidence should be such that, if believed, it could reasonably, when taken with other evidence adduced at trial, be expected to have affected the result.

---

[216] *Hayward*, 1993 CarswellOnt 1162, 86 C.C.C. (3d) 193, 67 O.A.C. 379 (C.A.).

[217] *Kowall*, 1996 CarswellOnt 3091, 108 C.C.C. (3d) 481, 50 C.R. (4th) 271, 92 O.A.C. 82 (C.A.); leave to appeal refused [1997] 1 S.C.R. viii (note), 111 C.C.C. (3d) vi, 208 N.R. 319 (note), 98 O.A.C. 400 (note); *I. (A.)*, 2010 CarswellAlta 2702, 265 C.C.C. (3d) 22 (C.A.),

9
PRESUMPTIONS AND BURDENS OF PROOF

1. PRESUMPTIONS GENERALLY

Everyone involved in the field of criminal law knows the fundamental rule that a person accused of a crime is presumed innocent, and that the burden of proof upon the Crown is to establish the guilt of an accused beyond a reasonable doubt. These well-known examples of presumptions and burdens of proof, however, do not easily explain the distinction between the two.

An instructive definition of presumptions was offered by Chief Justice Dickson of the Supreme Court in *Oakes*:[1]

> In determining the meaning of these words, it is helpful to consider in a general sense the nature of presumptions. Presumptions can be classified into two general categories: presumptions without basic facts and presumptions with basic facts. A presumption without a basic fact is simply a conclusion which is to be drawn until the contrary is proved. A presumption

---

[1] 1986 CarswellOnt 95, 1986 CarswellOnt 1001, [1986] 1 S.C.R. 103, 53 O.R. (2d) 719, 24 C.C.C. (3d) 321, 50 C.R. (3d) 1, 26 D.L.R. (4th) 200, 19 C.R.R. 308, 65 N.R. 87, 14 O.A.C. 335, relying upon *Cross on Evidence*, 5th ed., at pp. 122-23).

with a basic fact entails a conclusion to be drawn upon proof of the basic fact . . .

Basic fact presumptions can be further categorized into permissive and mandatory presumptions. A permissive presumption leaves it optional as to whether the inference of the presumed fact is drawn following proof of the basic fact. A mandatory presumption requires that the inference be made.

Presumptions may also be either rebuttable or irrebuttable. If a presumption is rebuttable, there are three potential ways the presumed fact can be rebutted. First, the accused may be required merely to raise a reasonable doubt as to its existence. Secondly, the accused may have an evidentiary burden to adduce sufficient evidence to bring into question the truth of the presumed fact. Thirdly, the accused may have a legal or persuasive burden to prove on a balance of probabilities the non-existence of the presumed fact.

Finally, presumptions are often referred to as either presumptions of law or presumptions of fact. The latter entails 'frequently recurring examples of circumstantial evidence' . . . while the former involves actual legal rules.[2]

Presumptions are thus really aids to assist a court in determining the issues before it. They are not, in themselves, either evidence or argument, although they may be based on general experience or probability, or even on policy and convenience. A few examples, using the categories outlined by Chief Justice Dickson, offer assistance.

Section 354(1) of the *Criminal Code*[3] makes it an offence for anyone to have in his or her possession any property knowing that it was obtained by the commission in Canada of an indictable offence. To succeed on this charge, the Crown must establish the following: first, that the accused had the property in his or her possession; second, that the property was obtained by the commission in Canada of an offence punishable by indictment (usually stolen); and third, that the accused knew that it was obtained by the commission in Canada of an indictable offence, in other words, that he or she knew that it was stolen.

The doctrine of recent possession, a common law rule, states that where an accused is found in possession of goods proved to have been *recently* stolen, the judge or jury, as the case may be, may infer not only that the accused had possession of the goods knowing them to have been stolen, but also that he or she participated in whatever offence was committed to obtain them. All the Crown has to establish is that the goods were found in the possession of the accused and that they were recently stolen. Common experience tells us that people in possession of goods that were recently stolen

---

[2] *Ibid.*, at pp. 330-31 [C.C.C.].

[3] R.S.C. 1985, c. C-46.

or obtained illegally should have some knowledge of how they were obtained.

The law then casts upon the accused a presumption of guilty knowledge unless, during the course of the trial, an explanation is offered. The rule is that the judge must tell the jury (or him or herself if judge alone) that they *may*, not that they *must*, in the absence of an explanation that might reasonably be true, find the accused guilty.[4]

This is a permissive presumption. It leaves optional the question whether the inference of the presumed fact (that is, guilty knowledge) should be drawn following proof of the basic fact (possession by the accused of goods recently stolen). It does not require the inference to be drawn.

Another example may assist in understanding what is meant by a mandatory presumption. Section 354(2) of the *Code* specifically provides that where an accused is found in possession of a motor vehicle that has the identification number wholly or partially obliterated, two presumptions will arise: the first is that the vehicle was obtained by the commission of an indictable offence; the second is that the accused knew that the vehicle was obtained by the commission of an indictable offence. However, this statutory presumption, unlike the common law doctrine of recent possession, is a mandatory presumption of law because section 354(2) provides that where the basic facts are established (possession of a motor vehicle by the accused with the identification number wholly or partially obliterated), this will amount to *proof* that the accused had the vehicle in his possession *knowing* that it was obtained by the commission of an indictable offence. Unlike a permissive presumption, a mandatory presumption requires the judge or jury to conclude that the presumed fact has been established unless there is evidence to the contrary. It is true that the evidence to the contrary need only raise a reasonable doubt. However, if the accused fails to raise a reasonable doubt, the judge is required to instruct the jury that they *must*, not simply *may*, convict the accused.[5]

Before leaving this area, two important presumptions should be discussed briefly.

---

[4] *Ungaro*, 1950 CarswellBC 5, [1950] S.C.R. 430, 96 C.C.C. 245, 9 C.R. 328, [1950] 2 D.L.R. 593.

[5] *Boyle*, 1983 CarswellOnt 88, (sub nom. *Boyle v. R.)* 41 O.R. (2d) 713, 5 C.C.C. (3d) 193, 35 C.R. (3d) 34, 148 D.L.R. (3d) 449, 5 C.R.R. 218 (C.A.).

2. SPECIFIC PRESUMPTIONS

(a) The Presumption of Innocence

The presumption of innocence has been long recognized under the common law. In *Woolmington v. Director of Public Prosecutions*,[6] Viscount Sankey L.C. wrote:

> Throughout the web of the English Criminal Law one golden thread is always to be seen, that it is the duty of the prosecution to prove the prisoner's guilt subject to what I have already said as to the defence of insanity and subject also to any statutory exception. If, at the end of and on whole of the case, there is a reasonable doubt, created by the evidence given by either the prosecution or the prisoner ... the prosecution has not made out the case and the prisoner is entitled to an acquittal. No matter what the charge or where the trial, the principle that the prosecution must prove the guilt of the prisoner is part of the common law of England and no attempt to whittle it down can be entertained.[7]

In *Oakes*,[8] Chief Justice Dickson explained that,

> The presumption of innocence protects the fundamental liberty and human dignity of any and every person accused by the State of criminal conduct. An individual charged with a criminal offence faces grave social and personal consequences, including potential loss of physical liberty, subjection to social stigma and ostracism from the community, as well as other social, psychological and economic harms. In light of the gravity of these consequences, the presumption of innocence is crucial. It ensures that until the State proves an accused's guilt beyond all reasonable doubt, he or she is innocent. This is essential in a society committed to fairness and social justice. The presumption of innocence confirms our faith in humankind; it reflects our belief that individuals are decent and law-abiding members of the community until proven otherwise.

This presumption received international recognition in the Universal Declaration of Human Rights adopted December 10, 1948 by the General Assembly of the United Nations and by the International Covenant on Civil and Political Rights, 1966, article 14(2). It has also been constitutionally

---

[6] [1935] A.C. 462, 25 Cr. App. R. 72 (U.K. H.L.).

[7] *Ibid.*, at pp. 481-82 [A.C.].

[8] 1986 CarswellOnt 95, 1986 CarswellOnt 1001, [1986] 1 S.C.R. 103, 24 C.C.C. (3d) 321, 50 C.R. (3d) 1 at para. 29.

guaranteed in Canada by section 11(d) of the *Charter Rights and Freedoms*. Section 11(d) provides:

> Any person charged with an offence has the right
>
> > (d) to be presumed innocent until proven guilty according to law in a fair and public hearing by an independent and impartial tribunal.

The presumption of innocence simply means that there is no obligation upon an accused to respond to a charge either by giving evidence personally or by calling other witnesses. It is a presumption that remains with the accused from the very beginning of the trial until the very end. There is no burden of proof upon the accused. That burden is on the Crown to prove each and every essential element of the offence charged against the accused beyond a reasonable doubt.[9]

(b) The Evidentiary Burden on the Defence

(i) Mental Disorder

Although the ultimate burden of proof always remains upon the Crown to prove the guilt of an accused beyond a reasonable doubt, the *Criminal Code* specifically casts an evidentiary burden upon an accused in certain instances. For example, section 16(1) of the *Criminal Code* provides that "no person is criminally responsible for an act committed or an omission made while suffering from a mental disorder that rendered the person incapable of appreciating the nature and quality of the act or omission or of knowing that it was wrong". However, section 16(2) goes on to provide that "every person is presumed not to suffer from a mental disorder so as to be exempt from criminal responsibility by virtue of subsection (1), unless the contrary is proved on the balance of probabilities". Subsection 3 of s. 16 thus imposes an evidentiary burden of proof upon the defence to prove otherwise. It provides that the "burden of proof that an accused was suffering from a mental disorder so as to be exempt from criminal responsibility is on the party that raises the issue". Although it is usually the defence that raises the defence that the accused was suffering from a mental disorder so as to be exempt from criminal responsibility, both the Crown and the defence have a right to raise the question. However, section 16(3) says that whoever raises the question must bear the evidentiary burden of proof.

This means that while the Crown must tender, as part of its case, evidence that will establish the existence of all elements of the offence with which the accused is charged, the Crown need not also adduce evidence in-chief to

---

[9] Per Lamer J. in *Dubois*, 1985 CarswellAlta 222, 1985 CarswellAlta 615, [1985] 2 S.C.R. 350, 22 C.C.C. (3d) 513, 48 C.R. (3d) 193 at p. 357 [S.C.R.].

challenge a defence of mental disorder that an accused might possibly raise. This principle is not altered by the fact that the accused may warn the Crown that it intends to raise that particular defence. A requirement that the Crown adduce evidence in chief to establish the sanity of the accused would defeat the presumption contained in section 16(2). However, the onus of proof upon the defence to establish a defence of mental disorder is only proof on a balance of probabilities.[10] This lesser standard is not as onerous as the one upon the Crown of establishing the accused's guilt "beyond a reasonable doubt".

The onus of proof upon an accused where a defence of insanity was raised was not always on a balance of probabilities. Prior to 1921, the defence had to "satisfy" the jury that the accused was insane, which was akin to proof beyond a reasonable doubt. In 1921 the Supreme Court reversed the conviction of a man charged with murder after the trial judge told the jury that they ought to convict the accused unless he was able to establish that he was insane at the time of the murder *beyond a reasonable doubt"*. The Supreme Court held that he had erred because the onus of proof was on a balance of probabilities.[11]

Section 16 imposes on the defence (or the Crown if it raises the issue) both the evidential burden of leading some evidence to demonstrate that the accused was suffering from mental disorder at the time of the offence and the persuasive burden on a balance of probabilities.[12] In determining whether the evidential burden has been satisfied, the trial judge must ask whether there is any evidence upon which a reasonable trier of fact, properly instructed, could conclude that the defence could succeed. In answering that question, the judge does not evaluate the quality, weight or reliability of the evidence. That is for the jury to decide. Once satisfied that the burden has been met, the judge must then assume the truth of the evidence that tends to support it, leaving the reliability, credibility, and weight of the evidence to be determined by the jury.[13] The persuasive burden on the defence is discharged by proof on a balance of probabilities.

Where the defence is insane or non-insane automatism, there is also a similar evidentiary burden. The defence has an evidentiary burden of leading evidence upon which a properly instructed jury could find that the ac-

---

[10] *Chaulk*, 1990 CarswellMan 385, 1990 CarswellMan 239, 62 C.C.C. (3d) 193, 2 C.R. (4th) 1 (S.C.C.).

[11] *Clark*, 1921 CarswellNB 3, 35 C.C.C. 261 (S.C.C.).

[12] *Fontaine*, 2004 CarswellQue 814, 2004 CarswellQue 815, (sub nom. *R. v. Fontaine*) [2004] 1 S.C.R. 702, 183 C.C.C. (3d) 1, 18 C.R. (6th) 203.

[13] *Fontaine, ibid.*

cused acted involuntarily on a balance of probabilities. As Dickson J. said in *Rabey*,[14]

> In principle, the defence of automatism should be available whenever there is evidence of unconsciousness throughout the commission of the crime, that cannot be attributed to fault or negligence of his part. Such evidence should be supported by expert medical opinion that the accused did not feign memory loss and that there is no underlying pathological condition which points to a disease requiring detention and treatment.

This means that in all cases of insane or non-insane automatism, the defence must make an assertion of involuntariness and call confirming psychiatric evidence. The trial judge must weigh all of the available evidence on a case-by-case basis, such as the severity of the triggering stimulus; corroborating evidence of bystanders; corroborating medical history of automatistic-like dissociative states; whether there is evidence of a motive for the crime; and whether the alleged trigger of the automatism is also the victim of the automatistic violence. Again, the trial judge must ask whether there is any evidence upon which a reasonable trier of fact, properly instructed, could conclude that the defence could succeed. In answering that question, the judge does not evaluate the quality, weight or reliability of the evidence. That is for the jury to decide. Once satisfied that the burden has been met, the judge must then assume the truth of the evidence that tends to support it, leaving the reliability, credibility, and weight of the evidence to be determined by the jury.

It has been held by the Supreme Court that the presumption of innocence guaranteed by section 11(d) of the *Charter* is infringed by the shift of onus of proof in section 16(3), because it permits a conviction in spite of a reasonable doubt in the mind of the trier of fact as to the guilt of the accused.[15] However, section 16(3) constitutes a reasonable limit on the presumption of innocence.[16] The objective of section 16(3), *which is a purely evidentiary section*, is to avoid placing on the Crown the impossibly onerous burden of disproving insanity to secure the conviction of the guilty. This objective is

---

[14] 1980 CarswellOnt 71, 1980 CarswellOnt 35, [1980] 2 S.C.R. 513, 54 C.C.C. (2d) 1, 15 C.R. (3d) 225 (Eng.), 20 C.R. (3d) 1 (Fr.) at p. 552 [S.C.R.], ; affirming 1977 CarswellOnt 24, 17 O.R. (2d) 1, 37 C.C.C. (2d) 461 (C.A.); adopted in *Parks*, 1992 CarswellOnt 996, 1992 CarswellOnt 107, [1992] 2 S.C.R. 871, 75 C.C.C. (3d) 287, 15 C.R. (4th) 289. See *Stone*, 1999 CarswellBC 1064, 1999 CarswellBC 1065, [1999] 2 S.C.R. 290, 134 C.C.C. (3d) 353, 24 C.R. (5th) 1.

[15] *Chaulk* (1990), 1990 CarswellMan 385, 1990 CarswellMan 239, [1990] 3 S.C.R. 1303, 62 C.C.C. (3d) 193, 2 C.R. (4th) 1, [1991] 2 W.W.R. 385, 1 C.R.R. (2d) 1, 69 Man. R. (2d) 161, 119 N.R. 161, [1990] S.C.J. No. 139.

[16] Section 1 of the *Charter*.

of sufficient importance to warrant limiting a constitutionally protected right.

(ii) Other Evidentiary Burdens

Not all federal statutes that have imposed a burden upon an accused to disprove an element of proof normally required by the Crown have survived the section 11(d) constitutional imperative. For example, section 8 of the former *Narcotic Control Act* provided that if the court found an accused in possession of a narcotic, the accused was presumed to be in possession for the purpose of trafficking; and that, absent the accused's establishing the contrary, he had to be convicted of trafficking. In *Oakes*,[17] the Supreme Court decided that section 8 infringed the presumption of innocence in section 11(d) because it required the accused to prove he was not guilty of trafficking once the basic fact of possession was proven. The Court accepted that Parliament's concern that drug trafficking be decreased was substantial and pressing, and that its objective of protecting society from the grave ills of drug trafficking for the purposes of section 1 of the *Charter* could potentially, in certain cases, warrant the overriding of a constitutionally protected right. However, it was noted that there was no rational connection between the basic fact of possession and the presumed fact of possession for the purpose of trafficking. The possession of a small or negligible quantity of narcotics would not support the inference of trafficking.

Although a burden of proof upon an accused requiring proof on a balance of probabilities will usually run afoul of section 11(d), a lesser burden may not. For example, section 153.1 imposes an evidentiary burden on an accused charged with sexual exploitation of a person who has a mental or physical disability to show that the complainant consented. Section 153.1(6) provides,

> (6) If an accused alleges that he or she believed that the complainant consented to the conduct that is the subject-matter of the charge, a judge, *if satisfied that there is sufficient evidence* and that, if believed by the jury, the evidence would constitute a defence, shall instruct the jury, when reviewing all the evidence relating to the determination of the honesty of the accused's belief, to consider the presence or absence of reasonable grounds for that belief.

Here the requirement of satisfying the judge that "there is sufficient evidence" would probably run afoul of section 11(d) if it imposed an obligation upon the accused to demonstrate on a balance of probabilities that the

---

[17] 1986 CarswellOnt 95, 1986 CarswellOnt 1001, [1986] 1 S.C.R. 103, 24 C.C.C. (3d) 321, 50 C.R. (3d) 1.

complainant consented. Although what constitutes *sufficient evidence* to satisfy the burden will often depend upon the case which the Crown must present, a mere assertion by the accused that he thought that the complainant was consenting will not satisfy that burden. Common sense would require the defence to present some other evidence or circumstances that would demonstrate an air of reality to the assertion that the complainant consented in order for the judge to leave the issue with the jury.

An example of where an evidentiary burden is imposed on the defence arises in cases where an accused is charged with sexual assault and claims that he had an honest belief that the complainant consented. Here the Supreme Court has imposed a burden upon the accused to lead some evidence of consent other than a mere assertion that the complainant consented. In *Bulmer*, McIntyre J. delivering the majority decision of the Supreme Court pointed out,[18]

> There will not be an air of reality about a mere statement that "I thought she was consenting" not supported to some degree by other evidence or circumstances arising in the case. If that mere assertion were sufficient to require a trial judge to put the "mistake of fact" defence, it would be a simple matter in any rape case to make such an assertion and, regardless of all other circumstances, require the defence to be put.

Lamer J., concurring, agreed.[19]

> If that means that the trial judge is not required to put the defence to the jury merely because the accused's lawyer has referred to the defence in argument then I agree. There must be some evidence supporting the defence before it is put to the jury.

Once the defence leads evidence to satisfy the evidentiary burden, then the ultimate burden of proof lies upon the Crown to prove the guilt of the accused beyond a reasonable doubt.

3. BURDENS OF PROOF

The close relationship between presumptions and burdens of proof often make it difficult to distinguish between the two. It is probably easier to state what the burden of proof is rather than to define it. In a dispute between parties, the burden of proof is the evidentiary burden that the court imposes on one side or the other. The general rule is that the burden of proof lies on

---

[18] *B. (E.H.)*, 1987 CarswellBC 702, 1987 CarswellBC 149, (sub nom. *R. v. B.*) [1987] 1 S.C.R. 782, 33 C.C.C. (3d) 385, 58 C.R. (3d) 48 at para. 12.

[19] *Ibid.*, at para. 22.

the party who asserts the affirmative of the issue or question in dispute. The extent of that burden will vary depending on the nature of the trial.

For example, in a civil trial, where A is suing B for breach of contract, the burden of proof is upon A to establish that breach. In civil cases, the onus of proof is simply on a balance of probabilities. The most vivid example of that onus is the tipping of scales slightly in favour of the person who has the burden. If A tips the scales in his favour, ever so slightly, he wins. If the scales are tipped in favour of B, then A loses because he has failed to discharge the burden. A also loses if, at the end of the trial, the scales remain evenly balanced.

In a criminal case, the burden is always upon the prosecution and never shifts to the accused, unless there is a "reverse onus" defence such as mental disorder under section 16 of the *Criminal Code*. The burden is also more onerous. That burden is to establish the guilt of the accused beyond a reasonable doubt. The trial judge is required to make it clear to the jury that the Crown is required to do more than prove the accused guilty on a balance of probabilities.[20]

A traditional formula that judges often used in defining reasonable doubt for the jury was:

> A reasonable doubt is an honest doubt, a fair doubt, one based upon reason and common sense. It is a real doubt, not some imaginary or frivolous doubt conjured up in the mind of a juror to avoid an unpleasant or painful duty.[21]

In the past, the courts felt that the term "reasonable doubt" was self-defining and the trial judge need not go any further. In *Campbell*,[22] Martin J.A. wrote:

> The term "reasonable doubt" is, to a great extent, self-defining and its meaning is, I think, generally well understood by the average person. Attempts to further amplify its meaning have often proved unsuccessful and, as a general rule, it is both undesirable and unnecessary to elaborate upon its meaning by departing from the traditional and accepted formulations.[23]

---

[20] *Starr*, 2000 SCC 40, 2000 CarswellMan 449, 2000 CarswellMan 450, [2000] 2 S.C.R. 144, 147 C.C.C. (3d) 449, 36 C.R. (5th) 1, 190 D.L.R. (4th) 591, [2000] 11 W.W.R. 1, 148 Man. R. (2d) 161, 258 N.R. 250, 224 W.A.C. 161, [2000] S.C.J. No. 40; *K. (S.)*, 2003 CarswellOnt 2325, 177 C.C.C. (3d) 90 (C.A.).

[21] *Roloson*, 1978 CarswellOnt 1210, 42 C.C.C. (2d) 262 (C.A.); *Tuckey*, 1985 CarswellOnt 100, 20 C.C.C. (3d) 502, 46 C.R. (3d) 97 (C.A.).

[22] 1977 CarswellOnt 5, 17 O.R. (2d) 673, 38 C.C.C. (2d) 6, 1 C.R. (3d) 309 (C.A.); varied 1977 CarswellOnt 6, 17 O.R. (2d) 673 at 699, 38 C.C.C. (2d) 6 at 32, 1 C.R. (3d) S-49 (C.A.).

[23] *Ibid.*, at p. 25 [C.C.C.].

For many years, trial judges frequently defined reasonable doubt by indicating that absolute certainty was not required. However, in *Starr*,[24] the Supreme Court said that this was wrong. A judge must make it clear to the jury that the Crown is required to do more than prove the accused's guilt on a balance of probabilities. By asserting that absolute certainty was not required, and then linking the standard of proof to the "ordinary everyday" meaning of the words "reasonable doubt", a jury might be lead to believe that a probability standard was the applicable standard of proof. The Court in *Starr* said that an effective way to define the reasonable doubt standard for the jury is to explain that it falls much closer to absolute certainty than to proof on a balance of probabilities. Since *Starr*, the use of adjectives such as "lingering" or "nagging" applied to a reasonable doubt has been frowned upon.[25]

Trial judges have run into difficulties whenever they have attempted to give the jury examples from everyday experience. In *Bisson*,[26] the trial judge gave the jury as an example the steps in detail that should be taken to determine the level of oil in an automobile. He suggested that when proper checks had been done, a person could feel certain "beyond a reasonable doubt" that there was enough oil in the car to enable it to run. The Supreme Court said that the trial judge should not have done so and ordered a new trial. To suggest that jurors may apply examples from everyday life in determining proof beyond a reasonable doubt could be misleading and lower the requisite standard. Often, those everyday decisions made by ordinary persons are made by using a standard of probability. Moreover, examples tend to be applied subjectively and will vary with the life experiences and background of every individual juror.

In *W. (D.)*,[27] Cory J. said that, ideally, a trial judge should instruct a jury along these lines:

> First, if you believe the evidence of the accused, obviously you must acquit.

---

[24] 2000 SCC 40, 2000 CarswellMan 449, 2000 CarswellMan 450, [2000] 2 S.C.R. 144, 147 C.C.C. (3d) 449, 36 C.R. (5th) 1, 190 D.L.R. (4th) 591, [2000] 11 W.W.R. 1, 148 Man. R. (2d) 161, 258 N.R. 250, 224 W.A.C. 161, [2000] S.C.J. No. 40.

[25] *Scott*, 2001 CarswellOnt 287, 153 C.C.C. (3d) 87, 140 O.A.C. 95 (C.A.).

[26] 1998 CarswellQue 66, 1998 CarswellQue 67, [1998] 1 S.C.R. 306, (sub nom. *R. v. Bisson*) 121 C.C.C. (3d) 449, 14 C.R. (5th) 1, 155 D.L.R. (4th) 531, 222 N.R. 365, [1998] S.C.J. No. 21.

[27] 1991 CarswellOnt 1015, 1991 CarswellOnt 80, [1991] 1 S.C.R. 742, 63 C.C.C. (3d) 397, 3 C.R. (4th) 302, 122 N.R. 277, 46 O.A.C. 352, [1991] S.C.J. No. 26.

Secondly, if you do not believe the testimony of the accused but you are left in a reasonable doubt by it, you must acquit.

Third, even if you are not left in doubt by the evidence of the accused, you must ask yourself whether, on the basis of the evidence which you do accept, you are convinced beyond a reasonable doubt by that evidence of the guilt of the accused.[28]

In *Lifchus*,[29] Cory J. went further and indicated what should and what should not be said to a jury about reasonable doubt. He felt that the following references to the required standard of proof should be avoided:

1. Describing the term "reasonable doubt" as an ordinary expression which has no special meaning in the criminal law context;

2. Inviting jurors to apply to the task before them the same standard of proof that they apply to important, or even the most important, decisions in their own lives;

3. Equating proof "beyond a reasonable doubt" to proof "to a moral certainty";

4. Qualifying the word "doubt" with adjectives other than "reasonable", such as "serious", "substantial" or "haunting", which may mislead the jury; and

5. Instructing jurors that they may convict if they are "sure" that the accused is guilty before providing them with a proper definition as to the meaning of the words "beyond a reasonable doubt".

Cory J. said that the trial judge should explain that:

1. The standard of proof beyond a reasonable doubt is inextricably intertwined with that principle fundamental to all criminal trials, the presumption of innocence;

2. The burden of proof rests on the prosecution throughout the trial and never shifts to the accused;

3. A reasonable doubt is not a doubt based upon sympathy or prejudice; rather, it is based upon reason and common sense;

4. It is logically connected to the evidence or absence of evidence;

5. It does not involve proof to an absolute certainty. It is not proof beyond any doubt nor is it an imaginary or frivolous doubt;

---

[28] *Ibid.*, at p. 310 [C.R.].

[29] 1997 CarswellMan 392, 1997 CarswellMan 393, [1997] 3 S.C.R. 320, 118 C.C.C. (3d) 1, 9 C.R. (5th) 1, 150 D.L.R. (4th) 733, [1997] 10 W.W.R. 570, 118 Man. R. (2d) 218, 216 N.R. 215, 149 W.A.C. 218, [1997] S.C.J. No. 77; amended (1998), 120 C.C.C. (3d) vi (S.C.C.).

6. More is required than proof that the accused is probably guilty — a jury which concludes only that the accused is probably guilty must acquit.

Cory J. went on to suggest that instructions to the jury might be given along the following lines:

> The accused enters these proceedings presumed to be innocent. That presumption of innocence remains throughout the case until such time as the Crown has on the evidence put before you satisfied you beyond a reasonable doubt that the accused is guilty.

What does the expression "beyond a reasonable doubt" mean? He explained:

> The term "beyond a reasonable doubt" has been used for a very long time and is part of our history and our traditions of justice. It is so ingrained in our criminal law that some think it needs no explanation, yet something must be said regarding its meaning.
>
> A reasonable doubt is not an imaginary or frivolous doubt. It must not be based upon sympathy or prejudice. Rather, it is based on reason and common sense. It is logically derived on the evidence or absence of evidence.
>
> Even if you believe the accused probably guilty or likely guilty, that is not sufficient. In those circumstances you must give the benefit of the doubt to the accused and acquit because the Crown has failed to satisfy you of the guilt of the accused beyond a reasonable doubt.
>
> On the other hand you must remember that it is virtually impossible to prove anything to an absolute certainty and the Crown is not required to do so. Such a standard of proof is impossibly high.
>
> In short, if, based upon the evidence or *lack of evidence*, you are sure that the accused committed the offence you should convict since the evidence demonstrates that you are satisfied of his guilt beyond a reasonable doubt.

Unfortunately, Cory J. fell into error in the last paragraph of the model charge that has been italicized. Clearly, a jury should not be satisfied of guilt of the accused because of a "lack of evidence". That error was later corrected.[30]

It has been held that the *W.D.* formula must be applied where the Crown has introduced a statement that is both exculpatory and inculpatory. For example, in *Bucik*,[31] H and B were charged with the murder of A and identification of A's assailants was in issue. The Crown had alleged that H had hit A with a small sledge hammer while B had punched and kicked him. H had

---

[30] (1998), 120 C.C.C. (3d) vi.

[31] 2011 ONCA 546, 2011 CarswellOnt 7654, 274 C.C.C. (3d) 421, 87 C.R. (6th) 309.

given a statement to a police officer admitting he was present at the beating of A but denied that he was the person who had hit A with the hammer. On appeal, it was held that the jury should have been told that unless it rejected that portion denying that he had hit the victim with a sledge hammer as untrue, it could consider H's exculpatory statement in the context of the rest of the evidence when deciding whether the Crown had discharged its burden of proof. The Court pointed out that an exculpatory portion of an accused's statement is of value for the defence, even if it was not believed, as long as it was not rejected by the jury as untrue. It was not necessary for the jury to decide that the statement was true before that statement could, considered in the context of the entirety of the evidence, provide the evidentiary basis for a reasonable doubt as to whether H was the person swinging the hammer. The jury should have been told that the exculpatory portion of the statement had potential value to the defence even if it was not believed as long as it was not rejected by them as untrue.

> [33] The lesson from *W. (D.)*, is that assessments of the credibility or reliability of exculpatory evidence in a criminal case do not raise either/or choices, but must reflect the application of the burden of proof placed on the Crown to prove its case beyond a reasonable doubt. An instruction to the jury to the effect that exculpatory evidence can be the source of a reasonable doubt even if not affirmatively believed is particularly important because it is arguably not the kind of common sense reasoning that jurors would apply in making credibility assessments in their day-to-day lives.

The *W.D.* formula has not been without difficulty even for trial judges sitting alone in cases of sexual assault where there are only two witnesses to the alleged offence. The issue often comes down to — who is telling the truth? An application of the formula would mean that if there was a denial by the accused and no evidentiary reason not to believe him, even if the complainant was credible, the judge must acquit. In *K. (S.)*,[32] the complainant's friend testified that the accused and the complainant went for a walk and, when they returned, the complainant looked really upset. The accused denied going for a walk with the complainant and assaulting her. The judge said that he believed the evidence of the complainant and the evidence of her friend corroborated the complainant's evidence. In convicting the accused, the judge said that the Crown had led evidence shifting the evidentiary burden to the accused who had not met that burden. In allowing the appeal, it was held that the judge had erred in shifting the burden to the accused. Even though the judge did not believe the accused and even though his evidence did not raise a reasonable doubt, the trial judge should have asked whether, on the basis of the evidence he did accept, he was

---

[32] 2003 CarswellOnt 2325, 177 C.C.C. (3d) 90 (C.A.).

convinced beyond a reasonable doubt that the accused was guilty. In other words, the trial judge is required to go through the steps set out in *W.D.* in arriving at his conclusion.

The Supreme Court has also said that it is important to distinguish between what is an evidential burden and a persuasive burden of proof.[33] An "evidential burden" is not a burden of proof. An "evidential burden" only determines whether an issue should be left to the trier of fact. A "persuasive burden", on the other hand, determines how the issue should be decided. On a trial before a judge and jury, the judge decides whether the evidential burden has been met. In doing so, the judge does not evaluate the quality, weight or reliability of the burden. The judge simply decides whether there is evidence upon which a properly instructed jury could reasonably decide the issue. It is then up to the trier to decide whether the persuasive burden has been met based on the burden of proof.

The persuasive and evidentiary burdens are not necessarily on the same party. For example in the case of "reverse onus" defences, such as mental disorder automatism, the accused bears both the persuasive and evidential burdens. However, in other cases, such as alibi, duress, provocation and self-defence, the evidential burden will be discharged where there is some evidence that puts the defence in play. There is no persuasive burden. The defence will succeed unless it is disproved by the Crown beyond a reasonable doubt.

4. CONSTITUTIONAL GUARANTEES

As was pointed out earlier, section 11(d) of the *Charter* guarantees every person charged with an offence the right "to be presumed innocent until proven guilty according to law in a fair and public hearing by an independent and impartial tribunal". Since the enactment of that section, there have been a number of cases in Canada attacking presumptions, both permissive and legal, as breaching section 11(d). These presumptions, described as reverse onus provisions, have been attacked on the basis that they have whittled down the presumption of innocence. The position of the Crown has generally been that these presumptions have been created by statute because there is a close connection between the basic fact and the presumed fact. Unless the presumption is allowed to stand, there will be instances where the Crown may be unable to prove its case. Section 1 of the *Charter*, it has

---

[33] *Fontaine*, 2004 CarswellQue 814, 2004 CarswellQue 815, 183 C.C.C. (3d) 1, 18 C.R. (6th) 203 (S.C.C.).

been argued, protects presumptions as a reasonable limit in a free and democratic society.

In *Downey*,[34] Cory J., delivering the majority judgment of the Supreme Court, summarized the principles governing the constitutionality of statutory presumptions:

1. The presumption of innocence is infringed whenever the accused is liable to be convicted despite the existence of a reasonable doubt.

2. If by the provisions of a statutory presumption, an accused is required to prove or disprove on a balance of probabilities either an element of an offence or an excuse, it contravenes section 11(d) of the *Charter*. Such a provision would permit a conviction in spite of a reasonable doubt.

3. Even if a rational connection exists between the established fact and the presumed fact, this would be insufficient to make valid a presumption requiring the accused to disprove an element of the offence.

4. Legislation which substitutes proof of one element for proof of an essential element will not infringe the presumption of innocence if, as a result of the proof of the substituted element, it would be unreasonable for the trier of fact not to be satisfied beyond a reasonable doubt of the existence of the other element. In other words, a statutory presumption will be valid if proof of the substituted fact leads inexorably to the proof of the other. The statutory presumption will infringe section 11(d) if it requires the trier of fact to convict in spite of a reasonable doubt.

5. A permissive assumption from which a trier of fact *may* but not *must* draw an inference of guilt will not infringe section 11(d) of the *Charter*.

6. A provision that might have been intended to play a minor role in providing relief from conviction will none the less contravene the *Charter* if the provision (such as the truth of a statement) must be established by the accused.[35]

---

[34] 1992 CarswellAlta 56, 1992 CarswellAlta 467, [1992] 2 S.C.R. 10, 125 A.R. 342, 2 Alta. L.R. (3d) 193, 72 C.C.C. (3d) 1, 13 C.R. (4th) 129, 90 D.L.R. (4th) 449, 9 C.R.R. (2d) 1, 136 N.R. 266, 14 W.A.C. 342.

[35] *Keegstra*, 1990 CarswellAlta 192, 1990 CarswellAlta 661, 61 C.C.C. (3d) 1, 1 C.R. (4th) 129 (S.C.C.).

In *Oakes*,[36] the Supreme Court set out the test that should be applied in determining whether a section of a statute that breaches the *Charter* is saved by section 1. One consideration was whether the measures adopted were carefully designed to achieve the objective in question. In other words, a presumed fact in a statute could not be saved by section 1 unless it was rationally connected to the basic fact. At issue in the *Oakes* case was whether the former section 8 of the *Narcotic Control Act*[37] (now the *Controlled Drugs and Substances Act*[38]) which required an accused found in possession of a narcotic to disprove on a balance of probabilities that he had the narcotic in his possession for the purpose of trafficking, violated section 11(d) of the *Charter* and was not saved by section 1. The Court found that section 8 did violate section 11(d). It was held that there was no rational connection between the basic fact of possession and the presumed fact of possession *for the purpose of trafficking*; the reverse onus clause could give rise to unjustified and erroneous convictions for drug trafficking of persons guilty only of possession of a small quantity of narcotics. Section 8 was held to be unconstitutional as infringing the presumption of innocence in section 11(d) and was not saved by section 1.

In *Boyle*,[39] which involved the constitutionality of the presumption in section 354(2) of the *Criminal Code*, the Court of Appeal of Ontario considered the rationality of the connection between the basic fact (possession of a motor vehicle with a wholly or partially obliterated identification number) with the two presumed facts (that the vehicle was obtained by the commission of an indictable offence and that the accused had guilty knowledge) and found the first presumed fact constitutionally valid but not the second. It was held that the only conceivable reason for removing or obliterating a vehicle identification number was to conceal the fact that it had been stolen or had been obtained by the commission of an indictable offence. On the other hand, since the presumption of guilty knowledge was not restricted to persons such as car dealers, who might reasonably be presumed to be knowledgeable with respect to the location of vehicle identification numbers and to be alive to the desirability of making an examination to ascer-

---

[36] 1986 CarswellOnt 95, 1986 CarswellOnt 1001, [1986] 1 S.C.R. 103, 53 O.R. (2d) 719, 24 C.C.C. (3d) 321, 50 C.R. (3d) 1, 26 D.L.R. (4th) 200, 19 C.R.R. 308, 65 N.R. 87, 14 O.A.C. 335.

[37] R.S.C. 1985, c. N-1.

[38] S.C. 1996, c. 19.

[39] 1983 CarswellOnt 88, (sub nom. *Boyle v. R.)* 41 O.R. (2d) 713, 5 C.C.C. (3d) 193, 35 C.R. (3d) 34, 148 D.L.R. (3d) 449, 5 C.R.R. 218 (C.A.).

tain whether there had been obliteration of such numbers, there was no rational connection between the basic fact and the presumed fact.

10
PARTICULAR PROBLEMS OF PROOF

1. JUDICIAL NOTICE

(a) Generally

Not every fact in issue need be proved by the introduction of evidence. The law has long recognized that some matters are so notorious they do not require formal proof. As one judge has said,

> Courts will take judicial notice of what is considered by reasonable men of that time and place to be indisputable either by resort to common knowledge or to sources of indisputable accuracy easily accessible to men in the situation of members of that court.[1]

As this definition notes, common knowledge will differ with time and place. What was notorious in the last century or even 50 years ago may no longer be the appropriate subject of notice. Moreover, what may be of common knowledge in one community may be unknown in another. What may be of common knowledge among certain professions involved in the finan-

---

[1] *Bennett*, 1971 CarswellNS 5, 4 C.C.C. (2d) 55, 15 C.R.N.S. 28 (Co. Ct.) *per* O'Hearn J. at p. 66 [C.C.C.]. See also *Potts*, 1982 CarswellOnt 56, 66 C.C.C. (2d) 219, 26 C.R. (3d) 252 (C.A.); leave to appeal refused (1982), 66 C.C.C. (2d) 219n (S.C.C.)

cial world, such as bankers and stockbrokers, may not be of common knowledge among tradesmen such as plumbers or electricians.

Judicial notice dispenses with the need for proof of facts that are clearly uncontroversial or beyond reasonable dispute. Facts judicially noticed need not be proved by evidence under oath nor tested by cross-examination. As the Supreme Court has said,

> Therefore, the threshold for judicial notice is strict: a court may properly take judicial notice of facts that are either: (1) so notorious or generally accepted as not to be the subject of debate among reasonable persons; or (2) capable of immediate and accurate demonstration by resort to readily accessible sources of indisputable accuracy.[2]

This does not mean that the taking of judicial notice of a fact or matter can never be disputed. Judicial notice is nothing more than *prima facie* recognition of the matter as true without requiring the side who asserts it to prove it. However, the other side is not required to accept the matter as being proved. The other side is entitled to dispute it if they believe it to be disputable.[3]

(b) Judicial Notice of the Law

Judicial notice may be taken, not only of a certain fact, but also of the law. For example, the common law requires courts to take judicial notice of the common law and all Acts of Parliament and of the provincial legislatures without those statutes being specifically pleaded. Legislative expression of this rule is contained in sections 17 and 18 of the *Canada Evidence Act*.[4] Sections 20 to 27 of the Act also provide a method of proving Imperial proclamations, orders in council, treaties, orders, warrants, licences, certificates, rules, regulations or other Imperial records, Acts or documents, as well as those issued by the Governor General or Governor in Council and the lieutenant governor or lieutenant governor in council of a province, judicial proceedings and official or public documents. In all other cases, the common law requires formal proof. However, the *Canada Evidence Act* does not restrict a party to proving such documents under that Act. Docu-

---

[2] *Find*, 2001 CarswellOnt 1702, 2001 CarswellOnt 1703, [2001] 1 S.C.R. 863, 154 C.C.C. (3d) 97, 42 C.R. (5th) 1 per McLachlin C.J. at para. 48.

[3] *Zundel*, 1987 CarswellOnt 83, 58 O.R. (2d) 129, 31 C.C.C. (3d) 97, 56 C.R. (3d) 1, 35 D.L.R. (4th) 338, 29 C.R.R. 349, 18 O.A.C. 161 (C.A.); leave to appeal refused [1987] 1 S.C.R. xii, 61 O.R. (2d) 588n, 56 C.R. (3d) xxviii, 23 O.A.C. 317n.

[4] R.S.C. 1985, c. C-5.

ments may still be proved at common law or by resorting to an applicable provision of another statute.[5]

(c) Judicial Notice of Facts

What constitutes common knowledge of a fact will be judged by reference to that which is common knowledge in the community where and when the issue is being tried, even though it may be unknown elsewhere.[6] For example, a judge sitting in the City of Kitchener may take judicial notice of the fact that Kitchener lies within the Regional Municipality of Waterloo, but not necessarily that a small village lies within the boundaries of the Region. A judge sitting in another community would err in doing so.[7] Other examples where judicial notice has been taken are that whisky, beer and wine are intoxicating,[8] that a large screwdriver is an instrument capable of being used for housebreaking,[9] and that bridges are publicly owned property.[10] On the other hand, courts are not yet allowed to take judicial notice of a distinctive cultural characteristic in the absence of evidence of that characteristic.[11]

Although a judge is entitled to take judicial notice of a fact, he or she is not necessarily required to do so, even if it is generally known and accepted. A judge is entitled to refuse to take judicial notice of a fact that is essential to the Crown's case where to do so would gravely prejudice the case for the defence.[12]

Unfortunately, fact-finding through judicial notice has risks. As Doherty J.A. observed in *Perkins*,[13]

> 37 . . . The "fact" judicially noticed may be wrong. Judicial notice can also jeopardize trial fairness in that it may deny the parties an opportunity to

---

[5] *P. (A.)*, 1996 CarswellOnt 3150, 109 C.C.C. (3d) 385, 1 C.R. (5th) 327, 92 O.A.C. 376, [1996] O.J. No. 2986 (C.A.).

[6] *Potts*, 1982 CarswellOnt 56, 36 O.R. (2d) 195, 66 C.C.C. (2d) 219, 26 C.R. (3d) 252, 134 D.L.R. (3d) 227, 14 M.V.R. 72 (C.A.); leave to appeal refused [1982] 1 S.C.R. xi (note), 66 C.C.C. (2d) 219n, 134 D.L.R. (3d) 227n.

[7] *Eagles*, 1976 CarswellOnt 955, 31 C.C.C. (2d) 417 (H.C.).

[8] *Moxley* (1928), 1928 CarswellMan 109, 50 C.C.C. 408, [1929] 1 D.L.R. 202, [1928] 3 W.W.R. 537, [1928] 3 W.W.R. 576, 38 Man. R. 27 (C.A.).

[9] *Robert* (1969), 1968 CarswellBC 241, [1969] 3 C.C.C. 165 (C.A.).

[10] *Rese* (1967), 1967 CarswellOnt 13, [1967] 2 O.R. 451, [1968] 1 C.C.C. 363, 2 C.R.N.S. 99 (C.A.).

[11] *W. (S.)*, 1991 CarswellOnt 105, 6 C.R. (4th) 373 (C.A.).

[12] *Zundel, supra*, note 3.

[13] 2007 CarswellOnt 5358, 223 C.C.C. (3d) 289, 51 C.R. (6th) 116 (C.A.).

challenge the existence of the fact of which the trial judge eventually takes judicial notice. These risks require careful limits on the reach of judicial notice.

In *Spence*,[14] a robbery case where the accused was black and the complainant was East Indian, at issue was whether the trial judge should have taken judicial notice that jurors have "natural sympathy" for victims of the same race. The trial judge had refused to allow a challenge for cause to include the race of the complainant. Binnie J. delivering the judgment of the Supreme Court held that the trial judge had not erred. The defence had not shown an "air of reality" to the assertion that the complainant's East Indian origin had the realistic potential of aggravating jurors' prejudice against the black accused. He went on to point out that judicial notice should be a flexible fact-finding device. The scope of judicial notice will depend on the nature of the fact of which judicial notice is taken. The closer a fact approaches the dispositive issue the more a court ought to insist on compliance with the stricter criteria for judicial recognition.

2. IDENTITY

It has been long recognized and accepted by the courts that identification based on personal impressions, that is, human observation and recollections, is notoriously unreliable. When a witness says "that is the man" without pointing out any distinctive features which single him out from others, that kind of identification will be given little weight or value. The reason is the possibility of honest error.[15] Experience has shown that even honest persons can be mistaken as to identification and recognition.

The trial judge is thus required to warn the jury (and him or herself) of the special need for caution when assessing the quality of identification evidence and the reason for the need of such a warning. For example, the judge might tell the jury that a mistaken witness can be a convincing one and that even a number of such witnesses can all be mistaken. Secondly, the judge must direct the jury to examine closely the circumstances of the identification. For example, matters such as how long the witness had the accused under observation, at what distance, in what light and whether the witness's

---

[14] 2005 CarswellOnt 6824, 2005 CarswellOnt 6825, [2005] 3 S.C.R. 458, 202 C.C.C. (3d) 1, 33 C.R. (6th) 1 at paras. 60-61. See *Manjra*, 2009 ONCA 485, 2009 CarswellOnt 3436; leave to appeal refused 2010 CarswellOnt 423, 2010 CarswellOnt 424 (S.C.C.).

[15] *Sutton* (1969), 1969 CarswellOnt 30, [1970] 2 O.R. 358, [1970] 3 C.C.C. 152, 9 C.R.N.S. 45 (C.A.); *Spatola*, 1970 CarswellOnt 4, [1970] 3 O.R. 74, [1970] 4 C.C.C. 241, 10 C.R.N.S. 143 (C.A.).

observation was impeded in any way, should be considered. Another factor that should be considered by the judge or jury is whether the witness ever saw the accused before, and if so, how often, and whether there was any reason to remember the accused. Any clear dissimilarity between the witness's description of the accused and the appearance of the accused should be pointed out to the jury.[16] Finally, the trial judge must point out to the jury any specific weaknesses or problems with the witness's ability to make the observations.[17] Although recognition of a person known to the witness may be more reliable than the identification of a stranger, the judge must remind the jury that mistakes can even occur in the recognition of a person that the witness knows, such as relatives and friends.

The most common example of identification evidence considered to be valueless is where a witness identifies an accused for the first time while the accused is sitting in the prisoner's dock. Another is where a witness is asked to look at the accused to see if he or she can recognize the accused as the person who committed the offence. Such identification has been called "unfair and unjust".[18] In *Browne*,[19] the British Columbia Court of Appeal described that kind of identification as:

> ... valueless in the sense that it is dangerous for a Court to act upon it in any respect. Its inherent tendencies towards honest mistake and self-deception are so pervasive that they destroy any value that could otherwise attach to it in a lesser role of 'some evidence'.[20]

---

[16] *Chartier v. Quebec (Attorney General)*, 1979 CarswellQue 48, 1979 CarswellQue 162, 48 C.C.C. (2d) 34, 9 C.R. (3d) 97 (S.C.C.). But see *Dimitrov*, 2003 CarswellOnt 5212, 181 C.C.C. (3d) 554, 18 C.R. (6th) 36 (C.A.); leave to appeal refused 2004 CarswellOnt 1770, 2004 CarswellOnt 1771 (S.C.C.).

[17] *Keane* (1977), 65 Cr. App. R. 247 (Eng. C.A.); *Turnbull* (1976), [1976] 3 All E.R. 549, 63 Cr. App. R. 132, Crim. L.R. 565, [1977] 1 Q.B. 224, [1976] 3 W.L.R. 445 (Eng. C.A.); *Edwardson*, 1993 CarswellBC 77, 77 B.C.L.R. (2d) 362, 79 C.C.C. (3d) 508, 22 B.C.A.C. 230, 38 W.A.C. 230 (C.A.); *Tebo*, 2003 CarswellOnt 1749, 175 C.C.C. (3d) 116, 13 C.R. (6th) 308 (C.A.)

[18] *Smierciak* (1946), 1946 CarswellOnt 26, 87 C.C.C. 175, 2 C.R. 434, [1947] 2 D.L.R. 156, [1946] O.W.N. 871 (C.A.) at p. 177 [C.C.C.].

[19] 1951 CarswellBC 25, 99 C.C.C. 141, 11 C.R. 297, 1 W.W.R. (N.S.) 449 (C.A.).

[20] *Ibid.*, at pp. 149-50 [C.C.C.].

Another danger with eyewitness-in-court identification is that it is

> deceptively credible, largely because it is honest and sincere. The dramatic impact of evidence taking place in court, before the jury, can aggravate the distorted value that the jury may place on it.[21]

The jury will be asked to look at *other evidence* that supports that identification before a finding of guilt may be made. For example, were there any distinguishing features, either physical, or in speech, or dress, which singled out that person from others? Unless there is some unusual or distinguishing feature that supports or confirms the initial identification, the trial judge must warn the jury (and him or herself when sitting alone) that a conviction based on such evidence is generally unsafe.

Where identity is in issue, the usual practice is for the police to show the witness a series of photographs (a photo-lineup), and ask the witness whether "anyone looks familiar". Alternatively, if a suspect is believed to have committed the offence, the police may conduct a lineup of individuals (an identification parade) which will include the suspect and ask the witness whether he or she can identify anyone. Appellate courts have stressed the need for constant vigilance on the part of trial judges and Crown counsel to ensure that nothing unfair to an accused person is done or put into evidence in connection with an identification procedure.[22]

The courts have also said that the police have a duty to ensure the integrity of the identification process by following procedures that tend to minimize the inherent dangers of eye-witness identification.

In *Goldhar*,[23] the Ontario Court of Appeal stressed that when conducting an identification parade, two matters should be clearly kept in mind:

> First, it should appear that there has been nothing whatever done to indicate to the witness the person in the line-up who is suspected by the police, either by showing the photograph or by description, or an indication of the position in the line-up. In the second place, it should appear that the selection of the other persons to form the line-up has been made fairly, so that the suspect will not be conspicuously different from all the others in age or build, colour or complexion or costume or in any other particular.[24]

---

[21] Per Arbour J. in *Hibbert*, 2002 CarswellBC 847, 2002 CarswellBC 848, 163 C.C.C. (3d) 129, 50 C.R. (5th) 209 (S.C.C.).

[22] *Miaponoose*, 1996 CarswellOnt 3386, 30 O.R. (3d) 419, 110 C.C.C. (3d) 445, 2 C.R. (5th) 82, 93 O.A.C. 115 (C.A.).

[23] 1941 CarswellOnt 227, 76 C.C.C. 270, [1941] 2 D.L.R. 480 (C.A.).

[24] *Ibid.*, at pp. 271-72 [C.C.C.].

In such instance, the court must be satisfied that the identification of the accused by the witness out of a series of photographs or out of a lineup was not influenced by any suggestion.

A similar obligation rests upon a trial judge to instruct a jury about the frailties of identification based on videotape evidence.[25] The jury should be instructed to consider whether the video is of sufficient clarity and quality and shows the accused for a sufficient time to enable them to conclude that identification has been proven beyond a reasonable doubt. Moreover, evidence by a police officer identifying the accused as the person in the video should not be received since the jury is in as good position as the officer to make an identification from the videotape.

A witness who is giving testimony is routinely asked by the prosecutor whether he or she sees the accused in court and, if so, to point out him or her. If this is the first opportunity for the witness to identify the accused in the dock, or if the witness made a prior identification that was influenced by suggestion rendering the identification in court worthless, the question arises whether the trial judge has the right under the *Charter of Rights* to exclude the identification evidence altogether as a breach of section 7 (fundamental justice) or section 11(d) (presumption of innocence). In other words, will a lineup procedure which is fatally flawed amount to a breach of the accused's *Charter* rights entitling an accused to the exclusion of the evidence altogether under section 24(2), or is it a matter that simply goes to the weight of the evidence and not its admissibility?

That issue was first addressed by the Supreme Court of Canada in *Mezzo*,[26] a rape trial. There the trial judge had directed a verdict of acquittal because the identification procedures carried out by the police had been flawed, casting serious doubt on the accuracy and reliability of the complainant's identification of the accused as her attacker. The Supreme Court ordered a new trial. McIntyre J., for the majority of the Court, regarded the issue as one of weight rather than of admissibility. He was of the view that to do otherwise,

> ... blurs or even obliterates the clear line separating the functions of judge and jury. Questions of credibility and the weight that should be given to evidence are peculiarly the province of the jury.[27]

---

[25] *Nikolovski*, 1996 CarswellOnt 4425, 1996 CarswellOnt 4426, 111 C.C.C. (3d) 403, 3 C.R. (5th) 362 (S.C.C.); *Cuming*, 2001 CarswellOnt 3140, 158 C.C.C. (3d) 433 (C.A.).

[26] 1986 CarswellMan 327, 1986 CarswellMan 403, (sub nom. *Mezzo v. R.)* [1986] 1 S.C.R. 802, 27 C.C.C. (3d) 97, 52 C.R. (3d) 113, 30 D.L.R. (4th) 161, [1986] 4 W.W.R. 577, 43 Man. R. (2d) 161, 68 N.R. 1.

[27] *Ibid.*, at pp. 107-8 [C.C.C.].

Although the Court ordered a new trial on the basis that there was some evidence that should have been left to the jury with a proper charge by the trial judge, Madam Justice Wilson, in a separate concurring decision (joined by Chief Justice Dickson), suggested that the proper procedure to consider improprieties was by way of a motion to exclude the evidence either under a trial judge's common law discretion to exclude prejudicial evidence having little or no probative value or under section 24 of the *Charter*. To date, similar views have been expressed by the Courts of Appeal of British Columbia in *Thomas*,[28] and of Ontario in *D'Amico*,[29] although in none of those cases was the accused successful.

With the recent proliferation of video-cameras in buildings, subways and on the street, the issue has arisen whether the courts should admit non-expert evidence of a witness who says that he or she can identify the person depicted in an alleged video of the perpetrator. For example, in *Berhe*,[30] the accused was charged with and convicted of indecent exposure just outside a TTC subway. The key evidence supporting his conviction was the non-expert, opinion evidence of a Toronto Transit Commission officer who testified that he was able to identify the accused from a video taken at the time of the alleged offences because he was familiar with the accused from "previous dealings" with him. Relying upon the decision of McLachlin J. in *Leaney*,[31] and Rosenberg J.A. in *Brown*,[32] it was held on appeal that the non-expert opinion is admissible provided that the witness has a prior acquaintance with the accused and thus is in a better position that the trier of fact to identify the perpetrator. However, it was stressed that before admitting such evidence, the trier must conduct a *voir dire* to assess under what circumstance the witness had previous dealing with the accused to determine whether that witness is in a better position than the trial judge to make the identification.

---

[28] 1993 CarswellBC 506, 24 C.R. (4th) 249, 32 B.C.A.C. 209, 53 W.A.C. 209 (C.A.) and *Fraser*, 1993 CarswellBC 1145, 80 C.C.C. (3d) 539, 26 B.C.A.C. 58, 15 C.R.R. (2d) 44, 44 W.A.C. 58 (C.A.); leave to appeal refused (1993), 83 C.C.C. (3d) vi (note) (S.C.C.).

[29] 1993 CarswellOnt 1087, 16 O.R. (3d) 125, 19 C.R.R. (2d) 309, 67 O.A.C. 396 (C.A.).

[30] 2012 ONCA 716, 2012 CarswellOnt 13254, 97 C.R. (6th) 213.

[31] 1989 CarswellAlta 131, 1989 CarswellAlta 617, [1989] 2 S.C.R. 393, 50 C.C.C. (3d) 289, 71 C.R. (3d) 325 at p. 413 [S.C.R.].

[32] 2006 CarswellOnt 8168, 215 C.C.C. (3d) 330, 45 C.R. (6th) 22 (C.A.) at para. 39 [C.C.C.].

3. INTENT

As was pointed out in Chapter 1, one of the issues that the Crown must prove is that the accused intended to commit the prohibited act. It is important to distinguish *intent* from *motive*. Intent in doing an act is shown when a person desires a particular result regardless of the reason for the desire. Motive is the reason that prompts the desire. The problem in establishing intent is that what goes on in a person's mind is often difficult, if not impossible, to ascertain. Nevertheless, the courts seem to have found no difficulty in making that determination. As Bowen L.J. said in *Edgington v. Fitzmaurice*:[33]

... the state of a man's mind is as much a fact as the state of his digestion. It is true that it is very difficult to prove what the state of a man's mind at a particular time is, but if it can be ascertained it is as much a fact as anything else ...

Some of the ways that a person's intent can be proved are by what he says or admits to others. However, it does not necessarily follow that such intention really existed in his mind because it may have been spoken in anger or mere bravado. Often acts or conduct of a person show the real intention and are more persuasive than words. The most common method of showing intention is by what is known as the presumption of intent. This presumption says that a man is presumed to have intended the natural consequences of his acts. In other words, if X shoots a gun at Y, it is open for the court to draw the inference that X did so intending to kill or injure Y. Such a presumption, however, is not considered to be a presumption of law, merely one of good common sense. As Roach J.A. pointed out in *Giannotti*:[34]

... a man is usually able to foresee what are the natural consequences of his acts, so it is, as a rule, reasonable to infer that he did foresee them and intend them. But, while that is an inference which may be drawn, it is not one which must be drawn. If on all the facts of the case it is not the correct inference, then it should not be drawn.

However, intent is usually proved by circumstantial evidence. For example, evidence of similar acts, motive, design or plan, malice or animosity, or preparation may show intent to commit an offence. Facts and circumstances accompanying an act are generally considered the most reliable evidence to prove the intent with which an act was done.

---

[33] (1885), 29 Ch. D. 459 (Eng. C.A.) at p. 483.

[34] 1956 CarswellOnt 11, [1956] O.R. 349, 115 C.C.C. 203, 23 C.R. 259 (C.A.) at p. 213 [C.C.C.].

4. MOTIVE

Motive must be distinguished from intent. Although the two words are often used interchangeably, they mean different things in the criminal law. Intent or *mens rea* refers to the mental element that the Crown must prove the accused possesses to establish its case. Intent, in criminal law, has been defined as "the exercise of a free will to use particular means to produce a particular result".[35] It may also, in some circumstances, refer to a foresight of consequences. In other words, an accused may not intend the consequences of his or her actions, but may be reckless as to the consequences and the courts will find criminal intent in this attitude.[36]

Motive, on the other hand, has been distinguished from intent as "that which precedes and induces the exercise of the will".[37] Motive may be the reason why a crime has been committed. Motive, in the words of Professor Glanville Williams:

> ... is ulterior intention — the intention with which an intentional act is done (or, more clearly, the intention with which an intentional consequence is brought about). Intention, when distinguished from motive, relates to the means, motive to the end ...[38]

Unlike intention, the Crown need not prove that the accused had a motive to commit the crime in order to succeed in its prosecution. Nevertheless, motive may be relevant and an important element along with other evidence to establish the three elements of every crime — the act; the identity of the perpetrator; and the perpetrator's intent.[39] As Chief Justice Duff noted in *Barbour*:

> If you have acts seriously tending, when reasonably viewed, to establish motive for the commission of a crime, then there can be no doubt that such evidence is admissible, not merely to prove intent, but to prove the fact as well.[40]

---

[35] *Lewis*, 1979 CarswellBC 520, 1979 CarswellBC 531, [1979] 2 S.C.R. 821, 47 C.C.C. (2d) 24, 12 C.R. (3d) 315 (Fr.), 10 C.R. (3d) 299 (Eng.), 98 D.L.R. (3d) 111, 27 N.R. 451 at p. 308 [C.R.].

[36] *Sault Ste. Marie (City)*, 1978 CarswellOnt 24, 1978 CarswellOnt 594, [1978] 2 S.C.R. 1299, 40 C.C.C. (2d) 353, 7 C.E.L.R. 53, 3 C.R. (3d) 30, 85 D.L.R. (3d) 161, 21 N.R. 295.

[37] *Lewis, supra,* note 35.

[38] *Criminal Law: The General Part*, 2nd ed. (1961), p. 48.

[39] *Barbour* (1938), 1938 CarswellNB 25, [1938] S.C.R. 465, 71 C.C.C. 1, [1939] 1 D.L.R. 65.

[40] *Ibid.*, at pp. 19-20 [C.C.C.].

In *Lewis*, Mr. Justice Dickson summed up the law as to motive this way:

1. As evidence, motive is always relevant and hence evidence of motive is admissible.

2. Motive is no part of the crime and is legally irrelevant to criminal responsibility. It is not an essential element of the prosecution's case as a matter of law.

3. Proved absence of motive is always an important fact in favour of the accused and ordinarily worthy of note in a charge to the jury.

4. Conversely, proved presence of motive may be an important factual ingredient in the Crown's case, notably on the issues of identity and intention, when the evidence is purely circumstantial.

5. Motive is therefore always a question of fact and evidence and the necessity of referring to motive in the charge to the jury falls within the general duty of the trial judge not only to outline the theories of the prosecution and defence but to give the jury matters of evidence essential in arriving at a just conclusion.

6. Each case will turn on its own unique set of circumstances. The issue of motive is always a matter of degree.[41]

5. CONSPIRACY

As was pointed out in Chapter 3, although what one accused says about a co-accused out-of-court is not evidence of the co-accused's guilt, there is an exception to this rule where two or more accused are charged with conspiracy. The exception allows the acts and declarations of one conspirator in furtherance of a common design to be given in evidence against all of the other conspirators even though such evidence is hearsay.[42] However, before such evidence is permitted, the trier of fact must follow three steps: first the trier be satisfied *beyond a reasonable doubt* that a conspiracy existed. Secondly, the trier must then be satisfied that the accused is *probably* a member of the conspiracy by evidence directly admissible against the accused without relying upon the hearsay exception. Finally, once the trier is satisfied as to this *probability*, the trier is then entitled to consider the acts and declara-

---

[41] *Supra*. note 35 at pp. 34–38 [C.C.C.].

[42] *Koufis*, 1941 CarswellNS 24, [1941] S.C.R. 481, 76 C.C.C. 161, [1941] 3 D.L.R. 657.

tions of co-conspirators on the final issue of whether the Crown has proven the guilt of the accused *beyond a reasonable doubt*.[43]

One might logically assume that because of this exception to the hearsay rule, conspiracy cases create a two-stage trial: the first stage involves evidence directly proving beyond a reasonable doubt the existence of the conspiracy and a determination by the trier of the probability of the accused's membership in the conspiracy; and then a second stage where hearsay evidence is allowed of the acts and declarations of co-conspirators to determine whether, based on all of the evidence, the accused's membership in the conspiracy has been proven beyond a reasonable doubt. Such a requirement would be fairer to an accused and would ensure that the jury did not erroneously consider hearsay evidence during their deliberation in the first stage. However, in *Carter*,[44] the Supreme Court of Canada held that this was not necessary because "the exigencies of the trial would make a chronological separation of the evidence impossible".[45] The Court said that it was only necessary for the trial judge to instruct the jury (and himself where he sits without a jury) that they were to sift through the evidence and carry out the following three-step process:

1. Consider whether on all the evidence, they are satisfied beyond a reasonable doubt that the conspiracy charged in the indictment existed. In other words, what must be considered at this stage is the existence of the conspiracy, not the accused's individual membership in it;

2. If they are so satisfied beyond a reasonable doubt that the conspiracy exited, then they must go on to decide whether "on the basis of the evidence directly admissible against the accused" the accused was probably a member of the conspiracy;

3. Only if they conclude that the accused was probably a member of the conspiracy can they then go on to apply the hearsay exception and consider the acts and declarations performed and made by co-conspirators, in furtherance of the conspiracy, to determine along with the other evidence whether the accused was, beyond a reasonable doubt, a member of the conspiracy.

---

[43] *Carter*, 1982 CarswellNB 13, 1982 CarswellNB 55, [1982] 1 S.C.R. 938, 46 N.B.R. (2d) 142, 67 C.C.C. (2d) 568, 31 C.R. (3d) 97, 137 D.L.R. (3d) 385, 121 A.P.R. 142, 47 N.R. 288.

[44] 1982 CarswellNB 13, 1982 CarswellNB 55, [1982] 1 S.C.R. 938, 46 N.B.R. (2d) 142, 67 C.C.C. (2d) 568, 31 C.R. (3d) 97, 137 D.L.R. (3d) 385, 121 A.P.R. 142, 47 N.R. 288.

[45] *Ibid.*, at p. 105 [C.R.].

Although the acts and declarations of one conspirator in furtherance of a common design are admissible in evidence against all of the other conspirators, *a plea of guilty by a co-conspirator* is not admissible for the purpose of establishing the existence of a conspiracy. Moreover, any mention by the Crown of a guilty plea by a co-conspirator requires a clear and sharp instruction to the jury that it ought to disregard that evidence in arriving at its verdict.[46]

Unfortunately, the distinction between what is direct evidence and what is hearsay evidence can be confusing for the jury, since it will generally depend upon the stage of their deliberations. For example, if X, one of the alleged conspirators, has declared that he, along with Y and Z, are part of a conspiracy to traffic in drugs, such evidence is direct evidence of the existence of a conspiracy and may be considered by the jury during their deliberations in step one. However, such evidence is also hearsay evidence against Y and Z of their membership in the conspiracy and may only be considered on the issue of the membership of Y and Z in the conspiracy if the jury reach step three.

The *Carter* formula has been criticized as confusing where there are only two alleged conspirators. In *Comeau*,[47] the Quebec Court of Appeal pointed out that where the conspiracy involves only two people, step one answers all the questions and steps two and three become irrelevant. In other words, the jury could not be satisfied of the existence of a conspiracy beyond a reasonable doubt unless they were satisfied beyond a reasonable doubt that both accused were members of it. Mr. Justice Tyndale summed it up this way:

> There cannot be a conspiracy of one person; two is a minimum; so if at step one the jury is satisfied beyond a reasonable doubt that the alleged conspiracy in fact existed, they must have found that the accused was a member,

---

[46] *Dixon*, 1984 CarswellBC 879, 16 C.C.C. (3d) 431 (C.A.); *Lessard*, 1979 CarswellQue 246, 50 C.C.C. (2d) 175 (C.A.); *May*, 1984 CarswellOnt 1158, 13 C.C.C. (3d) 257 (C.A.); leave to appeal refused [1984] 2 S.C.R. viii (note); *Paquet*, 1999 CarswellNB 470, 140 C.C.C. (3d) 283 (C.A.).

[47] (1991), 1991 CarswellQue 283, (sub nom. *Comeau c. R.)* [1992] R.J.Q. 339, 44 Q.A.C. 93 (C.A.); affirmed 1992 CarswellQue 129, 1992 CarswellQue 129F, [1992] 3 S.C.R. 473, 144 N.R. 229, 51 Q.A.C. 213. See also *Viandante*, 1995 CarswellMan 10, 40 C.R. (4th) 353, 102 Man. R. (2d) 126, 93 W.A.C. 126, [1995] M.J. No. 269 (C.A.); leave to appeal refused (1996), 115 Man. R. (2d) 160 (note), 206 N.R. 154 (note), 139 W.A.C. 160 (note), [1996] S.C.C.A. No. 243.

because he was one of the two members necessary to create the conspiracy.[48]

Although the logic of that criticism is compelling, unfortunately, the law of conspiracy is further confused by the rule that, even in a two-person conspiracy, it is open for the jury to convict one accused but not the other.[49] It may be logical to assume that if one accused is acquitted in a two-person conspiracy, the other accused should also be acquitted because one cannot conspire with oneself. However, a conviction of one and not the other has been held to be valid because it must be assumed that there was evidence admissible against A to establish his guilt but not sufficient evidence admissible against B to prove his participation.

Thus where the indictment alleges a two-person conspiracy, it has been suggested that the three-step procedure set out in *Carter* should be appropriately modified to ensure that the jury is not unduly confused.[50] The jury should be told that although it may seem inconsistent to convict A and not B in a two-person conspiracy, that inconsistency arises because there may be sufficient evidence against A to establish his guilt beyond a reasonable doubt, but not sufficient evidence against B to prove his participation.

---

[48] *Comeau, ibid.*, at p. 348 [R.J.Q.].

[49] *Barrow*, 1987 CarswellNS 344, 1987 CarswellNS 42, [1987] 2 S.C.R. 694, 87 N.S.R. (2d) 271, 38 C.C.C. (3d) 193, 61 C.R. (3d) 305, (sub nom. *Barrow v. R.)* 45 D.L.R. (4th) 487, 222 A.P.R. 271, 81 N.R. 321.

[50] *Viandante, supra*, note 47.

INDEX

371